Communication skills for effective management

Owen Hargie, David Dickson and
Dennis Tourish

palgrave
macmillan

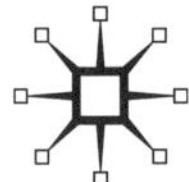

First published 2004 by
PALGRAVE MACMILLAN
Houndmills, Basingstoke, Hampshire RG21 6XS and
175 Fifth Avenue, New York, N.Y. 10010
Companies and representatives throughout the world

PALGRAVE MACMILLAN is the global academic imprint of the Palgrave Macmillan division of St. Martin's Press, LLC and of Palgrave Macmillan Ltd. Macmillan® is a registered trademark in the United States, United Kingdom and other countries. Palgrave is a registered trademark in the European Union and other countries.

ISBN 0–333–96575–2

This book is printed on paper suitable for recycling and made from fully managed and sustained forest sources.

A catalogue record for this book is available from the British Library.

Library of Congress Cataloging-in-Publication Data
Hargie, Owen.
Communication skills for effective manangement / Owen Hargie, David Dickson and Dennis Tourish.
p. cm.
Includes bibliographical references and index.
ISBN 0–333–96575–2 (paper)
1. Communication in management. I. Dickson, David, 1950– II. Tourish, Dennis. III. Title.

HD 30.3.H3653 2004
658.4′5—dc22 2003062245

10 9 8 7 6 5 4 3 2
13 12 11 10 09 08 07 06 05

Printed in China

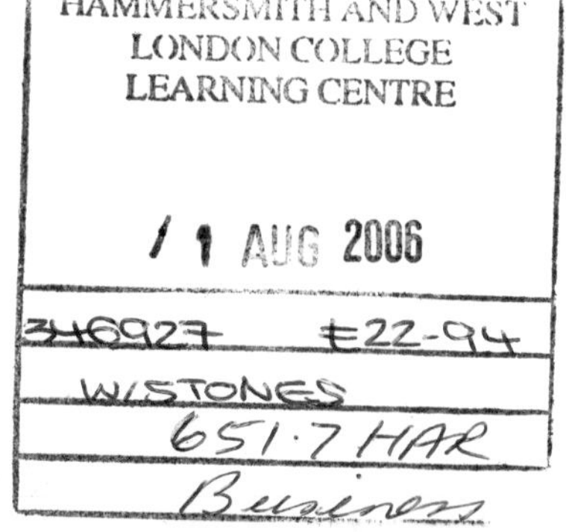

For our two late friends and colleagues, Colin Hargie and Christine Saunders. Working closely with them was both intellectually stimulating and fun. We remember them with fondness and gratitude. Thanks for all those lovely memories.

Contents

Preface

We live in a world that is ever changing. Some changes are for the better. When King Charles II had a fit in 1685 he received cutting-edge medical care from the 14 top men in the field. They shaved his head and applied a blistering agent to his scalp, fed him gallstones from a goat, had him drink 40 drops of extract from a dead man's skull, gave him a strong laxative, forced him to vomit violently, applied an enema containing *inter alia,* sacred bitters, rock salt, beetroot, fennel seeds, cardamom seed, saffron, cochineal and aloes, administered a sneezing powder of hellebore, applied a plaster of burgundy pitch and pigeon dung to the feet, and drew a pint of blood from a vein in his right arm, followed by an additional 8 ounce from his shoulder. As his condition failed to improve they forced Raleigh's mixture, dissolved pearl and ammonia down his throat. Two days later Charles was dead. Likewise, in the seventeeth century, pupils at Eton school were required to smoke before breakfast for the good of their health and were punished if they failed to do so.

Medical advice and clinical treatments have certainly changed, although one also wonders what those alive some 300 years from now will make of the care we currently receive. Equally, the pace of organisational change is supersonic. There are never-ending developments in technology that continually affect and alter the ways in which we send messages to one another. Management fads such as *business process re-engineering, just-in-time* and *total quality management* come and go. Financial systems ebb and flow. Production methods are regularly updated. However, one of the few things that stays constant in the workplace is the primacy of the human encounter. There is a deeply felt need among *homo sapiens* to communicate with one another. People are greatly influenced by, and remember, how others relate to them. If our interactions with another person are positive, then both working and social relationships with that individual are enhanced. Equally, a poorly handled interchange can damage relationships – sometimes irreparably. The core contention in this book is that communication lies at the heart of effective management.

Considerable evidence is provided to justify this contention. Successful managers employ the skills, styles and strategies as recommended in the chapters to follow.

The present text is a development and extension of our earlier one entitled *Communication in Management* (Gower). The contents represent our combined experiences of researching, teaching and consulting in the field of organisational communication. During this time we have worked with numerous private and public sector bodies on their communication strategies, devised training programmes to meet identified needs, carried out numerous research projects, and taught a wide range of courses to students and employees at all levels. Based upon our joint deliberations, we identified the areas covered in this book as being at the core of effective management. We also recognised that there was a need for a specific type of text to analyse these key dimensions. What we set out to produce was a user-friendly, yet academically rigorous, analysis of the main features of communication that are central to effectiveness in management.

This text has therefore been designed to meet the ever-expanding demand for valid and generalisable information on how best to relate to people in business and management situations. As such, it will be of interest both to practising managers and to students and teachers of organisational communication. The contents of the book are informed both by research and theory, and by first-hand experience. From working with practising managers and evaluating their central roles, and from analysing the work of other academics, we have selected 13 key areas for inclusion. These are: nonverbal communication, influencing and persuading, building teams, leading teams, making presentations, negotiating and bargaining, selling ideas, tele-communications, web-based and traditional writing skills, being assertive, helping and counselling, selecting the best applicants and appraising staff.

In the opening chapter we place the study of these skills and strategies within the broader context of the nature and functions or organisations, and the communicative role of managers therein. This provides a necessary backdrop against which the rest of the chapters can be placed. Then, in the final chapter we underline the importance of assessing communication performance. We recommend that corporations regularly measure and monitor internal and external communications within the workplace, and discuss the main audit methods whereby this can be operationalised. Given the recent ethical scandals that have besmirched many corporations, in concluding the book we emphasise the need for managers to communicate in a principled fashion, and itemise the key factors that must be borne in mind to ensure this is achieved.

The core objectives of the book are to:

- examine the main communicative contexts within which managers operate;
- identify and chart the key skills and strategies essential for effective managerial communication within organisations;
- review research findings pertaining to each area;
- allow students of management to sharpen their communication skills for the world of work;
- help managers to apply the material to their own particular workplace;
- enable managers to improve their day-to-day performance in their interactions with staff at all levels.

The style employed in all of the chapters encourages the reader to interact with the material covered. Each chapter contains a series of boxed text, diagrams, tables and illustrations, which summarise core points. Exercises are also provided to enable managers to put the material reviewed into practice. All of this is underpinned and supported by a firm foundation of research findings. The referencing style employed, using superscript numbers, does not impede the flow of text, yet allows the interested reader to identify and pursue relevant source material.

In writing this book, the authors would like to thank the editorial staff at Palgrave/MacMillan for all their help, advice and forbearance. Words of gratitude also to Philip Burch, Graphic Design Technician at the University of Ulster, for his help in producing some of the diagrams. Finally, we are indebted to our families who provided the necessary motivation, and who put up with us, throughout the production of this text.

OWEN HARGIE
DAVID DICKSON
DENNIS TOURISH

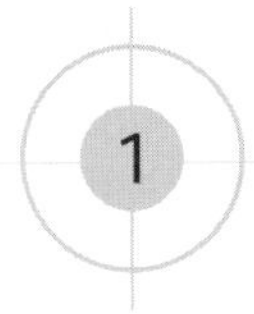

1 The world of the communicative manager

Introduction

The focus of this book is upon how communication in organisations can be improved. More particularly, it examines the pivotal communicative role of managers, who play a key part in maintaining effective information flow and promoting harmonious relationships within the workplace. Executives devote much of their time to interactions with staff. Manager-watching studies[1] have revealed that they spend over 60 per cent of their working time in scheduled and unscheduled meetings with others, about 25 per cent doing desk-based work, some 7 per cent on the telephone and 3 per cent walking the job. Indeed, it has also been shown[2] that 'communication, especially oral skills, is a key component of success in the business world ... executives who hire college graduates believe that the importance of oral communication skills for career success is going to increase'. The corollary of this is that today's graduates arrive with increased demands of what they want from companies,[3] not least of which is the expectation that communications will be two-way and cognisance will be taken of their views. Another example of the importance of communication was a survey[4] in which 2600 UK employees clearly expressed the view that what was most de-motivating of all was lack of communication from managers, citing issues such as a complete absence of interaction, a general lack of feedback, or meetings taking place behind closed doors.

In relation to employee satisfaction, the Gallup Poll organisation produced a scale (*Q 12*) comprising 12 questions, which are rated by staff on a 1–5 scale. These encompass issues such as the extent to which respondents feel they know what is expected of them at work, whether they are recognised for good performance, if their supervisor cares about them, and to what degree they believe that their opinions seem to matter. Thus, much of this *Q 12* scale relates to communication by managers. From its database of surveys of more than one million employees in the USA, Gallup found[5] a significant link between scores on this scale and business performance. Organisations where staff scored highly outperformed their rivals on a range of measures of productivity, such as employee retention, profitability and customer satisfaction. This again underscores the importance of effective internal communications.

In this chapter we plan to take you on a journey around the whole world of the communicative manager. You will be introduced to the climates and cultures of different organisations and see how these affect the disposition and behaviour of the inhabitants. On our tour we will visit the varying territories and terrains in which managers travail. We will witness how they can function as missionaries spreading the organisational gospel, and you will be encouraged to note the styles they adopt and the relative zeal they display. The signs and symbols they use to relate to and bond with their staff will be of particular interest. While the main emphasis is upon verbal and nonverbal rituals in these often strange organisational environs, we will also examine the written forms of communication in which the people engage. Among the interesting artefacts are new forms of technology (such as e-mail), which have transformed hitherto more primitive organisational hieroglyphics. To enhance our experience and inform our trek, we will also hear positive and negative stories from other experienced travellers. But first let us examine the organisational habitat.

Organisations

One thing that is clear, as we begin our travels, is that organisations are everywhere; our social world is unimaginable without them. They come in all shapes and sizes. There are large ones and small ones; flat ones and steeply hierarchical ones; those which are long established (the oldest company being Weihenstephan Brewery, founded in Germany in 1040) and those that are new to business; some of them are geographically spread out and others are located in a single building. The wealth continuum ranges from the very small business going bankrupt to the huge conglomerate with immense cash reserves, enormous power and ambitious plans for expansion. Furthermore, there is a high failure rate. Some 100 000 new products are launched every year in the USA, and more than 80 per cent of these fail.[6] As we shall illustrate, poor organisational communication is a major contributing factor to such failure.

But what do we mean by the term 'organisation' itself? We are all members of a whole host of organisations, yet often the closer you are to something the less you actually see. By taking a step back for a moment we can look at 'the organisation' in broader perspective. Ocasio[7] noted that 'it is easier to give examples of organizations than to define the term', but proceeded to conceptualise them as 'social systems of collective action that structure and regulate the actions and cognitions of organizational participants through its rules, resources, and social relations'. In like vein, Huczynski and Buchanan[8] iterated that: 'An **organization** is a social arrangement for achieving controlled performance in pursuit of collective goals'. Thus organisations involve:

- *Social arrangements*, where people come together to interact and organise themselves in a certain way. There are systems set in place whereby members interact with one another, both formally and informally.
- *Controlled performance*, which entails the setting of standards for outputs, measurement of performance against these standards, and the implementation of corrective action as required. Rules are laid down and employees have to accept and abide by these. This is facilitated by a managerial structure, and the pooling of shared resources.
- *Collective goals*, wherein members work together to achieve shared aims and common objectives. Organisational members are expected to hold certain values and to think in particular ways. It is the accepted norm that employees should contribute to the corporate 'mission'.

However, different organisations are formed for varying purposes and to achieve divergent goals. The function of the organisation inevitably shapes its nature, form and structure, and in turn influences the types of people who will want to work there. The classification made several decades ago by the social scientist Parsons[9] is still useful, where organisations are divided into those that pursue:

- *Economic production and profit-making goals* – these are primarily concerned with the market economy, in terms of maximising income and accumulating capital. Both manufacturing and service sector companies are involved in seeking these private enterprise goals.
- *Political goals* – these are determined by activities relating to the control and distribution of power in society. Examples here are government agencies, political parties, police and the military.

- *Pattern maintenance goals* – these relate to the facilitation of education and the dissemination of culture. Those involved in this sphere include the family, schools and colleges, religious denominations and cultural heritage groups.
- *Integration objectives* – these include the scrutiny of other groups and the mediation and resolution of disputes. This encompasses customer rights watchdogs, courts and legal offices, regulatory bodies and citizens' advice agencies.

More specifically, organisations can also be evaluated by using the 'I–We–Them–It' Principle.[10]

- *'I'* refers to how employees are regarded as individuals within the company. Are they all treated as equals? Is there disparity of treatment? What are the pay differentials? What kinds of people are rated most highly?
- *'We'* is concerned with how staff relate to one another. Is communication downwards only, or upwards and diagonal as well? Is there a rigid hierarchy through which communications must flow? Do managers encourage open and honest feedback from their supervisees? Is formal business dress required or is casual wear allowed? Is the firm one big happy corporate family?
- *'Them'* reflects the way in which external publics are dealt with. Are customers valued or seen simply as profit targets? What steps are taken to monitor and improve customer care? Are suppliers cared for as part of an extended business family, paid on time and treated fairly?
- *'It'* represents how the organisation feels about what it does. Is it proud of its products or services? What public face does it wish to display? Does it openly publicise what it does, or are there aspects of its work it would rather hide and not talk about? Are employees proud of what they do and where they work?

Managers should examine these four dimensions of their business, current value systems within each, their accompanying communication patterns, and how improvements could be effected.

As we traverse the organisational domain, it becomes obvious that the successful ones in any sphere are those that produce products or provide services that people want. They organise and manage their work efficiently, monitor costs and profits, market and publicise what they are selling, have good public relations, show concern for employees, customers and suppliers, and continually evaluate their performance. The one thing they all have in common is that they are composed of people. Organisations do not communicate – people do. Organisations do not have goals – the people who comprise them do.

For the organisation, communication has been portrayed variously as:

- its life blood
- its oxygen
- its brain
- its central nervous system
- its arteries
- the highways along which its business is transacted
- the mortar/glue which binds its parts together
- the fuel that drives its engine.

All of these metaphors highlight the role of communication in allowing messages to be transmitted rapidly and in connecting the different 'bits' together. The larger and more complicated the organisational structure, the greater the need for effective and efficient communication. Problems caused by breakdowns in communication are legion and have produced effects ranging from, at one end of the continuum, job dissatisfaction and stress, through to damaging strikes, operating losses, bankruptcies, production line injuries, shipwrecks, plane crashes and, at the other extreme, mass slaughter in the field of battle.

Communication is therefore a central component of effective business operations. Comprehensive reviews of relevant research[11,12] have shown the benefits of good internal communications, and these are summarised in Box 1.1. A review[13] of a range of leading companies including Federal Express, Xerox, IBM and AT&T identified the recurring best communication practices (see Box 1.2 for a summary).

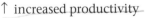

Box 1.1 Benefits of effective communication practices

↑ increased productivity
↑ better quality of services and products
↑ more staff suggestions
↑ higher levels of creativity
↑ greater employee job satisfaction
↓ decreased absenteeism
↓ reduced staff turnover
↓ less industrial unrest and fewer strikes
↓ lower costs

Box 1.2 Best communication practices in top companies

- Clear communication targets are set company-wide, together with accompanying accountabilities for their achievement.
- Regular employee attitude surveys are conducted and the results and action plans widely communicated.
- Senior management have high visibility among all employees – managers make, and take, time to talk with staff.
- Extensive face-to-face and two-way communication is fostered and employees are encouraged to communicate proactively with management; improvement suggestions are rewarded.
- There is a high use of technology, including an emphasis on videos and e-mail, to disseminate information and ensure it is understood.
- Communication training is an ongoing activity for all staff.
- All publications are carefully prepared and presented, each bearing in mind the specific purpose, goals and target audience.
- Management bonus takes cognisance of employee evaluations of communication performance and effectiveness.

Moskowitz and Levering,[14] in their analysis of the Top 100 UK corporations as perceived by employees, found that those that communicated well were the most effective. In the company that was number one, the supermarket chain Asda, the average salary was just £9000, yet staff turnover was a remarkably low 2 per cent for an organisation with 120 000 employees. The 'People Director' (a refreshing change from the mechanistic 'Human Resource Manager'), at Asda pointed out:[15] 'You cannot ask staff to behave well if they are miserable. And you cannot hide how you are feeling from 11 m customers a week. Asda is not a corporate family it is a [real] family.' Interestingly, the top performing business in a follow-up survey of UK companies,[16] Microsoft, also did not have a human resources department, but rather a division called 'great company'. Clearly there is a message here. Organisations should treat employees as *people* not as *resources*.

The importance of a people-centred focus was confirmed in research by Morley *et al.*,[17] which showed that organisations with conducive communication processes were more effective in achieving their task-related goals, and had more positive working environments, as perceived by employees. Furthermore, successful organisations were in turn more likely to devote resources to the development of best communications practices and the maintenance of a harmonious working environment. The linchpin in all of this is the manager, and, as we shall see as we now turn to examine this strange corporate creature, they take many guises and like chameleons come in numerous hues.

Managers

Put simply,[18] 'A manager is responsible for the work performance of one or more people in an organization.' The plethora of nomenclature for managers reflects the ubiquitous nature of the activity. In our travels we meet this animal under a range of genera. Titles include, *inter alia*, supervisor, team leader, division head, chief executive, foreman, dean of faculty, administrative officer, unit co-ordinator, production manager, school principal, bishop, master chef, director of research, prime minister and president. Equally, staff may be called by different titles such as crew members (at McDonald's), associates (Wal-Mart), cast members (Disney World), colleagues (Sainsbury's), partners (John Lewis), team players (B&Q), co-workers (Debenhams). Other terms include: parish priests, shop floor workers, employees, academics, technicians, secretarial staff and so on. The label used by an organisation to describe its employees often reflects its position on the continuum from highly interpersonal and harmonious to highly authoritarian and discordant, which in turn affects employee satisfaction and productivity. Likewise, consumers are referred to by various names, such as clients, guests, prospects, customers, fans, patients, students and so on. These usually reflect the nature of the role relationship. For example, it is interesting to note that as the 'market forces' ideology began to drive initiatives in the UK health service, 'patients' became 'consumers of services'. It is also vital that the titles people are awarded reflect the realities of organisational life. Calling people 'associates' but continuing to treat them liked hired and all too dispensable hands will be more likely to fuel cynicism than it is to enhance motivation. With that proviso in mind, the language used to describe people's jobs can be a powerful tool to underscore empowered and more enlightened social relationships.

Managers can be divided into two broad categories – those who manage shop floor workers, and those who manage managers. The former are first line managers, who have titles such as section leader, floor manager or supervisor. They are the managers to whom a section of the workforce is immediately responsible on a day-to-day basis. In turn, they report to middle managers, who hold positions such as head of computer section, sales manager or marketing co-ordinator. At the top of the hierarchy are senior managers, in positions such as deputy director, chief executive or vice-chancellor.

Managers at all levels engage in four main types of activity:[19]

- *Planning.* This includes deciding priorities, setting time-objectives and targets, and devising action plans to meet organisational goals.
- *Organising.* Here, the manager directs and co-ordinates the work of staff, makes decisions about their actual duties, monitors expenditure, and allocates tasks to individuals and teams.
- *Leading.* This involves motivating staff to work to their optimum level, directing and appraising them as they carry out tasks, maintaining good working relationships, and allocating rewards and sanctions to ensure compliance.
- *Evaluating.* In order to assess whether organisational goals have been met it is necessary to measure outputs and work performance, compare these to the set targets, implement corrective action to meet shortfalls and devise new plans as necessary.

Communication is involved at all four stages but is central to the organising and leading phases of the management process.

As shown in Figure 1.1 there are five levels[20] at which managers must employ their skills – upwards, downwards, across, outwards and self. Communication is essential in each of the first four. Managers have to communicate effectively in writing, face-to-face and on the telephone, with superiors, subordinates, peers and with people outside of the organisation. Furthermore, different forms of interaction are required at each level. An air of confidence is needed when managing staff, a more deprecating style may be appropriate when reporting to senior managers, a co-operative approach is best with colleagues and a professional manner should be displayed with customers. Style of management is perhaps the ingredient that most determines the success of the organisational mix. Management can be regarded as a continuum between two styles.[21] These are:

1. Management by *suppression.* This has been termed[22] *reactionary leadership*. Here managers treasure the status quo and perceive their

Figure 1.1 The five directions of management communication

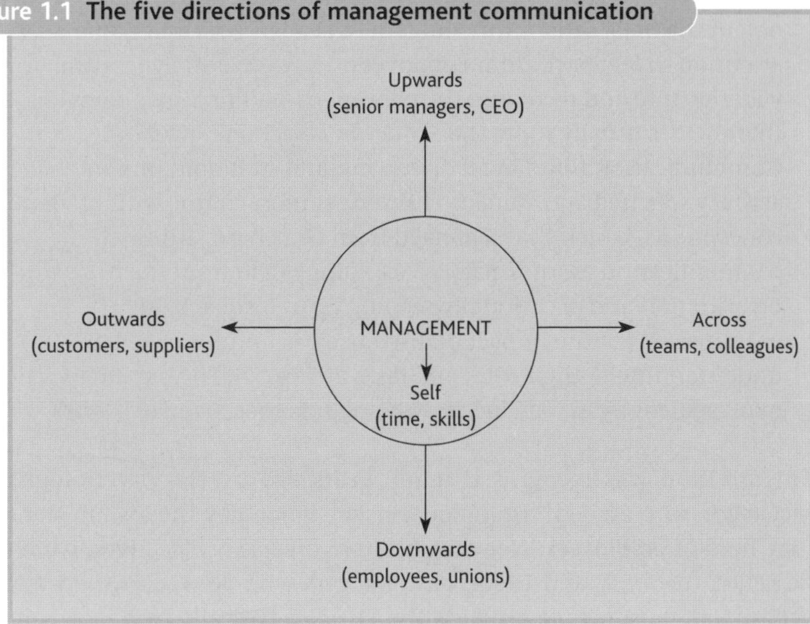

role as directive. Decisions are taken by management and imposed on subordinates, who are expected to obey orders. Their opinions are regarded as unnecessary at best and subversive at worst, unless they concur absolutely with the version ordained by senior managers. Information is seen as the property of management and workers are informed on a 'need to know' basis. Communication flows in one direction only – downwards, and this rarely amounts to more than a trickle. Workers feel that they operate so far below the senior management radar level that they rarely even appear as a blip on the organisational monitoring system. In essence, this style can be summarised in the maxim: workers work and managers manage. While this is an extreme scenario, traces of it can be found in many companies. Thus, one major survey[23] of 610 HR managers and 462 CEOs from a cross-section of 835 companies in the UK found that: 'Most managers only pay lip service to the idea that people are their most important assets.' While 70 per cent of respondents agreed that their organisation relied 'a lot' on their workforce as a source of competitive advantage, only 10 per cent strongly agreed that people issues were treated as a top business priority.

2. Management by *expression*. By contrast, in this style managers seek agreement. This is also known as *visionary leadership*.[24] Information

> is not seen as anyone's prerogative, but is shared in such a way as to obtain the most satisfactory outcomes. Leaders seek and pay attention to feedback from employees. They have an eye for the wider picture and recognise the concept of 'equifinality', namely that there is usually more than one way to achieve a goal. Communication flows in all directions, and staff opinions are actively solicited and valued. This style is more in line with modern conceptions, which have changed from perceiving 'internal communication as information cascading down from the top of an organization and occasionally seeping up as feedback, to examinations of the impact of discourses on employees, their understanding of their roles and tasks at work'.[25] The maxim of management by expression is: working together to make it work.

This division was recognised many years ago by the psychologist McGregor, who argued[26] that managers are guided by the assumptions they hold of employees. He identified two diverse perspectives, which he called theory X and theory Y. Managers who adhere to theory X believe that most people dislike work. They are basically lazy, have selfish self-interests, want to avoid responsibility, do not care about the organisation, try to avoid making decisions and prefer to be given firm directions. They adopt a perspective on their dealings with the workforce somewhat similar to that of Lenin who advised: 'Trust them comrades, but check on the buggers!' Theory X managers therefore continually monitor, scrutinise and regulate people's work and enforce a rigorous system of control, backed up by threats and punishment. By contrast, theory Y takes a much more benevolent view of human nature. The belief is that most people are responsible, wish to take an interest in their organisation and are eminently capable of self-direction. Given a conducive working environment, they actively seek responsibility, are industrious, like to make decisions and want to feel part of and contribute to the corporate effort. Theory Y managers do not threaten or coerce. They give employees encouragement to fully engage, freedom to be creative, and considerable delegated power and responsibility. The belief is that by so doing, staff will give value-added performance in return.

Iron managers, from the Theory X school, who rule by suppression, are likely to suffer from metal fatigue in the face of the corrosive power of ongoing negative staff reactions. Consensus management is eminently preferable. The theory Y, management by expression, approach is characterised by the flow of communication in all directions, participative decision-making and a high degree of informality. Managers using this style are supportive listeners who ascertain and address the needs and concerns of staff and discuss social as well as task matters. Actions that cannot be negotiated (e.g. compulsory legislative requirements) are fully explained. In democratic corporations that encourage expression, employees have a high level of identification with 'their' organisation and openly articulate dissenting views, knowing that these will receive full and fair consideration. The organisation is seen as an inter-related and inter-locking communicative system whose effectiveness is dependent upon good human relationships. All employees are encouraged to become active partners in the working enterprise, and to contribute to the overall operation. Success is a team game where all the players kick the ball rather than each other.

By contrast, Kassing[27] showed how in workplaces where suppression is the norm, employees have a low level of identification with the organisation. They are also less likely to openly express their views and so dissent remains latent. Thus, managers are kept ignorant of the true views of staff with the result that:

- unexpected conflagrations are liable to erupt;
- crisis management becomes the prevailing style;
- *boat rocking* is common, wherein employees frequently complain to one another about management and attempt to sabotage what are perceived as regulatory top-down initiatives;
- employees engage in *whistle-blowing* at the first opportunity, by notifying outside authorities about any irregular company practices (this issue is discussed in Chapter 15).

The theory X style is no longer acceptable. Communication programmes in the past were often simply concerned with announcing management conclusions, and ensuring that their messages were both comprehensible and delivered to all relevant employees. This will not suffice, since the following objectives have also been shown[28] to be crucial.

- stimulation of thinking, participation and ideas
- networking of know-how and learning across the organisation
- involvement of *all* staff in improving process
- identification of ways of providing added value to customers
- expansion of what all employees believe is possible.

To illustrate the validity of these points, let us take another short excursion, this time to one plant in General Motors (GM), to look at the effects of the introduction of a coherent, structured communication programme. Our guides here are McKeans[29] and Smith.[30] The GM programme included the following steps:

- Motivating senior colleagues to read about the basics of effective internal communications, so that at the outset they appreciated what the programme was about and the benefits which could accrue.
- Improving the existing newsletter, and introducing other publications including one jointly written and funded with trade union organisations.
- Setting up a communications review group, which met monthly to monitor performance.
- Producing a quarterly video news magazine, which was shown during working hours in scheduled meetings. This allowed managers to present business information on camera. These presentations served as a launch pad for subsequent discussions between supervisors and staff.
- Scheduling regular face-to-face meetings between managers and randomly selected small groups of staff, with the express purpose of facilitating open discussion on key issues.
- Implementing audits to track and chart the impact of the programme.

Performance improvements at this GM facility were quite dramatic.

- Within seven years sales had doubled.
- Budget savings were 2.8 per cent in the first year, 4.9 per cent in the second, then 3.2 and 3.7 per cent in the next two years.
- Within six years delays in delivering service parts had been eliminated.
- Suggestion savings per employee were \$864 in the first year, \$1220 in the second, then \$1306, \$1741 and \$5748 in subsequent years.
- Before the programme began less than 50 per cent of GM employees said they believed the information supplied by management. After four years of the programme in operation, this figure had risen to over 80 per cent.

While no causal link can be proved in such interventions, it seems more than likely that the communications programme was a key factor in this improvement. A notable aspect of this case study is that the measures adopted were simple to implement, yet their effects were significant.

Employees

Employees are the moving parts of the organisational engine. So, what do they expect in terms of communication? From a number of surveys[31–33] we can ascertain the key aspects of employee expectations in this area.

Access to information Staff want to be 'in the know' rather than being ill informed. This was confirmed by Shockley-Zalabak and Ellis, who, in their study[34] of over 2000 employees across 21 organisations in seven different countries, found that information reception was the factor most strongly related to organisational effectiveness and job satisfaction. Employees want to be kept apprised about key issues, especially those having a direct bearing upon their jobs. At the same time, and given the information explosion that has occurred in recent years,[35] they do not want to be flooded with detail. However, they certainly wish to be kept 'in the loop' with regard to all major corporate decisions, and at least know where they can access further detail as required. Where this does not occur, they feel underinformed and undervalued. If there is an information shortfall, the bush telegraph works overtime to fill it, and credence is given to gossip buzzing along the lines. As communications deteriorate, workers spend more of their time tuned in to the rumour station on the corporate radio, especially where they are subjected to the 'mushroom' method of management (kept in the dark and covered periodically with manure). To circumvent worst-case grapevine stories contaminating the organisation, firm and credible communication channels must be established for the rapid dissemination of information. In organisations spread across geographical locations particular efforts need to be made to avoid this pitfall.

Upwards communication Feedback is essential to effective performance in any endeavour, and so we benefit from optimising information from all available channels. Most corporations are aware of the importance of monitoring feedback from key publics to chart the success or failure of their products or services. Yet, when it comes to communications with staff, feedback is often seen as a top-down process, with little more than lip service being paid to the mantra of 'addressing staff concerns'.[36] However, for organisations to thrive, feedback must always be a two-way street. Furthermore, it is clear that employees attach considerable significance to upwards communication. In particular, they wish to report on initiatives taken in their area and request any information necessary for them to do their jobs effectively. They should therefore be encouraged to 'speak up' and managers should not get into a habit of 'talking down'. There ought to be a climate in which bottom-up communication is fostered and viewed as positive.

Regular staff attitude surveys and suggestion schemes are useful, as is upwards appraisal, provided that the information gleaned from such feedback is acted upon, especially by senior managers. If upwards communications disappear into a black hole never to be heard of again, the result will be staff cynicism and withdrawal.

Face-to-face contact In this era of mediated, technologically driven, communications it is interesting (and indeed refreshing) to note that employees consistently express a strong preference for face-to-face interaction with managers.[37] Yet, in many organisations, there remains a heavy reliance upon written communication. Senior managers have frequently been encouraged to engage in activities designed to increase their 'visibility' and encourage communication with the workforce – for example, 'Management By Walking About'. However, there are several drawbacks to this latter approach.[38] When prior notice is given, the senior executive is given red carpet treatment and the exercise become something akin to a 'royal visit' with the decks being scrubbed and the desks polished before the VIP 'inspects' the area. In essence this becomes management by walking past. Conversely, when the senior person arrives unannounced, such informal contacts can be viewed with suspicion by staff, who may interpret this as a form of 'snooping'.

One solution here is for senior managers to arrange regular formal meetings with groups of employees at which there is an opportunity for any issue to be raised. There should be a formal informality about these contacts – they should be round table, over coffee, for a set period (no more than one hour), should begin with a brief statement from the senior manager, and open out to allow anyone to raise any topic. This not only allows senior executives to 'address the troops', but also helps to foster a sense of openness and accessibility within the organisation. There is a cathartic effect in meeting and being listened to by those in positions of power and this should be facilitated.

Effective line managers Another prominent finding is that the key to organisational success is to have first line supervisors who are good communicators and who maintain high levels of contact with supervisees.[39] As summarised by Clampitt *et al.*,[40] in surveys: 'Employees routinely report that they prefer to receive information from their immediate supervisor.' A poor relationship between supervisor and supervisee has been shown[41] to have a very high association with intent to leave the organisation. It is hardly surprising that employees relate most closely to the person to whom they are immediately responsible on a day-to-day basis. If this relationship is positive, then there is a halo effect in that the organisation as a whole is positively evaluated, whereas if it is negative there tends to be a horn effect with the workplace being perceived negatively. In one audit of internal communications that we carried out in a large public sector organisation,[42] in response to an open question on the Audit Questionnaire that asked for details on communication strengths, one respondent noted rather enigmatically: 'My line manager always does his best to keep me informed, even when he doesn't know what's going on himself.' Clearly, the honesty of this person's line manager was a significant feature.

Good supervisors also serve as 'flak filters', in that they protect their staff from unnecessary and unwarranted hassle from above. In essence, employees want immediate managers who:

- take a personal interest in their lives
- seem to care for them as individuals
- listen to their concerns and respond to these quickly and appropriately
- give regular feedback on performance in a sensitive manner
- hold efficient regular meetings at which information is shared and freely exchanged
- explain what is happening within the company.

It is therefore important for organisations to provide comprehensive communication training for first line managers so that they can optimise the impact they have upon those that they supervise.

Training Staff recognise the importance of training in communication skills. They consistently express a wish for such training personally, and recommend that managers also receive such training. Communication skills training, which has been shown to be effective across a range of professional contexts,[43] should be organisation specific and should focus on how interactions can be conducted in the most supportive and encouraging manner. Management development programmes should cover the skills contained in this book.

Organisational tasks

But how do the inhabitants of the organisational world occupy their time? Their main role of course, is to undertake various jobs. For organisations to thrive, essential tasks must be executed efficiently.

Satisfied workers perform these tasks more effectively, and job satisfaction in turn depends upon six key dimensions.[44,45]

1. *Task significance.* This refers to the impact of the job on other people, and their perceptions of its importance. These factors determine its status. While this is influenced by pay, it goes beyond it. For instance a village vicar may have poor financial remuneration but be held in very high esteem and have a significant role to play in the lives of others. The vicar is likely to receive regular thanks and praise from parishioners for help and succour rendered, and be central to many community activities. All of this, in turn, gives a strong feeling that the job is worthwhile.
2. *Autonomy.* This is the extent to which the person has freedom to make decisions about how the job is to be done and is free to change it as necessary. For example, university lecturers in the UK traditionally had considerable freedom with regard to how they conveyed their discipline knowledge to students. This was a highly motivating feature of the job. However, it is increasingly being restricted and constricted by 'quality assurance' exercises replete with directives that prescribe exactly how higher education should be delivered. We confidently predict a negative impact for both lecturers and their students. Lecturers who traditionally 'were' their job are likely to consequently simply 'do' their job.
3. *Task identity.* Those who identify strongly with their work have higher job satisfaction. People, in turn, identify more with a job when it represents a whole piece of work as opposed to merely one small bit of a much larger process. Thus, an employee who feels part of the entire production procedure, will identify more with the job and have higher motivation and satisfaction than one who simply carries out an isolated task and feels removed from the whole.
4. *Skill variety.* Jobs should be as varied as possible to maintain commitment and motivation. Variety is determined by the extent to which the job requires a range of skills, rather than being a boring, repetitive, mechanical routine.
5. *Work demands.* Employees should feel that they are being challenged in what they do, so that they have a greater concomitant sense of achievement when tasks are completed. Routine work is likely to result in habituated responses and boredom. Conversely, innovation tends to be encouraged by increased job demands – people are then challenged to find new ways of facilitating their work. There is of course a happy medium

here, since task overload will eventually lead to stress and breakdown.

6. *Task feedback*. This relates to the amount of feedback on performance that the person receives. If someone is doing a good job, they should be told. Equally if performance is unsatisfactory this should be handled in a sensitive manner to encourage remediation.

Understanding communication

In the above analysis of organisations, managers, employees and tasks, we consistently emphasised the centrality of communication. However, if we are to effect improvements in this domain, we must first understand the process itself. In social science terminology[46] communication is 'The scientific study of the production, processing and effects of signal and symbol systems used by humans to send and receive messages.' This definition highlights three main dimensions:

1. Communication is amenable to scientific characterisation. It is a process that is open to measurement, analysis, evaluation and improvement.
2. The study of communication centres around how messages are produced, how they are then processed or delivered (e.g. by face-to-face interaction, in writing or through technological mediation), and what effects they have on those who receive them.
3. The importance of signs and symbols is highlighted. All interpersonal behaviour potentially serves a communicative function, and is judged on the basis both of verbal content and nonverbal signals. The overt message may be less important than the hidden meaning, or 'sub-text'. For example, a manager may express support for a policy of informal dress on Fridays, but, by personally turning up every Friday in full formal regalia, send the signal that actually conventional apparel is preferred.

These elements of the communicative process occur at four levels, namely intrapersonal, interpersonal, network/organisational and macrosocietal.

Intrapersonal communication is concerned with what goes on 'inside' the person – with the study of how individuals process, store and produce messages. This includes the elements of perception, cognition, emotion, beliefs, attitudes, self-image and self-awareness. How we interpret the behaviour of others and in turn respond is shaped by these internal processes. If a manager believes that workers are inherently lazy and dishonest and need to be constantly scrutinised, this belief system will inevitably affect how the actions of individual staff are interpreted.

At the *interpersonal* level the focus is upon the study of communicative relationships in one-to-one and small group contexts. It includes the analysis of relationship development, maintenance and breakdown; the acquisition of communicative ability and skills; communication dysfunction; and the study of professional communication. While there is some debate about the exact nature of the process, it can be argued[47] that interpersonal communication is:

1. *Inevitable.* When we are in the presence of others we cannot not communicate. Even by saying nothing we are making a 'statement' nonverbally. The senior manager who appears unexpectedly on the shop floor at different times of the day, does not speak, but carefully watches workers in action for five minutes, makes some notes on a sheet of paper, and then leaves, is also making a pointed 'statement'.
2. *Purposeful.* There is usually a reason for interaction, with the interactors pursuing definite goals. People may not be consciously aware of their goals as they communicate, but these nevertheless guide actions. The most effective managers are more aware of the goals they are trying to achieve, and of what they need to do next to be successful.
3. *Transactional.* When we interact we simultaneously send and receive messages in a continuous process of mutual influence and adjustment. Manager and employee concurrently monitor the actions and reactions of one another as they relate, and moment-by-moment responses are affected by the ongoing behaviour of both parties.
4. *Multi-dimensional.* Communication occurs on many levels simultaneously. There is the actual content of conversation itself, but linked to this is the way in which it is discussed. Respect, liking and relational power are but three of the aspects communicated by interactors. For instance, a common goal of employees is to impress their manager. Self-presentation and impression management concerns are therefore universal in organisations, as workers attempt to present themselves in the best possible light to those in power.

5. *Irreversible.* Once we make an utterance or a nonverbal behaviour (e.g. a particular facial expression) we cannot hit the picture search reverse button and wipe it. As the Roman poet Horace expressed it: 'Words once spoke can never be recalled.' We can apologise for what we have said or done, but in a very real sense the damage remains. Once the interactive toothpaste is out of the tube it cannot be retracted without some mess remaining. Initial care with words and actions prevents lasting hurt and dented relationships.

The third communication level is the *network* and *organisational* realm. Here, larger collectives are studied in the context of ongoing relationships. This encompasses the study of group norms and how they are developed, disseminated and enforced; the formation of organisational identity and its expression through symbols; value formation and the diffusion of values internally and also their external expression; formal and informal communication channels and networks; rewards and sanctions; processes which facilitate bonding and a sense of belonging; and the development of corporate image. The past decade has witnessed an explosion of interest by communication scholars in the world of work. Likewise, organisations are increasingly aware of the benefits of effective internal and external communications.

The final communication route leads to the *macrosocietal* or *mass* level. Here the focus is upon the communication properties and activities of large social systems. Examples of events studied at this level include: the nature, role, production and effects of the mass media; political structures and networks; dissemination and expression of national values, norms and identity; and the diffusion and continuity of language and culture.

The functions of communication in organisations

As a result of decentralisation, de-layering and reduced bureaucracy, it is clear that 'Management will be a function carried out by increasing numbers of people in the organization.'[48] The old line–management pyramidical hierarchy is being replaced by a flattened structure based upon project-based initiatives. Leaders of projects will change depending upon expertise and ability to do the task. This means that more people need to understand managerial functions, and the importance of communication therein. Communication has been shown[49] to serve five key functions in organisations.

1. *Task/work function.* The completion of tasks on time and to a high standard depends upon a steady flow of co-ordinated communications. Staff should know the goals and objectives of the organisation, information has to be shared widely, instructions must be given in a meaningful and comprehensible way, inter-departmental co-ordination of assignments needs to be facilitated, and problems openly identified and shared. Smooth two-way communication between managers and employees ensures that the job is done efficiently and effectively.
2. *Social/maintenance function.* In harmonious organisations, employees are friendly and colleagues become work*mates*. While some degree of creative conflict can be a positive dynamic especially towards innovation (see Chapter 7), where the conflict is not controlled, there is likely to be disharmony, and reduced output. The workplace is not just somewhere we go to do a job, it becomes an important and valued part of our life and helps to shape our sense of self-identity and worth. Good organisations develop this function through activities such as staff outings, social evenings, clubs, family days, parties and staff Newsletters. As Axelrod[50] noted there is a 'growing tendency to see work as a source of personal satisfaction' with the result that 'the workplace has become the center of American social life'.
3. *Motivation function.* Valås and Sletta[51] illustrated how motivation-enhancing strategies and techniques have attracted considerable interest within the organisational field for many years. They pointed out that the motivation of subordinates is probably the biggest challenge for managers. At a basic level people work to secure a means of income. But employment also provides other desirable goals such as a socially acceptable way of structuring time, a network of social contacts and a source of self-fulfilment. In all organisations, employees need to be motivated to perform at optimum level. In the military sphere, compliance with directives can simply be ordered – yet even here if the foot soldiers are not motivated to carry them out there will be calamity on the field of battle. However, in most organisations workers have to be encouraged and supported to ensure they produce their best efforts. While salary is one aspect of this, it is also the case that people are not primarily motivated by money. Motivation can be extrinsic, in the form of overt rewards (e.g. financial bonuses), or intrinsic (e.g. feeling that one is doing a valuable and worthwhile job). The latter form of incentive is best, since if people are driven solely by

extrinsic rewards, when these reduce or cease, work performance is swiftly and adversely affected. It has been shown[52] that intrinsic motivation is encouraged by facilitative line managers who take an interest in employees and who listen to their ideas and concerns.

As university academics, the authors have experienced many instances of mature individuals who have given up very well paid jobs to pursue a route that will lead to less pay but more perceived satisfaction and personal fulfilment. One review of this field[53] concluded that 'Those who derive pleasure from their work are considered most fortunate, and those who change their lives to obtain more satisfaction from work are most admired.' The most effective organisations are those that maximise the potential for intrinsic motivation in the work of employees, particularly through supervisors who encourage autonomy.

4. *Integration function.* Employees should feel they are an integral part of their organisation, and be proud to tell others who they work for. The more they experience a sense of belonging, the greater will be their commitment to work. Conversely, when workers feel dislocated from the organisation, they devalue their work and the organisation, so that output and quality are reduced. *Branding* and *bonding* are very important processes in achieving integration. The name of the organisation, its logo, mission statement and its reputation, all facilitate overall brand identity. Bonding to the brand is achieved through measures such as involving staff in the development or review of its mission statement and logo, having a system of effective team meetings, ensuring maximum upwards communication, engaging in outreach and community activities, as well as through aspects of the social function discussed earlier.
5. *Innovation function.* In his review of research in this field West[54] pointed out that 'opportunities to develop and implement skills in the workplace and to innovate are central to the satisfaction of people at work'. Employees do not want to feel that they are readily replaceable cogs in an organisational machine. Rather studies show[55] that they value greatly the chance to bring their own initiatives to bear on what they do. All businesses must move with the times, since there is truth in the old maxim 'innovate or die'. New products need to be developed or more effective ways of producing the current ones must be found. The workplace is a potential seedbed of sprouting ideas. However, they need to be nurtured, rather than trampled over by the slow, heavy, leaden, feet of bureaucracy, or poisoned by the harmful herbicide of apathetic,

antagonistic or autocratic management. Suggestions schemes, quality circles, focus groups, 'idea of the month' awards, and problem-solving fora, are all methods whereby innovation can be fostered. Since no one knows a job as well as the person who does it every day, it is absurd not to encourage ideas from those with such a depth of insider knowledge. Studies in this area[56] have shown that employees are a storehouse of ideas for improving all aspects of the business. However, these are stymied where restrictions are placed on personal autonomy, mistrust between members of the workforce is rife and there is a lack of clarity on goals. Nevertheless, it remains the case that even elementary forms of suggestion schemes are often infrequently or poorly used in many organisations. We regularly ask managers during workshops to indicate how many of their companies implement employee suggestion schemes. The proportion who respond positively is staggeringly low. In essence, creativity is more likely to occur when individuals:

- feel free from stringent time pressures
- do not experience high levels of stress
- feel safe and secure in their work
- understand the aims and objectives of the company
- are positive about their job
- know that personal face or identity will not be attacked
- work with receptive and supportive managers.

Thus, all five of these functions are important, and the role of communication in achieving them is central.

The elements of communication

As our gaze sweeps across the wide geography of communication, we can observe a number of peaks that define the terrain. It is to an analysis of each of these that we now turn.

Communicators refer to the people involved. Personal attributes such as the age, gender, dress, physique and disposition of those involved influence both our own actions and our reactions to the behaviour of others.[57] An important attribute is what Goleman[58] termed 'emotional intelligence'. After examining studies involving hundreds of large organisations, he concluded that this was the dimension that characterised star performers. Emotional intelligence includes the ability to persuade and motivate others, to empathise and build relationships, to handle one's own and other people's emotions, to give open and honest feedback sensitively, to form alliances, to monitor one's own behaviour, and to read organisational politics. It refers to the core skills of social awareness and communication. A working knowledge and understanding of the material covered in the present book will therefore enhance the reader's emotional intelligence.

Messages are the signals and symbols we use to convey what we mean. Communication messages are usually delivered in a visual, auditory, tactile or olfactory format. We are more conscious of the first three. Visual messages include written communication, as well as all of the nonverbal modes (clothes, jewellery, facial expressions, gestures and so on) prevalent in social encounters. Auditory communication may be face-to-face or mediated by telephone. Tactile communication refers to the use of touch and bodily contact (handshakes, hugs, kisses). Finally, olfactory messages include the use of perfumes, aftershaves, deodorants, and all the other types of scent, which in fact serve to disguise our natural body odours and project a certain image.

Channel describes both the medium and the means used to deliver messages. The 'means' of communication would include face-to-face, telephone, pager, written (fax, e-mail, snail mail, Newsletter), radio and video. In face-to-face contact, communication occurs through the medium of the visual, auditory and olfactory channels, while the tactile channel may or may not come into play. A skilled communicator will select, and maximise the use of, the channel most appropriate to the achievement of the goals being pursued, bearing in mind that, as discussed earlier, employees tend to prefer face-to-face communication with managers.

Noise is the term used to describe anything that distorts or interferes with meanings and messages. Dickson[59] identified a number of barriers to communication, the main ones being:

- *Environmental.* This includes a whole range of factors. For example, the layout of furniture can facilitate or inhibit interaction, intrusive noise may be disruptive, and heating and lighting can be conducive or uncomfortable.
- *Disability.* Physical, neurological or psychiatric impairment can make normal channels or patterns of interaction difficult, or even impossible. Examples include sensory handicaps such as sight or hearing loss, and conditions such as Parkinson's disease or severe depression.

- *Psychological.* These include the personal biases or stereotypes that influence how we perceive and interpret what a particular person is saying.
- *Semantic.* This occurs when the actual meaning of what is being communicated becomes distorted due to language or cultural differences between the communicators.
- *Demographic.* In particular, differences in age and gender have been shown to have the potential to cause problems during social encounters. To take but one example, when a male listener nods his head he is likely to be communicating to the speaker 'I agree', but when a female nods her head she may just be indicating 'I am listening' (but not necessarily agreeing).[60]
- *Organisational.* Barriers to communication can be constructed by the organisation itself. For example, we worked in one corporation where the CEO sent an edict to all employees that no one was in future permitted to send any e-mails directly to him. Rather, they all had to go through the line–management hierarchy. This was a very disabling and disempowering message and a definite obstacle to upwards feedback. Other examples of organisation barriers include the disparate physical location of staff who should be working closely together, a lack of a coherent strategy for team briefing, or overburdened, stressed and under-resourced supervisors who simply do not have sufficient time to devote to communication.

While some degree of noise is inevitable in communication, the objective should be to reduce this to a minimum.

Feedback This allows us to evaluate our performance. We receive feedback both from the verbal and nonverbal reactions of others, and from our own responses. This latter process, which is known as 'self-monitoring', involves being aware of what we say and do in social encounters, and of its effect upon others. Skilled communicators are high self-monitors who continuously analyse and regulate their own behaviour in relation to the responses of others. The messages we receive have to be decoded or interpreted by us. Meaning is perceived rather than received. In this sense, meaning is not an inherent quality of the message *per se*, but rather is something that is constructed in the mind of the recipient. For example, what we intended to be genuinely positive managerial feedback may be misconstrued as negative or patronising. Likewise, feedback may be ignored altogether, and indeed certain managers seem oblivious to the messages coming from staff – and to their meanings.

Context Communication does not occur in a vacuum. It is embedded within a particular context, which in turn has a major impact upon behaviour. A manager will behave totally differently when disciplining a member of staff in the office, as opposed to when calling at the home of the same person following the death of a child. In each case, the situation plays a key part in shaping the response.

Culture This is an aspect of organisational life that has been the focus of much discussion and research.[61] It has been defined[62] as 'the collection of relatively uniform and enduring values, beliefs, customs, traditions and practices that are shared by an organization's members, learned by new recruits, and transmitted from one generation of employees to the next'. An important defining feature of culture is that it is the basis for distinguishing one corporation from another.[63] There are six key aspects of organisational culture.[64]

1. *History*. Recent years have witnessed an emphasis on 'short-termism' in companies. Performance targets are rooted in time-limited criteria, such as sales volume this week, profits in the last month or change in share price over the past quarter. Yet, any depth of understanding of an organisation requires knowledge of the longer view. Just as people search for family roots in a genealogical pursuit for self-knowledge, so too do they appreciate a sense of being part of an established and ongoing 'organisational family' history. The notion of 'place identity' is now recognised as an important part of self, since 'questions of "who we are" are often intimately related to questions of "where we are" '.[65] Many established businesses have recognised this, and as part of the induction process recruits learn about the foundations and historical development of the organisation.
2. *Stories*. As children we are nurtured on a diet of stories – there seems to be an innate desire within us to hear tales of people and events. This does not really change with age. We may read different books or watch different films but in essence the central dramatic themes recur. At family reunions much of the time is spent recalling past happenings. Older family members relate tales about grandparents to younger ones who never knew these individuals, but still relish hearing about them. Likewise in organisations staff reminisce about major past events and pass these on to new staff. It helps to bond members and establish a sense of continuing corporate drama. Newsletters can facilitate this process by including stories from past times, as well as the dramas faced by current staff.

3. *Beliefs and values*. Deal and Kennedy[66] pointed out that 'Beliefs are shared convictions, widely accepted notions, of what's important. Values are what we stand for as a group.' Together they represent the philosophy and outlook of the organisation, and employees in turn are expected to share the corporate beliefs and values, and behave accordingly. Often businesses develop vision or mission statements to reflect these values and beliefs. However, the cynical view is that there is no mission control, and so these just end up in a frame on the wall, rather than as an action-guiding template in people's minds. A broad distinction is often made between Eastern cultures, which have collectivist values, and Western cultures, which are more individualistic. The former have tended to foster inter-dependence or a 'We' mentality, with importance placed upon aspects such as roles, position, status, fitting-in, being accepted and not offending the other's sensibilities. The latter encourage independence and an 'I' outlook, involving self-expression, assertiveness and being 'up-front'. However, care needs to be taken in generalising these concepts, since in Eastern cultures there are people who are primarily individualistic in nature, while in Western society there are those who are more collectivist in outlook.
4. *Heroes*. These are members who best typify the company's values. They are the organisational equivalent of the guru or evangelist. Indeed, one of the oldest organisations of all – the church – has long been cognisant of the importance of heroes, in the forms of a central guiding figure, notable disciples, martyrs, saints, etc. Staff at all levels should be considered in the search for such heroes. While work-based ones are essential to the success of the organisation (e.g. the 'founding father'), those who give stalwart voluntary service, gain community recognition or achieve other successes outside the confines of work (e.g. sporting prowess), and so contribute to the corporate social responsibility thrust of the company, should also be recognised.
5. *Rituals and ceremonies*. Our lives are based around rituals and we are creatures of habit. We do not like disruptions to our routines. For example, getting up and getting out of the house and into work is habituated. We do not have to think too much about it. Similarly, we develop work-based schemas to enable us to cope readily with what we do. Organisations must recognise this. For example, moving staff from one location to another may seem like a simple step to managers at a planning meeting in the boardroom. However, for the employees involved it is a major upheaval and stressful.

Humans, like all animals, are territorial. We need our own patch and become nervous when moved to new and unfamiliar ground. Rituals must therefore be dealt with sensitively. Likewise, ceremonies are an important element in organisational life. These are performed to celebrate and reinforce the organisation's values. Employee of the month awards, aerobic exercises for staff before store opening and university graduation ceremonies are typical examples. When a member of staff retires, a retirement ceremony is expected and serves the important functions of formal recognition of the individual's contribution and their transition out of the company. They are also important for remaining staff as they underscore a sense of corporate 'family' ties.

6. *Networks.* These are the informal channels that are used to indoctrinate staff into accepting prevailing norms. The staff bowling club, a particular table in the canteen or the pub down the road after work, are all situations where informal contacts are made, work roles and expectations are discussed, and gossip, opinions and information are exchanged. Deal and Kennedy[67] argued that 'The real business of a business gets done by the cultural network.' They identified six types of character within the network (see Box 1.3).

With rapid developments in all forms of communication the world is now in many senses a global business village. Yet, differences in culture persist and are of crucial import. Meanings can differ widely, as many multi-national corporations have discovered. To give an example, when Ford introduced the Pinto model in Brazil it flopped. The company, upon discovering that Pinto was Brazilian slang for 'tiny male genitals', quickly changed the name to Corcel (horse). An awareness of cultural norms, meanings and values is clearly crucial to business success. At a simple level, staff in those telephone call centres in the USA which handle consumer calls from the UK have to learn to refer to post codes rather than zip codes. Furthermore, techniques that work in one society may be anathema in another (see Box 1.4 for an example). Likewise, it has been well illustrated[68,69] how consultants frequently recommend various business philosophies (or fads) which while appropriate at one time or in one culture yield disaster when implemented in another.

Daniels *et al.*[70] pointed out that 'a culture exists when people come to share a common frame of reference for interpreting and acting toward one another and the world in which they live'. This means that

Box 1.3 Central characters in the organisational network

- *Storytellers.* Entertaining raconteurs who relate organisational happenings in an interesting manner. They interpret events for everyone.
- *Priests/priestesses.* These are those employees who take a principled stand on what they see as core issues (e.g. perceived unfair treatment of an employee; a proposal to cut down a mature tree in the grounds).
- *Whisperers.* They are often the power behind the throne, as they have the ear of senior managers and can decide what information to impart.
- *Gossips.* These are individuals who love to hear and spread the latest title tattle. They can play an important information dissemination role.
- *Spies.* People who gather information for senior managers. Often not popular with colleagues, but they can be useful conduits for those who want certain information fed up the line.
- *Cabals.* Two or more people who conjoin to plot a common course. In most organisations cabals of staff form, but it can be dysfunctional if they become competitive and enmities develop.

within organisations there are often sub-cultures. The Board of Directors, CEO and senior managers may perceive one culture to exist, whereas employees in various departments inhabit a very different milieu. We have worked with corporations where managers believed that there was openness and honesty about all aspects of what they perceived to be a democratic organisation. Shop floor staff, on the other hand, held a very different view seeing communications as top-down only, with a transparent veneer of democracy covering an autocratic style of management. The 'them and us' attitude then prevails. Communication is essential to bring these two worlds closer together. In effective organisations the gap between managerial and worker perceptions of culture will either not exist or be very small. This is particularly important in split-site organisations where locational culture may take precedence over corporate culture.

Box 1.4 Cultural clashes – the Wal-Mart German experience

Wal-Mart, the US supermarket chain, experienced severe cultural problems in Germany with losses of some £100 million per annum.[71] They imported their American system of 'golden rules', such as if a customer comes within a distance of 10 feet, staff should smile and offer help, and customers' bags should be packed at the checkout. However, the Germans were suspicious of the invasion on their personal space invoked by the 10-foot rule, and were most unhappy about someone handling their property (they had just paid for it) at the checkout. The typically taciturn German shoppers were also spooked at being confronted by grinning, garrulous, 'greeters' at the store entrance. German consumers see shopping as utterly boring and a waste of their time. They do not understand the point of cheerful service and just want efficiency. Neither did the German Wal-Mart employees relish the morning pre-opening meeting with ritual chanting of the company name 'Give us a W ... Give us an A ... etc.' replete with a wiggle for the hyphen. Reports abounded of employees hiding in the toilet to avoid what they saw as a humiliating spectacle. As Rushe[72] noted, the Wal-Mart 'one size fits all' approach to global retailing simply did not work. Indeed, Lee Scott, the CEO, admitted[73] 'We could write a training manual about our experiences in Germany ... We really did more things wrong than right.' The problem was that Wal-Mart had failed to take into account the cultural differences between the two societies.

The structure of the book

The core objective of this book is to provide a review of the main communication contexts in which managers operate. It is written in such a way that each chapter can be read on its own. To avoid unnecessary duplication we do at times cross-refer to material explained more fully in a different chapter, but the intention is that each chapter is self-contained. Thus, before conducting an appraisal interview the manager can turn to Chapter 14, when planning a presentation the information is contained in Chapter 6 and so on. At the same time, when taken as a whole, the book offers a wide panorama of communication in action.

To continue with our analogy, in the course of our travels the attractions you will encounter as you explore each chapter are:

- *Nonverbal vistas.* As humans we have developed that most sophisticated of communication devices – language. However, we are often so focused on *what* we say that we forget that *how* we deliver spoken messages is crucial. Our body language complements, adds to, underlines specific features of, and indeed can contradict and change the meaning of, the overall message. Nonverbal communication vistas that we will investigate in Chapter 2 include facial expressions, gestures, posture, gaze and eye contact, the use of interpersonal space, dress and physical appearance. These are in essence the contours of the interpersonal dimensions of the organisational communication landscape. The manager who understands them has a deeper insight into the entire interactive terrain.
- *Persuasion river.* One of the main functions of both verbal and nonverbal communication is to effect influence. Indeed, to be successful, managers must be persons of influence. Persuasion river runs through a variety of methods – both subtle and sometimes less subtle – which can be used to influence others. The core influencing and persuading strategies are summarised in Chapter 3, and the application of these techniques in one-to-one and small group situations explained. One important sub-section here is the role of relationship-building skills in successful influence. To borrow a well-known book title, managers need to know how to win friends and influence people.
- *Team games.* Winning organisations develop effective teams for the specific game they have to play. Managers must ensure that workers actually believe they are part of the team, rather than feeling like substitutes on the bench or, even worse, spectators in the stand. Techniques for fostering the development of cohesive teams are the focus of Chapter 4. It examines the stages involved in the formation of teams, the establishment of team identity, ways of encouraging loyalty, the role of 'celebration' and 'treats' and decision-making processes.
- *Leadership peaks.* It is true that the fewer the moving parts the less chance there is of anything breaking down. However, in large organisations delegation is inevitable. People must be given responsibility for specific areas of work, and for other staff. Meetings, while often portrayed as the *bete noire* of business, are

unavoidable, and, like the poor, they will always be with us. Indeed, there is considerable evidence that workers wish to be consulted and have their say on decisions being taken. It has been said that meetings take minutes and waste hours, but, as Chapter 5 illustrates, with effective leadership skills this is not the case. By climbing the leadership peaks, through gaining knowledge of the key skills involved, managers will be able to chair meaningful (and even enjoyable) meetings.

- *The presentation performance.* Studies of adult fears consistently show that having to give a formal presentation is rated as one of the most feared activities in life.[74] Standing on your hind legs and performing in front of others raises levels of anxiety considerably. There has long been a fascination with this aspect of communication. In fact, the oldest written document, dating from about 3000 BC, consists of advice to Kagemni, the eldest son of Pharaoh Huni, on speaking effectively in public. Thus, the central skills of effective public speaking have been analysed and written about for some five thousand years. There is no mystery about how to be successful in oral presentations – the expected performance can be well planned. Chapter 6 incorporates an analysis of presentational skills both in small groups (e.g. committees) and with larger audiences. It also offers useful advice on relaxation and anxiety-reducing techniques for those for whom stress may become distress.
- *The negotiation match.* Managers have to negotiate and bargain with their own staff as well as with those from other organisations. Indeed, these are important strategies in everyday life. Executives must understand the differences between negotiating and bargaining, and be cognisant with the range of approaches to negotiation (such as win–lose, win–win). To be successful in the negotiating match the manager needs to be familiar with methods for producing concessions. The core skills and strategies of effective negotiation are detailed in Chapter 7.
- *The sales challenge.* The focus in Chapter 8 is upon the skills of selling. However, this chapter is not intended just for sales people. Rather, it focuses upon selling as a challenge which all managers face regularly – selling ideas, enthusiasm, commitment and on occasions selling oneself. The well-established sales model of opening, establishing needs, presenting, overcoming objections, making additional points and closing, is presented as a template for action in many business situations.

- *Telephone land.* The fact that telephone calls are almost always much briefer than equivalent face-to-face encounters means that managers must know how to use this medium to best effect given the reduced time frame. Chapter 9 provides background information on the central norms of behaviour in telephone land, and outlines the communication differences between conversations on the telephone as opposed to face-to-face. It also deals with how best to make and receive calls, ways of facilitating immediacy, techniques for making impact and advice on how to overcome what has been termed the 'coffee and biscuits problem' of the other communicator not actually being physically present.
- *Written plains.* The key differences between written communication and the spoken word are outlined in Chapter 10, where the specific requirements of the former are highlighted. Included here is an analysis of reports, letters, e-mail, memoranda and the design of forms. The role of fonts, spacing, diagrams, illustrations, forms of emphasis, abstracts, sub-sections, appendices and structure are all examined. Given increased litigation, the importance of written information on appraisal forms, letters of reference, e-mails and so on is also underlined.
- *Assertion state.* Assertion is a set of skills rather than a trait of the individual. While once thought of as an American fad, which had little applicability in Europe, assertiveness is now widely recognised as a skill central to the effective management of relationships. Standing up for one's own rights while recognising the rights of others takes skill and tact. Assertive managers are tightrope walkers who tread a careful middle ground between aggression and submission. The techniques for achieving this are discussed in Chapter 11, where assertion as a response style is explained and distinguished from aggressiveness and submissiveness. The impact of factors such as situation, gender and beliefs is also detailed.
- *The helping melodrama.* Organisational physiognomy reveals that effective corporations have an emotional side to their face. At times of crisis such as divorce, serious illness or bereavement, employees may need and wish to share the problems and concerns raised by these melodramas. Thus, managers often have to deal with such very sensitive and emotive personal issues. When handled skilfully these helping encounters can enable the individual to cope better, while also forging a stronger bond of loyalty and trust between manager and employee. Skills of reflection, listening, empathy and rewardingness are analysed in the context of a helping format in Chapter 12.

- *Selection reefs.* When navigating the selection waters, care must be taken to avoid the many reefs on which decisions can flounder. In recent years there has been a great deal of research into the effectiveness of the employment interview and the identification of the main selection errors. These findings are summarised in Chapter 13. This is a vital stage in any organisation since the selection of staff involves a huge investment of money over a period of years and so mistakes can be very costly. At the same time, managers will also on some occasions be interviewees and so this chapter examines the selection process from the two perspectives of interviewing and being interviewed.
- *Appraisal mountain.* The appraisal precipice is one that must be climbed by supervisor and supervisee acting in unison. Two important employee questions are 'How am I doing?' and 'Does anybody care?' Formal and informal appraisals offer an ideal opportunity to answer both, as well as allowing staff to answer the key management question 'What can we do to help you do better?' Systems of appraisal are now part of the managerial operation of most organisations. In Chapter 14 an overview of research findings regarding appraisal systems is provided, the structure and content of this type of interview are outlined, and the role of the interviewee in the process is emphasised.
- *The tour path.* A final concluding chapter examines how the tour should be kept on the 'right' path, in two senses. First, the dawn of the new millennium witnessed a plethora of highly publicised cases involving unethical practices by corporations. Doing things right in companies therefore necessitates an awareness of the importance of the ethical dimensions of organisational communication. Second, most managers have a 'feel' for how well communication is in their organisation. However, this feel is often far from accurate. Therefore, ways in which the right communication pathways can be followed are explored, in terms of using an audit approach to objectively measure and monitor progress.

Overview

It is clear that communication is central to organisational life, and that ineffective communication leads literally to disorganisation. It is for this reason that 'Organizational communication is one of the fastest growing areas of academic study.'[75] Managers with effective interpersonal skills are better able to interact appropriately with employees at all levels. Research indicates that, as a result, many benefits accrue. Working relationships are enhanced and employees feel a greater sense of belongingness to the organisation. A positive team spirit prevails and there is an increased readiness to innovate. As well as greater job satisfaction there are bottom line benefits in terms of reduced costs and higher levels of profit.

Yet, there is nothing mysterious or esoteric about effective communication. As shown in this chapter, the main elements of communication have been identified and are amenable to measurement and evaluation. Indeed, communication is now a recognised social science discipline in which a voluminous amount of literature has been published. A great deal of research and study has been carried out in the interpersonal and organisational domains and the main skills, techniques and strategies that contribute to effective social encounters have been charted. These are discussed in detail in the following chapters. As we end this chapter we will also use our final tour analogy – enjoy the trip!

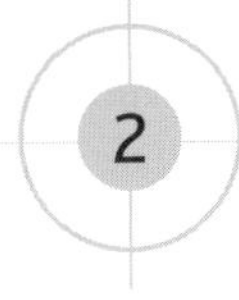

It's not what you say ...: communicating nonverbally

Introduction

A useful starting point for this chapter is a quotation from Abercrombie[1] in which he reminds us that 'We speak with our vocal organs, but we converse with our whole body.' Characteristically, we think of the process of communicating in terms of what we *say*. Did we speak with sufficiently authority? Was some complex issue clarified? Was a choice of topic ill judged? Could a word have been misconstrued? In short, we are inclined to focus upon *verbal* communication, upon words used and their sequencing and structure. Messages relayed in other ways while we speak, through glances, gestures, facial expressions, posture, tone of voice and dress, will most probably completely escape our attention. Yet it is often such *nonverbal* communication (NVC) that proves decisive in conveying information and forming judgements about others. The significance of this point is no less relevant in the workplace. While affirming the key role played generally by what he calls this 'silent language', Fletcher[2] continued by asserting that:

> ... nowhere is this more true than in management, where we are often uncertain about whether we have understood each other fully – and need every clue we can get to help us ensure we are sending and receiving messages accurately.

As we shall see, NVC performs these functions – and more.

The importance of NVC

Much of our relating to others is nonverbal and is in response to nonverbal cues picked up from them, albeit often with little conscious awareness on either part. To begin to get some idea of what interaction might be like if it were possible to strip the nonverbal part away and rely solely upon the verbal, think of the difference between simply reading a piece from the CEO in the in-house magazine and hearing that information delivered in a meeting with the workforce. How much more information about the issue (and the CEO) would be potentially available in the presentation? How would that extra information be conveyed? Relying upon the written word confines communication to the verbal medium, presentations include both the verbal and the nonverbal.

But what precisely is NVC? We can think of it *loosely* as communication without words: words are verbal while other forms of communication, by exclusion, are nonverbal. This seems fine, until we realise that, for example, some gestures that are part of formal systems of sign language, and might be regarded as nonverbal, function really as words. Likewise elements of speech such as rate and voice modulation (which might have been thought of as verbal) are not words *per se*, but rather have to do with how the words are delivered, and are therefore really better placed in the nonverbal category. According to Richmond and McCroskey[3] precise definitions that introduce hard and fast distinctions between verbal and NVC are illusory. Instead they suggested teasing the two forms apart by pointing up broad differences. As such, by comparison, verbal messages:

- rely much more heavily upon symbols (i.e. words) as part of an arbitrary code
- tend to be discretely packaged in separate words rather than represented in continuous behaviour, as in gaze
- carry more meaning explicitly rather than implicitly
- typically address cognitive/propositional rather than emotional/relational matters.

Remland[4] further noted that verbal interchanges must take place sequentially (i.e. participants must take turns) but interactors can communicate simultaneously using a nonverbal code. An important additional point of difference, stressed by Anderson,[5] is that NVC is largely the responsibility of the right hemisphere of the brain, rather than the left, unlike language.

In some ways, NVC can be thought of as playing a more pivotal role than the verbal in our social dealings, although it is not really sensible to regard these as two totally distinct systems, never mind two systems in some sort of perpetual competition.[6] Nevertheless, arguments supporting the importance of NVC include the following:

- NVC is undoubtedly a more primitive form of communication than language. Fossil records show that our early ancestors would have been unable to command language in the way that we do. Again, in terms of the evolution of the individual, as distinct from the species, NVC is primitive in the sense that it pre-dates language. Being more primitive, however, does not necessarily mean being more crucial.

- Much social meaning is conveyed nonverbally rather than verbally. Research suggests that in some cases nonverbal cues contribute more than half to the meaning of the overall message received.[7] This is particularly so where there is marked incongruity between *what* is said and *how* it is said; when expectations surrounding either channel are violated, and when there is an emphasis upon social/affective rather than cognitive/task issues.[8] When a manager bellows at an assistant that he is *not* angry, greater weight tends to be placed upon the nonverbal and paralinguistic message sources.
- We are inclined to be less aware of the nonverbal accompaniment of much of what we say, than we are of the actual words spoken. Indeed much NVC can take place outside of conscious awareness.[9] While we often carefully monitor what is said to achieve the desired effect, how we say it may escape censor thereby 'leaking' the reality of the situation. In other words, NVC is a more 'truthful' form of communication through the insights that it affords into what may lie behind the verbal message. It may be so, but only to a point.
- Of course, skilled interactors can learn to control what their bodies say as well as the messages sent in words. The work of 'Spin Doctors' with politicians and other influential people in the public eye does not stop merely at verbal manicure. Appropriate facial expressions, looks, gestures and tones of voice are all included in the packaged end product. Part of the training of staff in the service sector involves preparation for 'emotion labour'. Such outlets as McDonald's and Disneyland groom staff in how to appear pleasant, cheery and approachable to customers – the 'smile' industry.[10]
- Language is particularly suited to conveying ideas and information about our environment, our understandings and intentions in respect of it. Through the use of language *homo sapiens* has succeeded in such awesome feats of collaboration as building the pyramids and putting men on the moon. Only through language can we access and discuss the ideas of Wittgenstein, plays of Shakespeare, novels of Hemmingway and films of Fellini or Scorsese. NVC, in contrast, tends to convey information of a different type, to do more with feelings and attitudes. It is largely upon this sort of

detail that interpersonal relationships are built, sustained and sometimes terminated. These relationships, in turn, are the bedrock of institutions such as marriage, family and work, which go to make up society, as we know it.

- We can often make ourselves known in a rudimentary way through signs and gestures when communicating with people from differing cultural backgrounds who do not share a common language. NVC has therefore a greater universality than language. This is true but again only to a certain extent. As we shall see later in the chapter, failure to appreciate the nonverbal nuances of cultural diversity can lead to miscommunication and the breakdown of interaction, which is just as real as failure to use the proper words. Carol Goman,[11] a consultant in this area, stressed the importance of international business people doing their homework on the host culture before travelling abroad. It is crucial to give thought, she claimed, to 'What does it mean to make eye contact, to use hand and arm gestures, to smile, to laugh, to cross your legs, to put your hand in your pockets or on your hips, to touch another person, etc.? Especially, what gestures are taboo in this culture?'

NVC in management

The contribution of NVC in developing effective relational skills in the workplace must not be undervalued. Hiemstra,[12] who writes on the topic, made the point forcefully when she claimed that '... actions speak louder than words in business. Our nonverbal communications, including shaking hands in a professional manner, can be an important part of business success.' Using the amount of published material as a marker of interest, NVC is well represented in articles appearing each year in business periodicals. Furthermore, there is an ever-increasing stock of personal development/self-help type books for the committed businessperson keen to find out how a greater knowledge of both own and other people's NVC could help them operate more effectively.

In a survey[13] of 550 managers and staff in 50 organisations involved in manufacturing, health care, finance, retail and government, 92 per cent of respondents rated nonverbal aspects as either important or very important in group settings such as committee or departmental meetings. Overall, importance in dyadic (one-to-one) situations was rated even higher. Additionally, those who regarded themselves as being particularly sensitive to the nonverbal cues of others, when compared to colleagues who felt their abilities in this quarter were only average, placed greater importance on NVC in both dyadic and group situations. Incidentally, more than 50 per cent of those surveyed noted that their supervisors' verbal communication and NVC were either occasionally or frequently in conflict. It would seem that when managers attempt to disguise or mask their true feelings, all they succeed in doing, is to send conflicting signals which may readily be decoded by staff as confusion, subterfuge or duplicity and lead to the erosion of trust. Small wonder that Warfield[14] implored them to 'look at the body language you use and make sure it is congruent with your message'.

Effective management requires a high degree of awareness of one's own NVC as well as sensitivity to that of others. Without a doubt, what Carnevale[15] called the ability to 'people read' is a skill upon which depends the imaginative management of diversity in large companies and consequent success in the global economic order.

Functions of NVC

Why do we use NVC? We are, after all, the only species with this marvellously abstract and sophisticated means of communicating that we call language. Other species communicate, of course, but they all do so by means of various forms of nonverbal behaviour. Through changes in, for example, real or apparent size, posture and movement, odour and skin colour, and in a myriad of grunts, howls and roars, they signal social status, sexual receptivity, bodily and emotional states, and territorial ownership. But language is different. It frees us from the here and how, from the physical and actual. Without it we would find it difficult or impossible to refer to, never mind take into account:

- abstract concepts such as love, loyalty or honour
- happenings at this point in time in another place
- past events
- anticipated future occurrences
- things that have never happened and probably never will (including the whole literary genre of fiction).

So why do we bother with NVC? It seems that NVC serves a number of functions. These are summarised in Box 2.1 and elaborated in the remainder of this section.

Box 2.1 Main functions of NVC

- Replacing verbal communication
- Complementing the spoken word
- Contradicting the spoken word
- Expressing emotions and interpersonal attitudes
- Conveying personal/social/cultural identity
- Negotiating relationships
- Regulating conversations
- Contextualising interaction.

Replacing verbal communication

Some forms of NVC, especially gestures, are used as direct substitutes for words under circumstances where speech is either not feasible or desirable. In the Lancashire cotton mills, in days gone past when that working environment was particularly noisy, workers signalled when management was on the factory floor, by patting the top of the head.

Complementing the spoken word

Here NVC is used alongside what is said, especially when material is difficult to get across, in order to enhance the overall message (e.g. drawing an imaginary map in the air while giving directions) or to add impact. In the teaching of rhetoric in classical and mediaeval times, forms of specific gesture were identified along with their planned effects on an audience. Tone of voice may also accentuate the verbal message as witnessed by a charismatic captain of industry delivering a motivational address to the workforce.

Contradicting the spoken word

Forms of discourse ranging from sarcasm to humour often rely upon something being said 'in a particular way'. The words suggest one interpretation but tone of voice and body language something different. The NVC, as it were, provides a frame for interpreting what was said. This suggests the possibility of a specialist function for NVC to do with detecting deception. Are there particular nonverbal cues that signal when someone is lying, for example, avoiding eye contact, fidgeting, etc.? If the answer was 'yes', can you imagine the advantages that such knowledge would bestow upon the manager? Despite popular belief, though, research has failed to find such cues. As put by Vrij[16] '... there is nothing like Pinocchio's nose'. What we do have are indices of underlying internal processes that can be associated with deceptive behaviour. In this sense, lying can manifest itself in different ways including:

- increased physiological arousal suggesting heightened stress (e.g. raised heart rate and sweating);
- conspicuous attempts to control performance (e.g. appearing wooden or offering a slow deliberate delivery);
- displaying emotion which may be either caused by the deception (e.g. signs of anxiety and guilt) or the basis of it (e.g. pretending to be happy when sad);
- increased cognitive processing of information (e.g. more concentrated thinking revealed perhaps in gaze avoidance).

The relationship between deception and its nonverbal manifestation is more complex than folk wisdom would have us believe, and involves mediating circumstantial factors (e.g. perceived consequences of being found out) and personal considerations (e.g. skill in carrying the deception attempt off).[17]

Expressing emotions and interpersonal attitudes

How we feel, and how we feel about others, is revealed through NVC. Again the extent to which this is done intentionally and with awareness can vary. Some emotional cues such as pupil dilation in response to heightened arousal are largely beyond our control. Others suggesting anger or sadness are more manageable. Likewise we can convey attitudes about others nonverbally with little awareness of having done so, or on the other hand, deliberately decide to give another the 'cold shoulder'.

Conveying personal/social/cultural identity

In a complex of subtle (and not so subtle) ways involving habitat, dress, deportment and accent, we send messages about ourselves: who and what we are, and how we wish to be received and reacted to by others. *Impression management* or *self-presentation* are terms used to refer to this process of projecting an image that we want affirmed by those with whom we deal. In a piece of research involving 72 job applicants, Amy Kristof-Brown and colleagues[18] found that those who made use of nonverbal impression management tactics influenced interviewers' perceptions of interviewer–applicant similarity. Focusing specifically upon female professionals who were members of a chamber of commerce women's association, Trethewey[19] reported their use of their bodies together with what she called 'comportment skills' to create a sustainable professional identity at work. These women were keen to employ 'strategies of self-presentation that are at once engaging, though not too inviting, soft but not weak, and interesting, but not threatening'.

In business organisations with steep hierarchical structures of control, projecting suitable images of status forms an inevitable part of dealings with others both within and outwith the company. Features such as size of office space and opulence of furnishings take on a special significance in this process. Many firms have standards stipulating the minimum size and type of office for an employee at a particular level in the management pecking order.

Negotiating relationships

Communication is a multi-faceted activity. Two people discussing an issue are never *just* discussing that issue. They are doing other interpersonal things at the same time, both in what they say and how they say it. One of these 'other things' has to do with the relationship that they share. Is it positive or negative? Is there an equal or unequal sharing of power and control? In largely nonverbal ways, both parties establish, sustain or indeed terminate a particular type of interpersonal association. Generally those who get on well engage in more eye contact and interact at closer interpersonal distances, as will be explained later.

Regulating conversations

How do we manage to conduct conversations so that we don't keep interrupting or talking over each other but, at the same time, avoid awkward silences between speech turns? NVC helps to regulate turn taking.[20,21] Conversationalists are able to anticipate when they will have an opportunity to take the floor. The next time you are talking to someone, think of the cues that they give off that suggest to you that it would be acceptable for you to speak at a particular point. You will probably note changes in:

- tone of voice
- gestures
- gaze.

While there are important cultural differences, those from a North American/British background, in coming to the end of a speech-turn, will typically introduce a downward vocal inflection (unless they have just asked a question), stop gesticulating and look at their partner.[22] This information can be made use of in situations where one is keen not to hand over the floor. Since high status and interpersonal influence are usually positively correlated with extent of verbal contribution, there are occasions when retaining the floor in this way can promote a positive image.

Contextualising interaction

In the ways that people interact and communicate they, in a sense, create social situations. Again NVC has an important part to play. Through chosen dress code and layout of office space, opportunities are created for a meeting to become, for example, a very formal interview or a more casual chit-chat. As we shall see later, some managers organise their offices to include a formal workspace and social areas more conducive to informality.

Forms of NVC

How are these functions achieved? What are the most important forms of NVC by means of which these various interactive outcomes are reached? It is to answering these questions that we turn in this section.

Territory and personal space

We all have areas of the environment that we regard as ours in some way and to varying extents. These are spaces to which we claim special rights of access and 'ownership'. Such territories may include home, office or desk. Additionally, we all occupy an envelope of space that we move around in and think of as 'ours'. This is our personal space. As such, we feel very uncomfortable, even aggrieved, if it is violated. In other words, we like people to 'keep their distance'. The extent to which they do, depends upon a complex of factors including culture, personality, age, sex, status and dominance. It is more common, and 'permissible', for a person of high status to encroach upon someone of lower status than the other way around. For example, a production manager, on a visit to the shop floor may move largely unannounced into the personal/work space of a machine operator. Such tactics can be used intentionally for the purposes of impression management to stamp one's authority and gain an upper hand. Indeed there is evidence[23] to suggest that managers and other high-status members can actually *enhance* their credibility and attractiveness by violating spatial norms in this way. Were the machine operator to reciprocate in a visit to the manager's office, though, it would be regarded as very bad form and have completely the opposite effect.

But such management practice must also be tempered with caution. It should not be thought to invariably impress. Anne Warfield,[24] a leading organisational consultant, told of being asked to help sort out a problem of low morale in a particular workplace. The root of the problem was the extremely domineering stance of the manager, manifested largely nonverbally. She reported, for instance, how 'When he dropped by his employees' offices, he would take up the whole doorway or walk right in and up to their desk and look them in the eye – even if they were on the phone!' Failing to recognise the negative effects of intruding into personalised space can indeed lead to attributions of arrogance or boorishness and impact gravely on working relationships.

Switching from managing to selling, the received wisdom has likewise tended to advocate caution in moving into the customer's personal space during sales transactions. It has been found though, when put to the test, that such behaviour can actually pay dividends, but only under certain circumstances.[25] Moving very close to the customer can aid the sale when both involved in the transaction are female. Adverse effects occur, though, when both seller and customer are male. (See Chapter 8 for more information on selling.) This is in keeping with consistent findings about gender and NVC. Females generally tend to make greater use of a range of cues including:[26,27]

- eye-contact
- closer interpersonal distance
- direct orientation
- touch.

All of these suggest positive interpersonal qualities of engagement, openness and warmth. Women have also been found to be much more sensitive to the nonverbal behaviour of others, than the average man.[28] Perhaps this explains why, in part at least, female sales representatives, when compared with their male counterparts, have been reported to earn more sales awards at Prudential.

Interpersonal distance

This is the distance people maintain while interacting. It might be thought to be totally coincidental and largely insignificant. Neither assumption would be correct. Interpersonal distance, like personal space, is shaped by multiple factors as shown in Box 2.2. One of these is culture. Northern European and North American cultures tend to adopt relatively large interpersonal distances compared to those from Southern Europe, Latin America and the Middle East. These differences can lead to unfortunate consequences.

Hall[29] was one of the first to draw attention to difficulties in establishing mutually accommodating conversational distances with Arabs. The story is told of a group of British businessmen who formed a trade delegation to one of the Arabian countries at a time when wealth was pouring into that part of the world in the wake of the oil boom. A banquet was held in their honour, at which Arab and British had an opportunity to meet and make contacts. But something strange seemed to be taking place. All those present were seen circling the large banqueting hall, mostly in pairs, with the British businessmen in retreat, hotly pursued by their Arabian hosts. What on earth could account for this rather bizarre 'dance'. The answer was down to interpersonal distance. An Arab would approach a member of the delegation to introduce himself. Of course he did so in keeping with his culturally determined interpersonal distance, moving right up close to his guest. Somewhat taken aback, his uncomfortable guest, in responding, would take a few steps back to maintain his

Box 2.2 Factors shaping interpersonal distance

- *Cultural/ethnic background*
- *Gender* – females typically adopt closer distances than males
- *Personality* – extroverts adopt closer distances than introverts
- *Interpersonal relations* – friends adopt closer distances than strangers
- *Age* – the very young and old adopt closer distances
- *Topic of conversation* – taboo or sensitive topics that engender discomfort promote greater interpersonal distance
- *Physical features of the other* – people stigmatised through disfigurement or deformity evoke greater interactive distances
- *Physical/social setting* – the location places constraints on how far apart people can be (e.g. crowded party).

culturally determined interpersonal distance for such occasions. The Arab would, once more, close the distance, and so it continued.

Apart from the humorous side, the incident had rather unfortunate consequences in terms of each group's perceptions of the other. British businessmen were seen to be cold, distant, aloof and unfriendly. (Notice how we use expressions to do with distance, such as 'standoffish' and 'approachable', to describe how friendly or unfriendly people are!) The Arabs, in turn, were thought to be pushy, aggressive and domineering. Needless to say, that particular trade delegation met with little success.

Today, with globalisation and the onward march of international business, it is increasingly accepted that simply knowing the language is not enough, if one is to succeed abroad. A wider appreciation of communication and culture is required.[30] But differences in interpersonal distance also exist *within* a culture denoting contrasting relationships and social activities. As we have already seen, status differences are marked nonverbally. People of equal status tend to take up a closer distance between each other than people of unequal status.[31] In fact, where a status differential exists the lower status individual will allow the higher status individual to approach quite closely, but will rarely approach the high-status individual with the same degree of closeness. Based upon observations of predominantly white, middle-class American males from business and professional backgrounds, four distinct categories of distance emerged to characterise the range of interpersonal contacts.[32] These are:

1. *Intimate* (ranging from physical contact to about 45 cms) – reserved for very close friends and family.
2. *Casual-personal* (from 45 cms to 1.30 m) – typifies informal chit-chat with friends and acquaintances.
3. *Social-consultative* (from 1.3 to 4 m) – used for more impersonal business transactions.
4. *Public* (from about 4 m to the range of sound and vision) – used for making speeches and addressing large groups at formal gatherings.

Seating arrangements

The ways in which work space is arranged and utilised can send strong signals about the status and authority of occupants, the sorts of tasks and activities being implicitly proposed, and the desirability and appropriateness of focused communication in that situation.

Figure 2.1 **Seating arrangements and interaction**

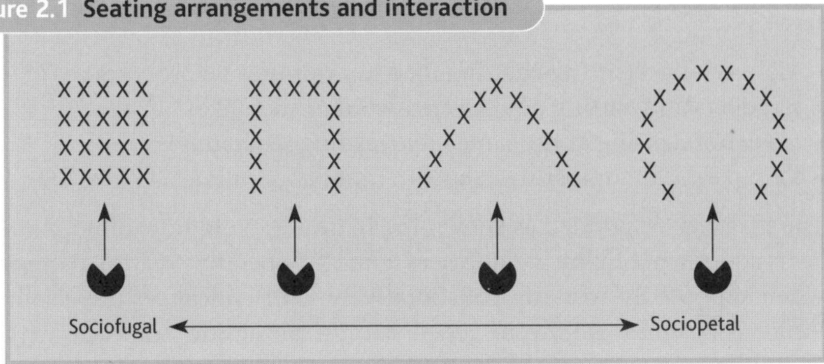

Promoting/inhibiting interaction Interaction can be made more or less likely in the way that the seating in a room is set out. A layout that encourages interaction is called *sociopetal*: one that has the opposite effect, *sociofugal*. It is imperative, therefore, that seating be organised accordingly by, let's say, using a sociopetal grouping to make it easier for those present to get to know each other and share ideas in free and open exchange. On the other hand, a sociofugal variant will be more accommodating if the intention is for the CEO to play a centrally dominant role through essentially one-way communication. Examples of types of seating varying along the sociopetal–sociofugal continuum can be found in Figure 2.1.

Denoting status and authority In at least traditional hierarchical organisations, those in authority and control commonly have their status acknowledged by the way they position themselves *vis-à-vis* other staff. As a rule they tend to adopt positions that are more elevated, isolated and 'head-of-table', than their lesser-ranking colleagues. Indeed it is common for the seats of power in organisations to be located in the top floors of buildings. It was said of Harry Cohen, the one-time president of Columbia Pictures, that he had his desk placed on a raised platform at the far end of a long, spacious room as a way of not only marking status but intimidating those who came to do business with him. We shall return to this issue when we discuss possible communicative effects of environmental features later in the chapter.

Conducting tasks It seems that people have firm notions of the sorts of seating arrangements appropriate to carrying out certain types of task. In one piece of research, workers in various organisations were asked how they would position themselves at a rectangular table with six chairs, if required to carry out a series of tasks with a friend of the same sex.[33] The tasks were:

- Conversation (sitting chatting for a few minutes before work)
- Co-operation (sitting doing a crossword or such like)
- Co-action (sitting at the same table reading separately)
- Competition (competing to solve a number of puzzles).

The majority responded as shown in Figure 2.2. Note how often managers adopt what many would see as a non co-operative seating pattern when supposedly working collaboratively with colleagues, especially junior colleagues. Failing to get physically 'alongside' someone with whom one is supposedly sharing a task may suggest a lack of harmony in the working relationship.

Figure 2.2 Types of task and seating arrangements

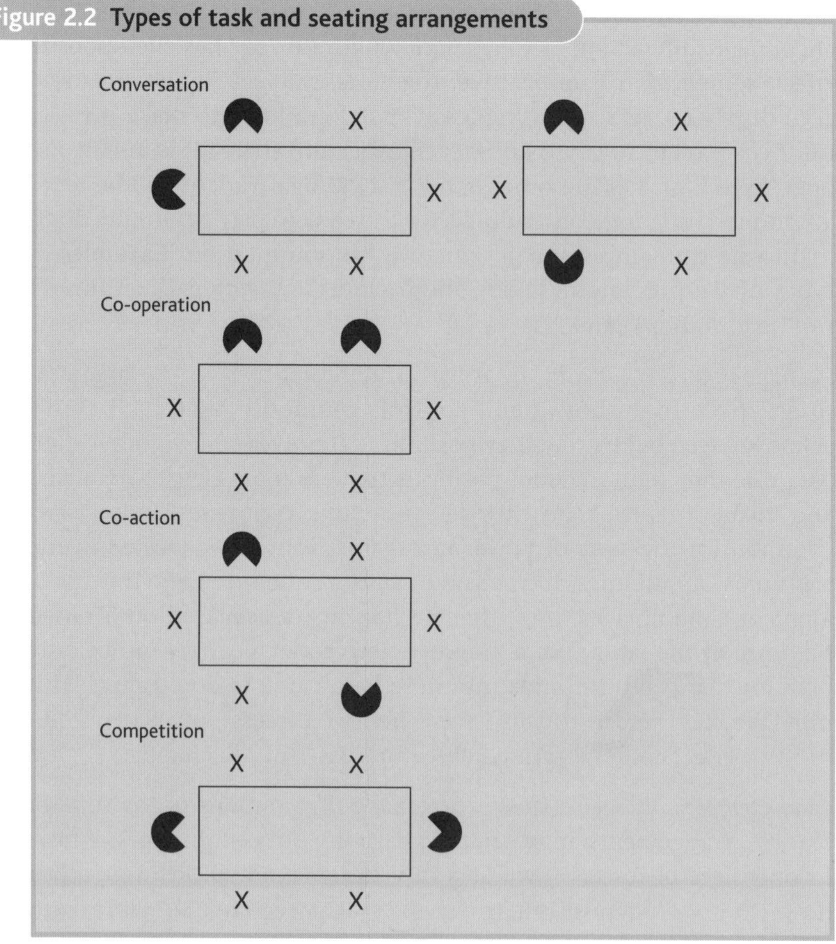

Facial expressions

The face is without doubt the most expressively significant area of the body, particularly the regions of the eyes and the mouth. It is through co-ordinated movements of over 20 different muscles that we encode some 1000 distinct expressions making the face a rich source of nonverbal information, particularly to do with emotion. Even with simplified schematic faces such as those in Figure 2.3, reading the primary emotions displayed, such as fear, anger, happiness and sadness, comes easily. Yet the differences in the faces are only in the lines representing the brows and the mouth.

More subtle emotional states such as *affect blends* are expressed when part of the face suggests one emotional state (e.g. surprise) but another region something different (e.g. anger). E-mail users will be familiar with adaptations of these faces, using combinations of key strokes, to relay emotional messages. Blake,[34] for instance, listed a variety of these

Figure 2.3 Facial expressions and emotional states

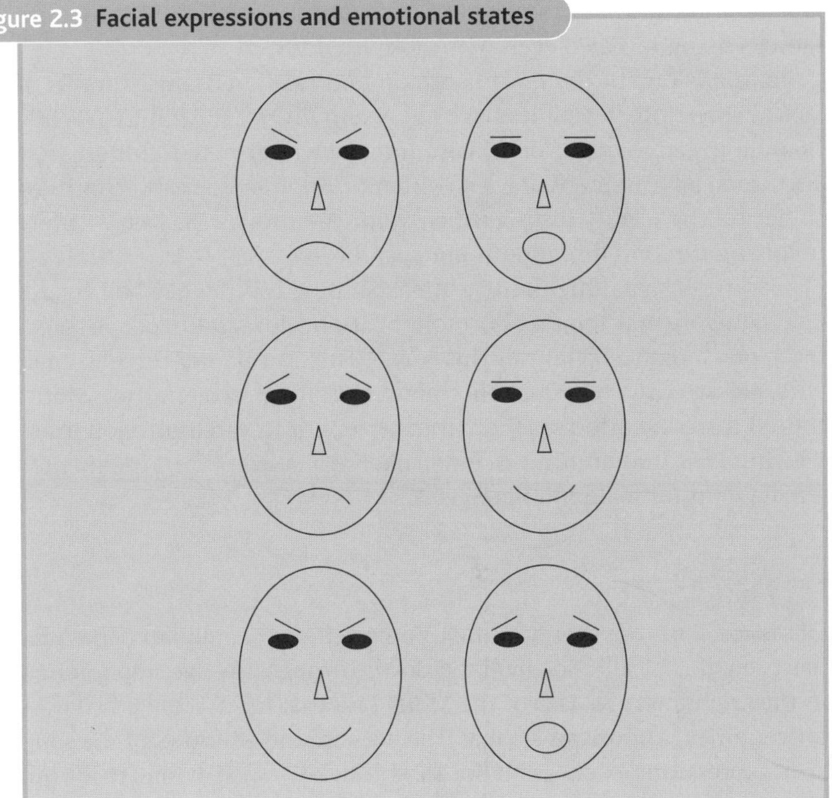

'emoticons' and described how they can reduce the emotional sterility of the medium and increase its 'bandwidth'. Examples are probably familiar to many and include:

:-) smile
:-(displeasure
;-) wink
:-D laugh.

We have already mentioned how different cultures use NVC differently. It seems, though, that facial expressions of primary emotional states, by contrast, are quite universal. In other words, everyone looks happy, angry or sad, in more or less the same way. But cultural norms dictate when and with whom it is appropriate to display emotion. The Japanese, for example, are renowned for their inscrutability. In an early experiment, Friesen[35] had American and Japanese students watch alone a gruesome piece of film while being videotaped. Similar expressions of disgust were revealed but when later asked about the film, only the American students persisted with these negative facial displays. Japanese are also less approving of emotions such as disgust and sadness being revealed even with close friends.[36]

Smiling is one of the most common and easily recognised forms of facial expression, yet smiles have many and diverse meanings.[37] While friendliness, enjoyment or affiliation may be interpreted, smiling may also signal appeasement or even contempt. Spontaneous and contrived smiles can be readily distinguished, with the former *Duchenne* variety involving not only the mouth but also the eyes.

Apart from signalling positive affect, smiling is influenced by gender and status in that females do more of it and low-status people seem more pressured to behave in this way.[38] This can poorly serve women who are striving to establish themselves in managerial positions. Indeed the conclusion reached from a piece of research into job interviewing was that smiling is more likely to suggest lower status for female than for male interviewees.[39]

Eye gaze

Obsession with the eyes and their potent effects on human behaviour has been graphically documented down through the ages, epitomised in the celebrated eye gaze of the Mona Lisa that has fascinated viewers for centuries. Aphorisms such as 'the eyes are the windows of the soul' and expressions such as 'if looks could kill', also come to mind.

Gaze (i.e. looking at another, especially around the face) and eye-contact (i.e. both parties looking each other in the eye), play several important roles in face-to-face interaction. In this way we:[40]

- *Initiate contact.* 'Catching someone's eye', is a first step to engaging them in conversation.
- *Define the interpersonal relationship.* Friends and those who like each other, typically gaze more than strangers or those who feel negatively. However, a gaze becoming a stare can mark extreme negativity.
- *Regulate the flow of conversation.* We have already seen how turn-taking is regulated, in part, through the use of gaze, with speakers typically engaging in eye-contact as they come to the end of their speech turn.
- *Monitor feedback.* Speakers gaze at listeners, from time to time, in order to gain feedback on the success or otherwise of their message. Listeners who reciprocate show that they are paying attention. There are cultural differences here, however, that can cause problems. As explained by Ilya Adler,[41] Principal of Kochman Communications and based in Mexico City, looking straight in the eye can be considered an aggressive act among Mexican males, and flirtation when between males and females, rather than a show of attention.
- *Orchestrate discussion.* In group situations, a speaker or someone in a chairperson role, may use gaze to invite certain members to speak at particular junctures, and tactfully discourage others.
- *Reflect thinking activity.* Speakers frequently engage in patterns of gazing with breaks at points in their speech-turn when they are concentrating on what to say next. Proponents of Neurolinguistic Programming claim that the direction in which a person looks away can reveal fascinating insights into what is going on at that point 'inside their head'. Depending upon a person looking up, to the side, or down and to the left or right in each case, insights can be gained into whether that person is busily remembering or constructing visual, auditory or tactile representations of events, real or imagined. Conclusive research evidence in support of these claims, however, has still to be provided. There may be some individual variations in patterning with left–right reversal for left-handed people. Still, this theory can be put to the test by asking a friend or colleague the questions in Figure 2.4 and noting if the eye responses correspond to those given.

Figure 2.4 Eye direction and thinking states

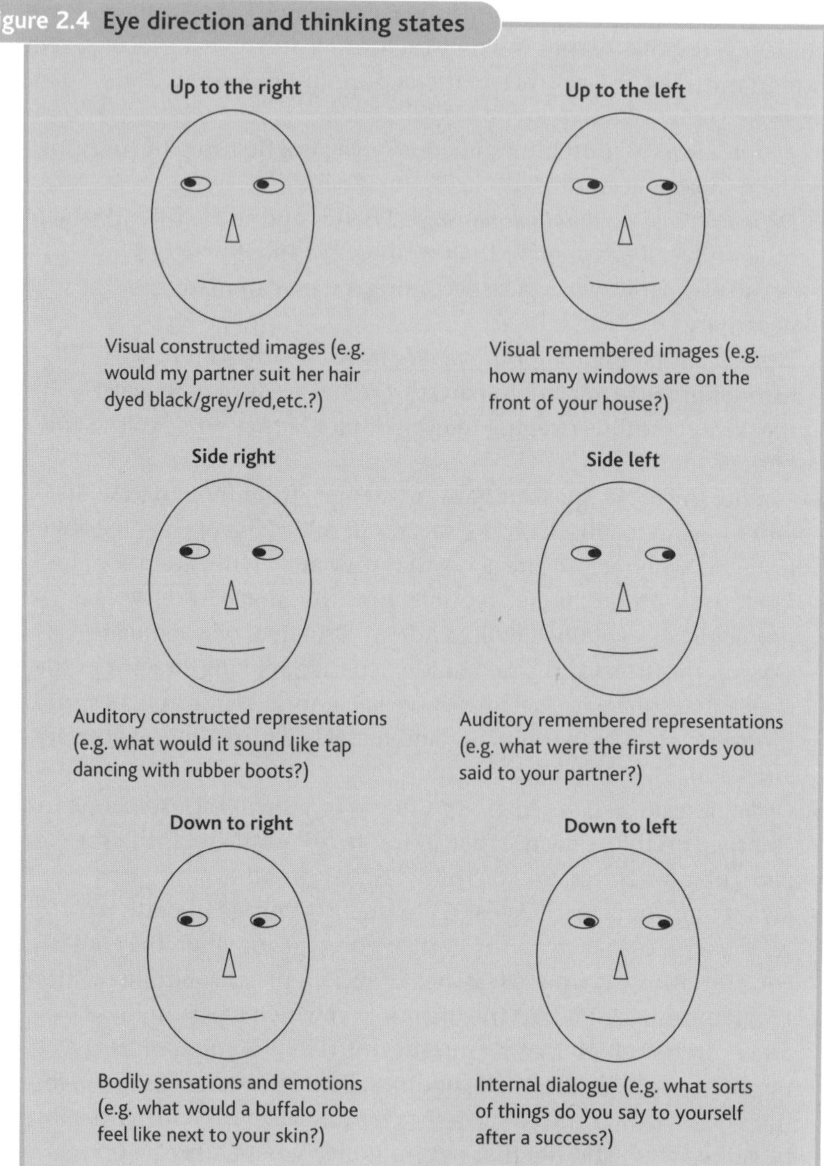
Up to the right
Up to the left
Visual constructed images (e.g. would my partner suit her hair dyed black/grey/red,etc.?)
Visual remembered images (e.g. how many windows are on the front of your house?)
Side right
Side left
Auditory constructed representations (e.g. what would it sound like tap dancing with rubber boots?)
Auditory remembered representations (e.g. what were the first words you said to your partner?)
Down to right
Down to left
Bodily sensations and emotions (e.g. what would a buffalo robe feel like next to your skin?)
Internal dialogue (e.g. what sorts of things do you say to yourself after a success?)

Gestures

Gestures are normally thought of as movements of the hands and arms, but can also be made with the head as when nodding approval. The extent to which they are put to use varies depending upon such factors as culture and situation. Italians are notorious users, while in

Britain, newscasters would seem to find little need for them at all. There are five main types of gesture.[42]

Emblems These semantic gestures and are one of the few types of NVC that function, to all intents and purposes, like words. Indeed, they could be more properly regarded as such, despite the fact that they are commonly discussed under the heading of NVC. Examples include the signs used by policemen to direct the flow of traffic, by those communicating with the deaf and by bookmakers at racetracks. In all cases, the gesture has a direct verbal translation that can differ, of course, from culture to culture. Since some have obscene meanings, one must be careful. Here lies a very slippery banana skin for the unwary businessman abroad. The sign with the thumb touching the tip of the index finger forming a ring and palm facing out, that in the UK means exquisite and is used as a compliment, in France and Belgium means that the thing referred to is worthless. In Turkey and Malta the gesture is an obscene insult with the ring representing an orifice – invariably the anus.

Illustrators These accompany speech, and are linked to it. On their own, however, they make little sense. Such hand gestures, in a variety of forms, can be used to enhance and facilitate what is said. They can take an *ideographic* form as when enunciating some abstract concept or idea (e.g. cupped hands when explaining the totality of the organisation). Similarly, *iconographic gestures* help describe some happening, place or thing (e.g. describing an action sequence from a mechanical operation; the layout of an office; or an irregular shape). Additionally, pointing to an object or place while referring to it involves *deictic gestures*.

Baton gestures are a slightly different type. If you spend time watching managers who are good at public speaking, you will notice that gestures are often used to add emphasis and create impact. This is usually against a backdrop of ongoing gesticulation that seeks to simply mark out the beat of the delivery in rhythmic movements.

Regulators These orchestrate conversation and ensure that turn-taking is switched smoothly. As speakers finish a speech-turn they will probably drop their hand as they bring a gesture to an end. Not to do so, despite the fact that they may have stopped speaking, is usually enough to signal that they still have something left to say and have not conceded the floor.

Affect displays Hand movements can also convey emotional states, although the face is a richer source of such information, as mentioned.

Gestures can reveal emotional dispositions such as, embarrassment (e.g. hand over the mouth); anger (e.g. white knuckles); aggression (e.g. fist clenching); shame (e.g. hands covering the eyes); nervousness (e.g. nail and finger biting); boredom (e.g. hair preening); despair (e.g. hand wringing). Managers should be sensitive to these hand signals which, because of their often-spontaneous nature, may reveal more about the employee's feelings than words would permit.

Adaptors These are also called *self-manipulative gestures* and include such things as scratching, rubbing, hand wringing and hair preening. One school of thought suggests that they are signs of anxiety or unease. Others proffer a more Freudian interpretation and hold that they represent the acting out of deeper psychic conflicts. As such, excessive scratching or hair tugging becomes a form of symbolic self-mutilation. In either case, these gestures are quite different in function from the previous two types mentioned and are decoded accordingly. It is quite often cues of this type that are focused upon when judging what someone *really* feels.

Those who supplement their dialogue with good use of hand and arm movements, usually arouse and maintain the attention of their listeners, indicate their interest and enthusiasm, and tend to make the interaction sequence a stimulating and enjoyable experience for all participants. Adam Kendon[43] focused on the various conditions under which individuals use gestures in this way and concluded that the speaker divides the task of conveying meaning between words and gestures to achieve either economy of expression or a particular effect on the listener. For instance, a gesture can be used as a device for completing a sentence that, if spoken, might prove embarrassing to the speaker. It can also be used as a means of telescoping what one wants to say, when the available turn space is smaller than one would like. Alternatively, gestures can be employed to clarify some potentially ambiguous word or as an additional component when the verbal account is inadequate to truly represent the information being shared.

Posture

It was once thought that the primary communicative function of posture was to carry information about the *intensity* of emotional experience and, to a lesser extent, status and bearing. In the research study by Trethewey,[44] already referred to, women reported that a confident posture was one of the ways in which they laid claim to professional status and respect. But attitudes can also be revealed in this way.[45] Watch how people sit in chairs at meetings, for example. It is usually reasonably easy to tell from their posture who is riveted and who virtually comatose, who is in enthusiastic agreement with what is being said and who implacably opposed, who is relaxed with those around them and who uneasy.

The matching or mirroring of postures can also take place. This is where one interactor adopts a similar or mirror image posture to that of another. This may change to maintain congruence as the other's changes. Neurolinguistic programmers place great store by this process of matching as a way of establishing empathic rapport. Likewise, it is often possible in meetings to spot the cliques and coalitions by noticing the members who are matched. Those 'on the same side' will frequently adopt matched postures, especially if they have a well-co-ordinated strategy.

Vocalics

The point has already been made that NVC includes parts of speech as well as body language. These are the parts that accompany the spoken word, but are not verbal, as such. The general term *paralinguistics* includes such features as speech rate and intensity; pitch, modulation and quality of voice; and articulation and rhythm control. Other nonverbal sounds like moaning and sighing, speech dysfluencies and vocalisations such as 'uh-huh', 'er' and 'ahh' are also included.

By means of paralinguistics, judgements can be made (with varying degrees of accuracy) about:

- *The speaker* (e.g. age, sex, size, personality, emotional state and to some extent occupation)
- *The presentation of the message* (e.g. enthusiasm, excitement, competence)
- *How the message should be received* (e.g. tongue in cheek, soberly, respectfully). In *The Selling of the President 1968*, McGinniss[46] related how, before a broadcast, the announcer who was about to do the introduction asked if his voice was too shrill. 'Yeah, we don't want it like a quiz show', he was told, 'He's going to be presidential tonight so announce presidentially.'

But it isn't just about image and personal impressions. How information is delivered paralinguistically has important consequences for how much of the message is understood, recalled and acted upon.

Prosody is the term used to refer to those vocal variations associated with the words that serve to actually change the meaning of what was said. Take, for instance the following question: 'Did you attend the Design meeting last week?' If we decide to place more vocal emphasis on certain words we can alter what is actually being asked, together with underlying assumptions:

1. '*Did* you attend the Design meeting last week?'
   ('*I suspect you didn't*')
2. 'Did *you* attend the Design meeting last week?'
   ('*I assumed that John had gone on his own*')
3. 'Did you *attend* the Design meeting last week?'
   ('*I thought you were merely briefed afterwards*')
4. 'Did you attend the *Design meeting* last week?'
   ('*Wasn't it only the meeting with Production?*')
5. 'Did you attend the Design meeting *last* week?'
   ('*Why did I think it was the week before?*)

Extralinguistics is about, for example, variations in accent. This is an important marker of social identity and a rich source of opinions and value judgements about people. Once a person is located, by accent, according to ethnic background, culture or class, corresponding stereotypes can be triggered that in turn evoke favourable or unfavourable attributions. Accent is indeed a powerful catalyst for prejudice. So Glaswegians are aggressive, Yorkshire men doggedly determined but unimaginative, Essex women stupid, Irish drunken and so on. In a TV interview with the Labour MP, Dr John Reid, upon his appointment as Chairman of the Party at a time when hints of internal party disharmony were growing, it was put to him that he had been given the job on account of his reputation as a political bare-knuckle fighter. He responded in self-defence by saying that ordinarily a person with a doctoral degree is regarded as something of an intellectual, unless he has a Gaswegian accent, whereupon he instantly becomes just another bruiser.

One management context where this accent can become particularly problematic is in staff recruitment. You may want to complete Exercise 2.1 at this point. In the presence of a poor interviewer, such influence can lead to inferior selection decisions. It was found,[47] for example, that a foreign accent leads to lower ratings of suitability for a high-status job, but higher ratings for one of low status.

Interestingly, it seems to have become fashionable for some of the most successful in business to flaunt, rather than try to disguise, their regional

Exercise 2.1 Accents and stereotypes

Imagine that you have just picked up the phone. The caller wants to find out how your company goes about recruiting, as he is keen to apply for a job in sales. As he begins to speak, you readily pick up his strong accent. Jot down (truthfully) images and qualities that are triggered if the person was obviously from....

Accent	*Images/qualities*
Birmingham	
Glasgow	
Kensington	
Liverpool	
Pakistan	
Belfast	
Melbourne	
Jamaica	
Texas	

If you are unfamiliar with these accents, or if they do not surface any strong stereotypes, select alternatives that do, in your case.

accents. Perhaps it is seen as a further cue, setting them apart from the herd, and promoting their individuality. Alternatively, it could be a way of saying, 'I have made it, despite my handicapping background.'

Environmental features

Features of the environment we inhabit send immediate and very strong personal and social messages that can have enormous impact in business and management. They are also a significant source of work-based emotion experienced by staff.[48] The communicative significance of office size and design, including furnishings and décor, should not be overlooked. Such cues are very potent sources of information for making judgements not only about the power and status of individuals within an organisation, but about the organisation itself – its structure, culture and corporate image.

Traditional, hierarchically structured, bureaucratic corporations have their organisational charts metaphorically etched on the walls of the contrasting office space occupied by members at different operational levels. For example, Sundstrom[49] pointed out how window allocation acted as an environmental status marker in the Canadian Ministry. While the deputy minister had seven, some senior officers made do with only three. This preference is in marked contrast to contemporary moves towards flatter organisational structures, accompanied by increased equality and informality in working relationships, with less attention paid to status differentials. A good example is Gore Associates, based in Delaware, and makers of Gore-Tex fabric, among other products. Here there are neither titles nor organisational charts: everyone is designated an 'associate' of the company. Company headquarters are housed in a low, unassuming building, with executive offices described by Malcolm Gladwell[50] as '... small, plainly furnished rooms, along a narrow corridor'. This is perhaps an extreme example, however, since it seems that, despite the move towards greater egalitarianism begun in the 1960s, most offices still carry the trappings of status.[51]

Office design Office size and design, therefore, convey messages about the position and personality of the manager. According to Korda,[52] a recognised authority in this area of NVC, one of the factors that determines the power afforded by an office arrangement is the extent to which the manager can control space and readily restrict visibility and access to visitors. Furthermore, he believed that the arrangement and use of office space is more impactful in this sense than the size of the office *per se*, or how it is furnished. Other factors such as not being exposed, being able to look directly at visitors, and seeing visitors before being seen, are also held to be important. Having access monitored on one's behalf by someone of lesser status, a gate-keeping secretary, elevates this art to an even higher level.

Considering the office plans in Figure 2.5, it can be seen that A communicates most power, B next, with C the least power. What about your own office? How is it organised at present? What impression of you and your position in the organisation does it possibly convey? Is this the message that you want to send? How could the layout be changed to be more effective?

In larger offices, separate areas are often set aside for distinct purposes, enabling temporary adjustments to be made to project power and control. What Korda calls the *Pressure area* is centred on the desk and is the site of formal business transactions. It is here that hard bargaining and difficult decision-making takes place. The *Semisocial area* is set apart and furnished differently with, for example, a sofa or easy chairs, coffee table and drinks cabinet. Here visitors can be stalled, ingratiated or mollified, as necessary.

Figure 2.5 Office designs communicating power

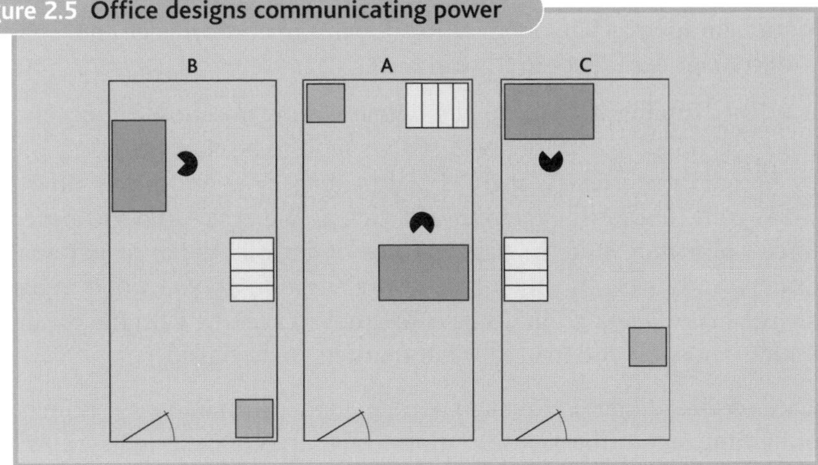

Furthermore, it seems that apart from impressions of power and authority, personality judgements are frequently based upon how managers make use of their office space. Ease in dealing with others, friendliness and extroversion tend to be attributed to occupants of more open office arrangements in which, for example, the desk is moved against a wall rather than used as a barrier.

Office 'props' Physical 'props' in the office such as state-of-the-art computers, Sales Manager of the Year awards, wall hangings and type of furniture, without doubt influence initial impressions of the manager, and more broadly of the organisation. This is particularly so in situations where the visitor has little prior knowledge of the person about to be met. Research has reported that such props generally shape impressions of comfort, warmth and friendliness, as well as status.[53] The presence of artwork, it seems, is a particularly potent symbol of power and influence.[54]

Certain props also influence impressions formed of the overall organisational climate.[55] These include:

- *Authority symbols* (e.g. flags, logos, pictures of organisational leaders) lead to impressions of tight structure, restriction and lack of employee involvement in decision-making.
- *Empathic symbols* (e.g. plants, magazines, family photos) create images of autonomy and comfort.

- *Reward symbols* (e.g. trophies, plaques, medals, certificates) are thought to reflect an organisation at pains to acknowledge and encourage excellence in its workforce.

A further finding is that, on the whole, an organisation's props also reflect its mission. Service organisations tend to be characterised more by humanising artefacts such as plants, magazines and pieces of artwork, while authority organisations such as the police and the armed forces, put more store in flags, photos of organisational or national leaders, and logos. In which type of organisation do you work? What are the major artefacts on display? Are they in keeping with the organisation's mission and image? What do they say to outsiders?

Colour, décor and lighting Colour of decor, together with intensity and type of lighting, are further considerations. In a series of case studies, Ellis[56] found that the aesthetic quality of office lighting, involving colour and contrast, affected the mood of staff and in turn their attitude towards work including subsequent absenteeism. Executives seem to have a marked preference for organisations that have reception areas decorated in shades of blue. Indeed blue has generally been found by psychologists to be associated with moods of pleasantness, security, transcendence, calm and tenderness.[57] Red, by contrast, is a more arousing colour, provoking more intense feelings of vitality, excitement and affection, or on the other hand, anger and hostility. In keeping with this finding, the colour of tablets has a corresponding influence on their perceived effects. Red and orange are good colours for stimulants while blue and green work better when marketing tranquilisers or sedatives.[58]

Physical appearance and dress

Perhaps the one feature of appearance that, above all others, influences how we are received is attractiveness.

Interpersonal attraction To the extent that we can make ourselves more attractive in the way that we present ourselves, we have a distinct advantage in most walks of life.[59] Physically attractive people are seen as more personable, popular, persuasive, happy, interesting, confident and outgoing.[60] In most work situations, attractiveness seems to be more influential in the advancement of women although, paradoxically, extremely attractive females may find their paths to the highest company positions blocked for that reason (among others). Perhaps they are thought to be too feminine for such a tough job. In any case, those who are not naturally gifted in this direction can compensate, to some extent, in how they dress. Several studies have shown that people are more inclined to take orders from, and accept the lead given by someone wearing 'high-status' clothing.[61]

Dress 'Most obviously, then, fashion and clothing are forms of non-verbal communication...', wrote Barnard.[62] He continued by explaining how some scholars in the area draw very direct parallels between dress and language. In the same way that words are combined into sentences according to rules, so items of clothing may be worn together as outfits, with a syntax that dictates which items can go together.

According to advice offered via the press by an image consultant to graduates looking for jobs, the single most important purchase they could make in going for interview is a new jacket.[63] It is difficult, though, to be precise about dress code. Fashions come and go shaping what is acceptable. The 'dressing down' trend at work seems to have come to an end, with suits back in vogue as part of an all-round sharper dress sense in both the private and public sectors. Gill Lucas, head of public sector headhunting for KPMG, is reported as saying people '... don't want to go to the housing office or social services and be seen by people who look as if they have been dressed by Oxfam'.[64] Perhaps if a rule had to be framed it would be to dress in accordance with the codes that apply in different situations as followed by significant others in the company, unless one has the status to flaunt such expectations with alacrity. Of course, many companies such as IBM have strict policies on dress, removing the option of individual choice.

Where less formal codes apply, look at what colleagues wear, especially if one is new to the organisation, and particularly at those in positions just above yours. If you have aspirations to move up through the organisation, are there some at the level of management just above who are more successful than the rest? Do they have particular styles of dress? If so, you may want to bear this in mind when you add to your wardrobe. Don't forget the old maxim, 'Dress for the job you want to be in, rather than for the one you are in!' Pauline Weigh, Cranfield School of Management, was also cited as suggesting that employees take into account the dress of those with whom they do business or provide a service.[65] She believed that many aim to dress broadly on a par. This thinking is echoed by Leigh and Summers,[66] who speculated that in a sales setting, comparability of dress between buyer and seller may be more telling for the seller that the particular type of clothes worn.

Despite the vagaries of fashion, in *Dress for Success*, Molloy[67] claimed men in business and managerial positions command greatest credibility when wearing ideally a dark-blue suit. In the famous television debate between Richard Nixon and John Kennedy, as part of the 1960 presidential campaign, Nixon appeared in a grey suit that contrasted poorly with the drab background of the studio. Kennedy, on the other hand, wore a stylist dark suit. While Nixon's failure to win the battle of image in this debate has been commonly put down to his infamous 'seven o'clock shadow', this sartorial contrast is also thought to have played a big part. Likewise Nancy Golden,[68] author of *Dress Right for Business*, recommended that the darker the suit, the greater the authority suggested.

As far as women are concerned, Molloy favoured[69] a business 'uniform' of blazer and skirt, although suits now seem to be the preferred option in many quarters. In colours such as navy, black and grey, this type of outfit projects an impression of competence and credibility on the part of professional women.[70] On the other hand, short skirts and plunging necklines were thought, by those women interviewed by Trethewey,[71] to jeopardise such an image. However, suitability depends ultimately upon the type of profession and the corresponding image cultivated. In *Looks That Work*, Janet Wallach[72] suggested three categories:

- *Corporate.* The corporate woman wants to be seen as competent, rational and objective (e.g., banker, accountant, lawyer). Here formal dress such as a suit is preferred and expected by customers.
- *Communicator.* This woman wants to project an image of warmth, sincerity and approachability (for instance, reporter, teacher, social worker, media person). Less formal attire, such as a skirt and blouse, tends to be selected here.
- *Creative.* Here the image is one of flair, originality and innovation (examples include, musician, artist, writer, fashion designer). The dress code in this instance favours flamboyance and above all individuality.

In summing up, the points of advice tentatively offered in Box 2.3 are based upon those by Cheryl Hamilton and Cordell Parker[73] in *Communicating for Results*.

Box 2.3 Dress rules in business

These tentative rules apply for both men and women in typical business environments.

- Always follow formal dress codes
- Pay heed to others going places in the company

Box 2.3 *continued*

- If unsure, dress conservatively
- Consider the style worn by those with whom you do business
- Simple, classic lines are usually best
- Neutral colours (e.g. grey, blue, beige, etc.) work well
- Dark colours command greater authority
- Dress as expensively as you can afford
- Do not dress wildly above your stratum in the organisation
- Wear real products rather than simulations.

Conclusion

As summarised by Fulfer,[74] increasing ones sensitivity to NVC '... can enhance understanding and thus greatly improve interpersonal relations in a wide variety of situations. At work, it can be a useful tool to facilitate decision making and ease work processes – for example, during interviews or at meetings.' The major uses to which NVC is put and how this is accomplished, together with the relevance of this to business and management practice, has occupied us in this chapter. The various forms of NVC including gestures, posture, facial expressions, gaze, personal appearance and environmental features, were also explored. The quality of management communication will suffer without a firm appreciation of NVC, both from the point of view of sending messages and being sensitive to the total message received in return.

While we have isolated NVC from the verbal dimension in this chapter, it must be stressed that operationally the two are inextricably interwoven in almost every instance of face-to-face interaction. This does not mean, though, that they carry meaning in exactly the same way. For the most part they don't. Most nonverbal behaviour carries meaning in a less explicit or precise manner than does words. The sociologist Erving Goffman[75] described the process as 'giving off' rather than 'giving' meaning. As such, cues can be picked up enabling judgements to be made about, for example, emotional state, interpersonal attitudes, information processing, status, occupation and personality. As we have seen, conversations are also regulated in part nonverbally.

Before leaving the topic, it should be appreciated that NVC plays an inescapable part in the activities that form the core of almost all of the other chapters of this book.

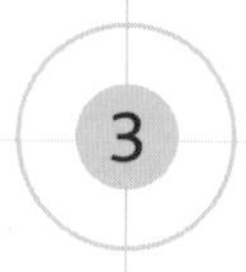

They could be persuaded: using your managerial influence

Introduction

Life would be much easier if other people would only do what we wanted, and just get on with it without any negative comment or complaint. Unfortunately this is far from the case, since we continually have to persuade and influence those with whom we come into contact that what we are recommending is the path they should take. Indeed, influence is a central thread in the fabric of social life. We devote a great deal of our interactive time with others to this aspect. To take but one simple example, when we are with friends we smile, laugh, listen to what they are saying, and give them sympathy, encouragement and support. A main reason why we do this is to influence them to maintain their positive relationship with us. In this sense, influence is pervasive. As summarised by Forgas and Williams:[1] 'All forms of human interaction involve mutual influence processes, and these function at a variety of levels.' In this chapter we shall examine these levels of influence.

This is an important topic, since the essence of effective management is the ability to influence and persuade others to behave in certain ways. Indeed Bragg[2] argued that, 'Influence has an impact on absolutely every aspect of managerial work.' In the modern workplace, employees cannot simply be forced to do what management decrees and so, as illustrated by Morris *et al.*:[3] 'Coordinating the efforts of employees in complex organisations relies on influence rather than coercion.' Indeed, the business vehicle is fuelled by the power of persuasion. Managers must use various forms of influence and persuasion to ensure that employees complete specific tasks, behave in certain ways with other staff, and with customers, and meet set targets. This does not mean that supervisors should be like little Hitlers, goose-stepping around the workplace and barking out orders which must be obeyed at all times. A key aspect of persuasion is the ability to gently bring people along and to convince them (often in subtle ways) that your point of view has merit. This necessitates sophisticated levels of interpersonal skill. As noted by Keys and Case:[4] 'Effective communications become interwoven coils of silk in the web of influence that help ensure the success of tactics.'

Persuasion has been defined[5] as 'an ongoing process in which verbal and nonverbal messages shape, reinforce, and change people's responses'. In the literature in this field, the person attempting to effect influence is referred to as the 'agent', while the person who is the subject of the attempt is known as the 'target'.[6]

Although the terms 'influence' and 'persuasion' are often used as synonyms, there are in fact four main differences between the two processes.

1. *Consciousness.* When we attempt to persuade others we do so consciously, whereas we can influence others unintentionally. For example, a pop star who smokes a cigarette during a TV show may influence young viewers to believe that it is 'cool' to smoke – yet no intentional or conscious persuasion attempt was being made. A manager may persuade staff to work until 8.00 p.m. by openly asking them to do so, by offering them special rewards for so doing, by leaving dated/timed requests for information on the desks of those who have left earlier, or by only involving staff who stay late in key projects. A similar influence may well be unintentionally effected simply by the manager always working to 8.00 p.m., thereby acting as a powerful, yet unstated, role model that other staff feel compelled to emulate.
2. *Resistance.* Persuasion is the form of influence that is employed when the target shows some degree of resistance to the message. If people are already convinced that the recommended action is the right choice, they can readily be influenced to undertake it, and do not need to be persuaded.
3. *Direction.* Persuasion is one-way, whereas influence is more reciprocal. During social encounters one person tries to persuade another, whereas both parties simultaneously engage in a process of ongoing mutual influence.[7] If both sides are concurrently trying to persuade one another then the interaction becomes a negotiation (see Chapter 7).
4. *Success.* The final difference is that persuasion is successful influence. We can influence others without persuading them. They may listen carefully to us and accept that we have a point, but they may then still reject our message. However, if we assert

> that we have persuaded others, this means that we have succeeded in getting them to do what we wanted. It does not make sense to say 'I persuaded them to do it, but they didn't do it.'

As shown in Box 3.1, persuasion techniques are used to achieve six main goals. But not all attempts at persuasion are successful. As

Box 3.1 Six main goals of persuasion attempts

1. *Adoption.* Here the aim is to encourage the adoption of new responses – to persuade others to *start doing something*. This may involve retraining – for example, in the case of a new computer system being introduced.
2. *Continuance.* Here efforts are expended to reinforce existing responses; in other words to persuade others to *keep doing it*. Where people are performing well, steps should be taken to maintain this level of performance. Such steps may include both praise from managers as well as material rewards (bonuses, awards).
3. *Improvement.* In this instance the purpose is to encourage greater efforts, that is, to get staff to *do it better*. If existing targets are not being met in terms of quality or volume, then efforts need to be expended to rectify this situation.
4. *Deterrence.* The goal here is to deter others from starting a new practice – that is to ensure that they *do not start doing it*. A company with an all male staff which is about to recruit females may run equality awareness seminars to explain to the existing workforce exactly what constitutes harassment, what the implications of such behaviour will be, and to prevent it from happening.
5. *Discontinuance.* In this case the objective is to discourage existing responses – to persuade others to *stop doing something*. This is often very difficult, since 'old habits die hard', and once existing patterns of behaviour become habituated they are very resistant to change.
6. *Reduction.* If it is deemed that it would not be possible for people to stop something immediately, then an interim goal may be to get them to *do it less*. If there is a high level of wastage in the production department, and it is unrealistic to attempt to eliminate it entirely in the short term, targets may be set to progressively reduce this.

shown in Figure 3.1, there are four main outcomes from any attempts by managers to persuade staff.

1. *Immediate success.* The undertaking can be instantly effective, in that employees agree with the manager's recommended course of action and carry it out. Of course, influencing is a two-way process and so employees may also successfully influence their managers to behave in certain ways.
2. *Eventual success.* While not immediately successful, seeds may have been planted in the target's mind. After a period of time spent 'sleeping on it' the seeds start to grow, and the employee later

Figure 3.1 Processes and outcomes in organisational persuasion

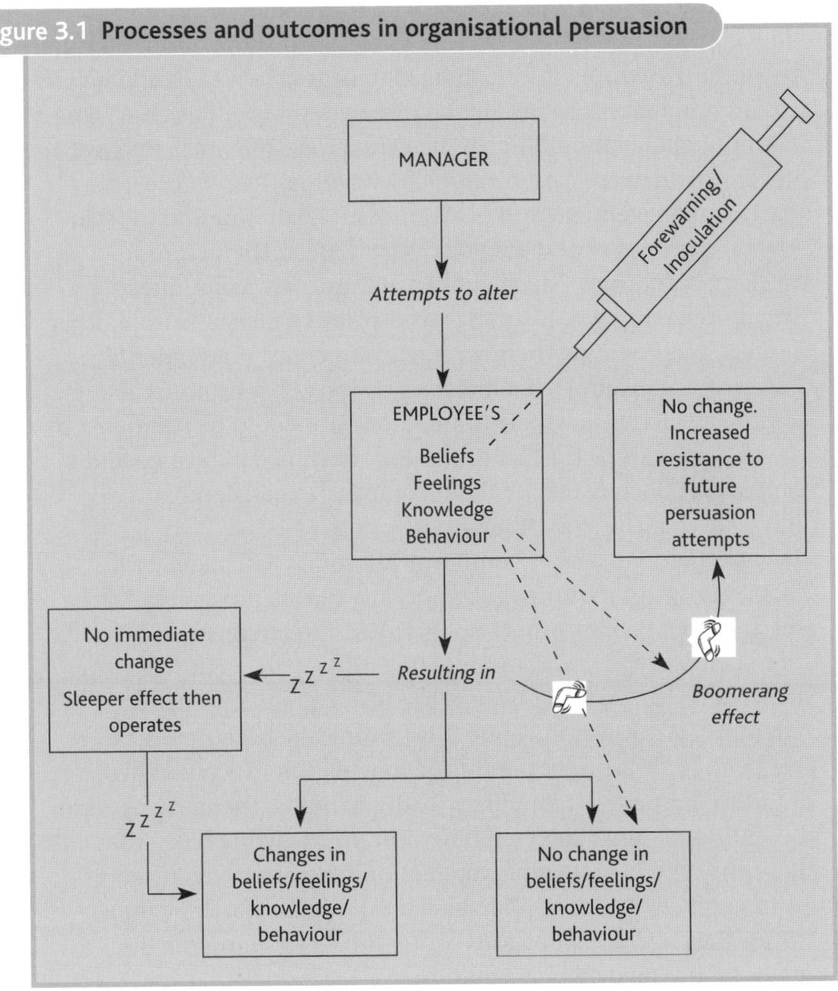

complies – the influence attempt has eventually borne fruit. Such acceptance may be a subconscious process of incubation, with the arguments gradually sinking in to effect change. This *sleeper effect,* whereby the target initially rejects the attempt, yet after a period of time eventually accepts the message, has been shown[8] to be an important phenomenon in persuasion. It is not realistic to always expect immediate compliance from employees on every issue. Thus, managers who do not obtain successful outcomes to the first persuasion effort should not necessarily despair. Given time, attitudes can and do change.

3. *Failure.* The attempt may fail, in that employees simply refuse to comply with the manager's wishes on this subject. One reason that persuasion may fail is as a result of a process known as 'inoculation', whereby targets are forewarned about a forthcoming persuasion attempt, are encouraged to be resistant to it, and given counter-arguments to negate the messages they will receive.[9] For example, trade union officials may encourage members to reject an upcoming management proposal by warning them of the 'true' goals of management, and explaining in detail how and in what ways the proposed deal would adversely affect their current working conditions. Managers can also use this technique to strengthen employee resistance to persuasive messages from other sources, by providing them with relevant counter-arguments in advance. For example, if a manager is aware that rumours about closure are about to appear in the press, this could be countered by alerting workers to the fact that the story will be published and providing concrete details about company expansion plans, to illustrate that the story is false.
4. *Deterioration.* Persuasive communication may fail badly, or 'boomerang', in that the target not only rejects this particular message, but is then suspicious of any future attempts at influence from this agent. This *boomerang effect* is likely to occur when the target becomes aware of what is perceived as a manipulation attempt.[10] As shown in Figure 3.1, this may be because the target has been forewarned as part of the inoculation process. Where an effort to persuade is particularly badly handled, the messenger can be 'contaminated', and credibility lost. In the workplace, what happens then is that employees not only become even more entrenched in their original views on the particular issue under focus, they also are suspicious of any future recommendations made by the manager.

Box 3.2 Sequential stages in persuasion

1. exposure to the message
2. attending to the message
3. becoming interested in it
4. understanding it
5. learning how to process and use it
6. accepting it
7. memorising it
8. retrieving it when required
9. using it when making decisions
10. carrying out these decisions
11. reinforcing the actions
12. consolidating the decision based upon the success of the actions.

McGuire[11] illustrated how successful long-term persuasion involves a number of sequential stages. These are summarised in Box 3.2. These begin with the initial exposure to the message, and progress through attending to it, understanding it, remembering it and eventually adopting it on a long-term basis. A distinction has been made[12] between *private acceptance* where an influence attempt leads to changes in your attitudes or beliefs, and *public compliance*, which involves simply changing your overt behaviour without altering your internal attitudes. People can feign attitude change and display what they perceive to be expected behaviour. For instance, a highly autocratic manager may influence staff to behave in certain ways, through fear. However, at the first opportunity these staff will take delight in behaving in the contrary style. In other words, they will have internalised a resistance to that which they are forced to do. For enduring change, private acceptance is necessary, and so the goal of persuasion should be to alter covert attitudes as well as overt behaviour (See Reflective exercise 3.1).

Knowledge of the range of influencing tactics that can be used to increase compliance is clearly of importance for managers. The ancient Greek philosopher Aristotle was the first person to present a comprehensive analysis of persuasion. He categorised persuasion attempts as being of three types, namely those that:

1. emphasise the rationality of the message (*logos*)
2. evoke the emotions of the listener (*pathos*)
3. underline the credibility of the persuader (*ethos*).

Reflective exercise 3.1 Persuasive people

Think of the individual whom you regard to be the most persuasive person you know. This should be someone who has successfully influenced you *personally*. What is it about this individual that gives them the power to persuade you? What interactive style does this person use with you and with others? How does this person present arguments? What is it about the presentation that makes it convincing? How does this individual present self in terms of dress, body furniture (watch, rings, necklace, bracelets, spectacles, ear studs and so on), hairstyle and make-up? How do these complement the overall image?

These are now known respectively as *logical proofs, emotional proofs* and *personal proofs*. Although, for the purposes of analysis we will examine each separately, when using persuasion we can combine techniques from each area to maximise our case. Indeed, Aristotle argued that the most effective persuasion attempts incorporate elements of all three.

Logical proofs

An appeal to reason and logic is the cornerstone of many persuasion efforts. In their analysis of different strategies in persuasion, Kipnis and Schmidt[13] concluded that: 'people who rely chiefly on logic, reason and compromise to get their way are the most satisfied both with their business lives and with their personal relationships'. It is therefore useful to examine those strategies that can be employed to maximise the impact of this approach.

Logical argument

Reason has been defined[14] as 'a strategy of influencing which relies on the presentation of data and information as the basis for a logical argument that supports a request'. There are well-established features of arguments, and of the way they are delivered, which increase their persuasive power[15] (see also Chapter 5):

- The message should be fully *comprehensible* – the meaning must be clear and unambiguous.

- The important aspects of the argument should be *emphasised* to underline them.
- The *advantages* of the recommended course of action, and the *disadvantages* of the alternatives, should be firmly stated and supporting evidence cited.
- Whether the disadvantages of the recommended course of action and the advantages of the alternatives should also be mentioned depends upon the situation. This is referred to as *sidedness* in message delivery. Two-sided messages while emphasising the positive aspects of the message also recognise negatives, whereas one-sided ones are partisan and only accentuate the positive. As shown in Box 3.3, one-sided and two-sided arguments are effective under different circumstances. One thing that is clear, however, is that while the recognition of counter-arguments can raise speaker credibility, this must always be accompanied by a refutation of the opposing views.[16] If not, confusion and doubt will be planted in the minds of listeners.
- Presentations benefit from the use of *case studies*, which has been shown to be a powerful technique for effecting influence. From childhood we identify with, enjoy and are moved by powerful stories.
- While the use of *statistics* to support an argument can be an effective technique, it can also seem detached, and even boring. However, when statistics are combined with the use of a pertinent case study this has been shown to be a very potent influencing cocktail.[17]

Box 3.3 Sidedness in message delivery

Two-sided messages are more effective with:

- those who are initially opposed to the message
- people who are already *au fait* with the issues involved
- those who are better educated
- attempts to refute what the listeners have been told earlier
- those who will hear the opposing views later.

One-sided messages are more effective with:

- those who already support the message
- those with lower IQ.

- Research has clearly shown[18] that, to ensure maximum comprehension and effect, explicit *conclusions* from the arguments presented should be drawn for the listeners.

Repetition

There is truth in the maxim 'something worth saying is worth repeating'. However, in management contexts, research has shown[19] that managers do not rate *persistent* tactics – which involve repeated reminders, continually checking up on whether something has been done and becoming a nuisance – to be effective. Instead *insistent* tactics, whereby requests are made in a firm, assertive fashion, are viewed as more effective (see Chapter 11). The lesson here is that repetition needs to be used with care. When presenting a reasoned argument, it is useful to underline the main points through judicious repetition. However, someone who bombards others with repeated reminders of requests is liable to be seen simply as a pest. As summarised by Lewicki *et al.*[20] 'repeating a point is only effective for the first few times. After that, additional repetition does not significantly change attitudes ... and may become annoying and lead people to react against the message.'

Reciprocation

An exchange norm of reciprocity operates in human encounters. Since we do not like to feel in debt to others, if we receive something we feel under pressure to reciprocate. If someone buys us a drink in a bar, we feel obligated to buy a round of drinks in return. Similarly, when someone discloses a piece of personal information to us, we then feel under pressure to tell them something about ourselves. This exchange phenomenon means that we are more likely to accede to requests from those who have previously done something for us. Thus, one way to effect influence is to use the 'trade-off' method, through an exchange of favours. It can take the form of *pre-giving* where the target person is 'buttered-up' by being given rewards before any requests are made. This tactic is used by sales companies when they give away free samples of their goods in the knowledge that this will (often dramatically) increase their overall sales. An alternative approach to reciprocation is *to make a promise* ('You do this for me now, I will do that for you later') before requesting something. Promises are more likely to be successful where there is an existing close and trusting relationship between the interactors. Persuasion is also easier where both sides make reciprocal concessions, as opposed to the expectation that they should be one-way only.

Scale of the request

Two separate strategies have been identified in terms of scale of request. The first is *door-in-the-face* (DIF). This tactic involves initially making a large request, knowing that it will probably be rejected. The ensuing refusal is then followed by a scaled down request. This is more likely to be successful since the target feels under pressure to reciprocate what appears to be a concession (indeed the DIF technique is also known as 'reciprocation of concessions') – the lesser request looks much more reasonable in comparison to its predecessor. For example, if a manager wants staff to work overtime for one evening, a DIF strategy would be to ask them initially to work overtime every evening for one week. When this is refused, the target request is introduced as a concession. DIF is most successful[21] when the same person makes the requests, in a face-to-face encounter (as will be shown in Chapter 9, it is easier to refuse mediated requests such as those made by telephone), the person or body that will receive the benefit from the request remains the same, and there is not an undue delay between the requests.

The second tactic is *foot-in-the-door* (FID). Here a small initial request is made, and, if successful, is followed by further requests gradually increasing in size. Continuing with the above example, the manager may initially ask a member of staff to work overtime for one hour. When this is agreed the manager returns later, says how good it was for the person to agree to work overtime and how helpful it will be, and then asks if two hours would be a possibility. FID has been found to be successful providing the initial request was acceded to voluntarily, no inducements were given and the size of the follow-up requests is not disproportionate.[22]

While both FID and DIF are effective sequential influencing strategies, in change management it is generally better to introduce changes gradually and so the FID approach is often most appropriate. In this sense, change has been found to be more likely to succeed when it is evolutionary rather than revolutionary. It should also be 'devolutionary', in that responsibility for, and ownership of, the implementation of change should be cascaded down the hierarchy.[23] We are, in general, more committed to a new course of action if we feel involved in its development. Yet, change is often management-driven and dominated by coercive top-down strategies.[24] While on occasions such a 'revolutionary' approach is unavoidable as a result of urgent business necessity (e.g. survival), it is not to be widely recommended in terms of securing worker commitment.

Scarcity value

The scarcity principle dictates that opportunities become more valuable when their availability is restricted. We tend to want what we cannot have – and the more restricted the item the greater its appeal. The fact that old masters are long dead and have produced a set number of paintings greatly increases the desire for and price of their works. Gold is scarce and therefore precious. Exclusive clubs charge exorbitant rates (Groucho Marx famously invoked the scarcity principle when he remarked that he would not belong to any club which would have him as a member). Collectors across a wide diversity of fields pay vastly inflated prices for particularly unusual or unique items. Firms publicise 'limited editions', 'time-limited' deals, and 'once in a lifetime' offers to increase their appeal, urging customers to 'hurry while stocks last'. Managers can therefore make staff feel important by telling them that the information they are about to receive is restricted and highly confidential. As shown in Box 3.4, there are three important factors associated with the scarcity principle.

One tactic used by retail salespeople who see a couple admiring a product in store is to approach them and tell them that the product is out of stock and the one on display has just been sold. This heightens their desire for it until eventually one of the customers asks whether another one could not be obtained. The salesperson, after underlining the difficulty of so doing, gets a commitment from the couple to buy at the display price if the product can possibly be obtained. After 'making some phone calls', hey presto the salesperson returns with a sales invoice having successfully located the item. Interestingly, at this point in the transaction it has been found that the customers' desire for the product decreases[25] but by then it is too late because they have made the commitment to purchase.

The effect of scarcity upon behaviour has been explained in terms of *psychological reactance theory*. Once something becomes scarce, our freedom of choice becomes threatened with restriction. We react against this threat to our freedoms by having an increased desire to have what has been presented as restricted. Reactance can be seen in children from the age of two. At this age, a toy that is forbidden often provokes

Box 3.4 Three important scarcity principle factors

1. Something that is *newly scarce* is seen as more valuable. This can either be an item that was formerly in greater supply but is now limited, or a completely new item. Manufacturers repackage products as 'new improved', 'new faster acting', 'new formula', or 'new longer lasting'. They do so because it works – consumers are attracted by the novelty dimension. If something is both novel and scarce it therefore has considerable persuasive potential. Staff are more likely to accept a transfer if it is to a brand new 'think tank' section of the organisation, which will be limited to a small number of key specialists.
2. If there is *competition* for a scarce resource it becomes even more attractive. For instance, people often bid more than they originally intended at auctions where others are bidding against them. Similarly, an employee will feel a much greater sense of satisfaction having secured a promotion that a large number of workers had also applied for, rather than one in which there was only the one applicant.
3. If the scarcity is presented as a *possible loss* it has more impact than if sold as a possible gain. People are more worried about minimising losses than maximising gains.[26] Thus, medical research has shown that it is more effective to warn smokers how many years of life they are likely to lose if they do not stop than how many years they will gain if they do, or that if they do not stop smoking their lungs will not heal, than to say if they stop their lungs will heal.[27] Likewise, people are more likely to insulate their homes when told how much money they are likely lose by not insulating, rather than how much they are likely to gain if they do.[28] Managers should therefore consider ways in which they can use 'loss language' when framing relevant messages to employees.

the child to scream for it unremittingly, until many parents capitulate in the interests of sanity.

Managers can make something appealing by selling it as a rare opportunity or a scarce resource. Access to the executive washroom, keys to certain doors, a personal computer or a larger office, can all become persuasive devices. Likewise, workers with special or scarce skills are in a position to wield greater influence. A study[29] by the

Conference Board of Canada found that one-third of the companies they surveyed adopted special pay strategies to recruit and retain people with scarce or 'hot' skills (such as computer programmers, scientists and professionals with special financial knowledge). While 'average' employees received raises of some 2.7 per cent, those with special skills received 4.8 per cent increases. The attraction of a scarce resource can of course be abused. It was Lenin who said 'Liberty is precious – so precious it must be rationed.'

Emotional proofs

While appeals to reason and logic can be very powerful, emotions are also potent determinants of human behaviour. Forgas[30] illustrated the central role that emotion plays in the influence process, but cautioned that not everyone is swayed by appeals to affect. Certain individuals (e.g. those high in tough-minded or Machiavellian traits) are much less influenced by this tactic. In addition, there is evidence that messages that include 'secondary' emotions, which are seen as unique to humans, have greater influence than those that employ 'primary' emotions that are also experienced by other animals.[31] For example, all animals experience fear, anger, happiness, sadness and surprise, but it is argued that feelings of disillusionment, cynicism, shame, pride and optimism, are specific to humans. Thus a manager saying to a group of employees 'I feel very proud of what we have achieved', is likely to have more impact than saying 'I feel very happy with what we have achieved.'

The following are the main emotional aspects associated with persuasion.

Threat/fear

The acceptance by a target of fear or threat messages is effective in influencing attitudes and behaviour.[32] However, a word of caution was sounded by Aristotle, who argued that 'Wicked men obey from fear; good men from love.' What seems to be the case is that the success of a fear appeal is dependent upon four key dimensions:[33]

1. It should really *scare* the target.
2. There should be a *specific recommendation* for overcoming the fear-arousing threat.
3. This recommended action should be accepted as *effective* in removing the threat.

4. The target should feel *confident* about being able to carry out the recommended action, and *willing* to do so.

If all four factors are present, the fear message is very powerful. Equally, if any one is missing, the potency of the threat is diminished.

Threat and fear are not always effective. This is because at very high levels, fear distracts the target and increases anxiety, leading to a rejection of the message. In using this tactic, managers need to avoid a strategy that may be perceived as bullying their subordinates. The results of such a perception tend to be that the workforce are unhappy, will try to sabotage production, and will take any opportunity to get their own back on the autocratic manager – including taking legal action against the bully. Since bullying is prevalent in many corporations,[34] managers should be aware of when the threat/fear tactic is being abused. Indeed, organisations should have policies in place to protect employees from bullying. Another problem is that the use of threats may only produce short-term behaviour change, and the target will abandon the new behaviour at the earliest opportunity.[35] While threats often produce compliance they rarely educe commitment. Where threats are made, it is better if these can be externally oriented. For example, a manager could tell employees that unless a certain course of action is taken competitors are likely to secure the contract, and that may mean that the company would have to close (see Chapter 7 for more information on this type of threat).

One investigation[36] into the influencing strategies employed by executives attempting to influence their superiors, found that with senior managers who interacted in an attractive fashion (were attentive, friendly, relaxed), reason was used most frequently. With those who interacted in an unattractive style, coalition formation with others to challenge the superior and appeals to higher authority, were more likely to be used. In other words, the threat/fear tactic will be reciprocated by the workforce, who may also threaten to take sanctions – such as going on strike, resigning or suing the company for harassment.

As a policy, therefore, hectoring and hounding is not to be recommended. This was recognised by Peter Birse, the chairman of a major construction company in England, who had to take steps to change a culture of fear that had developed in his firm.[37] He noted: 'From the friendly family firm I had started in 1970 it had become a backstabbing operation where managers ruled their fiefdoms with fear. No one learned from mistakes, never mind corrected them: instead there would be a witch-hunt for a scapegoat and some poor innocent would be blamed.' Things came to a head when the number of staff leaving each month reached 65 (out of a total workforce of 1000). Birse set about rooting out the bullies who ruled by fear, until he had 'weeded out the big egos, the arrogant bosses who got by on aggression'. The result was a much happier workforce, greatly reduced staff turnover and a massively increased annual profit.

Consistency and commitment

The *consistency principle* is a very powerful guiding force in human behaviour. We like to be viewed as being true to our word and doing what we say – in other words we want to be regarded as *consistent*. Those who change their minds are seen as fickle, indecisive or weak. This means that we are more likely to continue with a course of action once we have made a public declaration of *commitment* to it. There are three core aspects to commitment as a weapon of influence.

1. *Secure a public proclamation.* This can either be written or spoken. In general, however, the more people who witness a declaration of intent the stronger is the likelihood that the person will carry out the actions. If only one other person is present it is a case of 'your word against mine'. If a large number of people are there, it is then very difficult to recant. In our interpersonal communication training programmes, we employ a system of *Personal Action Plans* for trainees. This includes having trainees at the end of the programme identifying and writing down their three main strengths and how these can be further enhanced, and three main weaknesses and how these will be remedied. Each trainee in turn then reads these out to the training group. We have found this to be a very effective motivator of future action.
2. *Make the decision a voluntary one.* Research evidence clearly shows that freedom of choice is crucial,[38] since if any form of coercion is employed it is easier for the target to later recant and argue that they acted under duress. On occasions the voluntariness of actions can be slowly established. For instance, one large company we worked with had an Open Day for families of staff and members of the public. Some of the line managers were very sceptical about its worth. It was therefore organised in such a way that each line manager was given the task of preparing 'something special' in their department. At planning meetings, they were then asked to

give a short presentation on what they were preparing and how it was progressing. As the process progressed and they took ownership of their event, the implication of voluntariness was clear. At the evaluation meeting following the event, managers were asked to summarise and evaluate their input. By this stage every line manager, without exception, felt the Open Day had been a huge success.

3. *Get the person involved in practical activities.* It is one thing for people to make a promise and another for them to actually carry it out. Verbal statements can be misconstrued, but actions are less open to interpretation. When the 'cooling off period' legislation was brought in to cover sales in various sectors, companies discovered that numerous clients were availing of the opportunity to cancel the sale and receive a full refund. They discovered that one way to counteract this was to hand over the sales agreement form to the customer to fill out, rather than have the salesperson do this. The customer then felt greater subconscious ownership of, and commitment to, the deal, having actually written it out personally. The pressure to be consistent counteracted any later desire to revoke the sale. As a result there was a marked reduction in cancellations. Many ceremonies (marriage, swearing in, initiations) include public declarations of intent. Religious denominations employ various participation techniques (prayers, responses, chants, communal singing) to make their congregation feel a core part of the organisation. Entertainers are also aware of the importance of securing audience involvement, in the form of laughing, clapping or singing, for a successful show. Those who are involved are more likely to enjoy the activity and their involvement represents a form of commitment. Their participation also means they are less detached and have less opportunity to objectively evaluate what is happening. Managers should therefore think of ways of involving staff, on a voluntary basis, in presentations, meetings and other public forums.

Thus, these twin towers of consistency and commitment can be used to 'move' employees along a direction desired by the manager.

Moral appeals

The emotional impact of moral overtures can be very forceful.[39] As summarised by Kleinke[40] 'Research studies have shown that people can be induced to comply with requests if they are made to feel guilty'. Children at around the age of 3–4 years begin to show an understanding[41] of moral principles in terms of what is 'right' and 'wrong'. From this early stage they are able to invoke moral injunctions to influence their parents, with statements such as: 'It's not fair. You promised me.' Indeed, most parents live in dread of their children prefacing a remark with: 'But you said…' It immediately activates parental guilt instincts.

Moral appeals take a number of forms.

1. Reminding people that they have a *duty* to carry out certain actions. This technique is used by insurance companies to sell life policies, by highlighting to clients that they have a moral obligation to protect their family in the event of sudden death.
2. The use of *self-feeling* in either a positive ('You will feel good about yourself if you comply') or negative ('You will feel very bad about yourself if you do not comply') mode.
3. Emphasising how *esteem of others* will either be positive ('You will be highly regarded if you do this') or negative ('People will not think much of you if do that').
4. An appeal to *altruism*, which involves invoking the 'better side' of an individual ('Could you please help me? I wouldn't normally ask, but I am really in trouble').
5. *Altercasting* involves pointing out either that a good and caring person would carry out the proposed action, or that only a bad, uncaring person would not do so.

Few people like to be left with a feeling of guilt and so this is a potent ingredient in any influence mix. One drawback with this strategy is that we do not like to be made to feel guilty, and so tend to dislike the person who invokes this feeling in us. An interesting finding is that a mild insult about being uncaring from one person results in the target being more generous in the future, providing the next request is not made by the same person who made the insult. Here, people wish to 'prove' they really are caring individuals by acceding to the second request.

Personal proofs

A crucial feature of interpersonal influence is the nature of the persuader. If we are not convinced by the person, we are unlikely to be persuaded by their arguments. A number of the features pertaining to the persuader, and the relationship which exists with the target, impact directly upon the extent to which persuasion attempts are successful.

Power

The possession of power is a potent weapon in the armoury of influence. The 'Iron Law of Power' means that people with great power tend to wield it as necessary to get their own way. This does not mean that force is the first influencing strategy used, but rather that if other tactics fail then the power card is likely to be played. Six different types of social power can be used to influence others.

1. Expert power In essence, the more a person is viewed as an 'expert' the greater their potential for influence.[42] Managers are seen as experts in relation to the extent to which they possess expertise or knowledge that others do not have. This is because we perceive experts to be more credible, competent and knowledgeable. Credibility is a key feature in persuasion. The higher we rate individuals on this dimension, the more likely we are to pay attention to, and be persuaded by, what they say.[43] The two determining features of credibility are *competence* and *trustworthiness*. For example, it has long been known that medical doctors who have a competent, reassuring and warm, 'bedside manner', are most likely to effect improvements in patient health.[44,45] We are less likely to believe those we regard as untrustworthy, whatever their level of expertise. Likewise, if we perceive someone to be honest but lacking in knowledge we are unlikely to be influenced by the message. The impact of credibility is also affected by perceived vested interest. Someone who is seen to have a key stake in that which they are recommending will be viewed as less credible. For example, a Ford car salesman extolling the virtues of a Ford model will be seen as a less credible source of information on the car than a colleague at work who drives this model.

Expert power is underlined by what are known as the three t's – titles, threads and trappings. The use of *titles* such as 'product design engineer', 'systems auditor' or 'occupational psychologist', underlines the expertness of the individual. The power of titles is illustrated by the way they are sought and used. Two surveys involving a total of 3200 workers found that people often work much longer hours for very little more money just by being given a designated title such as 'director'.[46,47] They also revealed that another common tactic is to change the existing title to a grander-sounding one, such as a 'lavatory cleaner' who became a 'technical sanitation assistant'. Workers felt that their status was improved and their profile raised, both within and outwith, the organisation as a result of a new, more professional-sounding, title. Organisations, too recognise the import of the corporate title, and often spend huge sums of money on devising the optimum nomenclature (see Box 3.5). The second determinant of expertise is '*threads*', that is clothes, which also convey expert power. Common examples range from the hospital white coat, through the policeman's blue uniform, and on to the priestly black. The well-tailored business suit has also been shown to positively influence others regarding the wearer's credibility[48] (see also Chapter 2 for further discussion of dress). Finally, *trappings* convey expertise, in the form of diplomas on the wall, large tomes on a bookshelf or specialist equipment in the room. Other trappings, such as an expensive car, luxury house or private jet, also give the impression of general power and status.

Box 3.5 What's in a name? The search for corporate titles

Businesses often spend considerable sums of money on their corporate titles, but not always to best effect.

For example, in the UK the Post Office changed its name to Consignia. It then discovered that no one liked the new name, which was seen as meaningless and silly.[49] Indeed the postal workers' union pointed out that the word consign was defined by the *Oxford Pocket Dictionary* as 'To commit or hand over to misery, the grave, person's care.' It therefore changed it to Royal Mail Group. But this was the very name given by Charles I to the then new postal service some 365 years earlier. Meanwhile, the name changes had cost the company a total of some £3 million.

Similarly, Britain's largest insurance group, CGNU, spent £1 million on research in 50 countries, involving consultants and focus groups, before it decided upon Aviva as its new worldwide brand name. It then discovered that this was already the name of a dress shop some 300 yards from the insurance group's head office in Norwich. The shop owner had dreamed the name up over a 10 minute coffee discussion with two friends. Furthermore, Aviva was also found to be an Israeli floral delivery service, a Canadian lesbian group, and a brand of incontinence pads in the USA.[50]

2. Information power Here, the content of the message is the basis of the power. There is much truth in the maxim that 'information is power'. In organisations there can be a tendency for managers to control the flow of information on a 'need to know' basis. This may be due partly to fear – the belief that if subordinates know too much about what is going on then you will have less power over them. Yet, the available evidence shows that workers at all levels wish to be informed about what is happening within their organisation, and that levels of satisfaction and commitment increase where information flow is swift and open.

In organisations, there are three main types of information power:[51]

i. *Technical information.* This comes from knowledge of facts contained in reports and records, whether financial, administrative or operational. For example, unless you know what the budget is for a particular project it is difficult to evaluate it properly.
ii. *Knowledge of the social system.* This stems from having a large network of contacts who keep you up-to-date with everything that is happening in the organisation. Some employees are social animals who are reservoirs of information about who is doing what, where and with whom.
iii. *Personal insights.* Some individuals acquire a depth of knowledge about particular individuals. For example, personal assistants acquire quite intimate insights into the private lives of the executives for whom they work. For this reason, confidentiality clauses are often inserted into the employment contracts of these key workers.

A controlled study[52] of two worksites facing large-scale redundancies highlighted the importance of information. In one site the workforce was provided with comprehensive information about everything that was happening, while in the other, existing levels of information were maintained. The result was that absenteeism and other stress indicators remained significantly lower in the former site throughout the redundancy period. Another study[53] investigated the impact on the staff of an organisation that was being merged with a competitor to form a new company. Here it was found that employees valued most highly information which came from a known source and which gave them a sense of participation in the change process.

It is true that trade secrets should be kept from competitors, but it should also be remembered that employees are not competitors. Findings from a large number of audits of internal communication across a variety of organisational contexts show that one of the greatest consistent sources of dissatisfaction to emerge is an information shortfall.[54] While it may not be possible to disclose everything to all staff, the general maxim is to *be as open as you can possibly be*. This increases a feeling of empowerment amongst staff and encourages ownership of key issues.

3. Legitimate power Here the power emanates from the position occupied by the individual. A manager, by dint of job role, will have power over subordinates, but upon retirement this is relinquished. The authority is vested in the role or position, not in the person. Interestingly, subordinates also have legitimate power over managers, in that certain procedures must be carried out by the latter in accordance with set guidelines (selection, appraisal, discipline, etc.).

4. Referent power We are influenced by those whom we wish to be like and whose group we want to be part of – our reference group. As expressed by Tourish and Wohlforth:[55] 'Our membership in various groups helps us to determine who and what we are, and why... An intrinsic requirement of group membership is conformity.' We want to fit in and be accepted by our reference group, rather than being rejected or ostracised. This is why the process of highlighting the acceptability of a course of action by having it recommended and used by significant others is a highly successful technique.[56] Our desire to conform means that we are likely to copy the model. For this reason, advertisers use 'product endorsement' techniques whereby famous and socially desirable people are used to sell products. Among teenagers there is enormous peer pressure to conform to certain types of behaviour and to follow current fashions. Referent power has also, for centuries, been the driving force behind some notorious financial crashes. For example, in Holland between 1634 and 1637 the phenomenon of Tulipomania took hold. The tulip, then a fairly new flower in the West, became the focus of speculator madness, with some bulbs trading at the same price as the grandest canal house in Amsterdam. Of course, it all came to a sorry end with many people losing everything when the market collapsed. Similar processes occur regularly in events such as the South Sea Bubble and the more recent dot-com debacle. The herd instinct means that many people unthinkingly follow the lead of others and join in the rush.

In the workplace, referent power can take the form of peer pressure to follow set behavioural patterns (productivity rates, attitude to management). Reference groups are most powerful where two conditions apply. First, people are more likely to follow the actions of relevant others when they are *unsure* about what to do. The uncertainty is reduced by following the behaviour of our reference group. Second, people are more inclined to follow the lead of *similar* others. This means that in a workplace dispute, shop floor workers are more likely to follow the behaviour of fellow workers walking off the job, than that of senior managers staying at work.

5. Coercive power This type of power is based upon the extent to which someone has the capacity to punish others. Parents have considerable coercive power over their children ('If you do not finish your homework you will not be allowed to watch television tonight'). Managers will be able to wield coercive power to the extent that subordinates are concerned about receiving praise from them, or are dependent on them for other more material rewards ('If you get these contracts you will be in line for promotion, if not you will be spending the next year in the same job'). The further up the hierarchy, the more potential there is for coercion. Senior managers need to avoid overuse of power, since as noted by Edmund Burke 'The greater the power the more dangerous the abuse.' While sanctions can be an effective ploy in the persuasion game, they must be used carefully, sparingly and preferably as a last resort. Repeated use of sanctions will lead to resentment or overt hostility. Furthermore, where they are brought into play they need to be followed through, since a failure to execute the stated sanction can lead to a loss of credibility – the manager will be seen as all gas and no flint.

6. Reward power The corollary of coercive power is the capacity to reward others for performance. The power of reward is learned from an early age, and is again exercised by parents who have great reward power over their children ('If you behave today you can stay up late'). Likewise, a member of staff may comply with a manager's directives in order to receive a positive appraisal, and increase the chances of a bonus or promotion or other reward, such as employee of the month.

In relation to the administration of rewards and punishments, the advice given by Machiavelli in 'The Prince' is worthy of note, namely that managers should 'delegate to others the enactment of unpopular measures and keep in their own hands the distribution of favours'. Remember that persuasion is a two-way process. Subordinates influence managers through rewards such as social approval (praise, nonverbal acknowledgment, etc.), and by their work rate and volume of output. Conversely they can punish managers by withdrawing verbal and nonverbal rewards and by reducing their work efforts. The formal introduction of systems of upward appraisal of managers in many firms has also increased the reward and coercive power of subordinates.

Attractiveness

Personal attractiveness is a very important factor in the persuasion equation. Abraham Lincoln once said 'The Lord prefers common-looking people – that's why he makes so many of them.' However, the vast majority of people clearly prefer beautiful people.[57] There is truth in the old adage: 'beauty may be only skin deep but its effects run much deeper'. Research shows[58] that physically attractive individuals as compared to their unattractive counterparts:

- are perceived to possess higher levels of favourable characteristics, such as intelligence, friendliness, popularity and being interesting to talk to;
- are more successful in life, in that they achieve higher grades at school, are more likely to obtain secure employment, achieve higher earnings, date more frequently with (and marry) people of a high level of attractiveness;
- have more positive effects on other people, who wish to spend longer in their company;
- receive more positive responses from others – including requests for help;
- are more persuasive – they have greater credibility, being rated higher in perceived expertise, trustworthiness and likeability.

Given these findings, it is hardly surprising that people spend huge sums of money on fashion, jewellery, make-up, scents, hairstyle and plastic surgery, in an effort to increase their attractiveness. Ratings of beauty, which seem to be linked to judgements of youth and health, are consistent among judges and across cultures. In this sense it is not strictly true that 'beauty is in the eye of the beholder'. However, as with all aphorisms this one contains a modicum of truth, in that we all like different aspects of physical features, dress and embellishments. For example, some people find nose studs appealing while others abhor them. Furthermore, initial judgements of physical attractiveness are tempered by psychological, sociological, relational and contextual influences.[59] Features such as dress, scent, sense of humour, attentiveness, sensitivity and shared beliefs, all affect ratings of attractiveness. Managers should maximise their level of attractiveness to those whom they wish to influence.

The relationship

We are more likely to be influenced by people we like, are friendly with, or for whom we have high regard. To quote again from Abraham Lincoln: 'If you want to win a man to your cause, you must first convince him you are his friend.' Indeed, research in the field of assertiveness shows that one of the most difficult tasks is the refusal of a request from a friend (see Chapter 11). It is therefore important for managers to develop and foster a positive working relationship with staff. In large organisations the manager should develop a wide range of contacts across departments, and, where possible, be at the centre of networks by introducing staff to one another. This will facilitate influence attempts when required. A useful piece of advice is to offer help and support to as many people as possible, so that they will in turn be ready to reciprocate with favours. Communication networks are also related to staff turnover, since research has shown that individuals who have formed larger networks are less likely to leave their employment than those with a smaller number of contacts.[60]

An important component of relational communication is the appropriate use of *praise* and compliments. The receipt of praise leads to liking for the sender, which in turn facilitates the process of influencing. Where the manager has *similar attitudes* and values to staff, or a common interest or hobby, this facilitates the relationship. Similarity of language (accent, terminology and so on) has also been shown to aid compliance, and is part of what is known as 'communication accommodation'. In examining this similarity effect, Cialdini[61] concluded that: 'we like people who are like us, and are more willing to say yes to their requests'.

Using the person's *first name* is another useful strategy which, when not overused, leads to positive evaluations.[62] The judicious use of first name makes the person more attentive and also increases liking for the user. In the words of Rackham and Morgan[63] 'The oldest sales trick known to man involves making maximum use of the name of any person you wish to influence.' In his best selling book *How to Win Friends and Influence People*, Dale Carnegie advised using a person's name as one of the six key rules for encouraging others to like us (the other five rules being: be a good listener, show genuine interest in the person, talk about the person's interests, smile and make the other person feel important). When elected as British Prime Minister, Tony Blair made it clear to his colleagues that he wanted to be called by his first name. Despite the fact that the leader of the country wished to foster good working relationships with his subordinates by equalising the use of names, this was not widely practised in the workplace. A survey[64] of 557 workplaces in the UK employing more than a quarter of a million people in total found that 33 per cent of senior managers expected to be addressed by staff as 'Sir' or by their title.

Another important dimension in the establishment and maintenance of relationships is the use of *humour*. The common denominator 'among those whom I love' for W.H. Auden was that, 'all of them make me laugh'. Humour has been shown to be a key communication skill[65] and one associated with effective leadership.[66] One reason for this is that we like humorous individuals, and liking is in turn related to increases in the perceived credibility and authoritativeness of the source. Thus, managers who employ humour are rated more favourably by employees than those who do not,[67] and so their potential for influence is greater.

Finally, *eating with others* helps to facilitate the persuasion process. Eating is a vital part of human existence and essential to survival. In Western society where food is plentiful we forget its innate importance. We are programmed to seek food and to protect it as necessary from others. This is the case with all animals – just watch the feeding frenzy of birds in winter fighting over scraps of food on a lawn. In countries where food is scarce and hunger is rife, human behaviour tends to revert to this basic form. This means that eating has a special significance. We usually only invite special people to dine with us (family, friends, sexual partners), and we use these occasions to help develop and cement relationships. Hence, the importance of the business lunch or working breakfast. This means that we can use the power of shared eating to help persuade others.

Selecting an influencing strategy

Influencing as a strategy can be overt and hard or more subtle and soft. At this stage you should complete the Inventory in Exercise 3.2a. This measures your preferred style of influencing. The scoring for this Inventory is given in Exercise 3.2b at the end of the chapter.

Kipnis and Schmidt[68] carried out a study involving 360 managers in the USA, Australia and the UK, to investigate how and why they employed particular influencing strategies. Managers were asked to describe how they attempted to influence their subordinates, peers and superiors at work. The influencing tactics were then classified into three main strategies, namely hard, soft and rational (see Box 3.6). When employees wanted a personal favour from their superior they tended to use soft tactics such as flattery and behaving in a humble manner. On the other hand, when they wanted to persuade their boss to implement a new procedure they were more likely to use rational tactics such as giving reasons and outlining the advantages.

Another study[69] of employee compliance in branches of a multinational bank across four countries found that the one common determining factor was the relationship with the person making the request. But differences also emerged.

- In Spain, friendship was the key determinant of felt obligation to co-worker.
- If the requester was powerful or linked to a powerful other this had a significant impact in Hong Kong.
- Workers in the USA were also influenced by direct power and indirect power (i.e. the requester being linked to a powerful person), direct friendship and indirect friendship (i.e. requester linked to a friend), and authority. However, it did not matter whether the requester was a same branch co-worker.
- On the other hand, in Germany the factor of whether the requester worked in the same branch was important, as was whether or not the requester had personal power.

Other studies have also shown[70,71] that people choose different persuasion strategies depending both upon the situation and the target person. The choice is determined by a variety of factors including immediate objectives, relative power positions and expectations about the willingness of the other person to do what is being sought. In general, employees use five main strategies to influence their managers.

1. *Assertiveness.* Here, workers stand up for, and openly state, that what they are requesting is part of their rights (see Chapter 11 for a full discussion of this strategy).
2. *Ingratiation.* This is a very common tactic among subordinates. It involves the use of acquiescence, continual agreement with the

Exercise 3.2a Influencing inventory

Read each of the following statements carefully and select the rating that most accurately describes your response.

	Disagree strongly	*Disagree*	*Agree a little*	*Agree strongly*	*Agree very strongly*
1. The vast majority of people are good and kind and will help you as much as they can.	1	2	3	4	5
2. Even if you do not like someone you should use praise and flattery to pretend you do, so they will do what you want.	1	2	3	4	5
3. Principles are all very well in theory, but in practice business is by nature a hard-nosed world.	1	2	3	4	5
4. Cunning and manipulative people rarely prosper.	1	2	3	4	5
5. It is best to always tell others what your true goals are.	1	2	3	4	5
6. The end can never justify the means.	1	2	3	4	5
7. Most people like to be led and told what to do.	1	2	3	4	5
8. It is wrong to play on people's emotions so you can sway them to your way of thinking.	1	2	3	4	5
9. Most people need to be told what is good for them.	1	2	3	4	5
10. If you have power you should make it very clear to others that you will use it as necessary.	1	2	3	4	5

Exercise 3.2a ***continued***

11. Most people are conscientious and will work hard without being forced to.	1	2	3	4	5
12. Life in the world of work is a jungle where the strong do well and the weak suffer.	1	2	3	4	5
13. If you are kind and considerate to others, they will not take advantage.	1	2	3	4	5
14. Only a fool puts total faith in another person.	1	2	3	4	5
15. Everyone tells lies to get what they really want.	1	2	3	4	5
16. You won't get far in life if you worry about hurting people's feelings.	1	2	3	4	5
17. In business, doing things in an ethical way is more important than making profits.	1	2	3	4	5
18. Fear is not the best motivator of people.	1	2	3	4	5
19. Once a promise is made it must always be kept.	1	2	3	4	5
20. You should only do something if it is in your own best interests.	1	2	3	4	5

Total Score ___

Box 3.6 Influencing strategies

1. **Hard influencing strategy: exemplar responses of managers**

   'I threaten to give an unsatisfactory performance evaluation'
   'I get higher management to back up my request.'

   Hard tactics are more likely to be used when:

   - The influencer has the advantage/more power
   - Resistance is anticipated
   - The other person's behaviour violates social or organisational norms.

2. **Soft influencing strategy: exemplar responses of managers**

   'I act very humble when making my request'
   'I make the person feel important by saying s/he has the experience to do what I want.'

   Soft tactics are more likely to be used when:

   - The influencer is at a disadvantage/has less power
   - Resistance is anticipated
   - The goal is to secure personal benefits (e.g. time off work).

3. **Rational influencing strategies: exemplar responses of managers**

   'I offer to exchange favours: You do this for me, and I'll do something for you'
   'I outline the advantages of the recommended course of action.'

   Rational tactics are more likely to be used when:

   - Neither party has a real power advantage
   - Resistance is not anticipated
   - The goal is to get benefits for one's self and for one's organisation.

superior (the typical 'yes-person'), and flattery to 'butter up' the executive prior to making a request in a sycophantic fashion.

3. *Rational argument and discussion.* In other words they use logical proofs as discussed above.
4. *Sanctions.* This involves retaliation against the superior. This is part of the threat/fear tactic. Here, employees threaten actions such as litigation, work to rule, or strikes. They may also take time off ill.
5. *Coalition.* In this case, employees collude with others against the manager. This is a form of 'ganging up' against the executive, with others who have an interest in opposing this person.

In terms of the strategic choice of tactics, it is important to be aware that there are two cognitive routes involved in the processing of persuasive messages – the *central* and the *peripheral*. In the central route the individual engages in a careful and thoughtful consideration of the merits of the information as presented (asking questions, formulating counter-arguments and so on). In the peripheral route, little conscious effort is devoted to message processing or analysis, and the target is usually not aware that a persuasion attempt is being made. As summarised by Strack and Mussweiler[72] 'many influence attempts operate on an automatic level and lie outside the target's awareness'. For example, a television advert may sell a soft drink by presenting details of a research survey which found that in tests over 90 per cent of people preferred it to the taste of its rivals (central route strategy). An alternative approach would be to show lots of attractive people having fun in sunny and glamorous locations, with the soft drink in hand and upbeat music playing, while the voice-over tells us that this soft drink 'is the difference' (peripheral route strategy). The latter is an attempt to plant a subconscious association between the drink and being happy. If this were processed centrally the viewer would be asking questions such as: 'What exactly does it mean to say that a soft drink "is the difference"?' or 'Why are all these people grinning at nothing in particular?' However, the fact is that it does not tend to be so processed, but rather is dealt with through the peripheral cognitive route – and so it often succeeds. Indeed, research has shown that when people are in a positive mood they tend to process messages peripherally, whereas when their mood is negative central processing predominates.[73]

Managers should be aware of the impact of both routes. Aspects such as the attractiveness of the persuader, use of the target's first name, smiles, humour, eating with the person and so on, can all affect the outcome of persuasion attempts. In essence, these all contribute to a conducive 'feel-good' frame of mind in the target that in turn facilitates peripheral receptivity to persuasive appeals. Yet, these dimensions are usually processed by recipients through the peripheral rather than the central route. We are usually not aware, when they are used skilfully and appropriately, that these tactics are influencing how we feel about an issue. Of course, if we do become conscious of an influence attempt we may begin to resent the fact that our first name is being used, that the person is being humorous, or has invited us for lunch. In other words, the attempt may boomerang. Skill and tact are therefore required when persuading others.

Overview

We live in an era where we are deluged by a torrent of messages from professional persuaders. The average consumer in the USA is exposed to over 1000 commercial influence attempts daily,[74] in the form of TV, radio and newspaper adverts, billboard posters, etc. Interpersonal influence is also ubiquitous. Persuasion tactics are therefore valuable commodities in human interchange. Indeed, the ability to influence and persuade staff can be regarded as the *sine qua non* of management. If managers cannot encourage staff to follow directives, and use means other than force and threat to do so, they will inevitably fail.[75]

There is a rich variety of techniques which can be used in a subtle yet genuine manner to produce desired and desirable outcomes. These have been summarised under the three main categories of logical, emotional and personal proofs. While these have been analysed separately, inevitably there is overlap between the three categories. This reflects the fact that effective persuasion often necessitates a combination of tactics, which involve appeals to reason, emotion and personal relationship. The strategy used by a manager to effect influence should vary across situations and people. The possession of a wide repertoire of tactics, and flexibility in their usage, are therefore central to successful persuasion.

Exercise 3.2b Scoring for influencing inventory

Scoring

For items 1, 4, 5, 6, 8, 11, 13, 17, 18 and 19, reverse the numbers you have selected, so that *for these items only* a rating of 1 is converted to a score of 5, 2 is converted to 4, 3 stays the same, 4 is converted to 2, and 5 is converted to 1. Now sum all items to get your total score.

The score provides an indicator of your preferred style of influencing. Generally, people with scores *under 50* value a 'softer' style of influencing. The lower the score the more the person believes that humans are inherently good and kind, and will do things if they are properly explained to them. They feel that qualities such as honesty, sincerity, genuineness and truthfulness are essential for human interchange. They believe that this open and caring approach will be reciprocated by others, thereby increasing the likelihood of positive outcomes. By contrast, those with scores *above 50* are more hard-nosed individuals, and as the score increases towards *100* the more likely the person is to believe that people generally only act voluntarily out of self-interest. High scorers believe that one must therefore do what is necessary to 'move' others to their way of thinking and acting. They do not worry about hurting people's feelings, using subterfuge or pressurising people, to get things done.

Interpretation of scores

81–100	You have a very definite Machiavellian style of influencing.
61–80	You are much more Machiavellian than person-centred in your style of influencing.
51–60	You are slightly more Machiavellian than person-centred in your style of influencing.
41–50	You are slightly more person-centred than Machiavellian in your style of influencing.
26–40	You have a person-centred approach to influencing, and prefer an open and honest style rather than one involving subterfuge.
Under 25	You have a very definite person-centred, soft, style of influencing and do not like to use manipulative persuasion techniques.

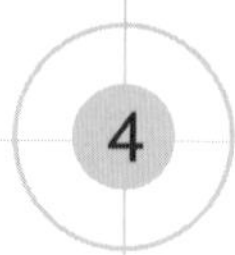

Let's get together: teams at work

Introduction

A team is a number of interdependent people bound together by a collective aim.[1] They may have a finite start and end date, or be intended as an indefinite part of an organisation's structure.[2] An essential feature of teams is that the members co-operate to achieve jointly agreed goals. They hold each other mutually accountable for success or failure. The underlying philosophy is that if one of them looks good, they all look good. Teams celebrate both personal and group achievements. In doing so, performance objectives are routinely exceeded. What was once considered impossible becomes viewed as inevitable. Given this, some leading researchers have argued that teams should be the standard unit of performance for most organisations, regardless of size.[3] Indeed, the research literature identifies a number of consistent benefits from team organisation. These include[4,5]

- Improved quality of work life for employees
- Enhanced work satisfaction
- Heightened levels of worker identification and commitment
- Enhanced flexibility
- Increased productivity
- Improvements to products and services
- Reduced staff turnover
- Increased industrial harmony
- A de-layered management structure.

However, in the rush to develop highly focused, productive and motivated teams, it is often assumed that groups are transformed into teams by a simple process of managerial decree: 'let there be team working'. A great deal of research has shown that the above listed benefits of team working do not automatically occur, and that in fact organisational performance may decline when teams are introduced. One study found that as many as seven out of ten US teams failed to produce the desired results.[6] In reality, positive change in this area requires clear goals, time and supportive communication. The purpose of this chapter is to examine each of these requirements, so helping managers transform groups into teams, and in a manner that improves performance.

This transformation is rarely easy. As Sartre once said: 'Hell is other people.' We regularly encounter his view in our work within organisations. Many people find that working in groups causes them more anxiety than anything else they do in the workplace. Rather than feel enthralled or stimulated, employees sometimes feel bewitched, bothered and bewildered by the whole business.[7] In addition, teams, committees and groups are often perceived as making poor decisions, while stifling innovation and creativity, and with spawning bureaucracy and inertia. As the well-known saying from the world's most prolific source of aphorisms ('Anonymous') puts it, 'A committee is a *cul-de-sac* down which promising young ideas are lured and then quietly strangled.'

On the other hand, teams are more widely used in the business world than ever before. Over 80 per cent of US organisations with more than 100 employees have been estimated to use teams, while a study of over 564 British manufacturing companies found that 55 per cent had made at least modest use of teams in the previous few years.[8] Such teams can consist of problem-solving groups (sometimes called quality circles), self-managed or natural work groups and cross-functional teams (such as short-lived project groups).[9] Complex business processes increasingly foster inter-dependency, and which give rise to new forms of team organisations. For example, there has been an enormous growth in industry of what is known as 'cellular manufacturing'. In this, all the equipment and people necessary to manufacture products that have similar characteristics are co-located, thus stimulating new forms of team working in contexts where it rarely existed before.[10] There may well be super heroes in most organisations, who regularly and single-handedly save everyone from catastrophe. But, in today's world, every Captain Kirk relies on a network of supporting teams, well organised, highly motivated, trained and committed to the goals of the organisation. Thus, inter-dependency inevitably leads to group development and the formation of complex relationships. The challenge for managers is to improve communication, transform groups into teams and free the human factor to fulfil its potential as the chief engine of business success.[11]

The human factor is crucial. Loyalty (on the part of employees, investors and customers) has been identified as more important in securing profitable growth than market share, scale, cost position or other key business variables.[12] This supports the conclusion that the promotion of trust within the workplace – as well as with external customers and publics – is crucial to success.[13,14] Teamwork is a powerful means by which trust and loyalty can be used to strengthen the foundations of your organisation. It is underpinned by values that encourage listening, supportive communication, responding positively to the input of others, and recognising everyone's interests and achievements. With such values in place individuals, teams and the whole organisation perform better. Teamwork is endangered by measures that threaten the underlying needs of employees. In that context, such management practices as downsizing (or, as it is sometimes termed, 'dumb-sizing') are inimical to the creation of trust and the promotion of loyalty within the organisation.[15]

Research has long established that well-managed and committed teams achieve much more than individuals working alone or in competition with each other. This is because workers in self-managed teams have greater autonomy and discretion in what they do. This in turn provides greater intrinsic rewards and job satisfaction, improves flexibility and stimulates innovation.[16] As a result, more than 75 per cent of workers surveyed on this issue who were currently in traditional work groups said they would prefer to be organised in teams. On the other hand, fewer than 10 per cent of those currently in teams said they would like to return to traditional supervision and methods of organisation.[17] Consequently, the reconfiguration of staff into self-managed work teams has been identified as one of the core characteristics of what empirical studies suggest can be defined as high-performing organisations.[18]

We list here some examples to illustrate the potential that teamworking has to offer:

- When Hewlett-Packard (HP) restructured its organisation around quality teams, efficiency across the company improved by 50 per cent.[19]
- A manufacturing operation in Ohio found that output increased by 90 per cent when production teams were created. Xerox headquarters reported that when a supervisory position was eliminated and the staff given more autonomy absenteeism fell by 75 per cent.[20]
- Teamwork has consistently resulted in greater achievement, productivity, innovation, quality and work satisfaction than 'competitively' driven management environments. This has been

demonstrated in studies ranging over scientists, airline reservation agents, business people, students and car assembly workers.[21]

- Nissan UK, based in Sunderland, has become one of the most successful manufacturing plants in the UK. At one point it had an absenteeism rate of 0.75 per cent compared to a national average of 4.7 per cent in manufacturing industry. Teamwork was a major factor in this success. For example, at the start of every shift each day all employees met together in their work groups to discuss tasks for the day. Accordingly, people-management and team-building skills were regarded as key requirements for potential supervisors.[22]
- A study of 128 claims adjusters from two insurance company offices found that the more employees communicated competently, listened skilfully and talked about the new computer system the more productive they were in using it. In short, the more formal and informal contact people engaged in with colleagues when a new process was introduced, the more quickly it was assimilated.[23]

Consider the example of quality teams in HP. The most important point to be made here is that HP supervisors received 40 hours of training in team building, and were allowed a great deal of autonomy in their day-to-day work. Success was due to training in key principles, intense communication and the empowerment of crucial change agents. A rigorous approach, and intense commitment to communication, is vital to build effective teams.

Such points are important even for teams whose members are widely dispersed – what are known as 'remote' or 'virtual' teams. This is a growing trend. At least two-thirds of Fortune 500 companies in the US employ telecommuters (i.e. people working from home),[24] while it has been estimated that over 100 million people throughout the world now work outside traditional offices.[25] Many of these interact with their colleagues in virtual teams. Such teams can be defined as groups of people who have a shared purpose and who work interdependently across time, space and organisation boundaries.[26] Here, members interact mainly via electronic media. Such teams are often seen as an additional route to improved organisational agility and hence a key tool in any effort at global expansion.[27] It is also clear that such teams face particular challenges in terms of building trust, cohesion, group identity and in overcoming isolation among virtual team members.[28] Overall, the emerging research on this topic suggests several problems and related strategies that should be utilised to overcome them. We summarise these in Box 4.1.[29]

Box 4.1 The challenges of virtual teams

- Building trust, cohesion, team identity and overcoming isolation is more difficult in virtual than in conventional teams.
- The general processes of team growth and building apply with equal force to virtual teams.
- Team members should meet face-to-face, for initial team building sessions, and be facilitated to develop norms to guide their work as a team.
- Members should continue to meet (again, face-to-face) at critical milestones in their team life cycle, to reflect on progress thus far and to set goals for the future.
- Rapid responses to electronic communication are essential. The team should agree and implement norms to facilitate this, such as a rule that all e-mails be answered within a specified timeframe.
- The team should be trained in managing meetings, problem solving and decision-making.
- Prospective members should be assessed on both technical *and* communication skills, with due weight given to the latter. It should not be assumed that only technical skills are important.

There are now many examples in the literature of how these principles can be put into practice. For example, the Ford Motor Company ran a complex design and engineering process of 1000 people in five continents. The manager responsible sustained communication through fortnightly one to one telephone meetings, weekly video-conference meetings with 25 key managers, and personal visits to each team at least once a year.[30] These and other imaginative measures are based on the recognition that technology solves some problems, while also creating others. Direct human interaction is indispensable for genuine team building to occur.

Stages of team development

Reorganising around a team structure is an inherently risky venture. To succeed, new relationships must be formed and the structure of the organisation will most probably need to be changed. There are hazards on every side – for example, if too much attention is paid to the task, people will feel neglected. But if too much attention is paid to relationships, the task will not be accomplished. Box 4.2 lists a number of

Box 4.2 Symptoms of team ruination

1. Members shirk responsibility. They constantly say 'This wasn't my fault.' 'Things were like this when I got here.' 'Why don't you ask Joe? That's his responsibility, not mine.' 'Here we go again.'
2. The team is always busy, but nothing ever gets done. There is no time for reflection or analysis. After all, reports have to be prepared for the higher-ups.
3. Members become obsessed by processes rather than outcomes. Lengthy procedures manuals emerge, but the team's goals recede even further into the distance. This allows the incompetent to engage in purposeful activity, but without any sense of purpose.
4. The team regularly fragments into sub-groups. Members exchange stories about each other's screw-ups rather than their successes. There are constant rumours of coups and counter-coups. Members spend their time recruiting reinforcements to shore up their own position. Secret treaties are regularly concluded, and instantly broken.
5. Members are terrified of making mistakes. They hope that when mistakes are made no one else will notice. New team members are taken aside and told to 'cover your back'.
6. Since nothing has ever worked before, everyone believes that disaster lies ahead whatever they do – a process that has been termed 'learned helplessness'.
7. Meetings start late and drag on past their closure time. Members drift out before the end. The same items keep cropping up on the agenda, with nothing ever being decided. The chairperson decides nothing, but does so decisively.
8. Noone else in the organisation knows what the team is up to. Furthermore, they don't care. It keeps some more bosses busy and out of their hair, while the real work gets done elsewhere.
9. The team mascot is Homer Simpson.

symptoms often found when teams have failed to get the right balance on such issues. The task for everyone involved is to steer team organisation through such rapids, avoiding the rocks that lie around each new bend. This process is helped if the inevitable stages associated with the development of teams are anticipated. One of the best-known contributions here was made by Tuckman and Jensen,[31] who proposed that effective teams go through a number of clearly identifiable stages. These are:

Forming At this early stage team members are confronted with maximum uncertainty. Their task is unclear, while the personalities, abilities and 'hidden agendas' of the others are relatively unknown. New members arrive in what is almost an arranged marriage, and see their prospective partners in this new role for the first time. People therefore try to define what the team's central task is, while also attempting to make sense of relationships between individuals. All of this involves sharing information, discussing subjects unrelated to the task and testing other members. Inevitably, misunderstandings occur and relationships sometimes become fraught. In fact, some would-be teams never go beyond such tensions – they sink as soon as they take to sea.

Storming Here, team members experience hostility and conflict as they struggle with the task. Defensiveness, competition and resistance to being a part of the team at all may occur. Internal conflicts break out, over status, power, and speaking or participation rights. Although our first instinct might suggest that this period, and conflict in general, is harmful the evidence suggests that it has a positive effect – if managed properly.[32] For example, a study[33] of 44 members in 14 teams found that project teams that began with very harmonious interpersonal relations did not perform as well as those which had early disharmonies. It has been theorised that this may have been because early conflicts teach people how to solve interpersonal disputes and become task focused. In short, some creative tension has a positive effect. However, it may also be that such conflicts helped the team avoid the natural tendency that also exists for the members to over-conform with its emerging norms. This process will be discussed later in this chapter.

Norming Here, there is growing acceptance by team members of each other's idiosyncrasies, and correspondingly less emphasis on enforcing absolute uniformity of thought or behaviour. A greater sense of belonging to the group is developed. New norms and methods of acceptable behaviour emerge. Co-operation and mutuality become more normal, in place of the conflict behaviours on display at an earlier stage.

Performing Once norms have been developed, team members work in a problem-solving manner to attain group goals. They also begin to evaluate their accomplishments. The review process has been described as the stage where members often engage in the creation of heroic legends. This may in itself become an important part of the whole organisation's growth. Peters and Austin[34] have argued that successful or excellent organisations are characterised, among much else, by legends of achievement and war stories of individual 'derring-do' which serve the purpose of illuminating and reinforcing the organisation's underlying value system.

Adjourning All good things must come to an end and groups are no exception. Teams may cease to exist because their task has been completed and their goals have been achieved. Alternatively, the group may, over a period of time, begin to lose its attraction or effectiveness, resulting in gradual adjournment and slow disintegration as members progressively leave. Where a team is being disbanded suddenly, care needs to be taken to lessen the psychological impact upon members. We become attached to groups to which we belong and termination can provoke bereavement-like symptoms.

Characteristics of successful teams

Building teams means moving a group of often disparate people through the stages discussed above, so that they all become committed to the group's goals, participate fully in decision-making, learn how to manage inevitable conflicts and feel complete ownership of the tasks in hand. At this point, team members will have found their sea legs. The research suggests that managing this transition requires a focus on a number of distinct issues.[35–37] These are:

The team should be a real team, rather than a randomly assembled assortment of individuals who barely know each other In particular, one of the foremost authorities on teams, Hackman, proposes that real teams have '… a team *task*, clear *boundaries*, clearly specified *authority* to manage their own work processes, and membership *stability* over some reasonable period of time'.[38] Boundaries refer to the need for a clearly designated team membership. Group meetings where participants are free to come and go, and frequently nominate other people to attend on their behalf, will not function effectively as a team. The need for a stable membership is also one that is frequently overlooked, often at horrendous cost. For example, Hackman found that 73 per cent of serious incidents involving aircraft occurred on the crew's first day of flying together, when people were still unused to close co-operation and communication. (You might, or might not, like to note that, typically, airline staff fly with someone they have worked with before once every five years!)

The team should have highly specific goals The importance of clear goals is discussed in Chapter 14, in the context of individual appraisal. Similar points apply to team objectives. President John F. Kennedy gave one of the most cited examples of a clear direction in the early 1960s. He told the American people that he wanted the country to 'commit itself to achieving the goal, before this decade is out, of landing a man on the moon and returning him safely to earth'.[39]

In the absence of a guiding sense of purpose teams become a bureaucracy, focused on self-preservation rather than the achievement of the organisation's objectives. A focus on clear goals can be established and reinforced by ensuring that meetings regularly address the following questions:

- What did we achieve last week, that contributed directly to the organisation's mission?
- What do we want to achieve this week?
- Who is responsible for what, when will it be done, and what will be different when they have finished?
- What specifically can we do better?
- What can we change in how we work?
- What can we change in the organisation?
- What added value have we brought to this enterprise, this week?

This approach reduces emphasis on status, facilitates clear communication, maintains focus, assists evaluation and creates symbols of actual accomplishment. Evaluation of the team's own workings is an essential part of its growth and development. The suggestion here is that such self-evaluation should be institutionalised into the team's deliberations, by ensuring that the above questions are openly addressed at each team meeting.

Effective teams number between 2 and 25 people, with most under 10 This supports constructive interaction, and enables an agreed focus on real, achievable goals. People can snooze peacefully in a crowd of 50, but their snores will be noticed in a room of 5. The smaller the team the harder it is to coast as a silent (or anonymous) member. By facilitating involvement, small teams also reduce members' frustration – when people cannot participate they feel disempowered. Disempowerment ensures that, after team meetings, the main discussion point on everyone's agenda is the need to grumble about the chairperson rather than action to solve real problems. Hackman,[40] reviewing the research evidence, has concluded that in general teams should not exceed six people, and function better when they have *slightly fewer numbers than the task actually requires.*

Effective teams hold themselves collectively accountable Peer 'pressure' is much more effective than pressure that is external to the team. It promotes ownership, without which no cohesion or commitment is possible. Ownership is central to sustained effort and involvement: when, for example, did you last mow your neighbour's lawn in preference to your own? One researcher[41] has argued that such team accountability is also promoted if teams themselves devise relevant measures for their activities: in short, a genuinely empowered team will have the lead role in designing its own measures. This is because the main purpose of such measures is to help the team gauge its progress, rather than those outside its ranks – including top managers. Furthermore, a team should adopt only a handful of measures. This keeps a few key and achievable tasks in focus. When teams have too much to do they do it badly or not at all, while producing reams of paper to camouflage their inactivity. More is a mess, while less is best.

A good start determines the team's prospects First meetings and actions create what is known as an 'expectancy effect' among team members. Is this a talking shop or an action forum? Are new ideas encouraged or punished? Will the team perform real work, or merely produce reports? First impressions and actions on these issues are vital. Thus, teams should:

1. *Set some readily attainable goals, and then declare an immediate victory.* Good generals know never to give an order that cannot be obeyed. Such orders lead to defeat, and the fearful expectation of further

debacles to come. Teams need to know they have goals that can be accomplished, and see steady progress towards them unfold at an early stage of their development.

2. *Set some clear rules of behaviour.* This would include issues such as confidentiality, punctuality, interruptions and the need to set action outcomes for all.
3. *Build evaluation of the team into all meetings.* This means habituating the team to ask questions such as:
   - What did we do well here?
   - What could have been done even better?
   - How can we promote greater participation at our meetings?
   - What outside help can we get to improve our decision-making?
4. *Do something radically different, at the outset, to that which members of the team would normally countenance.* Teams can unleash tremendous innovation, but only if a preparedness to change is the normal mindset of team members, and a characteristic of every task that they undertake. Business adviser Jim Westaway expressed the position thus: 'If you want change, if you want people to do something different, you must first stop them from doing what they are doing now. Once you do that, you have their undivided attention and it becomes possible to persuade them to do something else.'[42]

Encourage team interaction Successful teams spend lots of time together, engaged in both task and non-task activities. This investment in time promotes formal and informal communication, and so nurtures relationships. Expecting members to view the team as an add on to their real job ensures that they do not take it seriously. On the other hand, the quality of time spent together is more important than its quantity. As an old adage puts it, meetings take minutes but waste hours. Such a cynical view gains ground when teams lose their primary focus – the task at hand. In short, meeting for hours while deciding nothing is akin to athletes gathering at the racetrack but forgetting to run. All competitive edge will soon be lost.

Effective teams use positive feedback We are all heavily influenced by the power of rewards. People are social beings, and the feedback that we receive from others helps shape our sense of who and what we are, and the broader social environment to which we belong. A number of social rewards have been shown to have a particularly powerful effect on us, and these are therefore likely to be especially appreciated by team members.[43] Some of these are listed in Box 4.3. Although these could be viewed as particularly useful for team leaders, their frequent use by all team members is a vital means of strengthening overall relationships.

Box 4.3 How to use social rewards to build teams

- Make frequent use of praise and encouragement. Draw attention to people's successes. When a project ends with a setback, focus your feedback on what can be learnt from the experience, and what has been gained by the organisation as a result of the things which still went well.
- Send out regular thank you notes to people, for jobs well done.
- Telephone people and thank them, when you hear that they have done something well.
- Have a regular 'employee of the month'.
- Bring up specific examples of good performance at team meetings.
- Live by the 90/10 rule: 90 per cent of your feedback should relate to positive performance, and 10 per cent (or less) should relate to problem areas in people's work.
- Direct praise and encouragement towards individuals rather than the group as a whole. Seek out many individual instances of behaviour where such social rewards would be considered appropriate.
- Make rewards contingent on positive performance or behaviours. This increases the prospects that such behaviours will be repeated in the future.
- Apply rewards immediately after the behaviour has occurred, rather than after a long period of time has elapsed.
- Ensure that praise is sincere and appropriately varied. Use of the same expressions time after time diminishes their value, and is eventually seen as insincere.
- Encourage team members to engage in self-reinforcement and mutual reinforcement. Members should develop the habit of acknowledging when they or others do well.
- Utilise what has been termed 'response development'. This involves summarising in your own words what other people have said, and adding your own response, in order to validate their contribution to group discussion.

In addition, celebration is an important aspect of social reinforcement. It strengthens relationships among team members, and ensures that the focus on achieving goals remains to the forefront. Box 4.4 lists ways in which celebration can be promoted. There is some evidence that successful organisations institutionalise such an approach into the daily routine of how they work. For example, the cosmetic company, Bodyshop, has a Department of Celebration at its main headquarters. The UK mobile phone company, Carphone Warehouse goes so far as to organise a 'beer bust' for some 600 employees one Friday evening each month. They are held in pubs and wine bars, when for a period of one-and-a-half hours the company pays for all drinks, at a cost of some £4 000. These not only help team spirit, but have led to a number of romances and even marriage. The company also holds an annual ball for staff as well as specific team-building days. Results have been good. Turnover increased from £110 million in 1997 to £171 million in 1998, while a staff survey showed that 92 per cent of staff were proud to work for the company.[44]

It should also be noted that financial rewards are an important issue. In Chapter 14 we discuss problems with performance-related pay. One of the best documented is that rewarding *individual* performance endangers *collective action*. However, there is some evidence that high performance is encouraged when financial rewards are team-based rather than focused on the individual. For example, the thriving retail organisation in the USA known as The Men's Wearhouse offers team-based incentives.[45] Those teams that achieve or exceed their goals

Box 4.4 Ways to celebrate

- Publicise your successes.
- Create posters and put them around the workplace.
- Circulate newssheets advising of progress.
- Have award winners and ceremonies.
- Have wall charts showing levels of performance.
- Have a team lunch out.
- Plan evenings out, Xmas parties and team participation in charity fund-raising ventures.
- Create time and space for celebrations.
- Include celebration in your team agreement.
- At team meetings, regularly discuss what is good about the team and what could be even better.

are rewarded collectively, fostering a 'we're all in this together' sense of joint commitment.

Develop the practice of supportive communication In successful teams status differentials are noticeable by their absence. Communication is informal. Team members address each other by their first names. There is plentiful discussion, with everyone encouraged and expected to contribute. For example, a good team rule is that no one speaks twice until everyone has spoken once. Supportive communication facilitates civilised disagreement. The team is comfortable with this and shows no sign of avoiding, smoothing over or suppressing conflict. Box 4.5 lists some other commonly agreed characteristics of supportive communication.[46] These represent behaviours that everyone, not just the team leader, needs to promote if the group really is going to develop as a team.

Turn at this point to Reflective exercise 4.1 (See page 117), and answer the questions as frankly and honestly as you can. It will enable you to form some initial impression of the extent to which your own communication with other team members, and their communication with you, is either supportive or unsupportive.

Box 4.5 Principles of supportive communication

1. *Problem oriented, not person oriented*

Characterised by:	NOT:
'What can we do to solve this difficulty?'	'This is your fault, again.'

2. *Congruent, not incongruent*

Characterised by:	NOT:
'Yes, I am worried that we might not make the deadline.'	'Of course I'm not worried. Yes, I'm sure we'll make the deadline.'

3. *Descriptive, not evaluative*

Characterised by:	NOT:
'Well, this is what happened; this is how it made me feel; here are my ideas on how we can resolve it.'	'What you did was unforgivable.'

4. *Validating, not invalidating*

Characterised by:	NOT:

Box 4.5 *continued*

Characterised by:	NOT:
'What do you think needs to be done to solve this anyway, ' yourself?	'This is a bit beyond you so I'll get Joan to look into it. Do you know where she is?'

5. *Specific, not global*

Characterised by:	NOT:
'You interrupted me three times at today's meeting.'	'You never show me any respect.'

6. *Conjunctive, not disjunctive*

Characterised by:	NOT:
'Right, you've raised whether we can meet the first deadline. I think this relates to . . . .'	'The deadline has to wait. The thing here is whether you are staying within your budget.'

7. *Owned, not disowned*

Characterised by:	NOT:
'I've decided not to support your proposal, because . . .'	'I'd love to support your idea, and I fought hard for it, but the boss just wouldn't wear it. A pity.'

8. *Supportive listening, not one-way listening*

Characterised by:	NOT:
'Tell me what you think the problems are.'	'These sound like excuses. Let me tell you where you need to sharpen up.'

Main barriers to team development

We have looked, above, at some of the key steps groups need to take in order to become teams. It also has to be acknowledged that a variety of problems commonly arise when such attempts are made. Human beings are the most complex phenomenon in the known universe. It is hardly surprising that anything which involves people requires a great deal of work to get right. Some of the main difficulties which need to be addressed, and which have not so far been discussed, will now be considered:

Cohesion versus the need for dissent Teams need a consensus, on such vital issues as the nature of the task to be performed, how decisions are made, who performs various leadership functions and the extent of individual members' authority for different team functions. The resolution of these issues creates what are termed the norms of the group. However, it is also known that the quality of group decision-making is enormously improved when there is minority dissent. Nevertheless, groups have a tendency to suppress such dissent and punish, usually through the withdrawal of social rewards, those who challenge the conventional wisdom of the group.[47]

The benefits of minority dissent arise because decisions are improved when a variety of options are systematically explored and evaluated. Our first thought on a problem is rarely our best. Evaluation should occur at each stage of the decision-making cycle: for example, it pays for groups to return to first principles immediately before a final decision, and evaluate their options all over again. However, groups often avoid such debate and compel members to conform at an early stage to the perceived norms and values of the group. In short, it is difficult to play the role of minority advocate in a group of strong members already committed to a particular outcome. As Oscar Wilde once put it: 'We dislike arguments of any kind; they are always vulgar, and often convincing.'

A particularly important issue here concerns the extreme conformity which often settles on groups when they are involved in making important decisions, and which has been termed 'groupthink'. Janis,[48] who popularised the term, investigated a whole series of poor political and business decisions, and concluded that many of them could be explained by examining the decision-making process within the groups responsible. For example, the USA launched a disastrous invasion of Cuba's Bay of Pigs in 1961, using what was largely an army of Cuban exiles. On later reflection, it was apparent to many of those involved that they should have anticipated such a negative outcome. In explaining why they did not, Janis argued that the group taking the decision to invade shared the following characteristics:

1. *It was very cohesive.* Members valued being a part of the group, felt loyal to other members and to the leader (President Kennedy) in particular. This exaggerated their tendency to agree with each other. It takes more effort to disagree with someone than it does to agree. Moreover, it is harder to argue with a friend than an enemy.
2. *The group was relatively insulated from information outside its own ranks and had an inflated impression of its grasp of the facts.* The tendency to agree with other members also strengthened the

members' view that they already knew all they needed in order to make a decision. The group developed illusions of infallibility, reinforced by the failure of its members to question the general drift of its deliberations. In short, even the most bizarre ideas begin to look credible if a group of people talk only to themselves. This has been identified as a major factor behind the conformity to strange rituals and outlandish beliefs found in cult organisations, such as the Hare Krishnas and others.[49]

3. *Group members rarely looked systematically at alternative courses of action in order to evaluate their relative merits.* They put themselves under pressure to reach decisions quickly, which further predisposed them to 'agree' around a common position at an early stage of their deliberations. Their commitment to a decision reinforced their belief that it was right, since we all tend to seek positive reinforcement on decisions made. The group behaved like the man who leapt from the Empire State Building and was heard to mutter, as he passed each successive storey, 'So far, so good.'
4. *The group was dominated by a directive and charismatic leader: President Kennedy.* Group members therefore exaggerated the level of his insight, and this in turn reinforced the natural tendency to agree quickly with what they thought his main opinion was. The spectacle of others agreeing further added to the spurious illusion that they were agreeing to something which made sense.

Various factors have been discussed earlier in this chapter which often prevent groups from gelling into teams at all. Here, we are more concerned with what happens when the team has developed beyond a group of disparate individuals. The suggestion is that the opposite problem might emerge – the team is so cohesive that it becomes a choir with no room for soloists. People no longer think for themselves. What can be done to avert these dangers? Box 4.6 lists a number of suggestions, derived from the research literature, which all team members need to take on board.

Team productivity We are driven to work with others to achieve our goals, and frequently recognise that without such co-operation our efforts will not be as effective as they need to be. ('Many hands make light work.') On the other hand, we also often find that the imagined benefits from such co-operation fail to materialise. ('Too many cooks spoil the broth.') The question arises of whether productivity losses are common in teams, why they should occur, and what we can do to avert them.

Box 4.6 Measures to avoid groupthink

- The leader should adopt a more neutral role and avoid stating personal views at an early stage of group discussion.
- Encourage the expression of dissident viewpoints.
- Assign the role of 'critical evaluator' to every group member.
- After every big decision, ask three questions: What's wrong with this decision? How could it be improved? What alternatives have we overlooked?
- Assign sub-groups to independently develop proposals.
- Periodically bring in outside people or experts to review your deliberations.
- During important discussions, assign one member to play the role of devil's advocate.
- After formulating a plan, hold a 'second chance' meeting. Invite everyone to express residual doubts. Express doubts yourself.
- Always set tasks which involve everyone.
- Set clear performance goals for the group.
- Find a means of evaluating/measuring everyone's individual contribution.
- Encourage the expression of minority opinions. Cherish, reward and promote those SOBs who disagree with you.
- Provide rewards for individual as well as group effort.

First, the evidence does indeed suggest that productivity losses are common in team contexts. Each new person added to the group increases its potential productivity, but at a decreasing rate. Thus, increasing a group's size from two to three makes a bigger difference in potential productivity than when a twenty-fourth person is added to a twenty-three strong group.[50] A French agricultural engineer named Max Ringlemann at the turn of the century conducted one of the early studies into this.[51] Ringlemann persuaded students to pull on a rope which was attached to an instrument capable of measuring the force exerted on it. The students pulled alone, and then in groups of either 7 or 14. Ringlemann assumed that by adding up the individual scores for the level of force exerted by each member of the group he would have a total roughly in line with what the entire group would exert when it pulled. In actual fact, he found that the whole group only expended about 75 per cent of what the members' individual scores suggested should be its full capacity. A wide range of studies, varying the basic task, has tended to find the same: in groups, people just do not work as hard.

In case you think that this might be a matter of co-ordination losses (after all, everyone must pull at exactly the same time, for the maximum force to be measured) it should be noted that Ringlemann's basic experiment has since been repeated.[52] The difference here was that that only one 'real' subject was involved. He or she was placed at the front of the rope-pulling team, while the rest were instructed to make realistic grunting noises and only pretend to pull. Yet again, the luckless dupe at the front was found to pull at only about 75 per cent of his or her capacity when other people were involved. Studies of brainstorming have also found that people produce far more ideas on their own than they do when brain storming in the company of others. This is explained by the phenomenon known as 'social loafing' – our apparent willingness when in the company of others to slacken our effort, in the hope or expectation that they will compensate for our reduced effort.

On a positive note, it should be borne in mind that the evidence suggests groups are more effective in problem-solving tasks, production tasks, and learning and memory tasks than individuals. They also learn faster, make fewer errors, recall better, are more productive and produce a higher quality product than individuals. However, productivity per person is less in groups – the individual commits less effort than they would on their own. Thus, groups are generally more effective than individuals but are less efficient.

But all is far from lost. Box 4.7 contains some suggestions which if applied should ensure that social loafing can be eliminated, or at least drastically reduced.

Problems with top management teams

Some research has also looked specifically at particular problems with top management teams, defined as 'the relatively small group of most influential executives at the apex of an organisation'.[53] Five main problems were reported by a sample of CEOs drawn from the USA and Europe. These were:

1. Inadequate capabilities of an individual manager (e.g. short termism in outlook; poor organisational skills; interpersonal deficiencies).
2. Common team-wide shortcomings (e.g. a mismatch between a new competitive situation, and the style, experiences or training of the top team).

Box 4.7 Suggested measures for reducing social loafing

- The task should be one in which everyone must participate. For example, brain storming works better if people come up with their own ideas privately, and then pool them in the group, rather than start the process off in the company of others.
- The group leader facilitates involvement, rather than simply promotes their own ideas or engages in the task without waiting for others (see Chapter 5).
- The team regularly evaluates its own performance in terms of achieving its goals, and its functioning as a team. Issues of involvement, dominance and conflict are openly addressed.
- The task and the group are deemed attractive – by the participants. Remember that volunteers make more committed soldiers than conscripts.
- The task is intrinsically interesting. This tends to be the case when it impinges directly on the jobs of the people concerned, or what they regard as areas of core professional concern. For example, most nurses would be more likely to find the task of the team interesting if it is concerned with the quality of care on the ward, rather than the introduction of a computer system for monitoring personnel records.
- Social loafing decreases if members know each other well, interact informally before the task begins, and have some feeling of loyalty and durability about the group. On this issue, group cohesion is a force for good.
- Social loafing is less in evidence when the task of the group is more complex, since this tends to heighten involvement.
- Social loafing is reduced when the group sets its own performance goals and has the dominant say in devising its own measurement system.

3. Harmful rivalries, for status, position or decision-making authority.
4. Groupthink (as discussed earlier).
5. Fragmentation. This arises when the top team is a team in name only, functioning more accurately as a constellation of individuals engaged in minimal interaction.

As with other teams, it is clear that teams at the top are not formed simply by decree, and cannot be sustained by enthusiasm alone. Clear goals, proper training and regular review of team processes are essential preconditions for success.[54] Our own work with top teams suggests that a major barrier to this is that senior managers often assume they are immune to the difficulties that assail lesser mortal further down the organisational hierarchy. Moreover, some top managers imagine that to admit the need for training is to publicise a serious weakness, and thereby invite ridicule. In reality, weaknesses at the top are readily apparent to those on the tiers below. Management credibility goes up when problems are acknowledged and solutions are sought. Futile attempts at concealment, like pulling a mat over a hole in the floor, only prepares the way for even greater catastrophes in the future.

Overview

Business success is much more possible if people look forward to coming to work in the morning, if they are allowed to participate in decision-making, if they care about the people they work with, if they feel that the tasks they must carry out are worthwhile, and if they feel loyalty towards the organisation which employs them. Increasingly, research and practice points towards the adoption of more autonomous forms of working.[55] The pay-offs are considerable. Participation is associated with less resistance to change and a greater likelihood of innovation. The greater people's involvement in decision-making (through having influence; interacting with others; and sharing information horizontally, vertically and diagonally) the more likely they are to be committed to decision outcomes and also to contribute ideas for more efficient and effective ways of working.

Team organisation is a valuable means of promoting precisely such participation. Small teams, genuinely empowered to make decisions, have been shown to yield tangible bottom-line results. In particular, self-managed work teams are a vital method of achieving a powerful competitive advantage. However, if they are to achieve their full potential such teams require extraordinary operational autonomy, and enormous flexibility in establishing their own reward, incentive and appraisal systems.[56] It is impossible to introduce effective team working into organisations while maintaining old-style line command and control systems. One study into the issue reported the example of a successful yarn-making plant, in which there were only three levels: the general manager, a small number of team leaders and the team members themselves.[57] The CEO concluded: 'Pure and simple, the employees run that plant.' Hierarchy, traditions of deference and status differentials are also inimical to the approach outlined in this chapter. Teams transform work, and how work is done transforms organisations.

On the other hand, Sinclair[58] has argued that:

> the team ideology ... tyrannises because, under the banner of benefits to all, teams are frequently used to camouflage coercion under the pretence of maintaining cohesion; conceal conflict under the guise of consensus; convert conformity into a semblance of creativity; give unilateral decisions a co-determinist seal of approval; delay action in the supposed interests of consultation; legitimise lack of leadership; and disguise expedient arguments and personal agendas.

Others have also criticised what they have termed the rhetoric of empowerment, behind an agenda of escalating management control.[59] This chapter has presented a radically different agenda for action. We are discussing teams as a further means of promoting empowerment within the workplace, to the mutual advantage of the managers and the managed. The measures that work have nothing in common with the type of pretence discussed by Sinclair: in the long run, and even in the short run, you cannot fake empowerment. The effort required to disguise coercion as consultation is such that it is actually easier, not to say more satisfying, to promote 'the real thing'. In addition, there is no point in urging change in how everyone else works and demanding top class results, while remaining determined to sit astride the traditional organisational pyramid. Empowerment means managers identifying areas where they can relinquish power in favour of others – and then actually giving it up. Approached in this spirit building teams will be a powerful tool for both liberating the workplace and improving competitive advantage.

Reflective exercise 4.1 Evaluating communication quality in your team

You will be engaged in a variety of communication acts with individuals within your team. To assess how you and your fellow team members assess the effectiveness of communication in your team, distribute this exercise among everyone, and ensure that each of you completes it on your own. Please circle the response which most sums up the general quality of communication with individuals who fall into the categories specified. A scoring system

Reflective exercise 4.1 ***continued***

is given at the end of the chapter. Do not look at this until you have finished the questionnaire, and then completed this chapter.

1. When I communicate with other members of my team, we usually focus effectively on the problem and reach a common agreement about what has to be done.

   Sometimes *Rarely* *Frequently* *Always* *Never*

2. When my team performs a task, I usually go away feeling positive about the way in which we have encouraged and supported each other.

   Sometimes *Rarely* *Frequently* *Always* *Never*

3. When I communicate with members of my team, we would usually agree that the communication has been useful and helpful to all of us.

   Sometimes *Rarely* *Frequently* *Always* *Never*

4. When other members of my team communicate with me, they usually validate and encourage my work.

   Sometimes *Rarely* *Frequently* *Always* *Never*

5. I usually listen a great deal to what other members of my team have to say.

   Sometimes *Rarely* *Frequently* *Always* *Never*

6. Other members of my team usually listen a great deal to what I have to say.

   Sometimes *Rarely* *Frequently* *Always* *Never*

7. When other members of my team communicate with me, we usually focus effectively on the problem and reach a common agreement about what has to be done.

   Sometimes *Rarely* *Frequently* *Always* *Never*

8. When I communicate with other members of my team, my communication usually validates and encourages the work of the individual concerned.

   Sometimes *Rarely* *Frequently* *Always* *Never*

Scoring system for Reflective exercise 4.1

Score each answer as follows

Sometimes (3) Rarely (2) Frequently (4) Always (5) Never (1)

Add up your scores for questions 1, 3, 4 and 8 (Column A)

Then add up your scores for 2, 4, 6 and 7 separately (Column B)

You now have two separate totals. Your maximum score in each section is 20. Your minimum score is 4.

Column A is your own personal *perceived* level of communication effectiveness. The higher your score the more you perceive yourself to be an effective, supportive communicator within your team.

Column B gives what you *perceive* to be the general level of communication effectiveness of the other members of your team. The higher the score the more effective you consider their levels of communication to be.

Points for discussion

If your team is functioning well you should find:

1. Most team members score over 16 in each of the two categories.
2. Scores are very close for each respondent in both Column A and Column B. If most of you have scored over 16 in Column A but less than that in Column B, then it suggests that each of you think that individually you are very good communicators but that other members of your team are poor!
3. You now need to consider the following questions. Be as specific in your answers as possible in your answers. In the light of this exercise:
   - What are your team's greatest strengths?
   - What are your team's greatest weaknesses?
   - What practical, detailed steps are required to overcome these weaknesses?

5 Steering the way: leading meetings that work

Introduction

For many managers, work is one uninterrupted meeting, with only occasional changes in personnel to freshen the scene. One researcher has estimated that middle-level managers spend up to 30 per cent of their time in meetings, rising to 50 per cent for top managers.[1] Mintzberg goes further, calculating that managers spend 59 per cent of their time in scheduled meetings and another 10 per cent in unscheduled meetings.[2] These are often profitable, productive and pleasurable. At their best, meetings 'provide a means for participants to discuss and plan goals and objectives, keep up-to-date on events, encourage communication and pull resources together for strong decision-making and action planning'.[3] Unfortunately, many meetings are also held in a leaderless vacuum, in which all life forms perish. Roles are never defined. People feel powerless to influence events and eventually abdicate all sense of responsibility. Action is on a permanent leave of absence.

Still other meetings are dominated by highly directive leaders who attempt to impose 'the one right' way of doing things on every discussion and on all participants. The result is the same in both cases: meetings feel like the mother of all hangovers, rather than a forum for taking decisions and initiating action. Surveys carried out by the Wharton Centre for Applied Research have found that managers typically report that only 56 per cent of their meetings are productive.[4] They also believe that about 25 per cent of the meetings they attend would be more effective as conference calls, memos, e-mails or voicemails. Dysfunctional meetings are one of the biggest costs which business has to bear – and one of the most avoidable. The purpose of this chapter is to outline techniques for managing meetings that enable organisations to achieve their goals, strengthen relationships and reach high-quality decisions.

Achieving this requires a judicious blend of intervention and non-intervention, organisational support, instinct, careful planning and good chairing skills. We will explore the extent to which the leadership of groups is necessary at all, and how different styles of leadership are appropriate under varied circumstances. We will then examine the role of meetings in group life and how managers can improve their chairmanship skills, particularly in the context of decision-making. Most of us rarely consider how to improve meetings, precisely because they have insinuated themselves so thoroughly into the fabric of our working lives. It is time to take a fresh look.

When leadership is needed

Most managers perceive leadership skills as one of the main requirements of their job. In one survey of 250 British chief executives, who were asked to identify the most important management skills, leadership emerged as the top ranked item.[5] (The other top skills listed were vision, people management, communications and financial literacy, in that order.) Moreover, the research evidence generally suggests that 'Good management and leadership are fundamental to achieving sustainable growth and enhancing (a) nation's economic performance.'[6] It is therefore scarcely surprising that leadership has become a widely taught subject in business schools, a constant theme in business books and that more than a dozen academic journals are devoted to its study.[7] However, it is also true that most organisations remain dissatisfied with the level and spread of leadership skills that they possess. The areas of greatest weaknesses encompass strategic thinking, leading teams and motivating people.[8] This has also led to enormous dissatisfaction with the quality of leadership available. Leaders are often held to be the critical ingredient behind organisational success, while those holding top positions are simultaneously reviled as being incapable of the job. The pressures have generated a huge problem of what has been dubbed 'CEO churning', particularly in the USA. During one month, early in the new millennium, 119 CEOs departed their jobs in sizeable US companies, a 37 per cent increase on the same period a year earlier.[9] Plainly, requiring leaders to perform daily miracles while exuding the charisma of a Nelson Mandela sets both leaders and followers up for disappointment and failure. Moreover, an idolatrous approach to such leaders as GE's Jack Welch by the business press convinces some people that they are charismatic visionaries. More often than not, everyone else simply sees boring men in suits. Hubris, rigidity, scapegoating, an isolation from reality and eventual downfall ensues.[10] Focusing on the skills required to do the job well will help overcome such problems. In this chapter, we seek to explore the key skills that are required in leading more effectively, particularly in the prosaic but important context of running meetings.

In the context of groups, leadership can be defined as one or more people committed to the goals of the group as a whole rather than to those of any one part of it, and who are therefore also committed to improving relationships between the group members. Commitment to the goals of the group rather than to personal advancement is critical. Research into organisations that have made quantum leaps in performance suggests that although they are led by highly ambitious people, their sense of ambition is 'first and foremost for the institution, not themselves'.[11] This has been described as 'Level 5 leadership', and involves combining both professional will (or intense levels of determination) and some sense of personal humility. Such leaders know that they will only achieve their aims by harnessing the efforts of others, and thus strive to create many memorable win–win moments for themselves and those whom they lead.

Personality theorists assert that people are more likely to fulfil the range of roles discussed here to the extent that they exhibit the characteristics of self-confidence, empathy, ambition, self-control and curiosity – a set of traits sometimes referred to as 'the Big Five'.[12] These traits can be conceptualised as skills, and developed. It has also been suggested that leaders must have the capacity to:[13]

- *Develop a vision* – and generally engage in creative thinking.
- *Exercise sharp critical skills* – enabling the honest evaluation of problems.
- *Communicate* – in particular, the ability to ensure that others know precisely what you intend.
- *Manage expectations* – above all, the ability to be honest about what one intends, and what can be delivered.

Thus, leaders are figureheads, liaisons, monitors, disseminators, spokespersons, entrepreneurs, disturbance handlers, resource allocators and negotiators – roles that are interpersonal, informational and decisional in nature.[14] Given this, it is clear that more than one person can make a leadership contribution to the group's deliberations.

Group leadership is more important under certain conditions – for example, if the group is large.[15] In such groups there is a greater need to keep people informed, establish rules and make decisions. In turn, the job of leadership is made easier if the group believes it can achieve its goals, if it attaches value to the tasks being undertaken and if the tasks require co-ordination and communication. Since there is much emphasis on the supportive role of leaders, it is also appropriate to stress that leadership itself needs support in order to thrive. Introduced into an unhealthy climate, it will perish. People also prefer groups where leadership roles and functions are clear, since this reduces uncertainty, eases role confusion and relieves group members of such decisional nightmares as panicking about what to do next.

But how is such group leadership to be exercised? To appreciate this, we must explore the different styles of leadership and examine which are appropriate in different circumstances.

Tasks versus relationships

Leadership involves influencing the understanding, behaviours or decisions of other people. However, this need not become a display of overwhelming force, deployed in order to ensure compliance from others. Subject peoples can never be fully conquered, but they will frequently revolt. Organisations faced with perpetual insurrection lose out in competitive global markets.

Thus, organisations are coalitions, which work best when power is shared rather than regarded as the privileged preserve of a minority. Pfeffer[16] has argued that '... virtually all of us work in positions in which, in order to accomplish our jobs and objectives, we need the co-operation of others who do not fall within our direct chain of command. We depend, in other words, on people outside our purview of authority, whom we could not command, reward or punish even if we wanted to'.

As this suggests, the nature of leadership and management has been transformed. Management is increasingly about enabling others to take responsibility for critical thinking and decision-making, and so communication and human relations have assumed a higher priority. Thus, Kotter[17] has defined management as '... the process of moving a group (or groups) in some direction through mostly non-coercive means'. The language and paraphernalia of hierarchy, privilege and deference handicaps effective group functioning and meetings.[18]

This means that the effective management of groups and meetings needs to involve empowerment. Box 5.1 lists some of the signs which are commonly taken as indicating a feeling of empowerment among group members and wider layers of staff. It also contains a quotation from Lao-Tzu, which summarises the attitude an empowered group could be expected to have towards its leaders and the group's own

Box 5.1 The symptoms of empowerment

- People believe that what they do makes a difference. Real work is done. People feel that they can influence the decision-making process.
- Learning matters. Mistakes are viewed as offering feedback and improving the group's ability to do better next time. Mistakes are openly discussed rather than desperately concealed. Top people talk about their mistakes, modelling openness. People who make mistakes are promoted.
- People feel that they are part of a community. This can be called brotherhood, sisterhood or even family. Informal get-togethers occur regularly.
- Work is exciting. People enjoy work and look forward to coming in each day.
- Informal discussions are characterised by the sharing of good news, rather than gripes about 'how terrible this place is'.
- Managers have a consistently supportive style of communication. They praise in public and criticise in private. The emphasis, in any event, is on praise rather than condemnation.

Thus, an empowered team should feel as follows:

> Of the best rulers,
> The people only know that they exist;
> The next best they love and praise;
> The next they fear;
> And the next they revile.
> When they do not command the people's faith,
> Some will lose faith in them,
> Best of the best when their task is accomplished, their work done,
> The people all remark, 'We have done it ourselves.'

Lao-Tzu (sixth century BC)

achievements. The choice of leadership style is a crucial factor in determining whether such feelings are generated.

Early studies[19] suggested that two types of leader tended to emerge in groups – those principally concerned with the completion of tasks and those focused more on the nurturing of relationships between group members. However, it has since become clear that effective leadership depends on matching leadership style to the characteristics of the group, the cultural constraints within which it operates and the task it is undertaking. Thus, groups always need to work at strengthening relationships, even if their primary focus is task oriented. At the same time, groups which primarily have a relationship orientation (such as a therapy group) have work to do together, and must agree on objectives, how these will be achieved and how the group will evaluate its effectiveness.

Accordingly, more recent studies[20] look at how people have managed to integrate task and relationship maintenance and concentrate on one or the other in line with the prevailing needs of the group. Achieving a balance between focusing the group on its tasks while maintaining relationships is vital. Most of us have an inclination to emphasise either relationships or tasks, and it helps us adjust this preference more to the needs of the groups to which we belong if we can identify to which leadership style we are most attracted, and why.

Leadership styles

In addition, three main leadership styles have been consistently identified in the research literature.[21] Familiarity with these, and when they might be appropriate, is also crucial. The main styles are:

Democratic The democratic leader involves people during each phase of the decision-making process. A strong premium is put on consensus. Decisions are delayed until at least a majority of group members agree with them. A central goal is the maintenance of good relationships within the group. Sometimes, this looms larger than the immediate task, and sometimes such a stress on relationships is justified.

Laissez-faire A laissez-faire leader is fearful of making decisions. The group is left to set its own objectives, adopt a framework for decision-making and discover its own means of evaluating outcomes. The leader's responsibilities and hence those of other group members are never defined. Hard decisions are avoided or postponed, while initiative constantly waves a white flag to apathy. This could be termed the 'Let's cross our fingers together' school of leadership, in which closed eyes, hope and prayer attempt to compensate for foresight and planning. Order steadily surrenders ground to chaos.

Authoritarian An authoritarian leader is one who attempts to make the group's decisions for it, and whose definition of teamwork is 'lots of people doing what I say'. Such leaders have a strong sense of self-belief, and although they may sometimes be wrong they are never in doubt. When they shout 'jump', they expect people to answer 'how high?' There is little emphasis on the relationship side of the leadership function, combined with an obsessive and often debilitating stress on tasks. Team successes are rarely acknowledged, but lead to the imposition of new and even more demanding challenges. The leader behaves like an angry God, sitting in perpetual judgement of lesser beings.

Although some of these labels might seem pejorative, the weight of evidence suggests that what constitutes an appropriate leadership style depends on the nature of the challenge facing the group.[22] There are also factors concerned with the norms and general culture of the group to take into account. For example, despite its problems, those elements of an autocratic style concerned with making rapid decisions without intensive consultation may actually be justified when:

1. Something must be resolved quickly in the face of an impending catastrophe. If the Klingons have massed on the starboard bow and are preparing to fire, a democratic debate led by Captain Kirk is not a sensible response.
2. The meeting is dealing with a series of easy or routine items, such as agreeing the minutes. Not every issue invites controversy, needs comment or requires everyone's enthusiastic participation.
3. Higher levels of procedure and stronger control are needed in very large meetings. Such meetings are, in any event, often called purely to transmit information and do not need elaborate plans designed to achieve active participation.

On the other hand, a democratic style is useful when:

1. Political, legal or representational reasons make decision by consensus necessary. Here, Captain Kirk can usefully seek the views of Mr Spock.
2. An informal atmosphere is needed in the meeting.
3. The quality of the decision is less important than its acceptability.

It has been suggested, for example, that concern for the task should predominate at an early stage of group development, and that when the group is functioning well interpersonally, and achieving its tasks, a more relaxed leadership style is best. Deciding on which style to adopt therefore means analysing:

- the task facing the group;
- the nature and qualities of the group members;

- the past history of the group and those who comprise it;
- the pressures and demands of the external environment.

Personal flexibility and an awareness of the overall situation produce a happy marriage, whose offspring is greater and greater success. The challenge is now to consider how this might be applied in meetings.

Reflective exercise 5.1 is designed to get you thinking about the leadership roles and behaviours you routinely adopt in groups, and how they might be developed to widen the range of leadership behaviours you find yourself employing.

Reflective exercise 5.1 Evaluating your leadership effectiveness

1. In what *situations* do you perceive yourself as having a leadership role?

____

____

____

2. What are the *behaviours* you use when you are leading effectively?

____

____

____

3. Identify three different people whom you consider to be particularly effective group leaders.

(i) ______________________________

(ii) ______________________________

(iii) ______________________________

4. What behaviours do these people employ to *empower* the groups which they lead?

____

____

____

Reflective exercise 5.1 *continued*

5. Identify *three specific changes* in your own behaviour which you can immediately implement, that will improve your leadership effectiveness.

(i) ____________________________________

(ii) ____________________________________

(iii) ____________________________________

How leaders manage their time

Above, we identified a growing problem of leadership 'churn'. Two earlier researchers coined the expression 'the reluctant managers',[23] to describe those who concluded that the job was too challenging, and opted out. Part of the problem is that, as the *Harvard Business Review* has noted: 'Executives are busy people. They have too much to do, and certainly too much to read.'[24] Others have identified a growing pre-occupation with achieving a work life balance, including among middle and senior managers.[25] This clearly poses major challenges in terms of how leaders allocate their time, and for many has transformed the job of leadership into a heroic burden they would rather not carry. Even those who do not give up still struggle with the challenge.

We have developed a time distribution axis, to illustrate the problem. This divides how we allocate our time along two axes – one indicating the importance of the tasks performed, on a continuum from 'very low in importance' to 'very high in importance'. The other axis has a continuum on which tasks can be ranged, from 'very low in urgency' to 'very high in urgency'. Most management activities can be allocated to some point on the resultant grid. For example, we might have tasks to do (such as polishing a PowerPoint presentation) that are both low in importance and low in urgency, but that we like doing. Such tasks tend to find their way to the top of our 'to do' lists: generally, pleasure has a higher priority than duty. Other 'routine' tasks (such as finishing off a bog-standard report in time for a monthly meeting) might be highly urgent, but are still low in importance. Our diaries are often invaded and colonised by such deadlines. A third category identified in Figure 5.1 is that of fire fighting – tasks which won't make much difference to the long-term future of an organisation, but are nevertheless

Figure 5.1 The time distribution axis

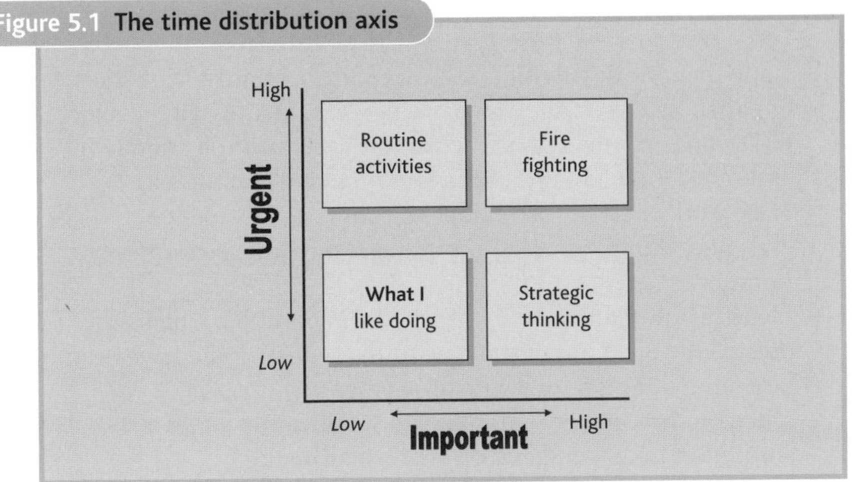

considered to be highly urgent, and incredibly important to the person concerned. Consider, for example, your response to the drama of a severed e-mail connection. E-mail addicts have been known to enter a state of paralysis, save for the sound of loud wailing, until their next fix is assured. Thus, the task of restoring the flow can feel both highly urgent and highly important: nothing else will be done until the problem is solved. Lastly, we arrive at the category of strategic thinking, where leadership mostly exercises itself. This involves asking the most critical questions of all about the future direction of an organisation – its core purpose, emergent markets, most likely competitive threats and pressing problems. This work is highly important – if no one performs such activities then somehow, someday the organisation will face a crisis it cannot surmount. Unfortunately, it is rarely urgent. If no one engages in strategic thinking today it is unlikely that anyone will notice, possibly up until disaster strikes the whole operation. However, leaders are under enormous daily pressure to do everything but engage in strategic thinking. Nevertheless, it is vital that those in leadership positions attempt to shift more of their energies into the fourth quadrant in the figure, in order to improve their effectiveness. The costs of a failure to do so will be high.

Reflective exercise 5.2 is designed to get you thinking about how you allocate your time on the time distribution axis and, most importantly, to do something about it.

Reflective exercise 5.2 Spending time on strategic thinking

- Copy the time distribution axis on Figure 5.1 onto a large sheet of paper. Take your diary for a recent week. Identify all the major tasks you performed (in particular, the meetings you attended) and transfer each to one of the four quadrants on the axis. Now, work out what percentage of your time was spent on each one – but particularly on strategic thinking. Be ruthlessly honest.
- Identify how many tasks to which you committed, which are outside the quadrant of strategic thinking, that could have been delegated – or dispensed with altogether.
- Agree on three major steps that will significantly increase the amount of time you spend on strategic thinking.
- Find at least three other colleagues, and get them to perform a similar analysis.

Leadership and strategic direction

It is easy to recognise that the job of leadership, often achieved in the context of meetings, is to develop and deliver 'a vision'. The idea has become commonplace, and hence devalued. Despite this, significant research into organisations that prosper and endure suggests that building a vision means leaders must guide the people they work with through a process designed to discover the following key elements:[26]

- *Core values* – the handful of guiding principles by which the organisation navigates. People want work that is meaningful, purposeful and has some social value.[27] Organisations that articulate a compelling set of core values to which people can subscribe, and which live up to them, have a strong competitive advantage in the marketplace.[28]
- *Core purpose* – the organisation's most fundamental reason for being. This is not what the organisation does at any particular moment (manufacturing widget Y): rather it is the sense of purpose that animates its strategic thinking and motivates people to haul themselves into work each day.

- *An envisioned future* – fundamentally, this is what has been dubbed 'Big, Hairy Audacious Goals' (BHAGs), that fire up the enthusiasm of the entire organisation. Collins and Porras cite the example of Sony in the 1950s, when Japanese products were a by-word for shoddiness rather than quality. Their BHAG became a vivid description of what the future would look like when the goal was achieved. In the first place, Sony's BHAG was to 'become the company most known for changing the world-wide poor-quality image of Japanese products'. This was made more vivid with the tag: 'Fifty years from now, our brand name will be as well known as any in the world … and will signify innovation and quality … "Made in Japan" will mean something fine, not something shoddy.'[29]

We recognise that leaders must address a myriad of other mundane issues on a daily basis. Yet those who fail to spend a significant amount of time on the issues discussed above are unlikely to possess a strong sense of direction, nor be capable of articulating a convincing strategy for achieving it. Leaders require both a target destination, and the ability to generate some underlying reason for others to join them on the journey. It is in this context that we consider the role of leaders in meetings.

The role of meetings

Research has shown that people are more likely to go along with a decision if they have been involved in its development.[30] Communication audits carried out by us have found that meetings often have a high personal value to people, and that there is a widespread desire in the workplace for more face-to-face contact with immediate and senior managers.[31] In short, it seems that people view meetings as an important means of participating in the decision-making process. Thus, meetings are both unavoidable and an important means of fulfilling fundamental human needs. The issue, therefore, is not one of getting along without them, but of how to manage them more effectively. Such management requires an understanding of when meetings should be called, the types of meetings appropriate for each occasion and the chairmanship skills which dismantle barriers to involvement while bringing people together.

When to call meetings People become frustrated when meetings are convened inappropriately – for example, when information could have been conveyed by phone or memo, when important players are not prepared, when all of the key people cannot attend, or when the meeting has been arranged purely as a matter of routine. We all grow exhausted and quarrelsome during a voyage from nothing to nowhere. It should never be the case that 'the Monday morning meeting' is held simply because it has always been held. By contrast, Box 5.2 lists some of the circumstances when meetings are generally deemed productive, and can usefully be called.

The general weight of the evidence is that most successful meetings are characterised by participant involvement, with the exception, as has been mentioned, of very large meetings convened simply for the transmission of information. Such involvement may be achieved through sub-groups formed to look at particular issues, in brainstorming sessions, or through straightforward debate. The role of the chair is indispensable, in facilitating participation, discussion and constructive disagreement. Crucial success factors include:[32]

- Goals are considered separately to maintain focus. The emphasis of the discussion is on agreeing *action* to achieve concrete goals.

Box 5.2 When to call meetings

- *There is real work to be done.* For example, important decisions must be made, or a work project needs to be reviewed.
- *There is a need for celebration.* Celebration in the workplace motivates and empowers. Meetings are a useful forum for public praise.
- *Good news needs to be shared with everyone.* When this is done at meetings managers acquire a reputation for openness, gain some of the credit for the good news they are spreading and create another occasion for celebration.
- *Uncertainty has to be dispelled.* When rumours are rife, silence adds to the impression that there is something to hide.
- *In the midst of a crisis.* When people are given information, even in the face of unsettling news such as an impending merger, they retain a much higher level of commitment than those kept in the dark.

- Participants feel utilised in a meaningful manner. Their contribution makes a difference. People are allowed to speak, contribute their ideas, disagree with the group leader and decide on objectives.
- Between meetings, real progress is made on important issues. Reviewing this generates an infectious feeling of achievement, which provides the rocket fuel for yet further success.
- Members feel that they have some personal responsibility for the success of the meeting. They are allowed to participate in the discussion, and a norm prevails that action outcomes will be declared for all participants.
- People learn something new and interesting. Ancient topics are not forced out of retirement, and compelled to jump over the same boring old hurdles – again. Action leads to success and new challenges.
- People enjoy themselves. Fun sparks creativity, comradeship and commitment.
- There is an atmosphere of commitment. The US banker, Walter Wriston, has defined commitment as *a dream with a deadline*.[33] Meetings should allow for the development of creative, innovative ideas – but then translate them into firm action plans, with time limits.

Blocks to effective meetings Unfortunately, not all meetings are successful. A number of barriers to effective meetings have been identified,[34] and include:

- *Domination by a single member.* Here, one person occupies centre stage and elbows everyone else into the wings. He or she attempts to keep the spotlight trained on his or her main object of veneration – themselves. Meanwhile, the real business of the meeting goes unrehearsed. Other participants become frustrated. Attempts to staunch the verbal flow are submerged under a mass of linguistic diarrhoea. Box 5.3 lists a number of typical behavioural problems of this kind, adapted from the work of Wheeten and Cameron,[35] and suggests various responses which might help to curtail them.
- *Critical norms.* This concerns the ratio of negative to positive comments made. Group solidarity disintegrates under a blitzkrieg of criticism, probably initiated by the leader. There is a relentless emphasis on difficulties and what has not been achieved, rather than what has. People fear that an ambush party lies in wait,

Box 5.3 Suggestions for interrupting destructive behaviours

Type	*Behaviour*	*Suggested response*
Hostile	'This is rubbish.' 'I'd expect a finance person to obstruct manufacturing in exactly that way.'	'Let's look at the evidence before reaching a decision.' 'How does everyone else feel?' 'I propose that we avoid labelling each other's ideas, and instead identify how they might or might not be helpful.'
Know it all	'As an expert in philosophy, perhaps I could be allowed to say …' 'No one knows more about Gizmos than me.'	'Everyone is here because they have something useful to say on this.' 'We need everyone's input to make the best decision.' 'What are the facts?'
Dominator	Speaks at length on everything and anything.	'Can you try to summarise your main point?'
	Brings in pet hobby horse, regardless of topic.	'Right, Jeff has now spoken twice and if I can summarise his main point as follows …'
Informal chatterer	Whispers to neighbours. Forms sub-groups	Stop talking, and create a silence. Ask everyone to pay attention to speaker. Point out that the rest of the group will miss out if information is not shared with everyone.
Disrupter	Comes in and out of meeting.	Establish ground rules such as no interruptions at an early stage.
	Receives faxes, messages and memos from secretary throughout meeting.	Agree that all should switch off bleeps or mobile phones.

Box 5.3 continued

	Arrives late, mutters apology and leaves early, possibly before crucial decision.	Establish finish time at the beginning, and get commitment from participants to stay.
Non-contributor	Sits silently, never speaks.	Address questions directly to person Bring up an area of special concern to them.

wherever they turn. They lose all faith in the possibility of finding a different and more constructive way of doing things. Eventually, they turn their anger on each other. The problem-solving abilities of the group are culled to the point of extinction.

- *Vested interests.* Here, the group has lost sight of its collective identity and responsibility to focus on organisational goals. Everyone is in the same vehicle, but they have each seized the wheel and are attempting to drive off in different directions. Individuals or sub-groups place a higher priority on their own needs, which may involve blocking constructive suggestions when they emerge from unapproved sources. Meetings become a war of attrition, with constant battles over strategy, tactics and the allocation of resources. Members leave bloodied and exhausted, rather than exhilarated by a feeling of accomplishment.
- *The dilemma of new members.* New members are generally expected to conform to the norms of the group, rather than express innovative new ideas of their own, particularly if such ideas challenge the conventional wisdom of the group. It is difficult to speak out, particularly when people feel that they are novices in the company of experts. However, groups often grow blasé and sometimes need corrective input from fresh sources.
- *Physical structure and space.* Nonverbal behaviour is a vital ingredient in effective management communication, including during meetings. Here, we can simply note that physical structure helps to determine whether the meeting invites participation and sustains free flowing dialogue between group members. Key needs include:
  - Comfortable seating arrangements.
  - Moderate heating.

- Circular tables, with no 'head of table' position – this is most facilitative and promotes equality of status.
- Physical proximity – this generates closeness, as sports teams huddling together before a match can testify.

The role of the chair

In one sense, presiding over meetings is straightforward. There are a variety of functions which the chair is routinely expected to fulfil. These include:

- ▸ Opening the meeting.
- ▸ Getting through the agenda, when one exists, in an acceptable time.
- ▸ Providing people with sufficient opportunity to express their views.
- ▸ Ensuring that decisions are taken, are agreed and that responsibility for their implementation is allocated.
- ▸ Conducting votes on resolutions, where necessary.
- ▸ Upholding the rules, constitution or 'standing orders' of the organisation.
- ▸ Regulating the discussion.

In practice, how these functions are executed is fraught with ambiguity. For example, discussions at meetings on important issues improve when the chair is neutral, at least initially. This prevents the emergence of groupthink and facilitates the expression of minority dissent (see Chapter 4). On the other hand, the chair is also in charge of the discussion, and has a responsibility to ensure that the goals of the organisation are realised. It would seem that successful chairpersons require the agility of a circus acrobat, as well as the verbal skills of a ringmaster and the thick hide of a performing elephant in order to succeed. In any event, a sense of balance is critical – as the following ancient testimony asserts:

> The best soldier is not soldierly
> The best fighter is not ferocious
> The best conqueror does not take part in war
> The best employer of men keeps himself below them
> This is called the virtue of not contending
> This is called the ability of using men
> The best chairman is not always conspicuously in control
>
> (Tao-Te-King scripture, China, sixth century BC)

In addition, meetings pass through a number of stages during which the role of the chair is particularly important. These are planning, helping group members get acquainted, managing the discussion and formulating decisions. Each of these is examined in-depth below:

Steps towards good planning Like many management activities the quality of the outcomes generated by meetings is correlated with the amount of effort invested in preparation beforehand. Planning for meetings is vital, especially if it is anticipated that major proposals will be met with opposition, that members are likely to turn up with serious grievances or that radically new proposals will be up for discussion. Box 5.4 lists a number of the most important steps which will help with this process. Consider, for example, the experience of one of the world's most creative companies – Intel. Anyone calling a meeting is expected to begin by assessing whether it is really necessary. They then e-mail ideas to selected people for comments, work out an

Box 5.4 Steps towards effective planning

- *Understanding the participants*
  - Who does each of the participants represent?
  - Why exactly have they been chosen for this group?
  - What is known about their goals and needs, their ego, their vested interests?
  - What special skills do they possess which may help the group achieve its goals?
  - What are their biases on the issues which this group will confront?
  - How do they feel about the group leader, and indeed about the organisation as a whole?
  - What are their strengths and weaknesses?
  - What is their track record in group work?
  - Are they what the advertising guru, David Ogilvy, referred to as 'extinct volcanoes', from which no further sign of life can be anticipated?
- *Assessing the history of the group*
  - How did everyone leave the last meeting? Was there a feeling of accomplishment, or one of learned helplessness?
  - What will people's expectations be of the next meeting?
  - What caused any problems, and what can be done about them?

Box 5.4 ***continued***

- *Setting realistic goals*
  - Have goals been set that are achievable?
  - Have goals been set that are within the 'terms of reference' of this group, or has the group gone off on an interesting but futile tangent?
- Have goals been identified that meet the group's collective needs, and the wider needs of the organisation?
- Will the goals adopted by the group command significant support within the organisation?
- What opposition to the group's goals can we anticipate?

agenda, and distribute it more widely for revisions. This results in a one-page document, setting out the meeting's purpose and goals, sub-topics and associated time frames, a list of attendees, and what each is expected to bring to the meeting. Clearly, this requires a considerable effort. But, as Michael Fors, the organisation's employee development manager, has accurately commented: '80 per cent of the hard work gets done before the meeting even begins.'[36]

Helping group members get acquainted As discussed above, problem-solving and long-term group cohesion is improved when steps are taken to improve relationships as well as maintaining a focus on the group's tasks. Thus, it is useful if:

- Before the first meeting, and if the members are relatively unknown to each other, the chair sends each member a biographical sketch of the other members, alongside some description of the group's origins, role and its intended outcomes.
- Again, just before the first meeting, the members should socialise, perhaps over coffee. We have worked with some public sector organisations where there is a policy that coffee is no longer provided at meetings, in order to save money. However, the evidence clearly shows that the informal dialogue which springs up around such social outlets improves the overall quality of group decision-making.[37] Chairpersons should expand opportunities for social interaction, not curtail them.
- At the first meeting, members should be introduced by the chair, or should briefly introduce themselves. Care needs to be taken to

prevent the proceedings becoming bogged down in exaggerated self-eulogies, or lengthy perorations in favour of pet projects. Among the advantages of the chair performing such introductions are that:

- A useful opportunity is created to publicly praise excellent performance
- This makes the recipient feel good
- The status of the manager delivering the praise goes up
- Control is asserted at the outset.
- During long meetings breaks should be provided, enabling members to resume the social conversations with which they began. This reinforces the human bond which underlies successful task performance.

Managing the discussion Early research identified 31 excellent chairpersons by observation, expert judge ratings, track record and the views of people they chaired.[38] This found that successful chairs made more proposals about managing the group discussion than other group members, expressed less support for various positions which emerged during debate, used a very high level of testing understanding and summarising, disagreed less frequently with members' ideas, were high in their use of information seeking and were relatively low in information giving. Overall, it appears that success occurs if the chair is aware of the value of neutrality early in group discussions, and encourages members of the group to ventilate their real opinions. A range of effective chairmanship skills have been identified, and these can be summarised as follows:[39]

- ▸ Begin the process before the meeting. For example, circulate important papers, and consult with key individuals. Prior activity improves the rate of discussion and enhances levels of satisfaction with the process. Box 5.4 has already listed a variety of tactics which help to achieve this.
- ▸ Begin your meeting on time.
- ▸ Clarify or refine what has been said when the discussion is underway. Use paraphrasing, summarising and probing questions as key skills. Show that you are paying attention to speakers.
- ▸ Ensure that all items on the agenda are discussed during the meeting for which they are scheduled. It is also generally good practice to ensure that the chair does not raise items for discussion under 'Any Other Business', although it is legitimate for others

to do so. Otherwise, it is possible to be seen as someone who manoeuvres controversial topics through, while allowing other participants insufficient time for preparation.

- Bring in non-participants and shut down those who attempt to dominate the discussion. A norm can be established that everyone who attends is expected to speak. Planned sub-groups help with this and enable people to feel that they have contributed to the eventual outcome. Time limits on contributions and presentations may also be necessary.
- Use 'key questions' to promote discussion. Ask open-ended questions rather than questions that can be answered with 'yes' or 'no'. Thus, say:

  'What are your opinions about the plan to increase production?'

  Do not say:

  'Do you agree with the plan to increase production this month?'

- Use rewarding behaviours and attentive listening to encourage greater participation.
- From time to time, shut up. The chair should not dominate the discussion or pursue pet hobbyhorses – others will quickly switch off.
- Repeat statements that seem significant. Make procedural suggestions for closing or opening topics. Never let the discussion drift aimlessly, without reaching a decision.
- Summarise and clarify regularly. Tell speakers what you think they mean – it might be right or wrong, but avoids post-meeting confusion. Use examples from your own experience to illuminate a topic.
- Ask group members for reaction to each other's points. When appropriate, involve group members in answering a question addressed to you.
- At the end of the meeting, summarise the points made, the decisions reached and indicate the way ahead. Focus on 'immediate next steps' and list action outcomes for all participants. This is a key chairing skill, and group members become aggrieved if the role is left to another participant in the meeting.
- End the meeting on time, or even shortly before your scheduled cut-off point. If you go over an agreed deadline your fellow participants will have already vacated the room mentally, thereby rendering continued discussion pointless.

- Stick to the agenda and a rough order for items. Develop, and keep, a long-range schedule.

Post meeting action The role of the chair does not end when the meeting closes. Follow up is critical, and determines whether your objectives are achieved, or felled by inaction.[40] There are five key tasks that still need to be completed. These are:[41]

- *Follow up quickly with minutes.* These should be pointed, short and action oriented. They remind people what they have agreed to do, and serve as a reminder that they will be held to account at the next meeting.
- *Meet the participants who felt unsatisfied with the results or feel they haven't been heard.* This extinguishes fires before they become raging infernos. It also gives you valuable feedback on what can be done better next time.
- *Send participants a memo on next steps.* This reinforces the message that something has been accomplished and maintains a bias towards action.
- *Provide any resources that you have promised.* When you announce that a play is about to commence it is a good idea to immediately show the actors and props on stage. This stops an audience from becoming restless. People grow anxious if they have been told that something will be provided or done, but nothing happens.
- *Act at once on decisions taken.* Immediate action by the chair is contagious. It radiates a determination to overcome obstacles. You will be judged more by what you do than what you say.

Encouraging learning Meetings are also often called in order to facilitate learning. This most obviously occurs during training sessions. It is also a feature of much decision-making, when it is imperative that people learn how to implement the decisions taken, to anticipate problems that may arise and to properly evaluate their consequences. Research suggests that most of us let two-thirds of our senses and emotions sit idle while we learn, and in consequence forget much of what we hear as soon as we hear it.[42] Lethargic meetings that fail to engage our senses are little more than a conspiracy to infect everyone with the virus of boredom. Many of us seize the opportunity to improve our doodling skills. Meetings should therefore appeal to the three dominant communication and learning styles – visual (learning through seeing), auditory (learning through hearing) and kinaesthetic (learning through physical activity in a hands-on way).[43] People should see, hear, speak, move around and touch. For example, if the meeting is discussing a new product then participants will engage more with the issue and carry more from the meeting if the product is there to be seen, if they hear its creator sing its praises, if they have the chance to comment themselves, and if it is passed around so that they touch it. Utilising the fully array of sensory inputs in this manner is also sometimes called stimulus variation.[44] In short, meetings should be designed to keep people awake, talkative, interested, tactile and mobile.

Managing conflict Chairpersons have a particular responsibility for managing conflict. Meetings are not always an oasis of calm reflection, amidst the turbulence of organisational life. We have alluded, above, to some behaviours that can engender conflict in a group. These dissipate its sense of purpose. Instead of uniting into a team, members form themselves into bitterly opposed factions. The effect is akin to that of a sports team who play against each other rather than the opposition. The skills we discuss in Chapter 11, relating to assertiveness and conflict management, are important here. In the context of meetings it has also been suggested that you have five main options, ranged in a continuum, that enable you to interrupt and defuse conflict-oriented behaviours. These are:[45]

- *Do nothing.* This might be appropriate if it is clear the problem or the disruptive behaviour is temporary, if it is inappropriate to correct offending behaviour in public, or if the problematic behaviour is of no great importance.
- *Engage in prevention.* This can include establishing ground rules (such as no interruptions when someone is speaking) at an early stage, re-stating the purpose of the meeting or having a one-to-one conversation with anyone you suspect might be likely to engage in disruptive behaviour.
- *Use of indirect methods.* These consist of asking questions, designed to tease out the broader purpose of the group and to illuminate the source of the conflict concerned. Examples include
  Why does this problem exist?
  What kind of data do you have to support that position?
  How will we know if we succeed in this effort?
  What is the purpose of this discussion?
- *Physical intervention.* Asking people to change seats, stand up when speaking or leave the meeting might be required, on very rare occasions.

- *Confronting and feedback*. Rather than focus on questions, this requires assertion, the reiteration of points made previously and a reminder of previously agreed ground rules. It might also require the giving of feedback on current behaviour combined with a request for a change (e.g. 'Thumping the table and shouting when you speak is not helpful at this point in the discussion. Please stop it, and sit down.')
- *Emergency halt*. This occurs when what is happening in the meeting is so disastrously counter-productive that it must be halted before it escalates any further. For example, if someone in the group has become the centre of an attack and is being scapegoated a tactic of 'full stop' might be appropriate. People attacked in public generally go on to cultivate an intense sense of grievance. Relationships may become permanently poisoned, and infect the wider organisation.

Formulating decisions and solving problems Teams exist to solve problems. A creative approach is indispensable. This suggests an action framework within which the team:

(A) Decides what it has to do.
(B) Discusses how this will be done, how the team will conduct itself and how it will evaluate its efforts.
(C) Starts doing it!

Our own observations of many groups suggest that the majority of them are inclined to start at point C. Teams tend to have such a thirst for 'action' that they engage in frantic (and usually chaotic) activity at the outset. This is often caused by external pressure, such as a boss screaming for instant results. After a further period of upheaval, teams then begin to discuss how they should be going about their task. Only after yet another period of fruitless but demanding activity do they begin to consider what it is they should be doing in the first place – a sequence, it will be noted, of C→B→A, rather than A→B→C. As one review of group decision-making has concluded:[46]

> One of the common dangers to group effectiveness is becoming 'solution minded' too soon; that is, generating solutions before a full understanding of the problem is available.

A central responsibility of the chair is to ensure that the group has sufficient awareness of its own behaviour to implement an A→B→C, approach to decision-making. This understanding can be promoted if the chair ensures that issues are discussed in the following fashion:

1. What is our goal on this particular issue?
2. How are we going to go about generating solutions?
3. What is the action that we have agreed to take on this issue?
4. When will it be done?
5. Who is going to be responsible?
6. What did we do well in this meeting?
7. What could have been done better?

There are, in addition, many techniques a meeting can use to enhance its creativity. Some of the key points are:

- *Consider how many people should be present.* For information-giving purposes a large number of people can be in attendance. But when the main objective is to decide on action, tackle a problem or invent a new process, between five and eight people are more likely to be effective.[47]
- *Imagine a schedule of the future scenario.*[48] Participants are asked to imagine either a brilliant future, or their organisation's eventual death, and to trace a sequence of events that caused such a happy or terminal outcome.
- *Conduct a vulnerability audit.* Members can be asked to imagine a proposal, product, service or idea failing, and then work out the top three reasons that might bring it crashing down.
- *Use armchair testing.* Possible scenarios are outlined, such as a doubling of customer traffic within an 18-month timeframe. Participants are then asked to evaluate whatever idea they are discussing against its capacity to withstand such a dramatic organisational change.
- *Make meetings fun*! Smythe has argued that the worst crime a CEO can commit is being boring, and jokingly suggested that the letters CEO should henceforth stand for 'Chief Entertainments Officer'.[49] As he points out, people (including most CEOs) are at their most creative when they are relaxed and having fun. Alternatively, meetings that become fear factories generate tension rather than solutions.

Overview

Leading groups is an exciting but often frustrating challenge for managers. However we feel about it, it is an unavoidable component of the management job. Success depends on a range of skills, attitudes and behaviours which encourage participation, generate excitement, inspire hope and result in concrete change. According to Warren Bennis,[50] one of the main researchers into leadership in management, this is facilitated if leaders possess the following characteristics:

- *A guiding vision.* There is a clear idea of where the leader wants to go. The vision is persisted with, in the face of temporary setbacks or obstacles.
- *Passion.* Enthusiasm energises, inspires and fortifies people in the face of adversity. Box 5.5 contains Henry Ford's views on this subject: one of the most powerful testimonials to enthusiasm ever produced.
- *Integrity.* The three main components of this are self-knowledge, candour and maturity. There is a breadth of learning, going beyond the basics of balance sheets, organisation design or marketing strategies. Broad perspectives are held and introduced into the group.
- *Curiosity and daring.* Life becomes a ceaseless quest for new knowledge and new ways of doing things. Innovative approaches to problem solving are introduced or encouraged in others. Stagnation is not an option.

Box 5.5 The power of enthusiasm

You can do anything if you have enthusiasm.

Enthusiasm is the yeast that makes your hopes rise to the stars.

Enthusiasm is the sparkle in your eyes, the swing in your gait, the grip of your hand, the irresistible surge of will and energy to execute your ideas.

Enthusiasts are fighters. They have fortitude. They have staying qualities.

Enthusiasm is at the bottom of all progress.

With it, there is accomplishment.

Without it, there are only alibis.

Henry Ford

Increasingly, it is also clear that what has been described as emotional intelligence on the part of leaders matters. As one of the foremost writers in this area, Daniel Goleman and two of his collaborators, have put it: 'The leader's moods and behaviours drive the moods and behaviours of everyone else. A cranky and ruthless boss creates a toxic organisation filled with negative underachievers who ignore opportunities; an inspirational, inclusive leader spawns acolytes for whom any challenge is surmountable.'[51] Encouragingly, their research suggests that leaders don't have to be superhuman, or on a permanent high – rather, that they will be emotionally effective to the extent that they are optimistic, sincere and realistic.

These qualities lift meetings, and group processes in general, out of the humdrum, giving them purpose and sparkle. Leadership should be fun, as well as productive. But there is a dark side. Leaders frequently set their followers up for failure rather than success, while desperately bemoaning the incompetence of their underperforming underlings. This happens when they form negative expectations of what people are capable, communicate these low expectations directly or indirectly, concentrate harsh feedback on instances of mistakes, fail to reward success, and refuse to share power with others.[52]

Effective leadership in groups inspires others to do more than they are ordinarily capable of. It creates a culture where what once seemed impossible now seems inevitable. The skills required to do this can be studied, learned and improved. Adopting the range of approaches discussed in this chapter will help to improve the quality of the meetings and the nature of the work groups in which we are all destined to continue spending so much of our time.

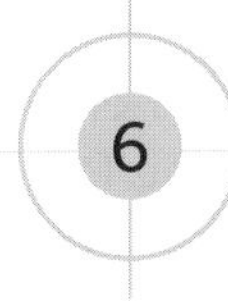

6 That silver-tongued devil ...: making presentations matter

Introduction

The sophistication of present IT and communications systems means that huge amounts of information can be offered up effortlessly and virtually instantaneously on a global scale. Despite the many different options that modern technology affords, the oral presentation with its roots in antiquity (see Chapter 1) has an enduring quality and appeal as a means of delivering ideas directly and with impact. Survey evidence attests to the growing recognition of the importance of graduates entering the job market with skills of this type. When 1500 corporate recruiters representing companies across the USA were sampled, over 50 per cent of those responding placed good oral and written communication top of their list of skills required of today's business applicants.[1] A further study[2] involved 500 managers in retail, wholesale, manufacturing, service industries, public administration, transport, and insurance and finance. Again, oral communication emerged as the type of competency felt to have the greatest currency for graduates entering the workforce. Furthermore, when the actual skills that constitute this competency were distilled down, those to do with making presentations ranked highly in both importance and frequency of use.

Being able to deliver up a stunning presentation has become increasingly important in the development of a successful managerial career. Getting appointed in the first place will probably depend upon it, since this element increasingly forms part of the selection process of many organisations.[3] Subsequent promotion has often been founded on the ability to catch the eye of those who matter. For junior staff, making an impressive delivery in the form of a briefing or a report is a prime opportunity to get noticed by those in senior positions. Research carried out at Stanford University found that the best predictor of success and upward mobility was a positive attitude towards, and effectiveness in, public speaking.[4]

Presenting also features prominently in the day-to-day schedule of executives in more elevated corporate positions. It can be a means of increasing staff morale, and directing and co-ordinating effort. When involving chairmen and board members, presenting typically forms part of the decision-making process whereby policy gets shaped. In the context of external relations new business approaches demand high-quality presentations in such areas as market research and advertising.[5] Contracts are not only secured in this way, but when the job is done, findings are commonly delivered through this medium. More generally, Sherman[6] made the point that executives are not only constantly selling themselves but also the company that they represent in the quality of the presentations that they deliver. These can vary in purpose, formality, exclusivity, and size and composition of the group, but are an unavoidable part of successful management. As put by Pullin,[7] speaking specifically to a professional engineering audience, 'It's a rare job these days that doesn't call for the ability to speak in public or make a presentation.'

Given what we have just said, it may come as something of a surprise to learn that the general standard of presentations tends not to be high. Aziz[8] made the point more stridently by claiming that, 'The average presentation made in British industry is woeful and we cannot go on this way'. He went on to describe the quest for the perfect performance in this respect as the 'final frontier when it comes to the executive's toolkit'. Part of the problem seems to be a deep-seated favouring of the written word over the spoken, coupled with the fact that still only a minority of managers receive formal training in how to address an audience for this purpose.[9] Grenville Janner identified both prejudices, together with their unfortunate consequences for the UK economy, in the following:

> The scientist must sometimes move out of the laboratory, the accountant from the office, the boffin from the drawing-board. They are forced into battle with overseas competitors who often have a far more practical, intelligent, informed and structured approach to presentation – formal or informal, public or private – than our old fashioned world of the public school and the ancient university where the learning of presentation skills bears the taint of the ill-bred.[10]

Many corporate personnel, therefore, fail to make the most of opportunities afforded. Due to a combination of causes including unmanaged anxiety, lack of planning and preparation, weak structure, and poor judgement of audience interests and need, what is often delivered up is nervy and discomforting, convoluted and confusing, or dull and tedious. Managers prefer business communication to be direct, easily understood and succinct[11] – although they are probably not unique in this respect! Oral briefings mostly fail because they are confusingly organised, contain too much technical jargon, are too long-winded, include too few examples, and are unattractively delivered.[12] But it need not be this way. Having the capacity to make a successful presentation is not a gift given at birth. It is a set of skills and techniques that can be learnt, practised and refined with further experience. While some are destined to be better than others, everyone can improve.

At this point let us pause for a moment's deliberation. Reflective exercise 6.1 is included to encourage you to think more deeply about presentations, assess your own current performance and reach decisions about your strengths and weaknesses.

Reflective exercise 6.1 Effective presentations: self-assessment exercise

This exercise is intended to help you identify some of the features of effective oral presentations, and the extent to which you make use of them. There are three stages.

Stage one

Think back to a presentation attended that readily comes to mind as having been particularly impressive. It is memorable perhaps because it was so useful, interesting, expertly delivered and so forth. Using the headings below, jot down a few comments that sum up what you experienced. Make a note of any other attributes that you feel made is successful, but that don't appear on the list below:

Presenter

Knowledgeable
Prepared
Credible

Presentation

Clear purpose
Gripping introduction
Relevant

Reflective exercise 6.1 *continued*

Structured
Integrated
Concise
Right pace
Good visual aids
Effective closure

Delivery

Engaging
Dynamic
Articulate
Suitable language
Appropriate style

Audience Reactions

Appreciation
Enthusiasm
Agreement

Stage two

Select the last presentation that you gave. Using the same headings, including those extra qualities that you may have added, analyse your presentation in a similar way.

Stage three

Compare your two analyses. On this basis, jot down three areas where you feel that you are generally strong and three that you suspect need improvement.

Strong	*Need improvement*
1.	1. ....
2.	2. ....
3.	3. ....

Types of presenters and presentations

Advice on public speaking has a well-established tradition in literature. The ability to capture the attention of an audience and deliver one's message in such a way that it is received with interest and changes beliefs, opinions and actions, is one that has been valued down the ages. But the prospect of having to face such an undertaking can be extremely daunting. According to research cited by DeVito[13] between 10 and 20 per cent of American college students suffer from severe and debilitating apprehension at the thought of communicating formally in public. A further 20 per cent are sufficiently affected in this way that their normal performance is interfered with. Furthermore, surveys of the adult population have found that fear of public speaking consistently ranks above that of heights, snakes and ill health. For some, having to make a presentation can be a fate worse than death. Little wonder the comment by Simons[14] that the natural reaction of most people is to want to flee.

Managers too are prone to the same emotional demands – at least to some extent. Survey results indicated that 76 per cent of business people responding, said that standing up in front of others and making presentations was the most formidable part of their job.[15] Furthermore, some 88 per cent of financial directors described this aspect of their professional role as the part with which they felt least confidence.[16] But not everyone is challenged in this way or demurs at the prospect of presenting. A few, at the other extreme, even relish the opportunity. Where do you place yourself on this continuum?

Mandel[17] identified four categories or types into which most of us fit when it comes to reacting to making presentations.

These are:

- *Avoiders* – those who will go to any lengths to avoid having to make a presentation, including going sick, or even finding another job. This option is becoming increasingly difficult, however, for those intent upon a career in management.
- *Resistors* – those who are extremely reluctant to carry out duties of this type and for whom doing so causes considerable unease.
- *Acceptors* – those who give presentations reluctantly, for the most part. They seldom volunteer to do so, but sometimes may enjoy it and feel good about what they have achieved.
- *Seekers* – those who actively seek out opportunities to appear before groups. They can turn initial anxieties into positive forms of energy and work at promoting competence in this area.

In addition to presenters, we can also recognise different types of presentation. Essentially there are four main kinds, although the first three mentioned are more relevant to the management context and will be concentrated upon here. These are:

- *Informative.* The primary purpose here is to deliver a body of material, including data together with interpretations and judgements, in such a way that it is well understood. The aim is to promote comprehension.
- *Persuasive.* In this case, attitudes, beliefs and opinions of the audience are targeted. The essential objective centres on either affirming and strengthening existing positions adopted by those present in relation to some issue, or trying to bring about a change in the opposite direction. In either case the intention has to do with influencing attitudes and held positions on issues. Much of what has already been covered in Chapter 3, Persuading, can be put to use here.
- *Energising.* Here the presentation serves to mobilise the group and spur them to action. It is a 'call to arms'. To be considered successful, the audience must leave with a firm commitment to do something – and then do it. Ideally it should be done with enthusiasm: the course of action should be warmly embraced. Needless to say, this can often be the most difficult of presentations to deliver. It runs on a heady cocktail of ingredients with generous measures of rhetoric and emotion. It is at its best when served hot with lots of charismatic appeal.
- *Entertaining.* Unlike the previous types that may have lively, enjoyable elements, the primary objective of this address is to entertain the audience.

We will now move on to consider the different components that go to make up the presentational process. In all cases, and simply put, there must be a presenter who presents to an audience in a particular setting. The presentation itself must have content and that content must be suitably delivered. Each of these five elements – presenter, content, delivery, audience and setting – deserves close attention. The remainder of the chapter will be structured by taking each in turn.

The presenter

Unless the presenter is perceived and received in an accommodating way, especially at the outset, it is highly unlikely that much attention will be paid to the message, let alone that the message will carry sufficient gravitas to have the impact intended. Here we can think of judgements made by the audience based upon:

- *How the presenter looks and sounds.* Initial impressions will be quickly formed around cues to do with dress, deportment and level of anxiety, for instance. These lead to estimations of expertise, confidence and sincerity.
- *What the presenter says and does.* Presenters, as part of the introduction, can enhance their credibility by mentioning, for example, prestigious companies that have called upon their expertise, professional associations of which they are members, qualifications obtained, books/research that they have carried out on the subject and so on. As with all attempts at impression management, they must be subtle if they are to work. Read as moves to ingratiate, they will invariably backfire and defeat the purpose. Without doubt, however, it is in how the main body of the talk is handled that the most enduring impressions are created.
- *What the audience already knows or is told about the presenter.* The situation where the presenter's name and reputation are already known to the audience and held in high esteem, is a happy starting point to any delivery. Short of that, it is usually acceptable to make the person who will introduce you to the group, familiar with some of your achievements. It is always more compelling to have someone else trumpet your successes.

Information gleaned in these ways will form the basis of impressions of personal qualities, dispositions and attributions such as outlined in Box 6.1. Many of these have to do with the fundamentally important issue of accepting the credibility of the presenter.

Box 6.1 What it takes to be a successful presenter

The more presenters come across in the following way, the more receptive the audience is likely to be to both them and their message:

Poised. The audience should be assured that the presenter is in control of self and the situation. If not, members become uneasy and lose faith.

Box 6.1 *continued*

Competent. The audience must be convinced that the speaker has some acceptable level of expertise in relation to the topic.

Trustworthy. Those present must be able to believe that the speaker is fair, reliable, honest, honourable, trustworthy and mindful of their interests rather than merely seeking self-gain. Gaining trust is something that frequently takes time to develop with a group.

Committed. The presenter must show commitment to the message delivered and, where applicable, to the course of action advocated. Being prepared to 'go the extra mile' with the group is one way of displaying commitment.

Dynamic. Dynamism carries its own message through energy, enthusiasm and forcefulness. It is displayed in words and action. Nonverbally it requires a more animated style in body movement and voice amplitude and variation. Dynamism is one of the attributes of that more ephemeral quality, charisma. It is particularly important in presentations designed to persuade and energize.

Sincere. Dynamism without sincerity is worthless. A trickster with a lively patter is simply seen as a more polished rogue. The successful presenter must come across as genuine, believing totally in the message. As noted in Chapter 2, incongruities between verbal and nonverbal messages can signal deception.

Respectful. The speaker must show respect for the audience, its views, opinions and knowledge base. Inexperienced presenters, often in an attempt to conceal their own feelings of insecurity and vulnerability, sometimes sound superior, even arrogant.

Attractive. Based upon what we know about the effects of interpersonal attraction, those presenters who have more of it, command for the most part greater attention and are more likely to enjoy a receptive hearing. But there are limits. If physical attractiveness exceeds expectations for that sort of occasion, it can have a 'boomerang' effect. The 'blond bimbo' stereotype can be triggered.

Apart from sheer physical attraction, the more similar the audience thinks the presenter is to its values, attitudes and outlook (but of course not expertise in the area of the presentation), the more attractive that person will be perceived to be (see Chapter 3).

Managing anxiety

One of the qualities of an effective presenter, mentioned in Box 6.1, is poise. Handling dysfunctional anxiety, as we have already seen, presents the greatest difficulty for many. But the point needs to be made that experiencing *some* level of stress when about to present is neither abnormal nor dysfunctional and familiar to even the most experienced. It is often even desirable. Without it we probably would not be sufficiently on our toes to give of our best. Keeping stress positive and within constructive boundaries is what matters.

Extreme negativity at the prospect of having to speak in public has a number of causes with associated implications for how to go about overcoming it. The three most important steps that can be taken are:

- *Find out how to present effectively and become more skilled at it.* Often fear is a consequence of knowing or suspecting that you have not the resources to put on a competent performance. There are number of useful 'how to do it books', together with video material, on the market. Better still, go on a course – then practise and reflect on your performance. If there are no courses locally, online alternatives are available.
- *Learn to relax.* There is no obvious reason why so many should be afraid in this way. Anxiety is something that is learnt. This may be from:
  - being 'spooked' by listening to others or perhaps, as children, sensing their unease about speaking in public;
  - watching others' faltering attempts;
  - giving a presentation that went horribly wrong and being humiliated in this way, so that a lot of trepidation and little self-confidence has formed around this activity.

But learning to relax is easier said than done. Box 6.2 offers some guidelines.

Box 6.2 Twelve steps to relaxed presentations

Mind and body share a complex relationship. Negative thoughts that we may scarcely even be aware of can produce a seemingly inexplicable visceral reaction. By the same token, excessive muscular tension as we go about our everyday work can cause us to *feel* 'up tight'. When this becomes habitual, we usually fail to even

Box 6.2 ***continued***

notice the tension in our body – just the psychological manifestation. One approach to overcoming this situation, therefore, operates along the lines of learning to relax bodily so that mental relaxation will follow. Better still, if we can replace accompanying negative with positive thoughts, the outcome is likely to be even more successful and enduring.

1. Find a quiet, dimly lit, comfortable room where you will not be disturbed for 15–20 minutes.
2. Take off your shoes and lie on your back with your body straight, arms by your sides. Make yourself comfortable. You may want to place a small pillow or folded towel under your head. Turn your palms upwards and let your feet flop outwards.
3. Breathe steadily and evenly. Now, beginning with your feet and calf muscles, take a deep breath and hold it as you tense those muscle groups. It is important that the rest of your body remains as relaxed as possible. Hold it for a count of four, breathe out and relax the muscles. Repeat three times, each time feeling more and more tension ease away with your out breath. (If you find this difficult, you may want to start with the right leg, then the left.)
4. Do the same for your thigh muscles again keeping the rest of your body relaxed. Bring your attention to those parts of your body that you tense and relax – appreciate the difference.
5. Move on to the buttocks and repeat, then the stomach muscles, hands and forearms, biceps, shoulders and chest, neck and face.
6. Now tense the whole body with an in breath and relax with an out breath, as before. Repeat several times. Your whole body should now feel quite relaxed. Check for any part where tension may still lurk.
7. Continue to lie quietly for a few minutes simply being aware of your slow, even breathing (without trying to control it) and your new state of relaxation. You should entertain no other intrusive thoughts. After sufficient repetitions of steps 1–7 over a number of sessions, to enable you to quickly establish a state of bodily relaxation, move on to step 8. You are now ready to introduce some thoughts about that troublesome presentation while in your new-found state of relaxation.

Box 6.2 *continued*

8. Draw up a list of situations in which you find yourself when conducting the presentation. Arrange them in order from the least to the most anxiety provoking (e.g. collecting material for the presentation may be the easiest, getting dressed the morning of the presentation more difficult, waiting to get to your feet in the Boardroom the most anxiety provoking).
9. Begin with the easiest. Work through steps 1–7 to established a relaxed state. While relaxed, begin to imagine yourself in that situation, doing that task. Stop if it becomes too anxious and return to steps 1–7. Once you can begin to visualise yourself complete that task relatively free from anxiety, tell yourself that you can do it. This begins the process of replacing negative with more positive 'self-talk'.
10. Once you have mastered the least difficult task, move on to the next on your graded list and repeat the process focusing upon it. Then deal with the next, and so forth. Always return to an earlier task if anxiety becomes intrusive.
11. Arrange to actually give a presentation to a small group of people with whom your feel comfortable and who can be trusted not to give you a hard time, selecting a topic on which you feel very confident.
12. Reward yourself for your achievement.

- *Don't talk yourself down.* Often those who are cruelly tormented at the thought of having to talk in public, engage in an internal chatter that runs along the lines of, 'I'll never be able to do this. I'll make a complete fool of myself. They will see right through me, and think that I'm stupid. I'll dry up in the middle of it. My mind will go blank. I'll never be able to face them again', and so on. In other words these people convincingly 'talk' themselves into believing that they are going to do poorly, and then get extremely agitated at the prospect. This serves to make them even more certain that failure is inevitable: and in truth under these circumstances it probably is. Negative ruminations must be replaced with constructive alternatives.[18] Concentrate upon your strengths and factors that can be exploited to your advantage. Substitute negative self-talk with reassuring reminders such as:

'I know this report back to front'
'I am well prepared and know exactly what I intend to do'
'The presentation will run smoothly, just as I have planned it'
'The audience will be hugely impressed.'

Remember that the objective is to manage your nerves, not eliminate them entirely, so be realistic in your expectations. As explained by Cristina Stuart,[19] MD of Speak First, a London-based company training in this area, 'Your nerves won't disappear, but an experienced speaker knows what it feels like and accepts it as part of it all.'

The audience

Success in presenting is measured not on a scale of how much is given, but rather how much is received. Each talk must be tailored, therefore, to the idiosyncrasies of the particular group to which it is delivered. Unfortunately, ineffective speakers often spend more time thinking about themselves than about their listeners.[20] This is entirely the wrong orientation. Trevor Zigelstein,[21] Regional Manger with Robert Half, a worldwide staffing services firm for accounting and financial services professionals, strongly advocated finding out about the audience as the first step in the preparation process. Here a useful starting point is with those who arranged the event. They might have a list of names of participants with some details on each. Information to gather includes:[22]

- Who will attend – age, sex, occupation and position in the company?
- How many?
- Why are they attending/what will they expect to get out of it?
- What do they already know?
- What is their position in relation to the issue/how will they probably react?

Gleaning further details during the course of the presentation is also a wise step. As far as predisposition in respect of the topic is concerned, audiences seem to fall into one of five types as outlined in Box 6.3. But ultimately they are made up of individuals and, at that level, members are likely to react differently within the group. For a start, it is usually unrealistic to expect all of those present to be constantly and totally

Box 6.3 Audience predisposition

1. *Indifferent.* This audience is possibly present under duress. They do not appreciate that they have a need, let alone a want, that can be met by anything that you have to say in this situation. Here the introductory part of your presentation has to succeed in quickly capturing attention and increasing motivation. This type of audience presents a particular challenge when the intention is to deliver an *energising* presentation.
2. *Uninformed.* The audience may know little about what you intend to cover and have developed no particular attitude towards it. This makes a persuasive presentation easier. It requires careful planning though in the case of the *informative* presentation.
3. *Undecided.* Unlike the previous, this group has information at its disposal but has not reached a position on the issue at hand.
4. *Antagonistic.* In this case, the audience is opposed to the line being taken in the persuasive presentation. This poses fairly obvious challenges to the presenter intent on dragging the group through 180 degrees in their thinking. It can also mean that the presenter may have less credibility in the eyes of those present and will possibly be less well liked. Under these circumstances, it is important that the presenter not be too ambitious in the objectives set. Maybe a lessening of audience entrenchment is the most that can be realistically hoped for at this stage.
5. *Supportive.* This is the presenter's dream: a group that already holds a position on the issue, in keeping with that of the presenter. There is considerable potential here for an energising presentation to succeed in mobilising the gathering into effective action. There is also considerable scope for an approach relying heavily on emotion, to be well received.

given over to what is being said. The fact that some show signs of being switched off can unnerve the inexperienced presenter. Again other participants adopt a confrontational stance, not because they dislike the speaker, or even that they disagree strongly with the content of the presentation, but to show perhaps that they are discerning. Their agenda may be one of impressing others rather than torpedoing your flagship performance, *per se*.

Also at the level of the individual and how s/he is predisposed to receive persuasive appeals and make decisions accordingly, Williams and Miller[23] tease out five categories into which they believe executives can be placed. They can be either Charismatics, Thinkers, Sceptics, Followers or Controllers. These types are fleshed out in Box 6.4.

Box 6.4 Types of audience: decision-making categories

According to Williams and Miller[24] executives fall into one of the following types when receiving persuasive presentations and making subsequent decisions.

Charismatics. Their natural inclination is to react to new ideas or proposals with exuberance and enthusiasm but eventually make a more considered decision based on the rounded picture. They tend to: move from broad considerations to analyse fine detail; be impressed by facts and straightforward argument; have short attention spans; place great emphasis on bottom-line figures.

Thinkers. They need to have as much detail as possible and to be able to appreciate the situation from different vantage points before arriving at an outcome. They are logical, rational and intellectual; swayed by lines of argument backed up by strong evidence; dislike risk; and take decisions slowly.

Sceptics. These are often dominant characters who instinctively challenge information put to them. They are likely to be confrontational; question the accuracy and validity of data and the justifiability of recommendations; and be open to influence once they accept the credibility of the presenter.

Followers. They are inclined to fall back on established practices for making decisions that have worked for them in the past, or for those whom they respect. They tend to shun risk; be responsible; be impressed by methods adopted by 'big players' and been shown to work; and be swayed by recommendations and testimonials from respected sources.

Controllers. These are often loners who are not particularly good at taking up the position of others or seeing the situation from their perspective. They tend to: take decisions on their own; make snap judgements; require good data that they don't always put to best use; agree on certain courses of action when they feel that *they* have reached that decision rather than been talked into it.

Content of the presentation

Baker[25] reminds us that all effective presentations demand two types of expertise on the part of presenters: content and delivery. They must know *what* they are talking about and *how* to do so to maximise the message. Being 'in command of your brief', is a core prerequisite. If you have only limited knowledge of the material then why should you be the person tasked with enlightening others? Later on we will concentrate on the delivery, but for the moment we are concerned with steps such as preparing the material to form the substance of the presentation, structuring it in an organised way best suited to increasing coherence and adding impact, and deciding upon visual aids to utilise.

Preparing content

As far as Davies[26] is concerned, 'Every good presentation is a well-prepared presentation.' The reason why presentations fail is largely due to inadequacies in this respect. Nor should it be thought that this vital stage can be skipped because the talk will be brief. In fact, having a short space of time within which to explain complex ideas, or make a compelling case, puts an added premium upon careful preparation. Winston Churchill is reputed to have said that he would spend ten minutes making ready a two-hour speech, but two hours if the speech was only ten minutes.

The preparation stage involves the following:

Identify the aim and clarify the objectives Begin by establishing firmly why the presentation is being made and what precisely it is intended to achieve. A useful way to think of objectives is to specify quite sharply changes that the presentation should bring about in the audience. These changes can be either in their knowledge, feelings/beliefs/attitudes or behaviour, and it is important that these be teased out and clearly sighted or it is highly unlikely that success will be achieved. While a single presentation may have more than one type of objective, each type points, quite naturally, to a contribution that should be primarily informative, persuasive or energising.

As mentioned, knowing your audience plays a pivotal part in preparation, as does establishing the length of time available for the address, and finding out where it will take place. The latter will be returned to later in the chapter. As far as the length of the presentation is concerned, if this is left entirely to the speaker to decide, something in the order of 20–25 minutes should be aimed for. Given that attention tends to wane after about 15–20 minutes, it will be difficult to keep the group engaged if this sort of time frame is excessively over-stepped.

Research the issue Once the purpose has been established, the next task is to decide what the audience needs to be made aware of in order for those objectives to be met. The point is worth repeating that, above all else, the presenter must be on top of the material. Audiences can be, and generally are, quite forgiving, but not if vast holes in that person's knowledge base quickly develop. This does not mean, of course, that *everything* must be known – few people do, about any topic – but the speaker's expertise in the area should be conspicuous. If not, the question will be asked, 'why are we expected to listen to this person'?

Researching the issue does not mean just collecting evidence to support the case being advocated. It must also cover alternative perspectives and possible counter-arguments, together with refutations. Not all, though, that has been found out must be included in the talk. The aphorism that 'the mind can only comprehend what the backside can tolerate', should not be dismissed lightly.

Select the method of delivery It is one thing to be familiar with the content, another to be able to deliver that material with best effect. How formal should the presentation be? Should it be all talk, and if so should you, as presenter, be the one doing all of it? Does the topic really require, on the other hand, a process to be physically demonstrated? Should you have visual aids to complement the talk? If so, which type? Should you try to get the audience actively involved? These are some of the decisions that need to be taken as part of planning. The actual process of delivery will be covered later.

Prepare visual aids Most presentations benefit from aids in one form or other to visually support what is said. These can range from physical objects and models, to pictures, tables, charts, graphs and diagrams shown either via video/data/overhead projector, film, computer, slides, flip-chart or white/blackboards. People take in information using different sensory channels. Some favour looking, rather than listening, and are particularly likely to appreciate the benefits of a multimedia approach.[27] Visual representations can, therefore, support the spoken word and, by introducing greater variety, make for a more attractive experience for the group. Speakers who use visual aids are perceived more favourably by their audiences, take less time to present concepts, and produce greater retention of what is learned.[28] Additional benefits are categorised by Pathak[29] as follows:

- Gaining and directing attention to key points.
- Providing a veridical representation of things – hence the expression, 'a picture is worth a thousand words'.
- Helping to organise material provided in text by contributing a visual framework displaying inter-relationships, etc.
- Offering an interpretation by illustrating the meaning of dense text.
- Graphic forms compensating for limited reading skills.

Computer software packages have now become a popular medium for delivering an attractive message with impact. The market leader is undoubtedly Microsoft PowerPoint, although alternatives such as Harvard Graphics, Corel and Astound are also available. Downing and Garmon offer some useful technical advice here.[30] Perhaps the golden rule when making out such software-based presentations is to avoid the 'all-singing-all-dancing' trap. In the hands of the over-zealous, the huge range of options available for varying font type and size, colour and design, as well as animation features, can quickly lead to a visual spectacular in which the core message gets lost amid the special effects and the presenter ends up sidelined. Such misuses can be avoided by following the guidelines for creating and using visual aids, to be found in several sources,[31–34] and synthesised in Box 6.5.

Box 6.5 Ten tips for creating and using visual aids

When making out and using slides or transparencies, including computer-generated presentations, remember the following:

Don't:

- have too many;
- obstruct the view of sections of the audience;
- keep the appliance on when not featured;
- clutter each slide/transparency with too much information. The 6 × 6 rule stipulates no more than 6 points each with a maximum of 6 words per line;
- use a small font size – normal-size lettering is useless. It usually takes 26/28 point with Times New Roman, for example, to avoid the audience having to peer;

Box 6.5 *continued*

- include colour in a random, unco-ordinated way;
- have 'wallpaper' designs/colours that are incompatible with the core message or type of audience or that camouflage superimposed text;
- use all the various ways of animation – having a line of text somersault unto the slide from above, this time, only to starburst from the centre on the next occasion, can be quite off-putting;
- rely solely upon text – visual aids taking more graphic forms can be even more effective;
- let the technology take over – remember these are just *aids*. They are merely a means to an end.

Decide how to handle questions Quite often inexperienced presenters look forward least to this element of the talk. The feeling is that at this juncture they are less in control and may be 'caught out' by an unanticipated query. But a question–answer session holds much potential for getting the audience actively involved, obtaining feedback, clearing up misunderstandings, consolidating learning, under-scoring the position advocated and securing a commitment to change.

The options here are to make it clear at the outset that all questions should be kept to the end or, alternatively, deal with them as and when they arise during the course of the delivery. Although the former reflects a more formal style, it does make it easier to control the progress of the presentation so that everything gets covered in the allotted time. The other possibility is simply to field question as they arise, on the way through. Incidentally, when a sensible answer does not come to mind it is invariably better to admit it and suggest getting back to the member later with a response, rather than try bluff or waffle. Remember, the speaker won't be expected to know *everything*. If you do promise to provide supplementary detail at some later date, though, you should do so.

Organising content and structuring the presentation

A simple, but useful, structuring heuristic is to think of the presentation happening in three phases. The first is the introduction; the second, the main body; the third, the conclusion.

Box 6.6 Functions of the introduction to the presentation

Introductions can serve to:

1. Make yourself known to the group and begin the process of building rapport.
2. Stimulate interest and gain attention.
3. Arouse motivation.
4. Create a suitable mood/climate for the meeting.
5. Outline clearly what the presentation is about.
6. Map the structure and progression of your talk.
7. Invite the audience to play a particular role, by suggesting activities that may be included for them.
6. Establish a common base with the group in terms of shared knowledge as a point for departure.
7. Project yourself and take control.

Introduction This first phase should not be overlooked or treated in a perfunctory way. Remember the importance of creating favourable first impressions. Rob Sherman[35] recommends 'starting with a bang', describing the first 30 seconds as 'make or break time'. You do not want this to be faltering or indecisive. If you fail to grab members' attention at this point and convince them that you, and what you have to say, are worth listening to, you may be in for an uphill struggle. The introduction serves a number of purposes, as outlined in Box 6.6.

Useful opening gambits which are effective 'attention-grabbers', depending upon circumstances, include:

- asking a challenging question
- providing a fascinating fact of particular relevance for the group
- using humour – but it should be relevant to the talk
- relaying a significant event or happening
- recounting a riveting story or dramatic event
- making a startling prediction
- reciting a pithy quotation from a respected source
- stressing the importance of the material for members.

In addition to grabbing attention and establishing relevance at the outset, the introduction should also serve to set the scene for what is to follow and provide a clear framework that can be used to organise the material.

The main body An adequate researching of the issue, as part of the preparation of the presentation, should reveal key points that need to be recognised, understood and accepted if the objectives are to be reached. These key points will be located amid other supporting information and evidence. It is crucial that they be identified as such. Having done so, the next concern is with how best to sequence them in the context of the delivery, to provide a cohesive, persuasive and well-formed address. The preferred organising structure depends both upon the nature of the material and the purpose to which it is put. Some alternatives are listed in Box 6.7.

Box 6.7 Alternative strategies for organising content

1. *Topical arrangement.* Here the issue is analysed into related topics and sub-topics to be presented – the key elements. These though have no particular relationship to one another apart from shared relevance. The order in which they are covered is typically shaped by going from (i) the known to the unknown and (ii) the simple to the complex.
2. *Chronological sequence.* Here the key elements of the material are ordered in relation to a timeline (e.g. describing how the company evolved to its present state or outlining the steps involved in a manufacturing process).
3. *Logical sequence.* There are two alternatives here. The deductive sequence moves from general principles to what needs to be done in certain specific cases of relevance to the group. The converse, inductive sequence begins with specific cases and from them moves to the derivation of broad principles that should be accepted and applied.
3. *Causal pattern.* Here the material is ordered in terms of a sequence of cause–effects relationships that explains events for the audience, and why they came about. It can be extended into the next possibility.
4. *Problem–solution.* This option structures the presentation into two sections. The first sketches the nature of the problem. The second maps the solution.

Box 6.7 *continued*

5. *The motivated sequence.* This is a more elaborate alternative than the previous. Like it, it is particularly suited when, as the name suggests, the intention is to change attitudes, beliefs or practices. It follows the sequence of gaining attention, establishing need, outlining how that need can be satisfied, helping the audience to visualise the satisfied need and finally stipulating what has to be done to accomplish that state.

The conclusion Audiences tend to remember more of what was said at the beginnings and endings of talks, than the bits in the middle.[36] The conclusion, therefore, offers a valuable opportunity to contribute something that will be taken away, retained and used to shape thinking or action. Quite often 'the sleeper effect' works (see Chapter 3 for further information): it is only some time later after mulling over what was said that a member decides to accept it. In any case, it is worthwhile thinking about how to end on a strong note. If there is a question-and-answer sequence after the main part of the delivery, it is seldom a good idea to simply finish on the last response. More impact is delivered by bringing proceedings to an end with a pithy summary comment.

Furthermore, the presentation should not come to an abrupt and unexpected finish. Rather it should be flagged, so the audience realises what is happening. Speakers will often use comments like, 'And now before I finish ...', 'Moving on to the last point ... etc.' to play the audience in to the end move. The following tactics should form part of this stage:

- review and summarise the key points;
- pull together any loose threads;
- reaffirm the conclusion reached and its importance (it can, sometimes, be highly effective to draw the 'inescapable' conclusion *from* the audience);
- elicit commitment to the advocated course of action (if the intention is to energise the group);
- get feedback;
- suggest ways in which the issues dealt with could be extended;
- clarify how the presentation will be followed up (if appropriate);
- disengage by thanking the group for their attention and co-operation.

Delivery of the presentation

In this section some thought will be given to styles of delivery and the techniques that can be used to make the presentation more attractive, comprehensible and impactful.

Styles of delivery

Basically there are four main types of delivery to choose from.[37] They are:

1. *Impromptu.* Here the address is given without any prior planning. This is best avoided if possible, especially for the inexperienced and those lacking confidence. Having said that, an effective style is often one that *seems* impromptu, in the sense of being relaxed and conversational – the well rehearsed *ad lib.*
2. *Extemporaneous.* This requires the presenter to flesh out the presentation, as it progresses, on the skeleton of key points and headings available in the form of notes or cue cards.
3. *Memorised.* In this case, a set script is memorised and regurgitated. While it is largely unfeasible for all but the shortest of presentations, there can be advantage in memorising your introductory statement to get you 'off the mark', as well as particularly pertinent points throughout that need to be delivered verbatim for reasons of accuracy or impact.
4. *Read.* This involves reading from a prepared script. Unless specifically trained to maximise the use of voice in this way, it quickly degenerates into tedium. It is best avoided despite the fact that it offers the greatest degree of control over the proceedings. In the case of highly technical presentations where accuracy is at a premium, the main findings can be covered using visuals, and if necessary the rest provided in the form of a handout.

Techniques of effective delivery

It is sometimes mistakenly thought that good speakers are born. The corollary is that if one has not been predestined in this way at birth, there is little that can be done to retrieve the situation. While no doubt there are people especially gifted in this direction, we can all improve. There are quite simple pieces of advice that can vastly enhance the quality of an address.

Appropriate language and avoidance of jargon If the audience cannot understand most of what is being talked about they will become detached, then bored and finally resentful. Jargon *per se* is not a problem. All professions have their stock in trade and this communication register eases information transfer amongst the discerning few. The problems arise when these professionals overlook the fact that the rest of humankind does not share with them this form of talk. Blocks to communication occur when what linguists call *code switching* takes place and jargon forms part of the dialogue with those not privy to this lexicon. The problem is further compounded by the fact that the same words sometimes appear in the vocabularies of both but with different meanings. Tiersma[38] gave examples of everyday words such as 'burglary' and 'assault' that have somewhat different and much more precise legal interpretations as well as common meanings. Under these circumstances jargon can serve to not only confuse, but to mystify and alienate.

Suitable pace of delivery Inexperienced presenters have a habit of speaking too quickly. This 'rush response' can be a nervous reaction. The feeling is that the sooner it is all over with the better. On the other hand, having the audience mark time while you catch up is a recipe for boredom. The pace to aim for is that with which the participants seem comfortable. As a rough guide, it has been suggested that listening tends to become difficult when the rate of speech exceeds 300 words per minute or drops much below 125 words per minute.[39] Where speed of delivery may be a particular concern, think about placing an accomplice in the audience primed to signal when you got too slowly or quickly.

Visual aids These are an immensely powerful tool for helping get the message across in an illuminating and attractive manner.[40] Established devices such as video, slides and overhead projections are now complemented by the enormous versatility of computer graphics packages. It must never be forgotten, though, that even the best of these are only aids to assist the speaker.

Sub-summaries, signposts and links It can be helpful, with complex material and convoluted arguments, to pause at transitional points in the flow of ideas to briefly summarise the material covered.[41] Explaining how this 'chunk' of information links with what comes next helps to signpost the path through the presentation and increases its coherence. Like all helpful signposts along the way, it shows where one is, the place that has just been visited and the next destination.

Additionally, most talks or explanations cover a series of sub-topics each designed to contribute to an audience's overall knowledge of a subject. Clarity of comprehension is improved if the speaker links these sub-topics into a meaningful whole. In addition, however, speakers should try to link their explanation to the experiences, previously acquired knowledge and observations of the audience. This is particularly pertinent when the primary purpose of the presentation is to inform.

Emphasis of key points Any given body of information contains points that can be graded in importance, as they apply to the audience. Participants cannot always be expected to instinctively appreciate the relevance of a piece of detail. If they could they would not need to be at the talk. It is therefore a requirement of the speaker to emphasise those key aspects that really must be grasped.[42] This can be done verbally (e.g. 'It is vital that you recognize....', listing main points, repeating core elements), nonverbally (e.g. gestures, changes in posture and position) and vocally (e.g. altering volume, speed of delivery, tone of voice).

Verbal fluency Effective public speakers do not have to be word perfect. Nevertheless, lots of 'umms', 'ahhhhs' and other fillers such as 'you know', 'sort of thing', can be highly distracting. Chaney and Green[43] referred to them collectively as 'speech tics'. Unfinished sentences, false starts and speech dysfluencies also erode personal credibility and switch off the group.

Precision As a general rule, speakers should strive to be precise in what they have to say rather than appearing vague and indefinite in the detail offered.[44] The latter style is, at best, unhelpful in enabling sensible decisions to be taken by participants. At worst, the speaker is seen as putting up a smokescreen to hide a lack of real knowledge on the topic.

Dynamic Impressive public speakers perform dynamically. Their irrepressible enthusiasm and compelling commitment make them powerful agents of influence. Nick Morgan[45] talks about the *kinaesthetic speaker* who is able to metaphorically reach out and touch the audience. Contact is made by removing barriers between speaker and audience, closing the distance periodically with members to heighten intimacy, and aligning gestures with content to reinforce the message. Contrast this with the most boring speaker that you have ever had the misfortune to be forced to listen to. Noticeable differences in punchy rhetoric, vocal variation and nonverbal animation will become quickly apparent. Being personally fired by the issue has to be the starting point here. If you are not enthused, how can you expect to be sufficiently enlivened to enthuse others? And if you cannot, how can you expect to persuade or energise?

Stimulus variation Try to introduce variety into your address. Intersperse talk with graphs, slides or pieces of video that the audience can look at, as a break from listening. If appropriate, encourage some discussion as an alternative to one-way communication. Asking the audience to work on a brief exercise, is a further way of introducing variety and increasing their active participation.

Appropriate examples Effective examples act as a bridge between what the listener knows and is familiar with and the new material being introduced by the speaker.[46] As such, examples must have a firm foundation on the audience's side if the breech in knowledge is to be spanned. Too often these bridges collapse through being supported on one side only – that of the presenter.

Immediacy This has to do with engaging interpersonally with the audience: being a real presence for them. It can be done by referring to individuals by name (if that is appropriate under the circumstances); using the type of language and forms of expression that resonate with those of the group (without appearing patronising); removing unnecessary barriers, such as tables, between the speaker and participants; moving close to them without making them uncomfortable; and using suitable patterns of direct eye-contact. Rather than staring blankly into middle distance, or allowing your gaze to sweep aimlessly over the group, making periodic eye-contact with individuals in the audience for short spells is recommended.[47]

Avoiding distractions These can be caused by pacing around, playing with a pen or pointer, and over-use of certain stock phrases or forms of expression. Not only do they get in the way of listening to the content, they can become incredibly irritating for an audience. But changing such habits can be difficult. Simons[48] captures the struggle to gain

Box 6.8 Features of effective deliveries

Effective deliveries tend to:

- use appropriate language and avoid jargon
- be suitably paced
- use visual aids without placing them centre stage
- make use of sub-summaries, signposts and links
- emphasise key points verbally, nonverbally and vocally
- be verbally fluent
- be concrete and precise
- be dynamic
- be varied
- include carefully chosen examples
- avoid distractions
- seem natural and uncontrived.

control of 'body language' in a humorous caricature:

> In speaking situations, your body is no longer an organic miracle, it is a traitorous wretch. When you want it to settle down, it acts up. When you need more energy, it wants to take a nap. When you want to look calm and confident, it wants to be a perspiring fool. On the podium your body is enemy No. 1 ....

Appearing natural and uncontrived To work as intended, all of the above pieces of advice, summarised in Box 6.8, must be acted on in such a way that the presenter does not seem artificial. They must become incorporated into the presenter's own style. This can take some time and practice.

Finally, before the delivery takes place the presenter is well advised to rehearse what is going to be said.[49]

The setting

Where possible, it is always worthwhile checking out the location of the presentation in advance and the actual room that has been set aside.[50,51] The size and position of the room, type of furniture and facilities, and available equipment should be noted. They can all influence levels of comfort and conduciveness to learning. They will also shape what it is possible for you to do with the group. Things to consider include:

- *Location.* Make sure you, as presenter, know precisely where you have to go on the day of the presentation. Get there early so that you can relax and meet the members as they arrive.
- *Size and shape of room.* It is usually better to have a room that is slightly larger than the bare minimum to accommodate the numbers attending: not too large though that your talk seems poorly supported. The actual shape may make some seating layouts difficult. (Issues to do with seating arrangements, and so forth, are covered in Chapter 2.)
- *Acoustics.* Are the acoustics suitable? Does the room have carpet and heavy curtains that can attenuate the sound? When full of people, will you be heard easily at the back? Do you need a microphone?
- *Equipment.* How is the room equipped? Can other equipment be provided? Will it be there on the day *and working*? Can you operate the equipment? Do you know where the various controls are? Will there be technical assistance to hand? Do you have a backup if the equipment lets you down? With computer-based presentations, it is always advisable to have both backup and a 'dry run' in advance, if at all possible, when you are relying, in total or in part, upon unfamiliar equipment.[52]
- *Power sockets.* The position and type of power socket should also be noted if it is intended that equipment be used.
- *Furnishings.* How is the room furnished? Is the seating comfortable and in keeping with what you intend to do?
- *Decor.* It is bright, airy and stimulating or have you been offered a dull, drab and rather sorry room? If the latter, your task of stimulating the group can be made more difficult. It sends all the wrong signals at the outset.
- *Lighting.* Is the lighting adequate? What type is it? Natural lighting often creates a more attractive ambience than the florescent variety.
- *Temperature.* Is the room sufficiently well ventilated and can the temperature be adequately regulated? Do you know how to find the controls and work them?

Overview

Making an effective presentation can be one of the most dynamic ways of getting your ideas across to others and influencing them.[53] It is also one of the most conspicuous ways of demonstrating your competence to those who matter in the organisation. For many, however, it is at best an unpleasant ordeal to be got over with quickly, or at worst an unacceptable part of an otherwise fulfilling job that eventually leads to a radical career reappraisal. But everyone can benefit from paying greater heed to their presentations and how they are delivered.

A useful framework for approaching this task, as we have seen in this chapter, incorporates a consideration of the presenter, the audience, the setting and the case to be presented. The importance of preparation and planning cannot be over-stressed. Thought must be given to ways of structuring and organising the material to be put across. The possible use of visual aids to help convey the message and enliven the performance should also be recognised. Finally, techniques of delivery during the introduction, main body and conclusion of the presentation can make all the difference between a well-received, stimulating address and a somewhat insipid talk with little or no ultimate impact.

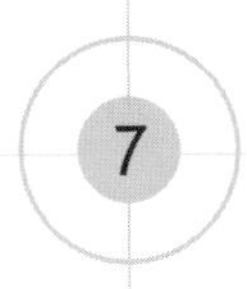

7 We can work it out: negotiating and bargaining

Introduction

Negotiations, or at least opportunities to negotiate, are an ever-present part of the manager's world. The fact was recognised by Simons and Tripp[1] when they declared 'Managers and executives negotiate constantly over issues as varied as hiring decisions and purchases, corporate resource allocations, and labor contracts.' There can be few aspects of the job that don't involve negotiating in some shape or form. The grand set pieces of industrial relations settlements or megabuck corporate takeover deals readily spring to mind. Negotiating features, though, on an ongoing basis in the day-to-day business of life at work with its myriad clashes of interests, disagreements and frustrations. Nevertheless, the smooth operation of the organisation depends upon the proper handling of such everyday situations. When recognised and dealt with astutely they do not compromise the smooth running of the organisation – indeed this may even be enhanced. When ignored or mishandled, an organisation that was making bold strides forward begins to hobble.

Although being a shrewd negotiator does not guarantee managerial success, the more accomplished you are in this sphere the more likely you are to manage effectively, regardless of work context. O'Hair and colleagues[2] recommended that, 'By learning productive methods of negotiation and conflict management, you can contribute a great deal to the groups, organisations and people with whom you work.'

But what exactly is a negotiation? For the moment it can be broadly thought of as a transaction between two or more parties, each of which is to some extent reliant upon the other to satisfy what seem to be incompatible goals. Examples include scenarios such as:

- Management proposes a wage restructuring for sales staff to reduce the standard element in favour of a performance-linked component; union representatives mount bitter opposition.

- Suppliers issue notice of a sharp rise in the price of their component parts in line with increased import costs; buyers complain that they can neither absorb such increased overheads nor pass them on to the consumer due to the depressed state of the market.
- A line manager attempts to influence a member of the workforce to accept a considerable extension of duties on the strength of a vague promise of promotion at some indeterminate point in the future. The member regards this as unreasonable and resist.
- An organisation is keen to downsize a section of its operation through natural wastage, and staff of a particular age are offered an early-retirement package. They find the package unattractive.

In all cases, each party has wants that are at odds with those of the other. Furthermore, each is dependent upon the other to satisfy those wants, producing the classic context for negotiating. Figures have been cited estimating that, depending on specific circumstances, those in management positions can spend from 20 to 50 per cent of their time dealing with situations of this type.[3]

Here we will consider the circumstances that give rise to negotiations and the contrasting approaches that can be taken. The stages which negotiators work through as they move towards a resolution will also be addressed. A considerable part of the chapter will be given over to revealing a range of tactics and techniques that can be put to effective use, especially in bargaining.

Conflict at work

Why should negotiating feature so prominently in management? The answer can be traced to conflict and its endemic presence in and between organisations. But it isn't just the workplace that is affected. For Wilmot and Hocker,[4] 'Conflict happens. It happens on the job, between groups in our society, within families, and right in the middle of our most personal relationships. Conflict is ever present and both fascinating and maddening.' Be that as it may, the work environment seems particularly susceptible. Staff typically find themselves at odds with each other when 'one party perceives that the other has frustrated, or is about to frustrate, some concern of his'.[5]

But the prospect of work being conflict-ridden should not distress us unduly. It was once thought that such disharmony was grit in the bearing of an otherwise smooth-running machine, all traces of which had to be removed before permanent damage was caused. This is now accepted as unrealistic and unjustifiably alarmist. Indeed some hold that even if it were possible to wipe away all traces of discord, it may not be desirable. Conflict may be good – at least in measured doses. It may promote increased effectiveness, strengthen relationships and further goal achievement.[6] Darling and Walker[7] cautioned that 'Managers who try to eliminate conflict will not last long', and continued by proclaiming that '... those who manage it well will typically experience both organisational benefits and personal satisfaction'. The trick, therefore, is not to ignore it but to manage it so as to maximise its constructive potential. Negotiation is one way of so doing. As put by Fraser and Zarkada-Fraser,[8] 'Every negotiation is in essence a conflict resolution exercise, where competing expectations are balanced against each other in order to produce satisfaction of the parties' needs.'

Negotiation: characteristics and preconditions

A variety of definitions of the term 'negotiation' can be located, each placing an emphasis upon slightly different aspects of the process. Here we will distil out what are commonly recognised as central elements.[9–11]

Differences of interests, ideas or objectives

A precondition for negotiation is the presence of conflict, *or at least the perception of conflict*. Unless parties view their positions as incompatible, there will be no need to contemplate negotiating. The fact that differences when probed can turn out to be more superficial than substantial, should not be overlooked. What initially seems to be an intractable impasse can sometimes be resolved speedily and amicably, once the issues have been more fully explored, as the example in Box 7.1 demonstrates.

Box 7.1 Message in a bottle

They grabbed the bottle of wine at the same moment, each unaware of the other until then. They looked surprised, then embarrassed, then annoyed.

'I think I had it first', he said, with an awkward smile.

Box 7.1 *continued*

'No', she countered 'I saw it before you', realising quickly that it was the last bottle of Chateau De Plonk 99 on the shelf.

'But you don't understand', he persisted, 'I simply must have this wine.'

'I've been looking all over for a bottle of Chateau De Plonk 99', she stiffened, 'and now that I've finally found it, I'm certainly not prepared to let you simply walk away with it'.

'I'll buy you any other bottle of wine in the shop – forget about the price', he pleaded.

'You can have two, any two, but not this one', she came back at him.

'Why does this rather modest wine matter so much to you?', he queried, continuing

'You see, my wife and I shared a bottle on the night we met and tomorrow is our first wedding anniversary. I've tried everywhere and had almost given up. I really must have it for sentimental reasons.'

'I collect unusual wine bottles and I really need this one to complete my collection', she explained.

'So you don't want the wine, as such?'

'No, can't really stand the stuff. What do you intend to do with the bottle, once you and your wife have enjoyed the wine?', she queried.

'Probably throw it out', came the reply.

'Can I suggest that we share the cost of the bottle and exchange addresses', they rhymed together, laughing.

Joint resolve

Negotiation may resemble debate, group problem solving or shared decision-making and indeed may sometimes encompass elements of all three. What sets it apart, however, is the unique dynamic of forces that surrounds it, some antagonistically pulling the parties apart, others collaboratively pushing them together. While, at one level, there may be conflict of interests, at another both sides strive towards the same goal of reaching resolution, *if they are negotiating in good faith*. Rubin[12] talked about the role of 'ripeness' in this regard, meaning that conflict must have reached a stage where both parties are prepared to look for more constructive ways of resolving their differences.

Shared interests

Sometimes the fact that opposing parties will seldom be at odds on *all* issues is overlooked. More characteristically, areas can be found where they are at one. When these get overshadowed by points of disagreement, the results can be bleak for all concerned. Even in the supposedly cutthroat world of business, rivalry is rarely untrammelled. Brandenburger and Nalebuff[13] coined the term 'coopetition' to more accurately describe the judicious blend of co-operation and competition that best serves present-day business relationships. When companies get sucked into all-out war, there are few victors. When one player cuts the price of its product, the authors explained, it may produce a temporary benefit. But 'the gains will evaporate if others match the cuts to regain their lost share. The result is simply to re-establish the status quo but at a lower price – a lose–lose scenario that leaves all the players worse off.'[14] They estimated, for example, that the price war in the years between 1990 and 1993 cost the US airline industry more revenue than previously made since the days of the Wright brothers.[15]

Interdependency

For a negotiation to take place, each side must be reliant on the other to meet its requirements. If this were not the case, each could simply disengage at the first realisation that their requests were not being acceded to, and seek alternative routes to fulfilment. The dynamic of such a situation of interdependency empowers all parties. No resolution of the situation is possible unless and until each is prepared to say 'Yes'. This does not mean, of course, that all sides are empowered equally.

Concessions

Negotiating depends upon those entering being prepared to accommodate each other, if necessary, through 'give and take'. Indeed it has been suggested that, 'The basis of negotiation is exchange: every party gains and gives concessions until they reach agreement.'[16] But making concessions is not inevitable, as we shall see. What is important is that ultimately, and if required, all parties tacitly commit themselves to compromise if that is what it takes to reach a settlement.

Communication

Getting and giving information lies at the heart of the negotiating process. Indeed, McRae[17] placed this communicative element at the core of the process: 'A negotiation takes place any time two or more people are communicating and at least one of those persons has a goal in mind.' Likewise, Woo and associates[18] reminded us that 'verbal and nonverbal aspects of communication are usually regarded as vital components of the negotiation process'. Where levels of trust permit, information can be exchanged directly and openly. Where it doesn't, members have to rely upon more indirect channels, such as making inferences and 'reading between the lines'. But the process tends to operate most successfully when open and direct communication is possible.

Finally, those involved should be able to communicate party-to-party and face-to-face, although negotiating through a representative may be an option. Involving a third party in a mediating role is also a possibility, if negotiations get stuck. When that third party is empowered to propose a settlement, we move into the area of arbitration.

Misrepresentation

Following on from the latter point, negotiating often has a dark side of concealment, evasion and half-truths. For Morley[19] negotiation was 'an exercise in which parties struggle to exploit asymmetries of interest and power, each knowing that the other may disguise or misrepresent their real position'. While conventions differ from culture to culture, blatant lying is usually regarded as 'breaking the rules' and, if discovered, seriously jeopardises the whole process. That said, there is a commonly held assumption, especially when the transaction is a 'one-off' with strangers, that not all will be revealed and that what is will probably carry a strategic spin.

Inherent tension

Mnookin and associates[20] drew attention to three core tensions experienced by those in negotiation. They have to do with:

1. Maximising one's own personal profit while at the same time attempting to ensure equity and a fair deal for both sides.

2. Standing up for one's own position, yet showing concern for the interests and needs of the other side.
3. Safeguarding personal interests and client interests in situations where the negotiator is representing another party. For example, a broker may be operating in a climate where the product representing the best investment for a particular client may not be the one that carries the highest commission for the broker.

At the heart of these foci of tension is the more fundamental issue of balancing two basic concerns that can often be in direct competition. One has to do with maximising substantive gain: the other with maintaining a positive relationship with the other party. As we shall see, such relations can be extremely important, especially in the context of ongoing transactions. Their importance has tended to be overlooked, however. As stated by Rubin,[21] 'Much of the negotiation analysis that has taken place over the last 25 years has focused on the "bottom line": who gets how much once an agreement has been reached... This economic focus is being supplanted by a richer, and more accurate, portrayal of negotiation in terms not only of economic terms but of relational considerations.' Indeed, in certain non-Western cultures such as China, negotiations may only take place with those with whom a certain level of friendship has been cultivated[22] (Box 7.2).

Box 7.2 Preconditions for a negotiation

Negotiating between parties depends upon each:

- experiencing an initial incompatibility (or perceived incompatibility) of interests;
- relying on the co-operation of the other to meet needs;
- agreeing that negotiating is a more satisfactory way of resolving the conflict than any possible alternative;
- being able to interact and communicate, preferably face-to-face;
- considering it possible to influence the other to modify their position;
- having some degree of power and influence over the other side;
- being prepared to accommodate the other's requirements, to some extent;
- being hopeful of an outcome acceptable to them in some measure.

Negotiating strategies

There is no one best way to negotiate, nor a single strategy that guarantees success. How the task is approached should be shaped by the circumstances of each encounter.[23] The skilled negotiator must ultimately be strategically flexible. That said, however, there are certain approaches that are more likely to lead to success than others. Four alternative negotiating strategies are now presented.

Unilateral concession

This plan can be caricatured as 'Come in peace'. The thinking here is to readily concede ground from the outset to appease the other side and fully accommodate their demands. This may be done for a number of reasons, such as:

- extreme discomfort in the face of conflict and an abiding desire to simply get it over with and get out;
- a belief that doing so may send a 'friendly' signal to the other side;
- an over-riding concern with relationship matters at the expense of material outcome;
- a move to make the other party feel obligated to reciprocate;
- lack of assertion (see Chapter 11).

Whatever the thinking (or lack of it) that informs the decision, unilateral concession is a highly dubious approach to take. In the vast majority of cases it leads to what Americans call 'giving the store away'. This approach is likely to fail because:

- you are not the best person to be negotiating if you have a phobia about conflict;
- an unforced concession will be perceived as weakness, naivety or inexperience, rather than as an amicable gesture;
- the relationship is unlikely to be strengthened, in reality, in a situation where the other ends up with everything;
- there is absolutely no reason why the other party should feel compelled to match a concession that you have volunteered unconditionally.

Competition

The caricature this time is 'Go to War'. This is undoubtedly the strategy traditionally associated with negotiating.[24] Indeed many people still believe that it is the only option. Here the aim is to defeat the other side: to get more from the transaction than they do. It is commonly premised upon a *zero-sum* distribution of payoffs, where a gain to one side represents a corresponding direct loss to the other. Think of a game of poker as an example. If both players start with €100 and at the end of the evening, one has €60 more than when starting, the other must be down €60. They both can't win. For this reason this strategy often leads to 'win–lose' negotiations.

But competing can lead to neither side getting much from the negotiation, as we have seen. Webber[25] cautioned 'When it comes to negotiating you can't let the Neanderthal side of your nature dominate. You need to rise above that.' Dawson[26] labelled a variant of this competitive way of thinking 'Power Negotiating'. The objective is to win while leaving the other side *thinking* that they are the victors.

Individual gain

This approach is 'Smash-and-grab'. The intention is not necessarily to beat the other side, but merely to get as much from the negotiation as possible. The motive is purely egotistical. It may lead to you 'scooping the pot' and leaving the other party with little. Indeed one of its disadvantages is the complete disregard for the outcome to them. But such neglect can prove short-sighted, especially if you find yourself in further negotiations with the same party at some point in the future. As we have seen already, under such circumstances you can't afford to dismiss relational matters.

Co-operation

The caricature this time is 'Brothers-in-arms'. The thinking is radically different from what we have considered so far. This strategy relies on co-operation, co-ordination and the integration of effort – on both sides working together to solve a shared problem to mutual benefit. The context is that of a *variable-sum* payoff, rather than zero-sum distribution typical of competitive situations, allowing both sides to benefit from the deal. Unlike distributive bargaining where the focus is upon how to 'cut up the cake' with each side intent upon getting the bigger share (or even all of it), the possibility of both working collaboratively to produce a bigger cake is acknowledged when co-operation is countenanced.

Box 7.3 I win–you win

Co-operative negotiating depends upon:

- accepting, as a goal, the best possible arrangement for both sides;
- separating the people from the problem – the latter rather than the former is the enemy;
- building mutual trust;
- avoiding deeply entrenched positions;
- exploring the needs behind the demands – sometimes those demands can be met in other ways;
- looking for new options that have added value for both sides rather than trying to grind the other side down in the concession-making mill;
- trying to reach agreement based on reason and principle, rather than the sheer weight of emotional pressure.

Thompson[27] regarded many negotiating situations as bedevilled by *false* or *illusory conflict*. This is a belief by those concerned that their interests are opposed, when in fact this is not necessarily so. With this removed the enemy now becomes not the other side but rather the obstacle that stands in the way of joint progress and is common to both. It is the problem not the person that must be defeated. This approach has also been referred to as 'Interest-based Negotiation',[28] and there is some evidence that it may be the one favoured by females in particular.[29] Furthermore, Olekalns and Smith[30] discovered that negotiating along these lines was more likely to lead to jointly beneficial outcomes.

The mind-set here is therefore 'win–win' and Fisher and associates[31] have outlined ways of bringing it about. These are summarised in Box 7.3.

There are four possible outcomes to these four strategies.

1. There may simply be no agreement with the negotiation breaking down.
2. One side can walk away with everything, while the other is left with nothing. This is more likely to happen with Unilateral Concession.
3. A compromise solution may be worked out in which each side ends up with something which is often less than they had initially hoped for. Competition often produces this result.

4. An integrative agreement is arrived at in which both sides enjoy higher joint benefits than could have been delivered through compromise. This is more probable when parties adopt a co-operative approach. Two competing retail outlets, rather than getting into a damaging price war, could launch a joint strategy to promote their part of town as providing the best shopping for the range of goods that they sell. In this way they increase the size of the cake for shared benefit. Where possible to achieve, this fourth outcome has obvious attractions underscoring its commonly acknowledged advantages.

Stages in the negotiation process

It is common to think of negotiations evolving through a recognisable series of stages or phases.[32,33] Kennedy[34] identified alternative models, ranging from those specifying a mere three, to more elaborate versions outlining as many as eight identifiable phases. However, in essence the five key sequential negotiation stages are as follows:

1. Planning and preparation
2. Opening
3. Exploring
4. Bargaining
5. Reaching settlement.

Stage 1: planning and preparation

Abraham Lincoln declared 'If I had nine hours to cut down a tree, I would spend six hours sharpening my axe.' This division of time is reflected in the attention that we will devote to the present stage in this chapter. An important maxim, therefore, is never to short-change yourself on making ready, in an impetuous charge to clash antlers with the opposition over the negotiating table. Lewicki *et al.*[35] expressed the point as follows:

> ... the foundation for success in negotiation is not in the game playing or the dramatics. The dominant force for success in negotiation is in the planning that takes place prior to the dialogue. While success in negotiation is affected by how one enacts the strategy, the foundation for success in negotiation is in how one prepares.

Indeed being skilled in this area was regarded, by a group of professional negotiators, as the most crucial attribute that they possessed.[36] Likewise, Jordan and Roloff[37] analysed the written pre-negotiation plans of those negotiators who were more attuned to the circumstances of the negotiation, with those less so. They discovered that the plans of the former were not only more elaborate but that they subsequently achieved a higher percentage of their initial profit goals. Broadly speaking, planning and preparation should cover goals; obstacles to the achievement of those goals; and finally, possible ways of overcoming these obstacles. As well as concerns over issues and outcomes, it should also include thinking about the negotiating *process* and how the encounter should best be handled.[38] These concerns are reflected in a more detailed way in the following components of the planning stage.

Clarify purpose and establish goals It is pointless going into a negotiation with only the vaguest of ideas as to why you are there or what you hope to come away with. Ask yourself the following questions:

- *Is negotiation necessary?* Can I get what I want in some other way? If I must negotiate, is this the most appropriate party to get involved with? You may discover, with some reflection, that you are less dependent upon the other side to achieve your needs than either you or, indeed they, had initially thought.
- *What must I come away with at the end in order to satisfy my needs?* This question deserves some careful thought. It requires you to identify precisely three positions:
  1. Your *target point* or *target range*. This is what you aim to get from the transaction, being optimistic, but realistically so. An alternative term is *aspiration level*. It can be conceived as a precise amount (target point) or as falling within limits (target range).
  2. Your *resistance point* or '*bottom line*'. This is the point beyond which you are not prepared to concede. For this reason it is sometimes called the 'walk away' point. As far as you are concerned you cannot accept a deal that falls below this point.
  3. *Your BATNA*. This is your Best Alternative to a Negotiated Agreement.[39] It is a response to the question, 'What if it's not possible to reach an agreement?', and should never be left until a breakdown actually takes place for initial consideration. Identifying what your best option would be if the negotiation fails, will help you position your resistance point.

> Remember, a poor settlement, from your point of view, may be worse than no settlement at all. Perhaps you simply can't do business with the other party at this time.

Of course you should bear in mind that the other side will most likely have target and resistance points as well. The space between the two sets of resistance points will set the parameters for a settlement, as exemplified in Box 7.4.

Identify the issues Time spent teasing out the issues to be negotiated on is always time spent well. Most negotiations centre upon a few key concerns for each party, and some additional issues that are less pressing. These must be unravelled and marked as such.[40] Useful guiding principles are to keep a picture of the total situation in mind and to be as flexible and open as possible in your approach.[41]

Box 7.4 Target points, resistance points and settlement range

Bob has just changed job. This involves commuting to and from work, thereby incurring a cost both in fares, time and energy. Property prices in the town where he works are comparable to those where he presently lives, as are amenities, quality of life, etc., so Bob decides to move. He puts his house on the market. Having done his homework, he decides that it is worth €180 000. This is his *target point*. Would he accept less? Yes, but he feels that anything under €150 000 would be giving it away, with the property market as it is. This is his *resistance point*. But what if he can't get a buyer to offer at least €150 000? Having done his sums, Bob decide that his *BATNA* would be to continue commuting until the spring and put the house back on the market then.

Along comes Bill. He quite likes the house and feels that it could be bought for €160 000. This is his *target point*. In any case he could not raise a mortgage of more than €190 000. This is his *resistance point*. His *BATNA* would be to wait for another similar house in the area to come on the market and rent accommodation in the meantime.

Their *settlement range*, therefore, lies between €150 000 and €190 000. Since both *target points* lie well within this range, Bob's set at €180 000 and Bill's at €160 000, it is likely that the house will change hands.

- *What are the different considerations that could or should be introduced into the process?* Negotiations that centre on just a single issue can prove extremely difficult and prone to deadlock. There simply are no other variables that can be brought into play to get around the main obstacle. However, few negotiations are inherently as limited as this when the negotiators step back from the key concern, for a few moments, to view the wider picture of their difference. Box 7.5 provides an example.
- *Are some issues more crucial to me than others?* The next step is to prioritise concerns. Which are central, which more peripheral? Answers to this question will enable decisions to be made about areas where latitude for compromise is greater.[42] Probing beneath the issue can reveal the actual need or value that it represents. Often these can be satisfied in different ways, introducing greater scope for

Box 7.5 Widgets and gizmos

Betty is in the business of making and selling widgets. Beth needs widgets for her gizmo plant. Beth offers Betty €10.00 per widget for her produce. Betty demands €20.00. Betty finally comes down to €16.00. Beth increases her offer to €14.00, but neither is prepared to concede further – deadlock!

What are the other issues that could have been introduced to broaden the negotiation and that could have been perhaps traded off, one against the other, in reaching an agreement?

The list might include such variables as:

- Volume discount – more for less.
- Quality of product
- Extended product guarantees
- Payment terms and conditions
- Assisted financing
- Transport
- Time/place of delivery
- Packaging
- Insurance
- Installation costs
- Buy-back arrangements
- Options on further contracts.

manoeuvre once the negotiation gets started. For example, if the main concern is over money, to what use will that money be put? Is it is to buy (at least in part) some product/s and if so, can a better deal be done focusing directly on those products?

- *Are issues linked? Can they be offset one against the other, if need be?* Are issues interconnected so that settlement on one cannot be reached without taking the others into account or can they be tackled on a stand-alone basis? Depending upon the other party's needs, it may be possible to concede on what to you are peripheral concerns at no substantial cost. Mattock and Ehrenborg[43] recommended that you locate target, resistance and satisfaction points, at the outset, for each of the variables isolated. You then have a basis for calculating where you stand as the picture changes in situations of intense bargaining where there is considerable linkage amongst the issues.

Gathering information It is impossible to be too well informed approaching a negotiation. That does not mean, though, that you cannot or will not be required to seek further detail once the negotiation gets underway. However at this stage two types of question can usefully be posed.

- *Do I know as much as I need to about my own position?* Make sure that you are *au fait* with the background to all relevant issues, including implications that various concessions might have for other departments of the organisation such as finance, production, sales or human resources. What are the arguments in support of the position that you will take? What is the supporting evidence for them? What are the areas of weakness and the counter-arguments? How can they be refuted? How long do you have to complete the negotiation? Must you reach a settlement and are you authorised to do so?
- *Have I unearthed as much information as I can about the other party?* Find out all that is possible about the other side, who they represent and the type of deal they are after. What is their track-record? What style do they prefer – highly competitive or co-operative? Which tactics tend to be introduced – brinkmanship, bluff, time pressures? In terms of personal qualities, are they, for example, honourable and trustworthy; impetuous and unpredictable; rational and calculating; patient and unflappable; or the opposite of these? What authority do they have at the end of the day to clinch a deal? Could this negotiator simply be a stalking horse, sent in advance of the proper negotiation to reconnoitre your position?

The sharper your vision of the other party's position, the more successfully you will be able to anticipate possible areas of agreement, conflict and compromise. What are the likely issues from their perspective? What are their underlying needs? Which issues are core to them and which more tangential? If necessary can you make concessions that will be valued highly, but at little cost to yourself? What are the strengths and weaknesses of their position as you understand it? What do they probably know of your position? Weber[44] stressed the need, therefore, to get inside the mind of the other party: to view the negotiation from their perspective. Echoing this sentiment, Davies[45] advised that 'You need to know as much as you can about your opposite number: who they are, what they want, how they are likely to act and react.' Metaplanning is therefore called for – planning that includes the anticipated plans of your protagonists.

Identify areas of potential agreement and conflict It is always wise to stake out common ground shared with the other party. It offers areas that can be retreated to, if the negotiation begins to falter, to affirm the basis of a settlement and strengthen spoiling relationships.

Areas of likely conflict must also be spotted. What is the crux of the difficulty? What are the possible avenues for overcoming conflict? What concessions can be made? Under what conditions will they be offered and accepted? Are there areas that can be conceded at perhaps no great loss, but that could lead to significant movement in more central areas?

Deciding upon the type of negotiation to pursue Given what has been gleaned of the other's approach, background to the negotiation and possible deals which it may spawn in the future, issues involved and the potential for conflict resolution, a decision has to be made about the approach to adopt. The basic choice is between competing with the opposition in a zero-sum macho battle of might, played out under win–lose rules to see who can wring the most from the other side and ultimately emerge victorious, or collaborating with them in a joint quest to find the best possible mutually beneficial outcome in the spirit of win–win co-operation. Associated ideologies have been referred to by Anderson[46] as 'Predation' and 'Symbiosis'.

Some of the shortcomings of ruthless competition are that:

- relationships with the other group can be damaged when it is left feeling defeated;

- repeat business can suffer if members believe that they have been treated unfairly;
- difficulties with implementation can arise when the other side is pressured into accepting a deal that they subsequently cannot sell to those whom they represent.

Corresponding advantages of a more collaborative stance have also been recognised where circumstances permit.[47–49] Conditions which promote collaborative negotiations include:

- trusting the other side not to take advantage of your willingness to co-operate;
- accepting the importance of the relationship with the other party;
- being involved with the other side in an ongoing, rather than one-off basis, or being in a situation that has this potential. Here it may be in neither party's best interests to engage in a protracted lose–lose war;
- seeing beyond a narrow zero-sum distribution of payoffs;
- coming from a particular cultural background. Hendon *et al.*,[50] discovered preferences for different styles when comparing negotiators from North America, advanced and less advanced (e.g. Philippines and Papua New Guinea) Asian countries, Latin America and the British Commonwealth. North Americans, for example, were much more likely to favour a tough approach that involved introducing concessions only at the very end when all else failed. Even those from similar cultures, such as the US and Canada, may approach negotiations differently.[51] Likewise, the French were more than twice as likely as the Spanish to recognise win–win possibilities, when surveyed by Salacuse.[52] The same author also found, however, that professional and occupational culture was as important in determining negotiation behaviour as was national culture.[53]

Formulating an agenda Now it is possible to draft a tentative agenda for the negotiation. This should list the issues to be introduced and the preferred order in which to consider them. Is it in your interests to negotiate item by item, or do you prefer to negotiate on a broader front? Being prepared to be flexible in the order in which issues are tackled is advisable. Brett and associates[54] found it to be a key factor in influencing 'win–win' negotiating encounters.

It should be appreciated, of course, that the other party will additionally have ideas about the shape of the agenda. Indeed the agenda may be subject to preliminary negotiations – so-called 'talks about talks'. For this reason, it has been suggested by Mattock and Ehrenborg[55] that the agenda be drawn up jointly, as a collaborative exercise. General ground rules, deadlines and such like, can be clarified as well.

Agreeing on how to work a settlement Settlement details are sometimes overlooked with the result that the deal ultimately unravels. To overlook issues of how the settlement should be documented, formalised and implemented as part of the initial stage of preparation, can often be to plant time-bombs set to go off when least expected just as participants are beginning to congratulate themselves on reaching a workable agreement.

Choosing a location Where the negotiations take place also has to be decided upon. Custom and convention may take care of this. It is more likely that the person selling will visit the buyer, than vice versa. Many negotiators feel more comfortable negotiating on 'home territory'. Alternatively, there may be advantage in seeing people you intend to do business with in their 'natural habit'.[56] One can quickly learn more about them and their standing in the company. Furthermore, in a worst-case scenario of negotiation breakdown, being in someone else's office affords the opportunity of 'walking out'.

As a final option, negotiations may be held on neutral territory. Indeed this is a favoured compromise in political negotiations that are particularly intractable and prone to breakdown.

Rehearsing If the negotiation is especially important you may want to have a dry run at it, as a culmination of your planning and preparation.

Before leaving this initial stage of the process, it should be stressed that negotiations represent what Wilson and colleagues[57] called 'a complex planning environment'. Little can be taken for granted so flexibility in preparation is the guiding principle. Consequently, it may sometimes be necessary to formulate multiple goals in circumstances where there are only fuzzy criteria for ordering priorities or where only vague assumptions can be made about the other's agenda. Again, while pre-planning is essential, initial decisions typically have to be revisited and revised when the negotiation gets underway.

Stage 2: opening

This stage begins when the parties meet at the negotiating table. It can be more difficult than might be imagined. The objectives are to establish a suitable climate, begin to build a facilitative relationship and orient proceedings to the business at hand.

Creating a suitable climate This will vary somewhat depending upon the type of negotiation envisaged, but for the most part it should be courteous, co-operative and businesslike.[58] Where circumstances permit the opportunity to negotiate within a win–win framework can be flagged. A significant finding is that negotiators often reciprocate each other's use of strategies and tactics.[59] This mirroring is known as *entrainment*, and it has been shown to be a valuable negotiating tactic.[60] Thus, if one party adopts a hostile opening stance, it is likely that the other will do likewise. On the other hand, a more integrative, co-operative and amenable approach is also likely to be responded to in kind.[61]

Such an atmosphere can be engineered in a number of ways:

- Initial contact involved in agreeing an agenda will set the tone and should strive to be positive and as non-confrontational as possible.
- The room set aside for the negotiation should be pleasant and comfortable with space available where people can mingle in a less formal setting.
- Use of 'We' language which suggests that parties have common concerns and are working together, 'We seem to be moving to a stage where ...'.
- Distractions, such as mobile phone calls or intruding secretaries should be minimised.
- Issues that are relatively uncontroversial can be introduced early to create some level of agreement at the beginning.

Building a facilitative relationship This is sometimes referred to as establishing rapport[62] and is related to the previous task. Relationship work can include:

- spending some time over routines such as personal introductions;
- respecting the other party's concerns and showing a commitment to taking them on board;
- emphasising the shared nature of difficulties faced;
- listening to what the other party has to say;
- sending the correct signals nonverbally as well as verbally;
- avoiding cheap one-upmanship ploys to gain initial advantage. These tend to be seen as just that and quickly sour the relationship.

Orienting proceedings towards business matters It is common for this stage to be brought to a close by both sides agreeing an agenda. This may involve acknowledging, ratifying and if necessary modifying earlier agreements in this respect, if framing an agenda formed part of preliminary work. Each may sketch the issues of concern and their stance in relation to them. In doing so they present their opening positions. The negotiation is now ready to move into the next phase.

Stage 3: exploration

This is a natural progression from the preceding stage. In it parties begin to explore in greater depth issues merely stated in Stage 2, and to seek a fuller appreciation of them. If these are dealt with fully, it may be possible to short-circuit the bargaining phase and move the negotiating process on expeditiously towards a win–win settlement. Exchanging quality information plays a significant part in revealing co-operative possibilities. If, on the other hand, a more competitive line is taken, at least each party should be in a position to make proposals and counter-proposals from a more fully informed background.

Probing beneath the surface level of wants and positions Here underlying needs and values are explored enabling seemingly incompatible stances to sometimes be accommodated and opportunities for collaborative negotiation recognised. What the other wants, on closer inspection, may not be what they really need. Additionally, needs can often be met in a variety of ways that neither party had recognised before they began to share deeper thoughts about the issues surrounding the negotiation. Going back to Box 7.5, Beth wanted to buy widgets for no more than €14 pounds each. What she really needed to operate in profit, however, was to have widgets installed in gizmos at or beneath a particular cost. This realisation would have brought the other variables listed in Box 7.5 into play enabling her, if necessary, to go beyond €14 on the amount paid per item. For example, let's say her trucks already made deliveries close to Betty's factory, coming back empty. Transport could, therefore, have been taken care of at very little cost to Beth. In return Betty, for whom having to deliver the goods would have been quite expensive, could have looked more closely at her per-unit price. This stage of exploring is pivotal in mutually beneficial integrative negotiating.

The exploratory phase should never be rushed. In some cases, had more time been spent exploring each other's requirements, bargaining could have been avoided or at least marginalised. Time saved exploring is often wasted ten-fold as the negotiation subsequently gets bogged down in dogged and protracted bargaining with characteristic deadlock and occasional breakdown.

Seeking a panoramic view of the other's issues It is important during this stage, to gain as broad a picture as possible of the totality of what matters to the other side. The unexpected introduction of a raft of new concerns later in the negotiation drags the whole process back to the stage of exploration and is highly frustrating. Lewicki and colleagues[63] were adamant that 'effective information exchange promotes the development of good integrative solutions', citing research evidence to substantiate their judgement. This includes both providing and seeking details of, in particular, the other side's preferences and priorities across the issues identified.[64] Furthermore, it is often possible to recognise, from the different values attached to concerns introduced by parties, ways in which both could benefit from particular outcomes.

Areas of agreement should be carefully noted when exploring. What seem to be points of conflict also need to be marked for perusal. As already mentioned, sometimes the conflict turns out to be more illusory than real, but not always. It is important, at this stage, to be able to unpack such issues without getting sucked into a process of bargaining on them. That comes later.

Listening to what the other party has to say is key. Conflict situations tend to quickly spiral out of control because neither side is willing or able to listen properly to the other. Listening is not just about hearing. It is about being as fully receptive as possible to the total message delivered by the other person. As such, it involves tuning in to how things are said, as well as what is said. Indeed noting what is not said can also be highly illuminating. Having carried out an analysis of the rhetoric used by managers and shop stewards during negotiations within a UK National Health Service (NHS) Trust, Hamilton[65] identified how listening keenly to implied as well as explicit statements played a crucial role in reaching agreement. Dunne[66] summarised it well: 'The best negotiators are good listeners who handle stress well and are able to argue logically and calmly.'

Stage 4: bargaining

Bargaining is commonly associated with a more competitive negotiating style. It typically begins when an agreed solution fails to emerge fully formed following the detailed examination of issues during the preceding stage. Having got a fuller appreciation of where each other stands, and being mindful of the fact that the other side may not have been completely open or honest, the next step is making a firm offer or putting a proposal for a settlement on the table. Opening positions need to be carefully thought out and presented appropriately.

Finding an opening level In classic win–lose negotiation involving distributive bargaining strategies the importance of beginning with the highest possible *realistic* asking price (if you are selling) or the lowest possible offer (if buying) is heavily stressed. There is firm evidence linking this tactic with the degree of success achieved.[67] But in both cases parties must be sensible and credible in the stances that they take. Interestingly, recent American literature tends to downplay this stipulation somewhat in favour of exaggerated opening gambits. This is consistent, no doubt, with the reputation, already referred to, of negotiators from this cultural background utilising hard-nosed tactics. Still, if houses in the street have sold for around €200 000 recently, this house is comparable and the property market has not changed significantly in the interim, there is no point putting this one on the market at €400 000. Opening offers cannot be so high or low as to appear ridiculous, ignorant of the market, unscrupulous or plain greedy. With that proviso, opening high (or low) has the advantages of:

- shifting the goal posts in favour of the party making the offer. The other side may be forced to modify its target point in that direction;
- providing ample space between the opening position and corresponding target point to enable concessions to be made, if necessary;
- revealing information about the other's target point. For example, do they seem shocked and reject the offer out of hand or do they seem essentially nonplussed;
- making the final settlement, when it is reached, seem even more attractive to the other side.[68,69]

A variant of the highest/lowest credible opening move is the 'final offer first' tactic.[70] This involves starting off with one's target point, making it clear that the offer is fair and reasonable and will not be improved upon, and sticking to that position. This ploy has also been called 'Boulwareism' after the eponymous Lemuel Boulware who adopted it as his hallmark when chief labour negotiator at General

Electric in the 1950s. The great danger of course is that the negotiation quickly reaches stalemate with both sides refusing to budge.

Opening proposals should be clearly stated so that Party A is left in no doubt as to what precisely Party B's opening position is. There should be no confusion or uncertainty. Switching perspectives, it is important for those on the receiving end to check the details of what is on offer. Opening positions should also be presented firmly. It is pointless making a high opening bid if it is presented in a weak, apologetic manner. If it is read as 'I want €8000 for my car – but realise that there is no way that I will get it and am prepared to accept substantially less if at all pressed', the seller will probably plummet to the 'bottom-line' in double-quick time.

Going first or second The concern here is whether to get in first with an opening offer, or wait for the other to make the running.

There are advantages and disadvantages attached to each strategy.[71] On balance, Thompson[72] strongly favoured taking the initiative and making the first offer, while Hendon and colleagues argued in favour of letting the opposition declare their position first.[73]

Advantages of opening first include:

- taking the initiative
- forcing the other to rethink their starting point
- putting the other party on the defensive.

On the other hand, disadvantages include:

- misreading the situation and failing to pitch in sufficiently high (or low)
- ending up being the first to make concessions
- being put on the defensive by the other side as they probe the offer.

A telling finding by Galinsky and Mussweiler[74] revealed a sizeable positive correlation between opening proposals and final settlements. Of course, offers can also be made on a conditional basis and Mills[75] pointed to benefits in this approach. For example, 'We would be prepared to let you have that grain for €120 per tonne if you can agree to pay in full within ten days of delivery.' While in win–lose negotiations, beginning in this way might confuse the deal, there are obvious advantages for win–win arrangements.

Making concessions Dawson[76] cautioned never to accept the other side's first offer, even if it seems reasonable. From a competitive negotiating point of view, it can invariably be improved upon. Once parties begin to yield their opening positions and trade in compromise to enable movement to take place across the middle ground, positional bargaining has begun.[77] Being prepared to make concessions is essential. A concession is a change in offer by party A in the direction of party B's interests that reduces the level of benefit accruing to party A. Concessions, therefore, lead to *position loss*: it is usually difficult to go back to a previously surrendered position. Moreover, being forced to move too far, too quickly, can result in *image loss* where the hapless negotiator begins to lose credibility. It has been recommended that bargainers be the first to concede on issues that are minor to them, but force the other to concede on those that are major.[78]

Being able to win concessions from the other party is a powerful weapon in the armoury of those caught up in competitive negotiations. Some of the tactics that can be used have been identified,[79,80] and are outlined in the remainder of this section.

Cultivate a friendly relationship Parties are more likely to be prepared to compromise if they have developed a positive relationship that neither wants to jeopardise. Indeed, buyers have been found to offer higher opening amounts, and sellers to make lower initial demands, when dealing with friends as opposed to strangers.[81] However, being seduced by friendship in this way can also have a down side in that there is a temptation to accept the first vaguely mutually beneficial solution to emerge when a little more persistence may have produced a better deal for both.[82]

Imposing deadlines Here the other side is made to believe that unless it is prepared to accept the offer on the table quickly, that offer will be promptly withdrawn to their disadvantage. Robinson[83] termed this 'the exploding offer' and the temptation is to grab it quickly before it is vaporised. When a more reasoned approach fails, the counter-tactic he proposed is the 'Farpoint Gambit'. This involves making a final acceptance conditional upon other concerns still to be ironed out. By carrying the negotiation beyond the imposed deadline, the power of that deadline is destroyed.

Appearing resolute Perceptions of firmness can be enhanced through de-coupling concessions from perceived weakness by:

- stating the one-off nature of a concession. It is never a good idea to fall into a predictable pattern of concession making;

- showing that the concession is a result of a unique circumstance ('I need the space for new stock');
- combining the concession with a strong move ('I'll lower the price if you take double the amount').

Reducing the other's resistance to making concessions This can be done by using:

- persuasive arguments;
- the promise of benefits (e.g. a trade union may argue that a pay rise will lead to increased productivity);
- reference to objective criteria (the 'book' price of a car; the pay of other professionals, the going rate for the job, etc.);
- an appeal to the disadvantages to the other party were an agreement not reached;
- an ultimatum – unless they are prepared to reconsider, the negotiation is over. This brinkmanship is a high-risk option and should be used with great care;
- face-giving devices that make it easier for the other side to concede without appearing to lose. Face concerns are particularly significant in certain cultures including China;[84]
- threat – nevertheless, this tactic can be counter-productive in the longer run. It inevitably spoils any working relationship with the other side and, even if successful, produces resentment. Research findings reported by Olekalns and Smith[85] clearly showed that threats are associated with less successful outcomes.

Salami slicing The significance of the title is that if you ask someone for a whole salami they will invariably refuse. Ask them for a single slice and they will probably comply. If they comply often enough, you end up with the whole salami.

Logrolling This is trading off pairs of issues that differ in importance to both parties. For example, the purchaser may agree the asking price of the car if the dealer is prepared to service it free for a year (a big savings to the purchaser but at little cost to the dealer).

Good guy/bad guy This tactic can be used in team negotiations where one member is particularly tough and uncompromising, another much more accommodating. If used subtly, accommodating the 'good guy' comes to be seen as the only way of working with the other side. The mindset created is that if we can't do business with the 'good guy', we have no chance.

Sometimes the 'bad guy' can be a third party who has to be placated ('Unless I get €135 for each, my boss will fire me on the spot as soon as he hears').

Fait accompli This is based upon the principle of 'act now and negotiate later'. Workers may come out on strike before negotiations with management get underway. As such, one party takes direct action in advance of the negotiation designed to put the other party on the defensive and make it more likely that they will concede.

In distributive bargaining situations, where each is essentially concerned with getting as much of the cake as possible, it is inevitable that there will be give and take. It is important, though, that concession making is governed by the golden rules of conceding listed in Box 7.6.

Box 7.6 Golden rules when making concessions

Do:

- allow sufficient room, when making an initial offer, to concede without jeopardising the target point;
- trade concessions rather than donate them;
- concede slowly;
- grant small concessions;
- concede in areas that are of less value to you;
- monitor concession making.

Don't:

- give concessions unconditionally – they will probably not be appreciated;
- set inappropriate expectations by starting off with sizeable concessions;
- be the first to make significant concessions;
- concede too early in the bargaining process;
- make concessions without having worked out their value to you and, to the best of your calculations, the other party;
- engage in tit-for-tat concessions. The fact that the other party has dropped its demand by €50 does not mean that you must reciprocate as a matter of course.

Stage 5: reaching settlement

Sensing that a settlement is within reach and moving in to grasp it is an impressive skill in its own right. If snatched at too early, the other party can feel pressured and resist. If delayed too long the opportunity is missed and a further round of even more difficult and protracted bargaining can ensue. At worst, the deal may be lost altogether. A number of central elements have been identified as being crucial to agreeing a settlement[86,87] and these will now be considered. For the most part, however, the advice offered has been based upon experiential rather than empirical evidence.

Cues suggesting agreement One side may begin to tidy up some papers, summarise points and confirm them, look excited, look tired or raise issues to do with implementation. Such cues should be noted as possible indicators from the others that a deal is not far off.

No further concessions Convincing the opposition that a point has been reached beyond which further conceding is not possible, is an important step in reaching agreement. If they feel that there is still a bit more to get, and it has been an uncompromising negotiation, they may not be satisfied until they have it. One difficulty here is that negotiators sometimes hold back a small concession to be conceded as a final inducement to settlement. Dawson[88] explained how negotiators are particularly vulnerable at this point to the temptation of making a final small gesture. One potential shortfall of this strategy is that a reputation can be gained of always having something else to concede if the other side bargains long and hard enough.

Closing the deal When both sides seem to have exhausted their concession making with neither prepared to move further, 'split-the-difference' is sometimes suggested as a basis for agreement. In a sales situation where the buyer apparently can't go beyond €500 while the seller must have at least €550, they sometimes settle for €525. This may seem a straightfoward solution to deadlock in a fairly basic negotiation, such as used in the example, but where issues are more complex it is not always applicable. In addition, the impression of fairness may be more illusory than real. If one side has already conceded a considerable amount and the other little, then the 'difference' is not just what is left. For this reason, negotiators have been cautioned against automatically resorting to this tactic in reaching agreement.[89]

Trial closure is a further technique used in selling to test if the customer is ready to buy. It may take the form of asking, say in a house sale, which child will occupy which bedroom, or if an appliance, whether the extended warranty will be taken up. The implication is that the deal has been done. If the assumption is rejected, it is still possible to backtrack.

As a final move what has been agreed so far can be summarised, concessions that the other party has obtained emphasised, and significant disadvantages were the deal not to proceed highlighted, as a way of successfully reaching agreement.

Positive endings A successful negotiation is one with which all parties should feel that they have benefited. It is important therefore that negotiations end on an upbeat note: that none feel they have lost out. This is important not only for future contacts but for agreement implementation.

Documenting the agreement Most agreements are formalised in a written contract and are legally binding, although the drafting and signing may take place at a later date. Pursuing disputes through the court, though, is a costly option and to be avoided. It is important, therefore, that all parties are clear on precisely what has been agreed. Going over the arrangements that have been hammered out making sure that interpretations are shared and differences of opinion resolved, is time well spent. But Fortgang and colleagues[90] also cautioned against getting engrossed in the fine print of the contract to the neglect of the spirit of the agreement. One of the difficulties with the Belfast Agreement, intended to usher in a new political dispensation for Northern Ireland, was that some political parties argued that they had fulfilled their commitments as defined strictly by the letter of the Agreement. Others argued that those same politicians were still in breach of the broader spirit of that Agreement, in respect of a commitment to wholly democratic and peaceful means of bringing about change.

Furthermore, Goman[91] recounted the story of a move by Ford to buy the production operation of Ferrari. Senior management from Ford visited Enzo Ferrari and an agreement was reached, sealed by a handshake. Shortly after, a team of lawyers and accountants descended on Ferrari intent upon fixing the fine detail. Enzo Ferrari felt that a gentleman's agreement had already been made and took exception. The deal was abandoned. While it is important, therefore, to give careful thought to the fine detail of the settlement, this should be done within the broader context of what was agreed.

Implementation considerations Ultimately, an agreement is only as good as its implementation. Good settlements therefore explicitly address these issues by considering difficulties that may be encountered at this stage and how these should be resolved if they do arise. Most contracts include grievance and arbitration elements, but these should only be invoked as a last resort.[92]

Negotiation skills

Negotiating is a complex activity that draws upon a range of associated skills and sub-skills.[93,94] Furthermore, for Koh,[95] all effective negotiators must have these at their disposal: '... a good negotiator, whether an Indian, an American, a Canadian, English, Gahnian, or whoever, is a person with certain definable skills ...'. There is also considerable agreement about what good negotiators should do. While some of this information is experiential and anecdotal, there is also a growing body of supporting research evidence available.[96,97]

Controlling emotion The most effective negotiators are those who are rational and can think logically. Getting dragged into a heated war of words with the opposition seldom leads to a mutually beneficial outcome. For Adler *et al.*[98] fear and anger are the two most intense negative emotions to which negotiators are prone. Building trust helps to counteract fear and will be returned to. As far as the anger is concerned, Rackham[99] identified two tactics that often have this unintentional effect and should be avoided.

1. *Irritators*. These are words or phrases used by one side which cause annoyance to the other. Examples of irritators include 'generous offer', 'fair and equitable arrangement', 'reasonable' (these imply that the other side is ungenerous, unfair or unreasonable). Skilled negotiators use significantly fewer of these. While few negotiators will directly insult or antagonise the other side, by using irritators the unintended net effect can be the same.
2. *Defend/attack spirals*. This occurs when Side A attacks the other using emotional terms ('It's your fault that these difficulties arose in the first place' 'Don't try to blame us for that') provoking Side B

to defend in similar vein. This, of course, is viewed in turn as an attack by Side A and defended likewise – and so the spiral escalates. Such events are not at all helpful and, not surprisingly, skilled negotiators are significantly less likely to become involved in this practice.

Building trust Trust is at the heart of relationships, and negotiation is no exception. It can be thought of as 'the extent to which a person is confident in, and willing to act on the basis of, the words, actions, and decisions of another'.[100] Where present, negotiations are enhanced. Sharing feelings and concerns with the other party is one way of developing trust, hence the importance of self-disclosure. Perhaps surprisingly, skilled negotiators tend to be more disclosing of feelings and emotions as the negotiation unfolds, compared with their less skilled counterparts.[101] In particular, the former are more likely to use a 'feelings commentary' by revealing their affective states about what is happening. Such feelings may be real or mentioned for effect, but this openness serves to reassure the other party that motives and intentions are explicit and above board.

Being able to place yourself in the position of the other, empathise with them in this way, and let them know your level of appreciation of their circumstances and aspirations, is also a positive feature of effective negotiators.[102]

Exchanging information Quality outcomes, especially in co-operative negotiations, depend upon both sides having a high-resolution picture of the other's needs, preferences and circumstances. In a competitive situation of distributive bargaining, of course, there may be areas of strategic concealment. Either way, having expertise in extracting detail is a key feature of good negotiators,[103] and being adept at questioning a key ability. Apart from gathering information, those who ask the questions are able to control the focus and flow of the interaction. The other side (Party B) is put on the back foot and forced to devote its attention to providing answers. This, in turn, gives Party A more thinking space to reflect upon what is happening.

Finally, questions can act as an alternative to an overt statement of disagreement. Compare the following:

A: 'No. We find this totally unacceptable.'
B: 'What do you imagine our members' reaction would be were we to accept this proposal?'

The response in B is much less confrontational and more likely to produce a reasoned response.

Promoting clarity Negotiations often falter and stall simply through confusion and misunderstanding. In the fog of battle, contributions can be misconstrued and positions misrepresented. It is therefore important to ensure that both sides are clear on what is taking place. Several tactics are facilitative in this regard.

1. *Behaviour labelling.* Skilled negotiators more often give notice of their intention in speaking, by labelling it. Instead of just asking 'How many units are there?' they preface this with: 'Can I ask you a *question* – how many units are there?' Other examples of behaviour labels include: 'If I could make a *suggestion* ...' and 'Could we *compromise* here by ...'. This process of labelling is advantageous in that it:

   - focuses attention on the behaviour to follow
   - puts social pressure on the other side to respond accordingly
   - slows the pace of negotiation
   - allows both sides to focus upon what will follow
   - reduces ambiguity by making clear what the behaviour will be
   - introduces rationality into the encounter.

   However, poorer negotiators are more likely to label instances of negativity, such as 'I disagree with that because ...'. By comparison, skilled negotiators, under these circumstances, give reasons why they cannot concur. These reasons are in themselves expressions of disagreement, but they avoid the need to state so overtly.

2. *Testing understanding and summarising.* Skilled negotiators often use these behaviours to facilitate the eventual successful implementation of any decisions. The less skilled tend to ignore ambiguous points rather than confront them directly – their main concern is often with immediate agreement, even if this is likely to raise problems at the implementation stage. Using *reflective statements* is one way to check for immediate understanding. Examples of reflections in negotiating include: 'So your main worry here is ...' 'This aspect seems particularly important for you ...' 'What you are saying is that this option is simply not acceptable.'

Summaries in the form of compact statements at the end of discussion, check that both sides concur about exactly what has been said and agreed.

Using reasoned argument In negotiations, the ability to sustain an image of rationality through logical argument and informed decision-making pays dividends. Two common tactics to be avoided here are the following:[104]

1. *Retaliatory counter proposals.* A mistake made by inexperienced negotiators is to respond to a proposal with an immediate counter proposal, for example:
   A: 'Our best price is €10 per unit providing we are your sole supplier for the next 12 months.'
   B: 'We cannot accept delivery costs and must have a buy-back clause.'
   Skilled negotiators are less inclined to succumb to this dysfunctional practice. Drawbacks are that such counter-proposals:
   - are put forward at a time when the other side is least receptive;
   - complicate the negotiation by introducing a new issue or option before the previous one has been dealt with;
   - are likely to be perceived as a blocking tactic or disagreement rather than a genuine proposal *per se.*
2. *Argument dilution.* Skilled negotiators give fewer reasons to back up their proposals. The more reasons given to justify an argument, the more likely it is that the other side will find (and exploit) weaknesses in one of them. Skilled negotiators have been found to advance a single reason insistently and only if they begin to lose ground do they introduce a subsidiary argument.[105]

Overview

Conflict in some form seems to be part of organisational life. The process of management invariably involves keeping this disharmony at a level where it does not intrude in dysfunctional ways into the smooth running of the operation. Negotiating is one approach to accomplishing this task and managers are unlikely to be successful if they are weak in this area. Negotiating is typically seen in classic pose as an essentially antagonistic activity in which those engaged play the roles of opponents or enemies, each out to defeat the other. But it does not have to be this way. In most negotiating situations there is scope for co-operation to secure a win–win outcome for the benefit of all.

In any event, the strategy adopted has implications for the shape of the negotiation and the characteristic stages that it passes through. Generally the process should begin with planning and preparing and move through phases of opening, exploring issues, bargaining and finally reaching settlement. The ultimate success of this outcome is dependent on the level of skill of the participants. Skilled negotiators tend to be able to control emotion, build trust, gather and share information effectively, introduce clarity into the proceedings, and operate through rationality and the weight of logical argument. In so doing, they engage in labelling behaviour, testing understanding, summarising, seeking information and disclosing their feelings and intentions (real or otherwise). They avoid the use of irritators, defend/attack spirals and immediate counter-proposals.

8 Will they buy it? Why managers must be able to sell

Introduction

The famous Scottish novelist Robert Louis Stevenson once said: 'Everyone lives by selling something'. This is indeed very true, but, of course, especially so in the world of business. In fact, in the USA alone, over 11 million people are involved[1] in jobs that involve direct selling, which is defined as 'face-to-face selling away from a fixed retail location'.[2] However, for all managers it is also necessary to 'sell' to others, whether what is being sold is in the form of an idea, or something more tangible such as a service level inter-departmental agreement. No business will survive without the ability of its key people to sell. As noted by O'Hair *et al.*[3] 'Selling products, services, or ideas occupies a great deal of time in organizational life.' At times we specifically have to sell *ourselves* – the obvious example being at selection interviews (see Chapter 13). However, in all instances where we are making a presentation (or sales 'pitch') others will evaluate us as well as what we are promoting – in other words they will 'buy' or reject us.[4] Exercise 8.1 contains a Selling Inventory that measures the extent to which you are likely to be a skilled salesperson. You should complete this now.

Exercise 8.1 Selling inventory

Please read each sentence carefully and select the number that best represents your communicative response with other people, using the following 1–5 scale:

5 = Almost always
4 = Often
3 = Sometimes
2 = Rarely
1 = Almost never

Exercise 8.1 ***continued***

1. I find it hard to put myself in another person's shoes so that I can understand how they think and feel. ____
2. I am very confident when I interact with others. ____
3. I am the type of person who wants to know everything about any topic I have to formally talk about to others. ____
4. I can only be myself and will not change my behaviour to adapt to the style of different people. ____
5. People regard me as a very trustworthy person of high integrity. ____
6. I am not a very organised type of person. ____
7. I am not very good at opening conversations with strangers. ____
8. If I want to get something from someone I will persevere with my efforts for as long as it takes. ____
9. If I am rejected by others I take it very much to heart and it upsets me. ____
10. I observe the verbal and nonverbal behaviour of others closely during interpersonal encounters. ____
11. I am very enthusiastic in the way I interact with others. ____
12. I am not a very good listener. ____
13. When I want something from someone I am very persuasive in my attempts to get it. ____
14. I am very good at using questions to control interactions. ____
15. I am not a very creative type of person. ____
16. If I do not succeed in an interaction with another person I use this as a learning opportunity and change my approach accordingly in future interactions. ____
17. I take a lot of care with my dress and appearance so that I always look my best. ____
18. I am a spontaneous individual and do not monitor my behaviour closely during social interaction. ____
19. I like to mull over decisions and am not happy if I have to make quick decisions. ____
20. People regard me as a very likeable individual. ____
21. I sometimes have a lot of trouble in bringing an interaction to a close. ____
22. I do not usually express my views very strongly in case other people would see me as 'pushy'. ____

Exercise 8.1 ***continued***

23. If I want something from someone I find it difficult to just come right out and ask for it. ___
24. I believe that most people subconsciously like to be persuaded as they make a decision. ___
25. I love the 'cut and thrust' of interpersonal encounters in the business world. ___

Total ___

The scoring key for this is given in Exercise 8.4 at the end of the chapter.

Managers therefore have to demonstrate good sales skills in many situations. Example include selling a new system to superiors, selling one's own ideas to peers, selling management decisions to subordinates, and selling the importance of change to staff at times of innovation. The process of selling is therefore a more specialised form of influencing and persuading[5] (see Chapter 3 for a fuller discussion of persuasion). Indeed, the key abilities of effective salespeople, as identified in a number of studies,[6–10] all apply to the role of management in general (Box 8.1). It is therefore no surprise to learn that good managers can 'sell'.

Selling is the process of persuading others that what you are offering is what they need and will be of benefit to them. In many situations this can be quite a difficult task, so that, as pointed out by McCarthy and Hatcher,[11] 'Selling your ideas, your goods, or your services is one of the most challenging and potentially creative communication situations you may ever be in.' This means that sales attempts have to be carefully planned and skilfully executed. In this regard it is important to be aware of a widely employed sales model[12] which, as illustrated in Figure 8.1, has six main processes or steps: opening the sale, establishing needs, presenting, overcoming objections, giving additional sales suggestions and closing the sale.

Although this is presented as a 'staircase' model, it should be realised that in practice the sales process does not always rigidly follow this sequence. For example, a sale may be clinched just after the opening phase if the buyer is willing and anxious to make a purchase, objections may arise at any stage of the sale and not just after the presentation, hidden needs may be uncovered as a result of objections, and so on.

Box 8.1 Key selling abilities

- Ability to learn
- Adaptability with different people
- Capacity to handle rejection
- Confidence
- Creativity
- Empathy/rapport building
- Enthusiasm/motivation
- Flexibility with different people
- Integrity and trustworthiness
- Knowledge and expertise
- Likeability
- Observation and listening skill
- Organisational skill
- Perseverance
- Persuasiveness
- Questioning skill – especially in relation to client needs.

Figure 8.1 The sales model

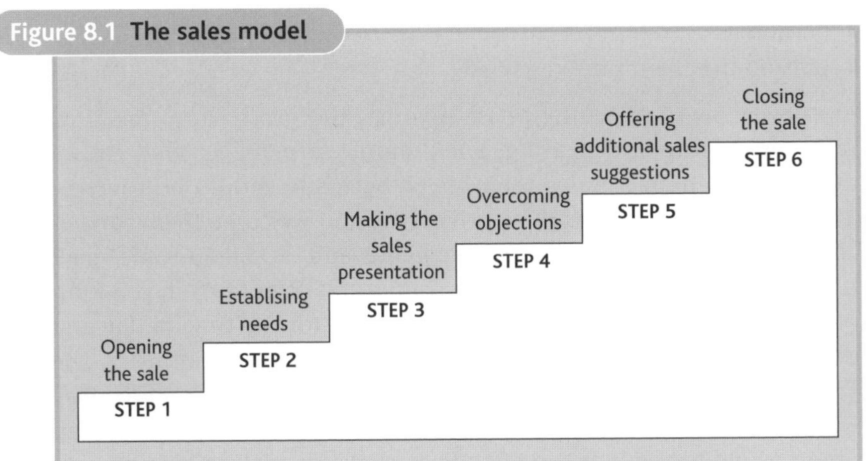

However, selling often does follow the sequence as portrayed in Figure 8.1, and so the staircase model serves as a useful template with which to analyse the stages involved. The operational use of this model can best be examined by considering each of the steps separately.

Step 1: opening the sale

This is an important stage of any interaction. Psychologists have clearly shown that the first (primacy effect) and last (recency effect) events in any sequence tend to be best remembered.[13] This means that the opening and closing stages of any sales attempt offer greater opportunities to make an impact upon others. The importance of effective opening is recognised in phrases such as 'Well begun is half done'; 'You don't get a second chance to make a first impression' and 'Start off as you mean to go on.' The initial perceptions that the target forms of the salesperson will influence the likelihood of success. How the individual is dressed, the posture adopted, facial expressions used and all the other forms of body language employed will affect judgements made on dimensions such as trust and confidence, which in turn impact upon buying decisions. In particular, trust is a key component of any sales situation, since people are very unlikely to buy from those they judge to be untrustworthy. Trust, in turn, is determined[14] by whether the client perceives the salesperson to be:

- honest and candid
- dependable and reliable
- competent
- likeable
- putting the client's interests first.

In sales terms the opening phase involves the processes of meeting, greeting, seating and treating. For example, a manager who calls a meeting at which a 'sales pitch' is to be made should be there in advance to *meet* others as they arrive, *greet* and welcome them (preferably using first names), smile, shake hands and engage in some small talk, have suitable and comfortable *seating* and offer *treats* in the form of tea/coffee/drinks/sustenance as appropriate for the time of day and occasion. Time spent at the opening phase is a good investment. The greeting and parting rituals are very important to human discourse. From an early age children are taught how to meet and part from others – told to say hello and goodbye, shake hands, smile and wave. These behaviours therefore become imprinted on us and we expect them. Those who use them effectively make a positive (often subconscious) impression upon us. We therefore ignore these social niceties at our peril. In the sales situation, the functional and social aspects are inextricably linked. The task of completing a successful sale is made much easier by the smooth lubricant of good interpersonal skills.

Making a positive opening impression is part of overall relationship building. Effective salespeople are enthusiastic and motivated individuals.[15,16] They are also rated highly in terms of sociability and likeability – this is a pre-requisite to successful social persuasion. In their book *In Search of Excellence* Tom Peters and Robert Waterman discussed one way in which the 'likability' tactic was used by Joe Girard, the top car salesman in the USA for 11 years running. Every month he sent out over 13 000 cards to his customers, wishing them, for example, Happy George Washington's Day in February or Happy St Patrick's Day in March. The front of each card simply read 'I LIKE YOU'. This tactic worked. The customers loved the cards, and by association, Joe, who in a typical year sold twice as many units as whoever came second. We also like people who are similar to us. It has been shown[17] that clients are more likely to buy from a salesperson they perceive to be similar to them in relation to factors such as age, politics, religion, interests, practices and habits. Salespeople, in turn, can build rapport by searching for, and focussing upon, similarities with clients at an early stage of the encounter.

After the initial 'social' stage of opening, there is the process of motivating others in preparation to receive your message. This involves gaining their attention and arousing interest in what you are about to say. The methods used to achieve this with larger groups (see Chapter 6) differ from those appropriate when dealing with one or two others. In both situations however, it is useful to mention a *tentative benefit* early in the encounter. For instance, the authors of this book were invited by the Chief Executive of a large organisation to make a sales pitch at a board meeting of the senior management team to run an audit of communications. Our opening gambit was as presented in Box 8.2, where the benefit mentioned very early in the process was that an objective audit by independent consultants was the best way of getting at the reality of what was happening with communications.

At this motivational stage the salesperson should check and probe for receptivity. Is the message being fully accepted – or totally rejected? Are listeners interested? Do some people seem supportive while others are more hostile? Information gleaned at this juncture can facilitate how the sales pitch will progress. It allows decisions to be made about which people to target and in what ways, and which ones may be allies who could be brought into the frame later to help clinch the sale. Approaches for opening a sale are outlined in Box 8.3, together with examples pertinent to the above example of selling an audit of communications.

Box 8.2 Opening phase of a sales pitch for a communication audit

'All of you here today are managers. You all communicate with your staff and you control how communications operate within your Department.

But do staff tell you the truth when they deal with you? How do you know they do?

There is a process called "The Boss's Illusion" which means that subordinates tell their superiors what they think they want to hear. Do you always tell the whole truth to the Chief Executive?

No one wants to be a dead messenger.

Yet if you don't know the real truth about the state of communications how can you remedy deficits and effect improvements? If you have a false diagnosis then the prescribed treatment is not likely to work.

So, how can we get information about what is REALLY happening in terms of communication within Departments.

There is a valid and reliable way of achieving this and it is called a Communications Audit. What an audit does is tell you exactly what is really happening on the ground. When carried out by independent auditors, with guarantees of anonymity for respondents, the audit allows employees to freely express their honest views. This in turn gives you a clear and objective picture of current strengths, weaknesses, blockages, and overall patterns of communication…'

Step 2: establishing needs

Having set the scene, this is the next important stage of the sales process. In the retail sector it has been shown[18] that effective salespeople employ three core tactics, namely they:

1. ascertain client needs and adapt their responses to address these needs
2. help clients to achieve their goals
3. present an image of being likeable.

Thus, the establishment of needs occurs right at the outset of the sales journey. Kossen[19] suggested that salespersons should remember the acronym **FUN** to emphasise that salespeople must **F**irst **U**ncover **N**eeds before making a sales presentation. Human behaviour is driven by motivation, which, in turn, is determined by needs and wants. Once

Box 8.3 Approaches to opening

Compliment The Customer
e.g. 'We know you are all committed managers who recognise the importance of good communications'

Ask A Question Leading In To What You Are Selling
e.g. 'How do you currently measure the effectiveness of your communications?'

Give A Tentative Benefit Of What You Are Selling
e.g. 'A communication audit will enable you to make quite dramatic improvements on present practice'

Emphasise That What You Are Selling Is Up-to-date
e.g. 'We use the most recent approach to auditing, which involves a combination of methods'

Show A Picture/Sample
e.g. Graphs of reductions in absenteeism, increases in staff suggestions, improved productivity etc. following an audit

Show The Acceptability Of Your Product
e.g. 'Large companies, such as WIZZO, AOK, and WHEEKER, all now use audits on an annual basis'

we know what another person desires then we can adapt our sales pitch to emphasise how what we have to offer will fulfil these desires. One of the most common errors made by ineffective salespeople is to attempt to make a sales presentation before identifying the real needs of the client.

A key selling skill is that of asking questions. It has been found[20] that salespeople ask questions in order to:

- establish rapport
- facilitate two-way communication
- gather information about the customer and their situation
- show concern for the customer's needs
- arouse interest in what is being sold
- build trust – perceptions of competence are influenced by apposite questioning.

Questioning skills have been shown[21] to be central at the stage of determining needs. Open-ended questions should be used at the outset to obtain maximum information (e.g. 'Could you tell me about how you presently do X?') followed by more closed-ended questions to check for accuracy (e.g. 'So you obtain some information through that method but you would like more?'). Throughout the stage of needs exploration, listening skills are also very important. In his analysis of the social skills of selling, Poppleton[22] identified the sequence used by demonstrably successful salespeople as that of asking initial questions, listening, then asking further questions, without embarking too early on the sales pitch.

The importance of listening has been demonstrated in a number of research investigations. Thus, Shepherd *et al.*,[23] in a study of 79 salespeople in a Fortune 100 international electronics company, showed that listening skills were central to effective selling. Likewise, Ingram *et al.*,[24] in a survey of 126 experienced salespeople, found that two of the most significant factors contributing to salesperson failure were 'poor listening skills' and 'inability to determine customer needs'. These findings were confirmed by Rosenbaum,[25] who illustrated that a key aspect of sales success was listening beyond immediate stated needs – the most effective salespeople probed deeper to identify all dimensions of these needs, so that they had a fuller understanding of where the customer was 'coming from' (see Chapter 12 for more details on effective listening). In this sense, it is important that the 'felt needs' of customers become 'expressed needs'. This process of engaging as fully as possible with the client throughout the sale has been referred to[26] as 'consultative selling'.

The best-known analysis of human needs is Maslow's oft-cited hierarchy[27] (Figure 8.2). At the bottom of the hierarchy and therefore most important are physiological needs, which are essential for the survival of the individual. Thus, if we are very hungry, cold or thirsty, we are highly motivated to rectify this deprivation and our immediate goal is to seek food, heat or water. If these needs have been satisfied, the next most important are those connected with safety, security and protection from harm. We meet these needs by a whole range of methods including locking our doors at night, purchasing insurance policies or obtaining secure and permanent employment.

At the next level are belongingness and love needs, such as the desire to be liked and accepted, and not to be lonely or isolated. Making and keeping friends, maintaining good relationships at work, joining clubs, getting married and having a family are all ways of satisfying needs at this level. After these are esteem needs which are met through occupational status and other achievements. Finally, there is the ultimate wish for self-actualisation by realising one's true potential.

Figure 8.2 **Maslow's hierarchy of human needs**

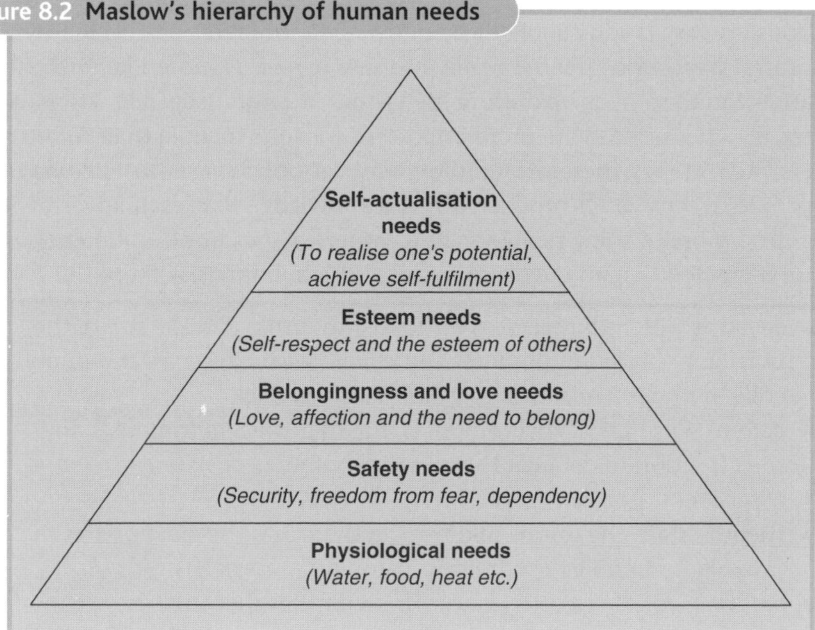

People continually seek new challenges (such as running marathons or pursuing courses in education), need to feel their talents are being fully recognised and utilised and want to realise their maximum potential.

Maslow argued that only when the basic needs are met does the individual become concerned with needs further up the hierarchy. Thus, someone who is starving with hunger will usually seek food at all costs, even risking personal security, and may show a lack of concern for self-esteem by begging. Equally, someone in secure, salaried employment may resign in order to open their own business and become 'self-actualised'. However, people can be manipulated either by promises that important needs will be met, or by threats that these needs will be unfulfilled. Politicians promise to reduce the 'appalling' crime rate and make the streets safe again for the people; insurance salespeople offer peace of mind from horrible events that may occur; and company management threaten a whole range of needs by warning that if workers go on strike the company may close and their jobs will be lost.

In western society many people have achieved most or all of these needs and they become more concerned with wants. I may not *need* a surround-around stereo system, but the fact that I *want* one is more important than the fact that I could live without it. Thus, both needs and wants can be related directly to buying motives. Someone whose house is very cold is liable to be more susceptible to a sales pitch by a central heating company, while a lonely person is more likely to pay attention to someone extolling the virtues of a dating agency. Also, different types of need are more important for some people than for others. Advertisers therefore employ a variety of adverts to encourage people to 'buy' their product – in the knowledge that each advert will appeal more to some people than to others. For example, different ads for a fast food chain encompass those which emphasise the:

- speed at which they serve their food and drink, and the size of the portions – 'A quarterpounder and cheese with large fries and jumbo coke in under 2 minutes' (physiological needs);
- careful selection of their products, the hygienic environment and the attention to detail at their outlets (safety needs);
- low cost of their fare (security needs);
- friendly staff, the fun people who go there and the great parties they provide for families and friends (belongingness needs);
- *pro bono* work for worthy causes and charities that they engage in – so supporting them by giving them your custom also results in a wider social good (esteem needs).

The key buying motives of individuals[28] are summarised in Box 8.4. Again, some of these are more important than others for any particular individual. Thus, 'getting value for money' may be an over-riding motive for a miserly individual or for someone in poor financial straits. Such individuals will be less concerned with 'having the best'. Managers, in making sales presentations, should attempt to ascertain

Box 8.4 The top 10 buying motives

1. Self-preservation
2. Attractiveness enhancement
3. Emulation of the successful
4. Being in style and up-to-date
5. Having the best
6. Being liked or accepted
7. Gaining knowledge and skills
8. Fulfilling a dream
9. Getting value for money
10. Revenge motives ('showing them').

and chart the level of needs, wants and motives of the target audience before moving on to the next part of the sale. This allows the presentation to be tailored more directly to meet the identified needs and style of the prospect.[29]

In essence, the sales encounter should be negotiated in such a way that people feel that they are *buying*, rather than that they are *being sold*, that which is on offer. As Rohrer puts it[30] 'people love to buy but hate to be sold [to] ... It is almost as though buying is a talent reserved for astute, clever persons, while being sold is a sign of weakness.' To buy is to engage actively in the process, whereas to be sold to is to be more passive. If prospects feel they have made the decision to buy they are more likely to feel responsible for the decision and satisfied with the outcome, than if they feel that they have been sold to. This is reflected in the numerous expressions that denote negative connotations to having been sold something unwanted (e.g. 'sold down the river', 'sold a pup', 'sold short').

Another key component of effective selling, as the following two quotations aptly illustrate, is the ability to recognise accurately what people will be prepared to buy.

> I think there is a world market for maybe five computers.
>
> (Thomas Watson, Chairman of IBM, 1943)

> We don't like their sound, and guitar music is on the way out.
>
> (Decca Recording Co. rejecting the Beatles, 1962)

Step 3: making the sales presentation

Having opened the sales encounter and established customer needs, the next step is to present a product or service that will meet the identified needs. Presentation is at the heart of the sales process.[31] Presentation is very important in underlining the advantages of what is on offer to clients. For example, the retailing giant Wal-Mart introduced a boxed computer-and-printer combo in the USA on the day after Thanksgiving – one of the busiest shopping days of the year.[32] They had great hopes for high sales of what was seen as a great value product. However, the central headquarters system showed that sales were very poor indeed, with the exception of one store. A telephone call to this store revealed that the manager had opened one of the boxes and displayed the contents – showing customers they were getting two separate products for one price. A message was sent to all stores to do likewise, and sales soared immediately.

In their analysis of persuading in a business context, Williams and Miller pointed out[33] that 'All too often, people make the mistake of focusing too much on the content of their argument and not enough on how they deliver that message.' As discussed in Chapter 2, *how* something is said is often as important as *what* is said. More detailed information on the skill of presenting is provided in Chapter 6, but in general a well-planned sales presentation has the following three main objectives:

1. *To create and sustain interest and attention in what is being sold.* The presentation should be vivid and attention-gaining. There is an old maxim[34] in the selling world 'Add a picture – Make a sale'. This means that the salesperson encourages the prospect to actively imagine and visualise the depicted scenario. For example a manager may say 'I want you to think carefully for a minute what it means to win this account. Our Department will then be at the top of the table for the second year running. We will win the incentive family holidays in Hawaii. The CEO will also have me in pretty quickly to negotiate the cash bonuses for all of you ...'. A related technique here is to use novelty. The manager of a firm selling poster-size adverts explained[35] how he used a novel technique to grab the attention of executives, who are often turned off by, or suspicious of, sales pitches. Given less than 60 seconds to make his sale, he took a poster-sized ad and folded it until it was very small. He then held it up and said that this size of ad in the local paper would cost £300. He unfolded it once and announced that it would now cost £600. He continued the process, with the increased rates being cited, until the ad was fully revealed and then announced that he would put this size of ad up for them at bus stops for just £40. The technique was highly successful. Executives both liked the presentation, and could see the value of what was being offered.
2. *To ensure client understanding.* A key aspect here is the fluency of the salesperson when making the presentation. Speech hesitations and dysfluencies interfere with the listener's ability to readily comprehend the message being delivered (see Chapter 6). A hesitant delivery is also rated by buyers as being less interesting and less persuasive.[36] Another important feature is that of flexibility. Effective salespersons must adapt their presentations to suit the audience,[37] and be able to switch tactics in mid-stream if necessary. One study[38] found that flexible salespeople endeavoured to fully understand the needs of each individual customer, were able to

change tactics if the initial approach was not working and were keen and able to try out a variety of sales approaches.

3. *To demonstrate how what is being offered can meet and satisfy established client needs*. During sales presentations a key distinction is made between *features* and *benefits*. Features refer to those characteristics inherent in what you are selling. They simply itemise and describe its attributes. Benefits refer to the advantages to the customer of what you are offering. Each of the features described should be converted into a benefit. This is because people are more likely to 'buy' benefits rather than features.[39] For example, they want to know how what is being sold can save time, money or labour, through being faster, easier to use, or more multipurpose.[40] In particular, where the benefits are shown to directly meet the needs (or wants) of clients, they are more likely to be influential. When making presentations, managers should therefore aim to convert features into benefits (see Box 8.5).

Box 8.5 Converting features into benefits: an example

Features	*Benefits*
This camera has a built in lens cover.	This means you don't have the hassle of looking after the cover each time you want to take a picture. Nor is there any danger of losing the cover.
It also has automatic focus.	So you don't need to worry about adjusting for focal length. The camera does the work for you. You just point and shoot and your pictures will always be in focus. No more fuzzy pictures.
It has a built-in automatic flash.	You don't have to bother with the nuisance of having to carry a flash gun. Also, the camera decides from the prevailing light whether the flash is needed – so you get the correct lighting for any situation. No more dark pictures.

The following lines vividly illustrate the power of benefits over features:

> Don't sell me gas lights.
> Sell me attractiveness, soft lights
> and full time service.
>
> Don't sell me gas ranges.
> Sell me modernity, fluffy cakes
> savoury roasts, juicy steaks.
>
> Don't sell me gas water heaters.
> Sell me temperature, sufficiency,
> reliability all day and night.
>
> Don't sell me gas furnaces.
> Sell me heating comfort, cleanliness,
> labour-saving convenience and health.
>
> Don't sell me air conditioners.
> Sell me trouble-free comfort cooling,
> efficiency and simplicity.
>
> Don't sell me industrial fuel.
> Sell me controlled heat, speed, production,
> quality and greater profits.
>
> Don't sell me Btu's.
> Sell me benefits and intangibles to
> convince me that I get more than I pay
> for with gas.
>
> (North Thames Gas Board)

This distinction between features and benefits is important. The 'Benefits or Features' quiz in Exercise 8.2 should therefore be completed at this stage.

Step 4: overcoming objections

Following (or sometimes during) the sales presentation, clients may raise objections or reservations about what is being offered (although objections may also occur at any stage of the sales process). To take but one example, any attempts by management to introduce change are usually met with initial resistance from employees. In Box 8.6 we list the 10 most commonly stated general objections to such change attempts.

Exercise 8.2 Benefits or features?

Indicate (✓) opposite each whether you think it is a feature or a benefit statement.

	Feature	*Benefit*
1. 'This video-recorder has a built-in satellite receiver'	☐	☐
2. 'Your promotion means you now have a key for the executive washroom'	☐	☐
3. 'This risograph makes 100 dry, high quality, copies from an original every minute'	☐	☐
4. 'The new structure will mean one Head for every 10 staff as opposed to the present 19'	☐	☐
5. 'These jackets are fully waterproof'	☐	☐
6. 'You will receive one free tape with each purchase of a pack of five'	☐	☐
7. 'Our security alarm system is monitored 24 hours a day and is linked to your local police station'	☐	☐
8. 'This new machine works at twice the operating capacity of the old version'	☐	☐
9. 'With our computer system you will be automatically connected to the Internet'	☐	☐
10. 'Our system has a full one-year parts and service warranty'	☐	☐

See Box 8.10 for answers

Box 8.6 Top 10 objections to change attempts

1. 'We're not ready for this'
2. 'We have too many other problems at present'
3. 'It is far too expensive/a waste of money'
4. 'Our staff will never agree'
5. 'We've been through all this before'
6. 'Our existing methods work perfectly well'
7. 'We will have to change our whole system of operation'
8. 'That doesn't apply to us'
9. 'We can use the facilities at Head Office'
10. 'We're far too busy to get involved in this'

However, as one analysis[41] of employee reactions to innovation and change pointed out: 'It is also important to accept that not all resistance is unhelpful. Well founded and constructive criticisms often result in improvements to the innovation or its implementation.' In this way, objections can serve a number of useful purposes (see Box 8.7). Indeed, in considering the importance of objections as a core part of the sales process, Williams[42] noted: 'If you think a sales objection is worrying, consider the implications of the prospective buyer who says nothing!'

Box 8.7 Advantages of objections

- *Indicate buyer attention and interest.* If the person is able to make objections this means they have listened to the sales presentation and are at least not apathetic.
- *Offer the opportunity to understand and sympathise with the client.* Showing concern and empathy for the expressed worries of the client can facilitate the process of relationship development.
- *Give insight into buyer attitudes.* The nature of the objection and the way in which it is expressed provide valuable information about what the person making the objection regards as important and what level of needs or wants they have.
- *Allow for the provision of reassurance* and *correction of any misunderstandings.* The objection may be based upon a misconception of what was being sold.
- *Are a useful form of feedback* as to the effectiveness of the sales presentation. For example, if all objections are based upon misconceptions then changes need to be made to the information provided and the way it is delivered.
- *Suggest potential product disadvantages* which need to be dealt with in future presentations.
- *Create further selling opportunities* in overcoming them. Some argue that if there are no objections then the customer is buying rather that the salesperson selling! Indeed where the buyer does not raise any objections the salesperson may do so and proceed to overcome them (e.g. may say 'Some people think that this is rather small, but in fact that is an advantage ...'). This approach has the added advantage of dealing with possible hidden objections which are felt but not overtly expressed.

Effective salespeople have been shown to have more distinctive and highly developed conceptual 'schemas' for handling different selling situations. A schema is a cognitive structure that provides the person with a store of knowledge and information about how to respond in any given context.[43] Schemas can take the form of 'scripts' which have been learned and are readily available for enactment as required. It has been found[44] that 'effective salespeople exhibit more sophisticated sales scripts than do ineffective salespeople ... [and] ... have more distinctive scripts for different selling situations'. In fact, experienced salespeople develop scripts for each part of the sales encounter. Thus, they will have scripts for opening the sale, uncovering needs and making the presentation. Likewise, in relation to successful sales outcomes, they should have developed carefully formulated scripts for dealing with objections.

Some companies no longer use the term 'handling objections' as part of their sales lexicon, and prefer instead to talk about 'responding to feedback'.[45] The argument here is that salespeople must always pay attention to the totality of feedback in terms of needs and feelings of prospects. While this is true, in reality it is dealing effectively with objections that most salespeople worry about. We therefore feel it is important to highlight this aspect of the sales process separately.

When handling objections the techniques used by effective salespeople are to:[46]

1. Listen carefully and let the person finish the objection without interruption.
2. Observe how strongly the person expresses the objection and if in a group context how many others offer verbal or nonverbal support.
3. Check for agreement about the exact nature of the objection and show understanding by verbalising it in summary form (e.g. 'So am I right in saying your main concern is ...?').
4. Provide some credibility to the objection and recognise its importance for the person raising it (e.g. 'I can see that this is a genuine concern and you raise an important issue ...').
5. Have a set of pre-prepared answers to counter possible objections.
6. Answer the objection directly and truthfully giving the minimum amount of information necessary to overcome it. Do not go on at length since this may raise suspicions that you are 'trying too hard'. The objective is to neutralise the objection, not to win a debate.
7. Avoid getting into a lengthy argument on any one objection.
8. Use each objection-handling episode as an opportunity to clinch the sale, or to learn what to change in future presentations.

A distinction can be made between *logical* and *psychological* objections. Logical objections include:

- cost (too expensive)
- negative product characteristics (too difficult to use, too slow, etc.)
- no need for it (if I am a vegetarian I won't want pork chops!)
- dissatisfaction with the source (e.g. 'We have had a lot of problems with *The Dodgy Computer Co.* in the past').

Psychological objections are more difficult to deal with since they may not even be fully recognised by the client. They include:

- a preference for established habits and a high resistance to interference in these
- negative feelings towards anyone who tries to 'sell' anything
- a tendency to resist what is perceived to be a persuasion/dominance attempt
- a general dislike of decision-making *per se*.

While decisions can quickly be made about whether logical objections can be overcome, psychological objections usually take longer to deal with, and require greater use of persuasive techniques (see Chapter 3).

A variety of strategies can be employed to deal with genuine objections (Table 8.1). It should be realised that buyers may be well-motivated towards what is on offer, but want to be fully persuaded – or at least reassured – that their decisions are appropriate. Alternatively, objections may be raised to test how convinced the salesperson is in the quality and appropriateness of the product. Dealing patiently and fully with objections therefore offers the opportunity of reinforcing the buying decision.

Step 5: offering additional sales suggestions

This step is not always necessary or appropriate in every sales encounter. However, in many situations, opportunities arise to make additional linked sales associated with the primary item. This is quite common in retail selling. For example, having purchased a piece of portable audio equipment, the customer at the point of sale may be informed 'It doesn't come with batteries included. Would you like these?' Similarly, shoe shops may offer cream or polish, clothing outlets often suggest accessories, and many retailers link the initial sale to an attempt to get the customer to buy related insurance cover.

Table 8.1 Dealing with objections – the 10 As

Technique	*Purpose*	*Example*
Acceptance inducing	To show the widespread acceptability of what you have to offer	'All the major agencies are using it. WISE & Co have had this system for the past 6 months'
Adapting	To convert the objection into a reason for buying	'It does seem expensive but it lasts twice as long and so saves money in the long run'
Advocating the advantages	To underline the benefits of what you are selling	Here the benefits as opposed to features should be stated or restated
Agreeing and neutralising	To empathise with the buyer while overcoming the objection	'Yes, it involves change and I appreciate that this will cause you some hassle, but it will make life a lot easier for you in the long run'
Anticipating the objection	To overcome likely objections before they are stated	'You may be thinking that this is rather expensive, but...'
Apprehension-raising	To underline the dangers of not buying	'Your competitors will be one step ahead of you if you don't install this system.'
Arguing logically	To appeal to logic	'Let me summarise the main reasons why you should buy this'
Asking for a trial	To encourage the buyer to give it a try	'Will you use it for a month and we can review what you think of it then?'
Attractiveness enhancing	To inspire confidence in the buyer towards the salesperson	Smart dress, good grooming, appropriate use of scents and so on
Authority stating	To inspire confidence in the buyer	'I have been in this field for over 15 years and I know what works'

Another example comes from a meeting of the senior management team in one of our consultancies with a large corporation. Here the Communications Manager, having persuaded his colleagues and the chief executive of the advantages of setting up an internal communication project team, proceeded to successfully sell the linked idea of having the chairperson of the team appointed from junior management.

It is important, however, not to push things too far at this stage. It is the main sale that is the key. If the linked sale might in any way jeopardise this, then it should not be attempted or should be quickly and gracefully abandoned. For example, it can be very off-putting to be met with a hard sale for unwanted insurance (from a salesperson on a large bonus to sell such policies), having just spent quite a lot of money on the initial product. This can leave an overall negative impression of the salesperson, or indeed the business as a whole.

One more subtle technique that is often used by salespeople is to offer a 'free' follow-up as a form of after-sales service (e.g. 'I'll call in next month just to check that everything is OK'). This then provides an opportunity to make additional sales suggestions on a later occasion, and so helps to avoid creating the impression of being a high-pressure salesperson.

Step 6: closing the sale

The 'close' is the process wherein the salesperson motivates the client to make an affirmative decision regarding purchase and proceeds to terminate the encounter in a smooth, friendly fashion – thereby facilitating future interactions. This is perhaps the most important step in the selling process, yet it is the one that often causes the most difficulties.[47] Some of the key problems faced in closing a sale are shown in Box 8.8. It should be realised that the close is an integral part of the process of sale and not divorced from it.

The salesperson needs to be aware of – and act upon – buying signals. These include:

- Questions such as 'When would this be available?'
- Statements like 'That sounds very useful'
- Nonverbal responses, such as agreeing nods, smiles and receptive facial expressions

Box 8.8 Main closing difficulties

- Lack of confidence in asking directly for a commitment
- Not wishing to appear 'pushy'
- Fear of rejection of sales suggestions (and by implication oneself)
- Accepting the first 'no' without persevering
- Inability to recognise and act upon buying signals
- Buyer not ready to close because
  - needs have not been fully established or met
  - the presentation was not convincing
  - objections have not been adequately dealt with
  - s/he is over-talkative and cannot make a decision.

- Physical actions, including handling the product possessively or testing it out (e.g. trying on a dress or using a new computer package).

In relation to the latter response, a skilful jeweller trying to sell a bracelet to a female will usually ask her to wear it and then compliment her on how well it looks and how much it suits her. Similarly, a salesperson attempting to sell a piece of equipment will encourage the customer to use it while simultaneously highlighting its benefits. This is why car dealers encourage prospective buyers to take a test drive.

As discussed in the previous chapter, trial closures are useful in sales negotiations. The salesperson can expedite closure by using what are known as 'assumptive questions'. Here the assumption is made that the buyer has decided and the question focuses on the formal close. Examples include 'How many do you want?' 'Would you like it wrapped?' as well as what are called dual positive assumptions, such as: 'Do you want to pay by cash or credit card?' 'Would you prefer the blue or the red?' When used skilfully these questions place subtle pressure on the client to agree to the sale.

The close is important in that it offers a final opportunity to reinforce and reward the buyer's decision.[48] All changes cause some degree of stress. When people make significant change decisions they therefore experience doubts and anxiety, or what psychologists have termed *cognitive dissonance*,[49] about whether they have decided correctly. Where the investment in time and cost is high, the more important the decision becomes, and so the greater the dissonance is likely to be. Cognitive dissonance eventually leads to one of two outcomes.

People may either decide that they took the wrong decision and revert to their former behaviour, or alternatively convince themselves that the new decision was correct and so embrace it. For effective sales, targets must be convinced in the long term that they have made the correct choice. Dissonance can be reduced by the salesperson providing reassurance and support, to ensure that the person stays committed to the buying decision and does not resolve the dissonance by abandoning the change and resorting to the original behaviour. Motivational exhortations[50] such as 'Your staff will be delighted when they hear about this'; 'You will wonder why it took you so long to get this'; or 'You have made an excellent choice', are all examples of dissonance-reducing interventions. The latter type of exhortation, which affirms and compliments the decision made, also serves to portray the encounter as one in which the client has made the active decision to *buy*, rather than one in which they have passively *been sold to*.

Overview

Selling is a complex process that involves a combination of skills.[51] The success of salespeople depends upon a complex myriad of variables, such as the personality of salesperson and customer, the product being offered and its appeal to the prospect, the sales experience and technical knowledge of the salesperson and so on. But one thing that is clear is that relational communication is at the heart of the process. The development of a conducive personal relationship with customers has been shown[52,53] to be central to effective selling. In terms of interactive style, buyers prefer sellers who are trustworthy (dependable and honest), task-oriented (main focus on the business in hand rather than on unrelated small talk) and composed (comfortable and relaxed) in their approach.[54–56] At the same time, they also wish to be treated with warmth and respect, and favour a co-operative to a competitive approach by the salesperson. A 'soft' sell is preferable to a 'hard' sell.

Managers do not have to earn their living as salespeople, but they do need to be able to sell. They have to convince their superiors, peers and subordinates of the benefits of courses of action they propose. They have to persuade all of these 'customers' to 'buy' what they are recommending. The importance of good sales skills is recognised at the highest levels of business. As one review[57] expressed it: 'you will now hear chief executives talk about their role in the selling of products, services, ideas and even the company'. In making such sales attempts, a knowledge of the process and techniques of selling is very useful. The sequential structure outlined in this chapter of opening, establishing needs, presenting that which will meet these needs, overcoming objections, making linked sales suggestions and closing, offers a template for action. These can be linked to Monroe's Motivated Sequence, which presents a pattern for selling ideas in an organisational context.[58] This has been summarised in a useful point format,[59] as shown in Box 8.9.

Exercise 8.3 provides a checklist, which can be employed before attempting to make a sale.

The skills and techniques highlighted in this chapter within each stage of the sales process are useful in the many contexts where managers have to influence and persuade others. Managers should bear these points in mind as they employ the skills covered in this chapter.

Box 8.9 Monroe's Motivated Sequence

Step 1: Gaining attention
Arousing listener interest in the topic
Focusing the listener's attention on the message

Step 2: Showing the need – describing the problem
Explaining what is wrong with the current situation
Clarifying the problems with examples
Showing the extent and seriousness of need
Relating the problem directly to the listener

Step 3: Satisfying the need – presenting the solution
Stating the proposed changes from the present
Explaining the mechanics of the solution
Showing how the solution solves the problem
Showing that the proposal is workable
Answering objections to the proposal

Step 4: Visualising the results
Describing future benefits if the plan is adopted
Describing future consequences if the plan is not adopted
Combining both positive and negative projections

Step 5: Requesting action or approval
Describing specific actions for listeners to take
Asking for commitment from the listeners

Box 8.10 Answers to exercise 8.2

They are *all features*. Each can be converted to a *benefit statement* and indeed the reader may already have done so when reading them. However, no benefits are *stated* in any of the items. In sales contexts the benefits should be clearly laid out for the customer. Thus, the *benefits* in each item are highlighted in the following statements.

1. 'This *saves you money* and is *much more convenient*. You do not have the expense of buying a separate satellite receiver, nor the inconvenience of finding space for two separate pieces of electrical equipment – the combined one is more compact and less cluttered.'
2. 'This gives you *convenient access to a scarce and desired resource*. It also gives you *higher status* than most of your colleagues.'
3. 'The speed of this machine *saves you considerable time* and gives you a much *higher quality product*.'
4. '*Access to the Head will be easier* and *your chances of promotion are greater*.'
5. '*You do not have to worry about the weather* since you *will stay dry should it rain* – no need to bother with an overcoat.'
6. 'This is a *direct saving for you of* €4 on each pack of five.'
7. 'This means that you *have no worries when you are away from the premises*. We *look after things for you* so *you have complete peace of mind*. If anyone tries to break in *we are there to protect your property at all times*.'
8. 'This *saves you both time* and *money*.'
9. 'It gives you all of the *advantages of the Web* (including e-mail) *without any further costly equipment* or connections.'
10. 'This means you have complete *peace of mind* and *security*.'

Exercise 8.3 Planning the sale

Think of a situation that you will have to deal with in the near future in which you will need to persuade others to actively 'buy' something that you will be advocating. Now consider each of the following questions.

- What will be the key techniques you will use at the *opening* stage?

Exercise 8.3 ***continued***

- How will you establish fully the *needs* of those whom you will have to persuade?
- In what way can you tailor your *presentation* to clearly meet these needs?
- Exactly what *objections* are you likely to face and how will you handle each of these?
- If your sale is successful, is there an opportunity for a *linked sale*?
- How will you *close* the sale to reward the buying behaviour and ensure that any cognitive dissonance is reduced?

Exercise 8.4 Scoring the selling inventory

1. Reverse the scores for items 1, 4, 6, 7, 9, 12, 15, 18, 19, 21, 22, 23. Thus, a score of 1 becomes 5, 2 becomes 4, 3 remains the same, 4 becomes 2, and 5 becomes 1 for these items.
2. Now add up all of the scores for each item to obtain your total score.

Interpretation of selling inventory scores

115–125	You have most of the qualities of a highly skilled salesperson, and will be able to use the key sales tactics in interpersonal encounters.
100–114	You are a skilled salesperson, and will be able to use many of the key sales tactics in interpersonal encounters. With a little effort, you can perfect these techniques.
75–99	You are above average in terms of selling skills, but need to work on particular aspects of your style to improve your ability.
50–74	You are below average in terms of selling skills, and need to work hard on particular aspects of your style to improve your ability.
30–49	You are well below average in terms of selling skills, and need to work very hard on particular aspects of your style to improve your ability.
Under 30	You are usually unsuccessful in terms of selling skills and will need to improve considerably to be successful.

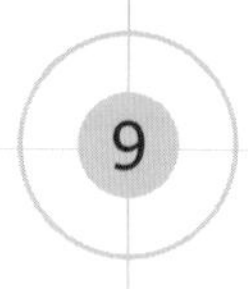

9 Calling all organisations: the business of the telephone

Introduction

One prominent aspect of recent organisational discourse has been the extended discussion about new technologies, and how and in what ways these have impacted upon communication patterns and practices. The effects of the internet and its electronic siblings, intranet and e-mail, have been widely debated, resulting in a voluminous and ever-expanding literature in this field.[1] Yet, the founding father of the technological revolution, the telephone, has received comparatively little attention. However, as noted by Bishop:[2] 'Although increasingly we are using alternative technologies to communicate, long distance, with each other, the telephone still plays a large part in every manager's life.' As we will demonstrate in this chapter, organisations need to be cognisant of the pivotal communications role played by the telephone.

The actual term 'telephone' is derived from the Greek words for far (tele) and voice (phone). It had long been the general consensus that it was invented by Alexander Graham Bell, a Scotsman who had emigrated to America and who had transmitted the first spoken sentence by telephone in Boston in 1876. However, in 2002 the US Congress formally recognised an impoverished Italian immigrant from Florence, Antonio Meucci, as the true inventor of the telephone.[3] Meucci gave a demonstration of his invention in New York in 1860, some 16 years prior to Bell's patenting of the device, for which he had the benefit of and access to Meucci's materials, as they shared a laboratory. Meucci could not afford the $250 required for a definitive patent, so had taken out a renewable notice of an impending patent in 1871 for his 'talking telegraph', but was unable to pay the $10 to renew it. When Bell took out his patent in 1876, he was sued for fraud by Meucci, who died before the legal action could be heard.

Since these early days of the invention, this now taken-for-granted device has gradually yet inexorably become part of our daily lives. For example just a few years after Bell's patent, eloquent poems were being penned about it, such as the following:

> The far is near. Our feeblest whispers fly,
> Where cannon falter, thunders faint and die.
> Your little song the telephone can float
> As free of fetters as a bluebird's note,
> Quick as a prayer ascending into Heaven.
> Quick as the answer, 'all is forgiven'
> The Lightning writes it, God's electric clerk;
> The engine bears it, buckling to the work
> Till miles are minutes and the minutes breaths...
> ('The Wonders of Forty Years': Benjamin Franklin Taylor, 1886)

This chapter provides background information regarding the development of the telephone as a communication device, examines the norms of telephone behaviour and highlights the key differences between telephone and face-to-face communication. It also outlines the main problems associated with telephone communications, and discusses techniques that can be employed to circumvent these.

The spread of the telephone

Shortly after its invention, the potential development of this innovation was summarised as follows:

> This 'telephone' has too many shortcomings to be seriously considered as a means of communication. The device is inherently of no value to us. (Western Union internal memo, 1876)
>
> 'My department is in possession of full knowledge of the details of the invention, and the possible use of the telephone is limited.' (Engineer-in-chief of the British Post Office, 1877)

So much for the skills of scientists as niche marketers.

Two years after he patented the invention, Bell demonstrated the telephone to Queen Victoria who was so taken with it that she immediately had a system installed at Osborne House. At that time the cost of the telephone for a household in the UK was £20 per year which was then a servant's annual wage. In real terms, the cost has reduced considerably over the years. For example, in 1934 the price of a three-minute cheap rate call from London to Edinburgh was one shilling (5p) which was equivalent to the cost of sending eight letters. In 1997 the charge for this call was 20p, the cost of postage for one letter. Likewise, in the USA a long distance call from New York to Chicago in 1892 cost $5 for the first three minutes, while a similar length call from New York to San Francisco in 1915 was $20.70. The first long distance calls from New York to London in 1927 were charged at $75 for the first three minutes. All of these rates are comparatively very much higher than at present.

The telephone system of communication has developed rapidly. In 1891 a telephone link between the UK and France was established; in 1927 the New York–London radio telephone service began; a similar radio service between New York and Tokyo was introduced in 1934; and in 1962 the first telecommunications satellite (Telstar) was launched. By 1975 there were 20 million telephones in use in the UK, with some 5 million of these in London. In the developed world, most private homes now have more than one telephone, many of which are cordless or include a 'handsfree' facility, and mobile phones are commonplace. Users are no longer 'tied up' to a base unit, and this in turn has helped to encourage its phenomenal growth.

The percentage of households with a telephone in the UK increased[4] from 42 per cent in 1972 to 92 per cent in 1992. Again in the UK, in 1985 there were only 25 000 mobile phone users, but by 1995 this number had risen to over 5 million, and by 2003 the figure had reached 50 million users.[5,6] The miniaturisation of mobile phones, coupled with the use of satellites as well as terrestrial transmitters, have enhanced their popularity – it is not surprising that this has been the fastest growing part of the telecommunications sector.[7] As expressed by Plant[8] during the 1990s the mobile phone 'leapt from obscurity towards ubiquity'. By 2002 the number of mobile phone users worldwide had reached the 1.4 billion mark, as compare to 1.1 billion fixed line telephones.[9] As Smith[10] observed 'Soon, only babies, toddlers and the very elderly (although I am not so sure about them) will be without a mobile.' In fact, children begin to use the telephone at around the age of two years, and by the age of five they have begun to master the nuances of this mediated form of communication.[11]

Billions of calls and text messages fly through the ether every year. In relation to the latter, in Japan teenagers have become known as *oya yubi sedai* (the thumb tribe). Evolutionary theorists speculate that texting will eventually result in changes to the shape of the hand, with increased dexterity of the thumb. Just as the fixed-line telephone arrived when it was required for the development of great cities and increased trade, so too the mobile telephone has both met the needs of a generation on the move and encouraged such mobility. Huge volumes of people travel across continents, knowing that access to family, friends and businesses is constantly available via their little electronic friend. Few people now travel any distance without their mobile. In addition, WAP (Wireless Application Protocol) technology allows access to the internet on mobiles, further developing the information-giving potential of this communication network. Some businesses, especially in the financial sectors of insurance and banking, have further experimented with videophone systems, where customers access staff via their television sets using cable TV. However the results to date have not been very positive[12] with customers giving the message that they prefer actual face-to-face contact when making financial decisions.

Paradoxically, the increased availability of telecommunications has had the effect of encouraging many people to seek shelter from the electronic storm. The exponential growth in use of voice-mail, mobile phones, pagers, faxes, e-mail, and so on, has heightened the danger of what has been variously termed 'techno stress', 'information fatigue syndrome', 'future shock' or 'multiphrenia'. In other words, we become overloaded and overwhelmed with the wide range and volume of communication information being sent to us. Not surprisingly, some people then take steps to protect themselves. One example of restricted access is shown in the fact[13] that the percentage of ex-directory numbers among residential telephone owners in the UK rose from 24 per cent in 1991 to 37 per cent in 1998. As would be expected, this trend was greatest in cities, where the level of such communications tends to be highest, so that 56 per cent of residential telephone users in London and 49 per cent in Birmingham elected to stay out of the book in 1998.

The impact of the telephone

In the business context it is impossible to imagine life without the telephone. The Direct Marketing Association has estimated that some 80 per cent of all financial transactions are carried out by telephone. Telecommunications is currently a trillion dollar business (i.e. one thousand billion dollars). This has been encouraged by the growth in freephone usage, a system pioneered by the telecommunications company AT&T in 1967. In that year Americans made a total of seven million toll-free calls. By 1997 AT&T alone carried 20 billion such calls.[14]

This growth is likely to continue. The Henley Centre's '*Telecultures Futures*' report found that customers view a freephone provision as a sign that a company is professional and wants their business, since this minimises the hassle and removes the cost of telephoning them. They also estimate that freephone numbers in adverts result in increases in customer enquiries of up to 140 per cent. One downside to the increased usage of freephones is their misuse. For example, in the UK every day some 47 000 people call the emergency services 999 number when it is not an emergency,[15] causing potential delays in dealing with the real distress calls. Overall, however, the benefits of freephone services far outweigh their drawbacks.

Economic wealth is dependent upon many factors, one of which is the effectiveness of communication between people in organisations. The telephone is of importance here since it facilitates instant communication, within and between organisations, across time and distance. Indeed the correlation between GNP and telephones per head of population is very high – for all countries and even for states within countries.[16] It is, however, unclear whether an increase in telecommunications somehow contributes to an increase in GNP, or whether greater wealth leads to the purchase of more luxury goods such as telephones. That this correlation does not hold for other electronic goods (such as televisions) tends to support the view that there is a causative relationship between total number of telephones and growth in industry. Indeed, as shown by Kellerman,[17] there is 'strengthening of economic cores when telecommunications means are enhanced. This applies to urban cores as well as to countries and continents.'

The causal link is further supported by the fact that most developments in new forms of telecommunications (fax, voicemail, conference lines, pagers, videophones) take place in industry before transferring to the domestic market. However, a social history of the telephone[18] reveals that initially it was perceived to be fit only for domestic usage. This limited view of its potential was in line with early conceptualisations of the telephone and other technologies. These were influenced by the concept of *technological determinism*[19] – the idea that communication technology has certain fixed effects on human behaviour. More recently this has been replaced by the notion of *reciprocal influence* – the view that technology influences how people behave, but people also then shape the technology and the way in which it is used. Thus, it was the early business users who started to employ the telephone for social purposes. As the domestic potential increased, some of the related innovations were then tailored primarily for the home market (call return, callback request, caller display, texting).

In his book on the subject, Frey[20] concluded that: 'The telephone is a technological innovation that has altered our social relations perhaps more than any other device.' Psychologists have clearly shown a strong relationship between physical closeness and the formation of friendships. We are more likely to become friends with the family next door, or opposite, than the family living on the other side of town. Within the workplace, higher trust evaluations are given to those with whom we interact more often.[21] Another finding is that increases in physical distance have been shown to impair friendships.[22] However, with the advent of mass usage of the telephone this is now no longer necessarily the case. Friends and family can maintain regular contact, provide topical informational updates and share experiences over distance without any great effort or expense. For example, the Federal Communications Commission has noted that there are 156 million telephone lines presubscribed to long distance services.

Research[23] shows that we tend to express a higher degree of liking for those we have met face-to-face rather than those we have only spoken to on the telephone. At the same time, friendships can and do *develop* over the telephone without the participants having met face-to-face (as tele-dating agencies have discovered). Furthermore, what is known as the 'synergistic effect' means that an increase in one medium of contact stimulates demand for contact through other media, that is the desire for synergy increases. Thus, for example, the opening of the Severn Bridge linking south-west England with south Wales soon resulted in the jamming of telephone trunk routes between these areas. Once we have made contact with others we want to communicate more and through all available media. Having met someone we are more likely to telephone them, write, send e-mails, and so on. Likewise, having talked to someone on the telephone we are more likely to want to see what the person actually looks like.

There are over one billion telephones in use in the world and billions of person-to-person telephone calls are made every year. In many cities there are now more telephones than people. Yet comparatively little attention is paid to the effects of this medium upon interpersonal behaviour. Paradoxically it is usually those at a lower level in the organisational hierarchy who receive training in telephone skills.

Thus, secretaries, receptionists and those handling consumer complaints or making tele-sales will be given training in how to improve their skills in the use of the telephone. However, middle and senior managers are somehow expected to be naturally skilled in its use – a state of affairs which is patently not the case. Indeed in reviewing this area, Argyle[24] concluded that 'The telephone... is a different communication skill, which has to be learnt.' In order to manage communications effectively, knowledge of telephone conventions and techniques are very important.

Norms of telephone behaviour

The ringing phone creates inner tension When a telephone rings our arousal level increases and we have an inner urge to 'answer the call'. The noise is intrusive and cannot easily be ignored – it *demands* attention. Indeed McLuhan[25] conceptualised the telephone as the *irresistible intruder*. The recipient is in a sense being *summoned* to answer. Indeed, people often actually *run* to answer the telephone. The reasons for this are a matter for speculation. It has been suggested that the noise of the telephone ringing is akin to a distress call – for example, the cry of a child or the alarm bells of an ambulance, police car or fire engine – and that we are therefore conditioned to respond. Thus, there is a compulsion to answer and even disrupt other activities. Sales assistants in smaller businesses (e.g. in travel agencies) will often interrupt face-to-face interactions to answer a ringing telephone. Why does this occur? This brings us to the second norm of telephone behaviour.

There is a mystery about a ringing telephone Not to answer may mean the loss of a reward or the receipt of a later punishment. As a result, tension increases. Who was that? Was it someone important? Will they call back? Should I have answered? This means that tele-sales staff have the advantage of knowing that at the very least their call is likely to be answered (since even if they have caller display, householders will not recognise the caller's number and so the mystery is further heightened).

Another norm is that in most interactions *the initiator shall terminate the call*. This is because hanging up by the recipient amounts to 'interaction homicide' – it kills the dyad. It is also a form of bad manners. In a sense a telephone caller is analogous to someone arriving unexpectedly with us. The caller becomes our guest. Norms of civilised behaviour dictate that we should be hospitable to guests and not ask them to leave unless they have upset us. We may make broad hints about them leaving in the hope that they are sensitive enough to act on them, or we will make excuses as to why we are ending the interaction ('I have to go to a meeting.' 'I am picking up my daughter'). To do otherwise will result in the guest feeling annoyed and offended.

Hopper[26] used the term *caller hegemony* to describe this phenomenon – as he put it 'the caller acts, the answerer reacts'. As a result, few respondents to a telephone call hang up without speaking. Rather, we negotiate our intention not to participate, or give a reason or excuse for being uncooperative. This may be done rather quickly – for example, if we receive a cold call from a double glazing company we may simply say 'No thanks I already have double glazing. Good-bye.' Interactional norms place pressure on recipients to participate at some level, since few of us like to be intentionally rude.

Of course, tele-sales staff can make use of these learned norms of politeness to try to establish a rapport with the recipient during that initial window of opportunity at the start of the call. Thereafter, those skilled tele-sales staff who can give length and life to the call will increase their opportunity for a sale. This norm also means that if someone whom we do not want to talk to for a long period phones, we should make an excuse such as 'I'm tied up with someone just now. Can I call you back in about 5 minutes?' Then when calling back, the norm is that *we* determine when the call will be terminated. This process also conveys the impression that we are very busy and helps to reduce what the other person will perceive to be the expected duration of the call.

Most person-to-person calls begin from a position of equity and callers then use what has been termed *image vending* to highlight their importance, impress the other person and sell their message. This norm can be changed, of course, by having one's secretary ring so that when the actual person-to-person call begins, the caller is already at a position of advantage (i.e. I am of high status as I have a secretary) – unless of course the call is mediated for the recipient by another secretary in which case the equity norm is restored.

Differences between telephone and face-to-face interactions

When we use the telephone we change our behaviour in a number of often subtle ways. These include the following.

☎ On the telephone we increase our use of what are called 'filled pauses'.[27] Linguists have identified two types of speech dysfluencies – 'Ah' and 'Non-ah'. Non-ah dysfluencies include stuttering, stammering, slips of the tongue, incompletions, spoonerisms, and so on. The 'Ah' category, also known as 'filled pauses', includes all those ubiquitous vocal fillers such as 'ums', 'ers', 'ahs', 'ams' – and of course 'ahs'. It is in this latter domain where differences arise, with filled pauses four times as likely to occur during telephone calls as in face-to-face interactions. This is because we use filled pauses to communicate to the other person that we have not finished what we want to say and that therefore we wish to continue speaking. In face-to-face interaction (and especially when making formal presentations) a high number of 'ahs' would be negatively regarded and seen as poor presentational style, but this is not the case in telephone encounters. The following is taken from an actual telephone communication and in this 10-second excerpt the speaker uses 3 filled pauses to maintain the floor:

> I could have it for you by Friday. ... ah. ... but there would be a cost implication. ... ahm. ... in that this would mean overtime for staff. ... uh. ... and re-organising the production schedule.

It should be noted that this is an example of the skilled use of filled pauses, since each one occurs just before a new and important issue is raised. Their use here allows the speaker not only to keep the floor but also to signal an important upcoming piece of information. This is an effective telephone technique since, when they are used skilfully and systematically, filled pauses help recipients understand and remember important information that comes next.

☎ There are fewer interruptions on the telephone and what is known as 'turn-taking' is smoother. In any interaction those involved have to negotiate who speaks when, and at what point one person stops and the other takes over. In normal encounters this turn-taking process is signalled by the speaker dropping voice volume and pausing; visual cues, not available on the telephone, are also important such as ending the use of gestures and looking directly at the listener. However, there can be confusion in that these behaviours may occur when the speaker wishes to continue and is just checking for feedback that the listener is still interested. At such points both people will begin to speak. On the telephone, however, where the speaker wishes to continue, an 'ah' filler will tend to be used as a clear indicator of more to come, and so there is less likelihood of confusion. In this way, the absence of visual cues actually reduces the opportunity for interruptions.

☎ On the telephone what are known as 'guggles' are crucial. Guggles refer to all those vocal indicators of listening such as 'Uh hu', 'Hmmm', 'Mm hm'. These are part of what is termed 'backchannel behaviour',[28] whereby the listener provides feedback to the speaker in an ongoing but unobtrusive manner. Backchannel behaviour also includes nonverbal cues such as head nods, eye gaze and facial expressions. Since on the telephone there are no visual cues to indicate how the other person is receiving our message, we judge interest on the basis of vocal cues. If no such vocalisations are forthcoming there will be a query such as 'Hello, are you still there.' The power of guggles also means that they can be used to 'shape' the behaviour of the other person. Since they are a form of reward, they can be used subtly to encourage the other person to talk more on certain topics and less on others. Giving more guggles and sounding more enthusiastic in the way they are used when the speaker is addressing the targeted topic is a way of shaping behaviour. When done skilfully the other person will not be aware that this shaping process is happening.

☎ On the telephone, single utterances are on average longer, yet as a whole interactions are much briefer. In this sense, telephone conversations are more 'business-like' and economical. For example in one study[29] of a total of 705 employees in 72 firms in central London, involving 1544 meetings and 5266 telephone calls, the results were as shown in Table 9.1. As can be seen, almost all of the telephone contacts lasted for less than 10 minutes. This finding was confirmed by us in an audit which we carried out on managerial communications in the health service context.[30] Here, we found that the average length of all telephone contacts between managers was well under 5 minutes.

Table 9.1 Length of contact face-to-face and by telephone

Length of contact	*Telephone %*	*Face-to-Face %*
2–10 minutes	87	19
10–30 minutes	12	29
30–60 minutes	1	19
1–2 hours	0	18
Over 2 hours	0	15

By contrast, when people meet eyeball to eyeball they tend to go on somewhat. In Table 9.1 over 50 per cent of the face-to-face encounters lasted for more than half an hour and 15 per cent were longer than two hours. The message is clear. If time is limited and something needs to be decided quickly, use the telephone. This does not mean that all telephone calls are always brief, as those with teenage children will testify. Thus, social usages of the telephone involve a longer period of contact, although again by comparison they will be shorter than comparable face-to-face meetings. One other finding is that length of utterances between each person on the telephone is positively correlated. The duration of a telephone conversation can therefore be reduced by employing briefer utterances.

☎ A number of gender differences in domestic telephone usage have been found[31] including the following.

- Females use the telephone more often and for longer periods; one reason for this is that women tend to take the lead in maintaining family relational contacts.
- The duration of calls for both males and females is longer when the other conversant is female.
- The shortest calls are male–male and the longest female–female.
- Men are much more likely to call men and women to call women.
- Caller–receiver duration is asymmetrical across genders, in that when a woman calls a man the call is significantly shorter than when a male calls a female.

In the business context these gender factors should be taken into consideration when planning which members of staff should be assigned to make or receive particular calls.

☎ Another part of the business edge associated with telephone calls is that they involve less chit-chat, are more formal, more task centred and less personal. There are fewer jokes and less humour overall in telephone interactions than face-to-face. In addition, more questions are asked during telephone interactions and therefore not surprisingly a greater proportion of utterances are replies to questions. Many of these features make it more difficult to develop relationships. Therefore, when the relational dimension is important, managers should make deliberate efforts to use humour, engage in small talk, and so on.

☎ Some studies[32] have shown that attitudes change more readily as a result of telephone communications. It is argued that during such encounters we pay more attention to the actual *message* and are not distracted by the *person* delivering it. In normal interaction we make judgements based not only upon the content of what is said but also upon the look and general nonverbal behaviour of the person delivering the message. In essence if we do not like the cut of a person's jib then we are more likely to reject what they are saying.

☎ It is easier to refuse a request over the telephone. For example, in surveys refusal rates to sensitive questions are higher on the telephone than in face-to-face interviews.[33] It is also easier to express anger in mediated communication. One study[34] found that 65 per cent of those surveyed were most likely to express anger over the telephone, as compared to 26 per cent in writing and 9 per cent face-to-face. Another investigation[35] revealed that over 50 per cent of respondents were able to say things over the telephone, especially expressing anger or making social refusals, than they would do face-to-face. The corollary here was that over 80 per cent of respondents had topics they would *not* discuss over the telephone, such as personal problems. Indeed, studies show that for almost all interactions people express a preference for face-to-face contact *except* when they are required to be assertive (such as in refusing a request), when the telephone is preferred.

☎ The incidence of aggression and rudeness is greater on the telephone. One review[36] of this area quoted a 9 per cent and 65 per cent chance of rudeness respectively for face-to-face and telephone communication. Part of the reason for this is distance and anonymity. It is easier to be aggressive with people we do not know and with whom we are interacting from a distance. In face-to-face situations, being rude or aggressive may lead to overt physical violence. However, on the telephone there is no such danger and so it is easier for either party to 'up the ante' without any imminent physical threat. Also, in eyeball-to-eyeball communication, other cues (such as facial expression, physical attractiveness) may help to take some of the potential heat out of the encounter. Managers should be aware of the temptation to become aggressive on the telephone and consciously monitor their responses to avoid this. There is truth in the old adage that if you lose your temper you lose the argument. Among the behaviours that callers find most annoying[37] are the following.

- ☏ *Stance indicators* – negative attitude towards the caller inferred by what is said ('Oh I hear what you are saying OK, but I find it hard to believe ...')

- *Controlled enunciation* – the practice of pausing briefly between each word, as if one were speaking to a child ('Please ... listen ... carefully ... to ... what ... I ... am ... saying.')
- *Being interrupted* in mid-flow
- *Increased loudness* of voice ('Just **LISTEN** to me.')
- *Metacommunicative directives* – commands or inquiries into one's ability to comprehend what is being said ('Can you not understand what I am trying to tell you?')
- *Confrontation/Denial* (Caller: 'I have been holding on the line for 10 minutes.' Recipient: 'It was nowhere near as long as that')
- *Assertion/Counterassertion* (Caller: 'I am not happy with the way I am being dealt with.' Recipient: 'Well, I'm not happy with the way you are talking to me either')

☎ One study[38] found evidence that the telephone is used most often in lateral communication between those at the same level in an organisation, rather than in upwards or downwards communication, where other media (face-to-face or written) are preferred. It was also found that managers rated the telephone as the most potent communication medium for influencing others.

☎ A problem with telephone interaction is that it must be synchronised in that the other person must be there to answer the call. An analysis[39] of intracompany calls in the US found that only one out of every four business calls was completed at the first attempt, resulting in what is known as 'telephone tag' where callers were chasing round trying to 'catch' the recipient. The cost of each call, including unsuccessful attempts, was calculated at $13. This is very wasteful. In fact, a US survey[40] of 200 corporate vice presidents estimated that one month out of the executive's working year can be lost through unnecessary or unproductive telephone communications. Increasingly, people end up communicating with each other's voice mail. Thus Hopper[41] pointed out that *serial monologue* has replaced tag – we leave messages for one another but do not have a dialogue. These messages are also referred to as *audio postcards* (or *oral postcards*).

While the lack of visual cues causes communication problems, information giving and problem solving are often as effective on the telephone. We can also accurately judge from vocal cues alone whether the other person is smiling, and we are able to make accurate estimates of their age, gender, emotional state and level of extraversion or introversion.[42,43] Businesses attempt to manipulate these factors. Thus, one computer systems sales company[44] requires that its salespeople stand up when dealing with customers, in the belief that they then dominate the conversation and have a better chance of making a sale. Another business that we worked with had mirrors placed in front of their sales staff to remind them to smile when dealing with clients.

As discussed in Chapter 5, explanations can be improved through the use of several well-established techniques. On the telephone the most relevant of these are to:

- State the most important points at the beginning and end.
- Emphasise the key points. This can be achieved through the use of changes in voice and by making good use of filled pauses.
- Have a logical structure.
- Present in a fluent style.
- Move at the other person's pace.
- Repeat key points and if necessary spell important words.
- Summarise what has been agreed.
- Check for understanding.

Telephone hates

In his book on telephone communications, Hopper[45] asserted:

> Ask any friend or colleague if they have pet peeves about the telephone. Allow time for tirades: against answering machines, against talking computers, against telephone solicitors, against telephone call waiting, against the fouled-up new phone system at the office, against people who tie up the phone with small talk, against people who get straight down to business with no small talk, against people who call too early or too late.

In other words, there are lots of aspects of telephone communications that irritate us. A number of surveys have revealed what people most dislike when using the telephone. From these it is possible to compile the top 10 most annoying telephone experiences (see Box 9.1). These need to be addressed, since a survey by British Telecom revealed that the reaction of nine out of 10 customers who experienced unanswered or poorly dealt with calls was to simply stop dealing with that organisation. They further estimated that some 4.6 million clients have been lost by firms in the UK as a result of negative telephone experiences. Conversely, and not surprisingly, if someone telephones a company with a problem which is then efficiently resolved, that person is much more likely to use the company's services in the future.

Box 9.1 The ten most annoying telephone experiences

1. A delay in your call being answered
2. Being greeted by voicemail rather than being dealt with in person
3. Being left 'hanging on' for a long time
4. Being put through to the wrong person
5. Being passed from pillar to post until being finally put through to the correct department
6. People who interrupt the telephone conversation to talk to someone at their end
7. People who deal with you in an offhand manner, and do not treat your call professionally
8. Leaving a message on voicemail and no one getting back to you
9. The call being terminated without being told what the follow-up will be
10. Listening to muzak when put on hold.

The top hate is a delay in the call being answered. In a survey conducted by the Financial Mail the length of time taken by companies to answer a call ranged from 1 second at best to 7 minutes 30 seconds at worst, and more than 25 per cent of calls took longer than a minute to be answered.[46] In the same year, a survey by British Telecom (BT) revealed that 31 per cent of calls to small businesses in the South of England went unanswered (the cut-off point in this survey was 15 rings). However, a survey of phone companies by the Consumers' Association revealed that BT was itself the worst offender, taking seven minutes to answer a call to its consumer helpline.[47] Many companies have recognised that this is unacceptable. For example, Citibank discovered that over 500 calls a day to the bank's London office were not being answered within target times of between 10 and 30 seconds. They then installed new equipment at a cost of £120 000 with the result that 95 per cent of the 5000 daily calls to the bank were answered within 10 seconds. The benefits of an effective telecommunications system have been well demonstrated by Direct Line, which launched its telephone insurance business in the UK in 1985. By 1997 it had become Britain's biggest insurer with 2.2 million customers, employing 4000 staff at call centres in six cities. Using automatic call distribution systems, 3000 calls can be answered simultaneously within a second.

After delays in calls being answered, customers next most dislike the call not being dealt with in person. Indeed in an NOP poll of what most irritated members of the public the third most frequently cited irritant (mentioned by 33 per cent of the sample) was 'companies where the telephone is answered by recorded messages'. (As a matter of interest the top hate was 'junk mail' and the fourth was 'people who use mobile phones in public places'.) The most disliked system has been termed 'voicemail jail' which is the situation where the caller is told by a recorded voice: 'Press 1 for X, Press 2 for Y....' Studies in the US show that such electronic answering services have on average a 67 per cent 'slam down' rate. A related hate here is the use of muzak when put 'on hold'. Whatever muzak a company chooses will be disliked by a percentage of its customers. The real problem, of course, is that callers simply do not like having to wait and the muzak becomes linked to the annoying delay, with the result that a conditioned negative association occurs.

The lesson for companies is clear – answer calls quickly and in person. Avoid voicemail where possible, and especially voicemail jail. An awareness of this fact has resulted in many businesses employing specialist call handling centres to deal with their calls.

Telephone call centres

In the UK some 400 000 staff are employed in call centres,[48] 70 per cent of whom are female. Government initiatives to make all central and local public services readily accessible have contributed to this growth.[49] Large companies have their own centralised call centres where staff handle enquiries from business customers and users in various countries, in a range of different languages. An increasing number of call centres are now located in lower-wage countries with an English-speaking workforce, such as India where savings of 30 per cent can be made on labour costs compared to the UK. However, the investment in call centres technology to allow such distal call-handling arrangements seems to have had an inverse relationship to customer satisfaction.[50]

One problem is that many call centres are multi-functional. They not only handle telephone enquiries, but also deal with e-mail queries, as well as trying to sell products or services. Customer needs can get lost in the resulting maelstrom, and calls can be perceived by customers as unfriendly or uncaring. Another problem is that, although workers in this industry generally earn much less than the average wage,[51] labour costs account for more than 50 per cent of the total call centre expenditure. As a result, companies try to replace as much of this with technology, such as voicemail jail. But, what almost all customers want is for their call to be answered swiftly and by a fellow human being.

In the financial sector, the 'big four' UK banks made major investments in call centres. They introduced systems whereby all calls, including those to local branches, were routed to the call centre. This meant that, much to the chagrin of customers, they were then dealt with by staff they did not know. This certainly saved on expenditure on jobs. For example, in 2002 Lloyds TSB's 'efficiency programme' resulted in it removing 3000 of its 81 500 staff. However, it also proved[52] to be unpopular with customers, who valued greatly the ongoing relationship they developed with staff in their local branch. Faceless call centre operators are no substitute. There has also been criticism of the way staff in these centres can be treated.[53] They are the most heavily supervised category of workers, with calls being constantly monitored and regularly recorded.[54]

Call handlers face a tension between giving the present customer as much time as needed so that the caller feels he or she has been dealt with in a satisfactory manner, and achieving set targets for total number of calls answered in a set period. More time per call, less calls overall. While one call person is being handled, the worker is ever-aware that another is waiting on the line. There is therefore a constant awareness of the need to get off the phone. Not surprisingly, levels of sickness absence and staff turnover in many centres are very high. One reason is that employees can suffer from a condition termed RBI[55] or 'repetitive brain injury'. RBI sets in after about six months, when some workers begin to experience a feeling of burnout. They just cannot bear to deal with yet more of the same queries and complaints, and so stop caring about how they communicate with customers.

Better call centres are aware of these problems and have taken steps to alleviate the problems faced by staff. Among the positive features[46,56] of the best centres are:

- ☏ open-plan office areas so staff can communicate readily with one another
- ☏ well designed, comfortable, workstations allowing flexibility of movement
- ☏ offices decorated in warm colours with attractive wall paintings, etc.

- picture windows overlooking scenic views (e.g. fields, trees)
- flexible working patterns
- free childcare facilities
- break and rest areas with easy chairs
- good cafe facilities
- a library
- team-building exercises, including 'fun days'
- free nights out where families come along (e.g. to movies)
- ready access to counselling for those who have to answer distressing calls (e.g. in the health service sector).

Telephone communication problems

In essence, the problems posed by telephone communication are all part of what has been termed 'the coffee and biscuits problem'.[12] In most business encounters, when people meet there is an initial social stage at which time refreshments are usually provided, there is some small talk, and the participants begin to settle in to the encounter. During this period, each side sizes up the other and makes judgements about aspects such as the receptivity and warmth of the other person, the degree of formality likely to ensue, and whether rapport can easily be established. This makes it easier when the conversation moves on to the business side of things. On the telephone, of course, there is no coffee and biscuits. Even on a video-conference link where both sides are simultaneously engaging in refreshments the social dimension is lost – socialisation tends to occur with those face-to-face at each end.

Three related theories have been put forward to explain the problems normally associated with mediated communication.[12] These have been termed 'Cuelessness', 'Social Presence', and 'Immediacy'.

Cuelessness refers to a reduction in social cues (visual contact, physical presence), which increases the psychological distance between the interactors. Thus, in face-to-face communication more cues are available (from nonverbal communication and the environment) than in telephone interactions. As cuelessness increases, the content of any interaction becomes more depersonalised, the interaction is likely to be task-centred rather than social, and the interactive style becomes more formal and less spontaneous. In other words, it is argued that the lack of social cues makes communication more stilted and less spontaneous. Interestingly, in telephone counselling,[57] such cuelessness helps to increase the anonymity of the conversation (as compared to face-to-face contact), which in turn facilitates 'psychological proximity'. Callers feel less embarrassed, since the counsellor cannot see who they are, and feel better able to discuss intimate problems. The discussion content can then more readily become personalised and self-revealing. This is an important advantage for helpline services such as the Samaritans.

Social Presence refers to the degree of *presence* of the other person in the interaction – the extent to which the other person is 'there'. Communication media vary in the degree of presence they afford. As shown in Figure 9.1, there is a descending scale of presence across media. On the telephone therefore the problem can be summarised as an absence of presence. Of course, one reason for this is the decrease in social cues along this scale, and so this theory has close links with the cuelessness perspective.

Social Immediacy refers to the degree of psychological distance between sender and receiver. The more information a medium can transmit the greater its intimacy. For example, someone two doors away in the organisation may telephone rather than drop in. This decreases the social immediacy and will shorten the duration of the interaction. Increased cues and greater presence in turn help to increase immediacy, and so these three theories are all closely interrelated. On the telephone, immediacy can be increased through the use of first names, references to family and friends, social chit-chat and gossip, non-task comments and the use of humour. An awareness of

Figure 9.1 Social presence in media

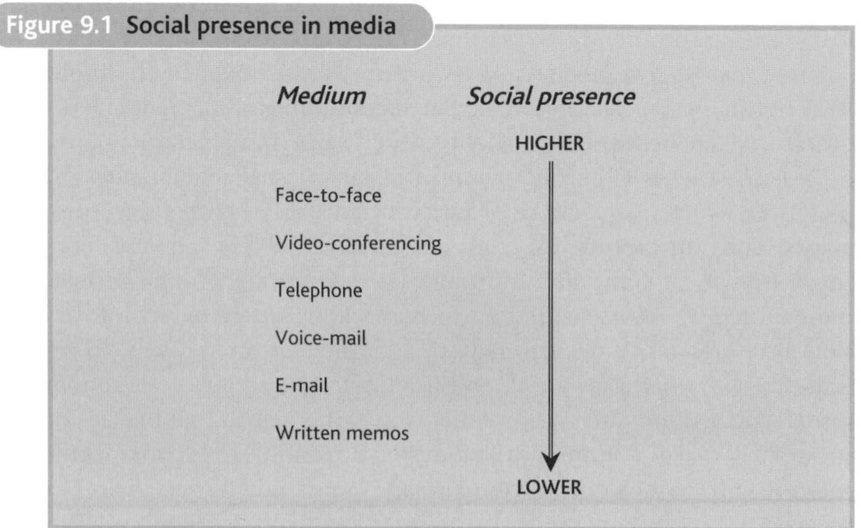

the importance of employing such immediacy-enhancing tactics on the telephone helps to compensate for the lack of coffee and biscuits.

More recently, these three elements have been incorporated into media richness theory.[58] This is concerned with the extent to which communication channels are 'rich' in terms of the information they offer. Judgements about the richness of a channel are based inter alia upon:

- the number and 'mix' of cues (visual, audio and written) it contains
- the availability and rapidity of feedback it offers
- the extent to which it facilitates what Burgoon *et al.* termed *interactivity*[59] and participation by all parties
- its capacity to provide affective as well as cognitive information.

Thus, face-to-face communication is the richest channel as it carries verbal, vocal and nonverbal cues, allows for shared written material to be examined, enables emotional tone to be scrutinised and facilitates instant feedback on message effects. By contrast, written communication is the 'thinnest' medium, while the audio telephone has a mid-level of richness. In the business sphere, the telephone has been shown[60] to be richer than voicemail, which in turn is richer than e-mail, with written memos the thinnest medium. For complex, time-consuming, interactions, where relational aspects are crucial, and it is important that uncertainties be reduced, the media rich face-to-face channel is usually most effective.[61] On the other hand, for briefer encounters, involving factual information, and even potential conflict or negative outcomes,[62] a mediated channel such as the telephone can be best.

However, studies of media choice indicate that while we should select the communication medium most suited to our goals,[63] in practice we choose the medium with which we are most familiar or use most often.[64] One important factor in relation to the telephone is the 'basic distinction between calls aimed at getting someone and those aimed at getting something'.[65] This dichotomy is also referred to as social v practical, intrinsic v instrumental, and emotional v functional. In other words, we may call others for relational (just to 'have a chat') rather than task-related reasons. Advertising campaigns, such as 'It's good to talk' and 'Reach out and touch someone', have successfully exploited this function to increase usage. For example, an analysis of usage in the UK shows that Thursday is the busiest day for calls,[66] one reason for this being because social plans are then being made for the weekend. In business terms, however, the instrumental function predominates and so task concerns or 'getting the job done' become the central goal. Thus, UK usage also reveals that most phone calls are made each day in the period between 4 p.m. and 5 p.m., as people try to complete their tasks before finishing work.

Making and answering calls

Studies of caller openings[67] have shown that we may use one or more of six main categories of behaviour at the beginning of a call.

1. A *greeting term* such as 'Hello ...' or 'Good morning ...'.
2. *Identification of the recipient* ('Who am I speaking to?' 'Is that Dee?').
3. A *reference to the recipient's 'state'* may be made ('Did I wake you?' 'Are you with someone?').
4. A *'switchboard' request* may be necessary ('Is Jo there?' 'Can I speak to the manager?').
5. *Self-identification* ('This is Mr. Jones speaking' 'It's me').
6. A *joke introduction*, in the social rather then business sphere. For example, asking 'Is that the undertakers?' or using a funny voice or accent when phoning a friend.

There are five categories of recipient opening behaviour. As above, the first of these is a greeting ('Good morning'). This aspect of telephone communication has been termed the *verbal handshake* and its importance is recognised by most businesses. Second there is departmental identification ('Marketing Department'), or in social calls this may just be the person's telephone number (954765). This is followed by personal identification ('David Fyfe speaking'). Fourth, there is an invitation ('How may I help you?'). As with caller openings, in social calls there can be the recipient joke introduction ('Mario's Pizza Parlour').

Answering and making telephone calls are an important part of any business and so it is important that all staff have good telephone skills. The key areas to bear in mind in making and receiving telephone calls[68,69] are summarised in Box 9.2 and Box 9.3. Good organisations should monitor and audit their performance in these areas.[70]

Overview

The telephone is now a ubiquitous piece of technology. In a relatively short space of time it has moved from being the preserve of the rich to

Box 9.2 Answering the telephone effectively

- Answer promptly – within three rings.
- Start the call by giving a greeting ('Good morning'), the Department ('Human Resources Department'), your name ('This is Mr. Jones …') and position ('… Departmental Admin. Officer'), and offer an invitation ('How may I help you?'). Also, remember to smile as you answer (remember this can be accurately judged by the other person) and to sound interested/motivated/enthusiastic.
- Establish the reason for the call.
- Ascertain and use the caller's name early in the conversation.
- If the call is inconvenient or you cannot deal with the enquiry, explain why, take the name and number of the caller and arrange exactly what will happen next and if appropriate when you will call back.
- Most Departments have a pro-forma for logging calls – remember to use it. Don't hesitate to suggest alterations to it if it misses out key points.
- If taking a message for someone else, again there should be a 'Messages' pro-forma. Remember to log the name of the caller, time and date of call, summary of message or topic of enquiry, and when the caller will be available to take return calls. Indicate to the caller when the person is likely to be available to return the call. Be accurate – check with the caller the spelling of names and addresses, repeat numbers, facts and so on.
- Take notes during the call and 'read back' key points so that the caller knows you are taking the call seriously. This also allows for an accuracy check.
- Show verbal and vocal signs of listening ('Uh hu' 'Hmmm' 'Yes' 'OK').
- Explain fully what you are doing if the caller is required to 'hang on'.
- If dealing with a complaint, speak gently and do not interrupt. Acknowledge emotions ('I can see that you are annoyed by this …'). Allow the caller to ventilate. Treat the call as a problem to be dealt with, and not as a personal attack.
- End the call by recapping on what exactly has been agreed and what each side will do next.
- Thank the caller and give 'action' reassurance that the call will be dealt with.
- Remember, callers like to close so try to structure the call to make it seem that *they* are closing.

Box 9.3 Making telephone calls

- ✆ Make notes before you make the call. What are your goals? Exactly what information do you require? Have a checklist of points to be covered. In case you have to leave a message with someone else, have the key points distilled.
- ✆ Start the call by stating your name (first name is important for relationship establishment), your Organisation/Department, your position and the main purpose of your call.
- ✆ Establish to whom you are speaking, and if not the right person ask to be put through to the latter.
- ✆ Use the person's name – and try to get on first name terms (though be sensitive to feedback here).
- ✆ Sound pleasant and motivated.
- ✆ Make your requests and have them answered or if not find out why they cannot be dealt with.
- ✆ End the call by recapping on what exactly has been agreed and what each side will do next.
- ✆ Remember the norms are that you made the call, therefore you should close the call.
- ✆ Use reinforcement if appropriate ('Nice talking to you'; 'You have been most helpful').
- ✆ Anticipate having to leave a message with voicemail. If leaving a message on voicemail, itemise what your main points are, speak at a slower rate, repeat key details (for example, your telephone number), emphasise the importance of a return call and give suitable times for this. If really important, try to connect with someone else (who may be able to contact the person) or telephone back to leave more than one message on the voicemail.

being an integral part of everyday life. As noted by Cairncross[71] the wiring of the world began with the development of the telephone. It is a core communication medium in its own right, but it has also been the fulcrum for the development of a wide range of related technologies (fax, e-mail, the internet, paging, video-phones, etc.). Advances in technology, a reduction in unit costs and the user-friendly nature of the product have contributed to an exponential growth in usage.[72] It is a communication device that has now been adopted and embraced by all levels of society and in all walks of business. Because we all use the telephone, however, it does not follow that we all use it wisely or well. The fact that most of us will have had personal experience of appalling telephone technique is testimony to this fact. In the business sphere the implications of such ineffective usage can be financially damaging. It is crucial that staff members in any organisation make good use of the telephone both internally for the accurate transmission of messages between colleagues to ensure the overall smooth operation of the business, and externally with customers and other key publics.

In relation to the latter, a large part of the work of most businesses will be transacted by telephone. How these calls are handled will be central to the overall public perception of the company itself. A firm which answers calls promptly and pleasantly, connects callers quickly with the right department, listens to the caller's concerns and explains what action will be taken, by whom and when, will leave the impression of efficiency and competence. Return business is likely to ensue. By contrast a company where calls are not answered for long periods of time, where the caller is dealt with in an offhand manner, transferred all over the place, and eventually receives little direct advice or satisfaction, will be perceived as slipshod and inefficient. Any return contact is likely to be in the form of complaints or notice of termination of business (Reflective exercise 9.1).

Reflective exercise 9.1 Effective telephone technique

Think of the person whom you have dealt with who, in your opinion, has the *best* telephone technique you have encountered. How does this person:

- open calls (a) when phoning you, and (b) when answering your call?
- establish rapport and reduce social distance (through humour, use of first name, personal conversations about family, holidays)?
- conduct the business side of the call?
- terminate calls?

How many of these techniques do you currently use? Which of them should you incorporate into your telephone style?

Reflective exercise 9.1 ***continued***

Now think of the person whom you have dealt with who, in your opinion, has the *worst* telephone technique you have encountered and answer the above questions. How many of the mistakes that this person makes do you make?

Finally, think carefully about how, and in exactly which ways, you need to change your present telephone style to maximise your communicative potential. Identify three specific improvements you could make in (i) making calls, (ii) receiving calls and (iii) terminating calls.

Analyse your telephone manner carefully over the next ten calls you make and receive, and produce a list of your strengths and weaknesses. Ideally record these (with permission from the other person) for more detailed analysis.

10 Writing matters: how to create the write impression

Introduction

The ability to communicate in writing has been one of the earliest and most significant achievements of human civilisation. Indeed, the Egyptians first used postal systems in 2000 BC. Since the invention of printing in the fifteenth century, written communication enables us to disseminate ideas and information widely, cheaply, clearly and (with the advent of e-mail) instantaneously. Formal written communication within businesses include audit reports, shareholder statements, marketing and promotional materials, annual reports, technical briefs, white papers and other forms of writing that interface with services and products.[1] In consequence, it absorbs a great deal of any manager's time. One study of 60 front line supervisors at a Midwest US steel manufacturing plant[2] found that 70 per cent of them spent between 8 and 14 hours per week in writing related activities. These involved producing disciplinary action reports, clarifying job procedures, dealing with formal grievances, writing memos, producing instructional documents to subordinates, drafting incident reports and writing external letters or reports to customers. In addition, managers spend significant amounts of time responding to the written communications of others. It is scarcely surprising that a survey of business departments in US universities found that departmental leaders regarded written communication as the single most important component in business communication courses for students.[3]

Perhaps because it takes so much time, and is viewed as being so important, written communication causes many people a great deal of stress. The survey of frontline supervisors discussed above disclosed a number of key stress factors in managerial writing (Table 10.1). It is, therefore, imperative that managers reduce such stress factors, while monitoring and improving their written communication. This chapter

Table 10.1 Major stress factors in management communication

Major problems in the writing of documents	*% of managers identifying difficulty*
Meeting deadlines	76
Identifying appropriate information for document	68
Organising information in document	65
Writing instructions that workers understand	58
Summarising information from other sources	46
Understanding grammatical and stylistic conventions	33
Creating effective tables, graphs and charts	18

seeks to facilitate this process by examining the strategic role which written communication plays in dealing with a business's internal and external customers. In particular, we look at how it should be evaluated, to ascertain whether it is doing its main job – enabling a receiver to understand, internalise and act upon the sender's message. Flowing from this, steps are discussed which managers can take to improve the major aspects of their written communication – producing reports, memos, letters and dealing with complaints. We also increasingly live in an era of e-mail communication. Therefore, a special section of this chapter is devoted to the main trends in e-mail use, and how it can support rather than undermine fundamental business goals.

The strategic role of written communication

Written communication activates customer recognition, purchases and loyalty. The reasons for this are clear. In one study, 70 per cent of businesses claimed to look forward to receiving their post.[4] Clearly, there is a pleasure factor in anticipating the plop of a letter hitting the mat. Most people rush to get their mail in the morning. This reflects our profound sense of curiosity about the unknown, to the extent that we are generally curious about the contents of mail intended for others. The Royal Mail in Britain surveyed 2000 people on this point. One third admitted to reading mail addressed to their partner, relatives or other people, while one in six even claimed to steam such letters open.[5]

This sense of curiosity can be used to attract and retain customers. The Henley Centre for Forecasting found that 68 per cent of customers actively wanted information from the companies they dealt with and 60 per cent were more likely to buy from suppliers who kept in touch.[6] This may be an illustration of what has been dubbed 'the availability factor':[7] information about something which is readily known to us is more likely to inspire action than information which requires considerable effort to access. Maintaining contact ensures that knowledge about products and services is more available to customers than what is on offer from competitors. Thus, sending newsletters, cards, calendars, circular letters and directly addressed letters activates the availability factor, cements customer loyalty and improves profits.

This effect is also achieved since written communication can engage what has been termed the norm of reciprocity (see Chapter 3). Once we feel that a positive attitude has been displayed towards us we are motivated to respond by expressing similar feelings to the other person. We might, for example, feel obliged to return a favour, even to a much greater extent than the one we originally received. Ninety-four per cent of respondents in one major survey agreed that when they received a letter from someone they felt that the sender had put time and thought into its contents.[8] Clearly, this predisposed them to feel favourably towards the sender, and respond in like fashion to what was perceived as a positive act. Thus, simply staying in touch influences people – and attracts their business. The one exception is what is perceived to be junk mail. Many recipients detest this precisely because its impersonal character conveys the impression that the receiver's individual needs were not considered when it was produced.

Retaining customer loyalty by writing to them is cost efficient. The Office of Consumer Affairs has calculated that it costs six times more to get a new customer than to keep an existing one.[9] Such findings put the costs of sustained communication in a proper perspective. It has also been found that small changes in presentation enable your written communications to stand out from the crowd. For example, the Henley Centre estimates that 80 per cent of people are more likely to open a personally addressed white envelope than a manila one.[10] As an illustration, the owner of a small family company which won an export award, Tanice Slater, reported that when she uses direct mail the envelope is hand written to give it a personal touch. Regular customers receive a birthday card.[11]

Such findings suggest that the impact of direct marketing mail can be intensified if you:

- Hand write the envelope.
- Use a white envelope rather than a manila one.
- Use the receiver's name, in your opening line.
- Include as many personal details about the recipient as possible.

Written communication is also a powerful means of rewarding people, publicly disseminating praise and encouraging an atmosphere of celebration inside an organisation's own ranks. It forms a crucial part of communication strategies aimed at building and sustaining positive relationships between managers and their staff. Some of the main options available include:[12]

- Newsletters (monthly/weekly/quarterly)
- Internal memos (particularly in response to crises, rumours or to instantly spread the news of a great success)
- E-mail postings, to everyone in the organisation
- Postings on corporate intranet sites
- Notice boards (although these tend to become cluttered, and often go 'unnoticed')
- Letters to individual staff members.

Tom Peters[13] gives an example of a manager of Marriott's in New Mexico, who made a firm policy of sending out 100 'Thank You' notes a month to members of his staff for jobs well done. However, caution is in order. Many staff have confessed, during communication audits conducted by us, that they automatically deleted e-mail postings from various people (including some senior managers), irrespective of the subject line. The message senders had acquired a reputation for verbal incontinence, one that is not easily shed. Thus, personal notes, or other efforts at promoting written communication, do not in themselves yield results. Personal competence matters, and will be addressed later in this chapter. But a systematic approach to evaluation matters more, and should form an integral part of a planned and systematic approach to written communications.

Evaluating written communication

What is effective communication? It is useful to explore some of the most pertinent myths we have about written communication, which prevent us from accurately estimating its impact.

1. More communication is better communication This assumption often leads to the distribution of multiple photocopies or indiscriminately circulated memos and e-mails, about everything. In reality, these are usually produced to protect the sender rather than inform the receiver. There is some evidence that communication between senior managers may be particularly prone to this fault.[14] In organisations where the dominant urge is to 'cover your back', paper is used to camouflage the lack of real communication. People drown in ink while gasping for facts. The result is information anxiety. One respondent in a communication audit conducted by us, a senior manager, complained bitterly of 'death by memo'. Typically, those working in such organisations are uncertain about what messages to attend to, and deal with this uncertainty by filtering out most communication emanating from senior managers. A blizzard of paper causes snow blindness, ensuring that the business's key aims and objectives continually drift in and out of focus. The result is inertia, internal feuding and missed business opportunities.

2. Written communication equals a fulfilled obligation The assumption here is that if a message is received, it is read, understood and acted upon. The sender can then always claim: 'But I told you about this, in paragraph 23 of my 14-page memo of last January!' In reality, *repetition* of key points (albeit in as *concise* a manner as possible) is as important as their initial *transmission* in determining impact.

3. Informing someone is the same thing as persuading them Most of us assume that more people agree with us than actually do, and that our opinions are more correct than is really the case.[15] We also assume that our arguments are more attractive to other people and hence more persuasive than they actually are. An additional difficulty is that people often view the needs of the reader as less important than their own credibility, possible financial rewards and scope for promotion.[16] In short, the writer's own agenda and ego needs over-ride the requirements of the audience. A golden rule is that the information needs of the receiver should be clearly established before messages are transmitted.

In one study, investigators[17] found that roughly half of keyboard and secretarial staff who regularly used erasing fluid did not know the content of the warning label on the bottle. A communication audit conducted by us in a hotel found that none of the receptionist staff knew the organisation's mission statement – although it was posted in large letters beside the reception desk. Thus, even if information is presented it is not necessarily attended to, understood, retained or acted upon. Effective communication involves mutual feedback. It is vital to build opportunities for this into our written communications.

4. Using one channel of communication is efficient – that is it saves money The consequence here is that important issues are often only mentioned once, perhaps in a company brochure, newsletter or an internal memorandum. In reality, effective communication requires us to:

- Employ multiple channels for important information.
- Use written channels several times.
- Engage in the systematic, planned repetition of key themes and messages.

In one survey,[18] a selection of women undergoing a hysterectomy and who received a booklet providing information about how to cope with anxiety and what to expect in hospital, experienced less post-operative pain and stress than those who did not. They also left hospital more quickly. In short, people can obtain added benefit when they receive written communication, even if the information it offers has already been made available to them by other channels.

5. Channel proliferation = increased informativeness This is the opposite but equally destructive mistake to that identified above. Particularly with e-mail technology an abundance of communication creates the illusion that real information exchange has occurred, and that messages have been understood, agreed with and acted upon.

Many surveys have shown that employees have a strong preference for face-to-face communication, above all else. The more vital the issue at stake, the more important face-to-face communication from immediate and senior managers becomes.[19] Written communication should reinforce contact between people, rather than paper over its absence.

Box 10.1 contains a number of evaluation criteria, which you are encouraged to apply to the written communications in which you engage.[20]

The rules of high impact writing

Effective writing does three main things.[21] It:

1. *Attracts the recipient's attention.* Ignored messages fail to persuade. Worse, messages submerged in the small print lose any sense of urgency, purpose or conviction.

Box 10.1 Evaluating channels of communication

1. Feedback potential: How quickly can the receiver respond to the message?
2. Complexity capacity: Can this channel effectively process complex messages?
3. Breadth potential: How many different messages can be disseminated through this channel?
4. Confidentiality: Can the communicators be reasonably sure their messages are received only by those intended?
5. Encoding ease: Can the sender easily and quickly use this channel?
6. Decoding ease: Can the receiver easily and quickly decode messages in this channel?
7. Time–space constraint: Do senders and receivers need to occupy the same time space?
8. Cost: How much does it cost to use this channel?
9. Interpersonal warmth: Does the channel have the potential to communicate interpersonal warmth?
10. Formality: Does the channel imbue a sense of formality?
11. 'Scanability': Does the channel permit the message(s) to be easily browsed or scanned to find relevant passages?
12. Time of consumption: Does the sender or receiver exercise the most control over when the message is consumed?

2. *Ensures that the arguments in the message are understood.* This means that key arguments should be simple, repeated, short and to the point. Waffle muffles your voice in cotton wool, and sends your audience into a trance.
3. *Enables the recipient to learn the arguments contained in the message and comes to accept them as true.* This means that the argument should promise the reader a benefit. We scan written messages with one question foremost in our minds – what is in this for me? The sender should keep the needs of the reader clearly in view, answer this cardinal question at once and repeat the answer several times.

In general, a 'high impact' style includes stating your main objective in an opening paragraph, using bold type headings and constructing simple but dynamic sentences. A more traditional bureaucratic style is characterised by abstract language, no personal pronouns and the general lack of an explicit purpose.[22]

In the quest to develop a high impact style there is no substitute for quality writing, and vivid presentation. A number of steps will enhance this effort. Here, we look at issues of writing style, and then of presentation.

Writing style

- *Use concrete words rather than abstract words and sentences.*[23] Aim to write the way that you speak. Do not say 'collateral damage was inflicted on his upper personage by an object'. Do say 'a brick hit him on the head'.
- *State presuppositions explicitly rather than refer to them implicitly.* For the most part, people can only understand evidence when they know what it is aiming to prove. The general rule is that you should put your conclusions first, and your evidence second.[24] Thus, lawyers tend to begin summing up by saying what they intend their evidence to mean ('My client is innocent'). Open with your big sell, and then reiterate and refine it throughout.
- *Use antithesis.*[25] This takes the form of 'not this, but this'. An excellent example comes from the oratory of President Kennedy, when he said: 'Ask not what your country can do for you, but what you can do for your country.'
- *Find the right tone.* If you are trying to fire people up, to energise them, engage their enthusiasm or win their support for change then your prose must be hot as opposed to cool.[26] This means that it should freely employ colloquial expressions that people can relate to and boldly outline lively scenarios that they can visualise. Passion is critical. Except when conveying bald factual information, your prose should aim to woo and wow an audience. We offer an example of a 'cold' written communication in Box 10.2, and what it looks like when livened up. Which version makes most impact on you?
- *New information should be related to what people already know.* This will make it more easily understood. Thus, put new information at the end of a sentence and old information at the beginning.[27]
- *Never use a metaphor or other figure of speech that you are used to seeing written down or spoken aloud.*[28] Metaphors should create a visual image for the reader, and so assist them to sharpen their thinking on the topic at hand. Clichés begin as an arresting image ('We need a level playing field'), but lose all colour, subtlety and shade through over-use. Why turn up at a dinner party in some one else's cast-offs, when you can wear a designer outfit of your own? Dress to impress.

Box 10.2 From cold to hot in writing style

Cold (and traditional)

You will have realised recently that our market share in Gizmos has fallen dramatically. This threatens our previously front-rank position in the Fortune 500, and puts a very large question mark over our competitiveness. I need hardly delineate the consequences. It seems that we will have to pay our shareholders a reduced dividend, while bonus payments may also be suspended and job cuts may even have to be contemplated. The senior management team will be devoting all its efforts in the next month to the development of a new strategy, and will communicate this to you as soon as it is finalised. As a first step, we have cut production of Gizmo A and invested more resources in a marketing strategy to support Gizmo B. Your support would be appreciated.

Hot (and lively)

The world has recently become a far tougher place. We used to dominate the market for Gizmos, and every one of us was damn proud of it. But a new bunch of competitors is out there. They're, lean, hungry and after our business. They want my job, and they want yours. We have to act fast and we have to act now. Otherwise, they'll have us for lunch and we'll all be standing in the unemployment line. First off, we will be cutting production of Gizmo A. We might love it, but not enough of anybody else shares our enthusiasm. We will be making more of Gizmo B, and investing every ounce of our sweat to make it the best Gizmo in the world. Nothing will stop us. Let's work together, and make sure that by the next quarterly report we're back where we should be – on top.

George Orwell, widely regarded as one of the finest ever prose writers in the English language, added the following recommendations to the above suggestion, and argued that they formed the foundation of effective writing skills:

1. Never use a long word where a short word will do.
2. If it is possible to cut out a word, always cut it out.
3. Never use the passive where you can use the active.
4. Never use a foreign phrase, a scientific word or a jargon word, if you can think of an everyday English equivalent.

5. Break any of these rules sooner than say anything outright barbarous.

- *Avoid vague modifiers*. These are imprecise expressions that leave an audience puzzled about what you expect them to do.[29] Padding illuminates an argument in the same way that a burnt out candle illuminates a darkened room. Instead, use specific, concrete language. For example, 'bottom line' means *final result*. 'Interface' means *meet*. Vagueness is also engendered when sentences are expressed in a negative manner. If someone says 'Computers are not as inexpensive in TopRam as they are here,' it takes some time to grasp what they mean. However, we quickly get the point if negatives are avoided and the person instead says 'Computers are cheaper here than in TopRam.' Interestingly, formal documents such as government welfare applications, often contain negation

Box 10.3 The anaemic impact of vague modifiers

Sample 1:

'Although an appropriate budget had originally been established, a slight financial over-run has been caused in the short to medium term, due to the consequences of unanticipated industrial action in our main supplier industry.'
Total words: 34

Translation:
'The project is now overspent. This is because of strikes in the machine tool industry.'
Total words: 15

Sample 2:

'He has a talent for self aggrandisement, obfuscation, and indolence, leavened only by the transparent nature of his intentions which renders it distinctly questionable whether his obvious ambitions will be realised.'
Total words: 31

Translation:
'He tells lies and is lazy. His main aim is self advancement, but since everyone knows this he will never be promoted.'
Total words: 22

such as: 'If the applicant is not earning less than € 15 000 she or he should not apply for this grant ...' and one wonders if the goal is to deliberately confuse the reader and so reduce uptake of available benefits. Box 10.3 contains two examples of writing that contain many vague modifiers, and then how they might appear if translated into a more vigorous style. Be ruthless while pruning your prose, and clear messages will bloom in the imagination of your readers.

- Make your writing *vigorous*, *direct* and *personal*. Compare the following two statements, and consider which would be likely to have the most impact: 'The job was completed on time and to the satisfaction of the customer' 'You did a top class piece of work and against all the odds you pulled it off well within the time frame. I am proud of you. Well done!'
- *Identify your central idea*. Write down the main purpose, theme or thesis that you are trying to convey. Then consider your expectations, what you intend to accomplish, the content areas that need to be addressed, the order of importance that they should come in and the amount of detail or information that will be required by the particular audiences that you need to address.[30]
- *Use the active rather than the passive style of writing.*[31] The active is more direct, more forceful, tends to use fewer words and is more likely to conjure up a clear picture of what you are talking about. Consider the following sentence:

  'The building was destroyed by the storm'.

  Here, the subject in the sentence (building) receives the action, and is hence described as passive. However, this could be amended to read:

  'The storm destroyed the building'.

  In this case, the subject (storm) does the destroying, and is therefore described as active. The overall impact is more vigorous, and the reader will be more likely to assume that such energy is a normal characteristic of the writer.
- *Build your writing around verbs*, like a theme park constructed around a spectacular central attraction. These are essential for active writing. Verbs 'show action, convey sense, and engage the reader'.[32] They are a visual image of something happening. Before you write something, think of what action it will convey, write it down as a verb and build the rest of the sentence around it. Do not say: 'We will do all that we can to achieve our goals.' Do say: 'We will storm heaven and earth and we will be victorious.'
- Consider at all times the importance of *accuracy, brevity and clarity*.

Presentation matters

- *Use headlines*. According to advertising guru, David Olgilvy, five times as many people read headlines as read the body copy. They grab our attention, and enable at least some of our message to get through. Headlines in quotes increase recall by around 28 per cent.[33] Headlines on memos, notices, e-mails or most other forms of written communication grab attention, without which no real information exchange occurs. As Sam Goldwyn reputedly once remarked: 'A good movie should start with an earthquake, and then work up to a climax.' Get the promise, claim you are making or the main point of the issue to hand into your headline, reaffirm it in the opening paragraph and repeat it at intervals throughout.
- *Insert frequent crossheads*. That is, use short headings to break up your text, and summarise the key issue of the next section. An army engaged in a long march needs regular stopovers for rest and refreshment. Crossheads create curiosity, but should also convey the gist of what is to follow in order to prepare the reader for your message to come. They improve both comprehension and recall.[34]
- *Insert illustrations*. Pictures and cartoons convey a human dimension to your message and attract attention, particularly if you are conveying information about particular individuals.[35] People love stories, however brief, about other people. As discussed in Chapter 3, case studies can be more effective than statistics in persuading an audience of your argument.
- *Use bullets, asterisks and marginal marks*.[36] This is particularly important when you are listing a number of disparate points on a range of issues, as we are doing here.
- *Indent the first line of a paragraph*. This increases speed of reading.[37]
- *Consider carefully the size of type that you use*. Type should be at least 10 point in size – this type is 14 point, while this is much smaller at 9 point and 12 point looks immediately much better.[38]
- *Printing in italics also reduces the speed of comprehension*, although it is effective for short passages of emphasis.[39]
- NEVER WRITE AT LENGTH IN CAPITAL LETTERS, *or prolong your use of italics, PARTICULARLY IN CAPITALS* – IT IS MUCH HARDER TO READ, ESPECIALLY IN A LONG MESSAGE. THAT IS WHY NEWSPAPERS ARE NEVER PRODUCED IN THIS STYLE![40]

- *Use the HATS acronym* to check the style of your document when finished.[41] This means looking at
  HEADINGS – Do you have enough of them? Do they reflect your subject matter?
  ACCESS – Is important information easy to locate? Does the method of presentation enhance the clarity of the message?
  TYPOGRAPHY – Do you use the appropriate typefaces and sizes, styles, and alignment options for both headings and body text?
  SPACE – Do you use sufficient white space, to avoid an impression of denseness and clutter?
- *Avoid errors in typing, spellings, in numbers and dates and misplaced apostrophes*. Presentational blunders suggest the presence of a sloppy thinker. Readers will reason that your careless attitude towards small issues betokens a careless attitude towards bigger issues: first impressions do count.

In praise of plain English

The 'Plain English Campaign' has made a major contribution to the campaign for clear writing. It has identified many examples of bureaucratic or otherwise mystifying jargon in company and Government documents and urged the use of plainer English as a means of conveying meaning rather than confusion. For example, European Union documents at one point redesignated a 'cow' as 'a grain-consuming animal unit'. Another described a plane crash as an 'involuntary conversion'. A British local authority replaced the evocative term 'bottlenecks' with 'localised capacity deficiencies', while another added the following erratum to its district plan: 'For the justification statement read the implementation note and vice versa.'[42] Other instances abound. An Air Accident Investigations Bureau Report on a near miss over Heathrow Airport in London concluded that 'Co-ordination between air arrivals and air departures was incomplete' – that is, the planes nearly collided. The Bureau for At-Risk Youth in New York produced hundreds of pencils for primary schools with the message 'Too Cool To Do Drugs'. Once these had been sharpened a few times they read 'Cool To Do Drugs' and later 'Do Drugs'. The pencils were withdrawn. Clearly, it is vital to think ahead when you write. Obscure language is often matched by long-windedness. The longest sentence the Campaign has found was in part of a sales contract and ran to 513 words. A New Zealand mortgage agreement only managed a 236-word sentence – but did get by without any punctuation.[43]

In addition to many of the points listed above, the Campaign urges the following in written English:

- a good average sentence length (about 15–20 words)
- everyday English (e.g. words such as 'we' and 'you' rather than 'the insured', 'the applicant')
- conciseness
- an average line length of between 7 and 23 words
- plenty of answer space and a logical flow (on forms).

The campaign now has a seal of approval – the Crystal Mark. This has become a much sought after symbol among major corporations who wish to use it on their documents. It certifies that they have been tried out on members of the public. But it is also evident that clear written documentation improves decision-making, and hence makes business sense. For example, with the Campaign's help, British Aerospace redrafted a 150-page international leasing agreement in just 50 pages. The first time the new document was used, a £120 million deal took just three and a half weeks to complete, instead of the previous average of six months. The benefits are enormous.

Letters and memos

Effective written memos and letters follow the guidelines listed above. They have a definite purpose, a specific target audience and convey clear information in as succinct a fashion as possible. When they are required to do more than simply impart information, they should use an appropriate blend of the levers of persuasion discussed in Chapter 3 to argue a case. One of their most important characteristics is length. Paperwork is an organisation's cholesterol. The arteries of even the healthiest organisation are generally clogged with far too much. Readers therefore respond with gratitude towards short communications, in which the primary point is nevertheless made absolutely clear. Elegant formula and exotic excursions have their place, but their primary role is to make the ultimate sacrifice in the interests of brevity (see Reflective exercise 10.1).

Writing reports

Most managers are called upon to produce reports during their careers. The ability to do so frequently determines whether your career has lift

Reflective exercise 10.1 Dynamic writing

Read the following memo carefully. Then rewrite it, in line with the guidelines for dynamic writing outlined above. An alternative is contained at the end of this chapter, but you should first of all craft your own version before reading it. Cheating is not allowed!

To: All employees of Rite Manufacturing Corporation
From: Managing Director
Date: 28th June, year

I am happy to advise you that representatives of the Board will be available next Friday 5th July to acquaint you with information about additional voluntary contributions to our existing occupational pension scheme. This will help all of you to plan for a comfortable retirement, and should take no more than a few minutes of your time. Feel free to contact my office for further details. The meeting with the Board representatives will be at 11.30 a.m. in the Boardroom. In addition, experts from our finance department will be on hand to deal with any detailed queries you may have on this issue. I hope to see you there.

Total words: 122

off, or whether it stalls on the launch pad. Reports can be viewed as 'primarily factual accounts that communicate objectively about some aspect of the business'.[44] One of the problems with writing them is that they typically have multiple audiences. For example, an account of financial audit reports estimates that they will typically have at least eight different audiences, including management, boards of directors and outside auditors.[45] Nevertheless, most reports come with certain expectations and standard formats.

In general, they are expected to be:

- *Timely*. This refers to both the production of the report, and its contents. Ideally, it should arrive before it is due (but certainly no later), and contain the most up-to-date information available on the problem at hand.
- *Well written*. The report should be clear, concise and interesting; it should grab the reader's attention and hold it throughout; it should avoid errors in grammar, spelling, punctuation and factual content.

One factual error damages the credibility of your whole case, much as a single episode of adultery shatters a reputation for fidelity. Above all, it should be driven by a bias towards action, which solves a problem, identifies the next steps your key audience can and must take, and relates to the underlying business objectives of the organisation.

- *Well organised.* A good report is designed to be read selectively, so that the reader can pay attention only to its most necessary parts. Most reports have multiple audiences, and will have few readers interested in its entire content. For this reason, with long reports, an executive summary is obligatory.
- *Attractive.* It should be clearly labelled, arrive in good condition and be presented with an attractive typeface and lay out. First impressions count. They shape expectations about the overall impact and import of the report. Thus, many of the issues concerning the power of attractiveness in communication between people, as discussed in Chapter 3, also apply here. A well-presented report projects a favourable impression of you, and creates an aura of attractiveness around your central propositions.
- *Cost effective.* The report's recommendations should be designed to solve real problems facing its readership, and should be clearly explained, possible to implement and cost effective. Although there are no guidelines on the maximum number of recommendations it should contain, it is important to remember that an organisation with 40 priorities in reality has none. On the other hand, a small number of key proposals is known as an action plan.
- *A report begins before the beginning,* with the terms of reference set for its production. These identify the problem(s) it will be expected to solve, set explicit limits on the range of issues to be addressed and identify specific outcomes towards which the report should aspire. Box 10.4 provides an example terms of reference that are more likely to produce a report with an agenda for action.

You are also asked to consider the terms of reference outlined in Reflective exercise 10.2, and contrast them with the options discussed above. Standard formats exist for the structure of a report, which will normally contain the following:[46]

- Title page
- Contents
- Acknowledgements

Box 10.4 Examples of effective terms of reference

1. Complaints from customers. To investigate why the rate of complaints from customers about the new payment system has increased by 20 per cent in the last three months and to recommend changes in procedure which will solve this problem.
2. The current computerised personnel management information system (PMIS). To explore alternative systems currently available, conduct a cost benefit analysis of the various options, and recommend whether to upgrade the present system or to keep it for a specified period.
3. Absenteeism. To establish our current level of absenteeism, compare it to industry wide norms, investigate its causes and recommend measures which will significantly reduce it.

Reflective exercise 10.2 Writing for objectives

Study carefully the terms of reference shown here, and then answer the questions listed below:

'To produce ideas which will enable the Board to refine a strategy for innovation in certain key resource areas, thereby increasing market penetration in our most important markets, enhancing quality, improving the efficient use of resources and increasing profits in the next financial year.'

Issues for consideration:

- List as many of the objectives contained in the above terms of reference as you can.
- Consider whether the objectives identified are compatible or in conflict with each other.
- Pick what you think are the top two objectives. Consider the criteria that influenced your decision. Would other people in your organisation employ other criteria, and reach different conclusions?
- Translate your main two objectives into terms of reference that match the style and specificity of those on offer in Box 10.4.

- Executive summary
- Introduction
- Methodology
- Findings/Conclusions
- Recommendations
- Appendices
- References.

❑ *The Acknowledgements* are an opportunity to identify key change agents within the organisation who have helped you with the most important aspects of the report's production. By sharing the credit you gain a valuable reputation as a team player. You also spread the responsibility for awkward issues raised and difficult decisions proposed: it is harder for people to reject your conclusions outright, if you can identify the Chief Executive as a key figure in drawing up your terms of reference and gathering your data. But avoid 'Oscar night syndrome': the urge to thank everyone, down to your remotest ancestors, who has made the slightest contribution to your night of glittering triumph. This tempts readers to fast forward before your peroration reaches its climax.

❑ *The Summary* should outline both the main findings and recommendations. Busy senior staff will read only this section. However, the rest of the report lends authority to the summary. Readers who query a particular finding or recommendation can delve into the appropriate section in more depth, to reassure themselves that you have done your homework, and that your conclusions rest on solid evidence rather than an unstable mixture of hype and hope. Such supporting testimony is excised from the summary, which needs to combine brevity with a comprehensive account of the most salient issues.

❑ *The Introduction* should explain who commissioned the report, who was responsible for the project or issue it is discussing, the purpose of the report, the method of inquiry which has been adopted and the terms of reference which have been set. It should also explain how the data have been assembled and arranged, how the report is structured and whatever general background factors you consider to be most crucial. In general, this means identifying the importance of the issue to the organisation at this stage. The temptation here is to assume that, since the issue is by now over-familiar to you, it will be equally familiar to everyone else.

❑ *The Methodology* outlines, in detail, the steps which you took to assemble your data – for example, who you interviewed, what questionnaires you used (and why), what other reports you relied upon, what tests you carried out and what other organisations you studied. Each measure taken should be explicitly related to your starting terms of reference. This helps you to build a convincing series of steps towards your grand design – the recommendations which you want the organisation to implement. They should appear logical, rest on irrefutable facts and be supported by a wealth of impressive detail. Would you buy a house if the builder had neglected to erect it on solid foundations?

❑ *The Findings/Conclusions* section details precisely what you have discovered. It should also present your analysis of their significance. If 70 per cent of your customers express a hostile attitude towards your new product, and a favourable attitude towards that of your main competitor, what precisely does this mean for your marketing strategy? Add interpretation to the facts. Draw clear conclusions.

❑ *The Recommendations* are the heartland of any report, and should emerge clearly from the findings, rather than appear unintroduced in the middle of your conclusions. Your principal finding (judged by its importance to your organisation, and as identified in your terms of reference) should attract the most emphasis in the recommendations. It is vital to frame recommendations so that they tell people the following:[47]

- ▶ Why were we doing the wrong thing before?
- ▶ How does this change fit with the previous changes?
- ▶ What will remain constant?
- ▶ How is this change grounded in our values and commitments?
- ▶ What will the organisation look like in six months? In a year?
- ▶ What will we gain or lose personally?
- ▶ What support will we get to make the change?
- ▶ What will executives do to make sure the change works?

Remember also that too many recommendations produce paralysis rather than action. In addition, anything that irritates your readers or does not support your case distracts from it. You should resist the urge to drag your own darling hobbyhorses centre stage: other people never find your children as fascinating as you do. Above all, answer this cardinal question: what can the organisation do differently to what it already does, and how will this make a difference to the main problem which it currently faces?

❑ *The Appendices* should contain supporting material which is important to your case, but which does not belong logically in the main body of the report. These include examples of data collection instruments (e.g. questionnaires), tables which are of interest to some readers but are marginal to the main issues being explored, or more lengthy extracts from interviews with people who have been surveyed.

- *The References* is a list of main sources cited in your text – books, reports, newspaper articles, journal articles or official statements. This reassures readers that your methods, findings and recommendations rest on a solid body of research and experience. It also enables anyone who wishes to explore in more detail a particular issue you have raised to do so by following up some of the sources you have cited. If they do, this is also likely to reinforce their interest and hence commitment to the issues raised in your report.

Breaking bad news

Reports must also sometimes tell people bad news. For example, they might have to explain that a crisis is looming, at a time when neither senior managers nor anybody else wants to hear about it. Only hypochondriacs visit a doctor praying for bad news. In fact, organisations frequently ignore warning signals that tell them something is dreadfully wrong.[48] How can reports alert them to warning signs in such a manner that they take corrective action, rather than guillotine the messenger?

Research suggests that when positive and negative feedback has to be communicated about a person, object, process or organisation the message recipient is more likely to believe the message when it begins with the positive comment.[49] This may be because a variety of self-serving biases cause most of us to routinely exaggerate our proficiency as communicators.[50] In consequence, a message that begins by confirming what we think we already know (i.e. *what I am doing well*) has a greater intuitive validity for most people, and leaves them more favourably disposed to accept what follows. A report should begin by accentuating the positive, in the form of stating whatever good news it honestly can.

It is also important to indicate how the findings compare with surveys of this kind in other organisations, or how much further improvement could be realistically expected at this juncture of its history. This will facilitate benchmarking. Context is vital to promote understanding and facilitate action.

Above all, the report should be written in non-inflammatory and neutral language, offering solutions rather than a grievance list. It should be sensitive to the internal politics, language and values of the organisation concerned. Rather than identify scapegoats, responsibility for problems should be shared as widely as is honestly possible, thereby encouraging a collective determination to do something about them. Naming and shaming leads to aggravation, conflagration and retaliation.

Reinforcing the previous point, it is vital that critical feedback be constructed as non-judgementally as possible.[51] This means that it should avoid negatively labelling the people involved (e.g. 'the marketing department in this organisation is causing blockages for every other department, and therefore creating nothing but trouble'). Such an approach attacks people's face needs, and is thus likely to provoke their immediate opposition rather than attract their support. On the other hand, a constructive focus on detailed behaviours which can be changed is likely to be perceived as helpful feedback, and spur further change. Thus, a report *could* usefully say: 'The Marketing Department is pivotal to the entire operation of the company. It currently has a very heavy workload, which leads to delays for other Departments. This problem should be addressed.' Non-judgemental feedback is generally perceived as one of the foundation stones of supportive communication.

E-mail, snail mail, more mail

The Internet has transformed business communication. At one point during the 1990s, there were 20 million US e-mail addresses, and more than half of these had gone on line during one calendar year: a phenomenal rate of expansion.[52] The advent of the new millennium witnessed e-mail becoming the dominant force in written communications, both in the office and at home.

E-mail enables the 'instant transfer of messages and documents worldwide between people on the same private network, or with access to the same public network'.[53] For example, in one calendar month the Royal Mail handled 258 million letters for domestic customers in the UK, while over twice as many e-mails (550 million) were sent and received from family homes.[54] This has done more than change the way in which we transmit information: it has also increased the volume we send. Most people now regard it as a vital link in the information chain, and a measure of the importance that managers attach to communication, both internally and externally. One respondent in a communication audit conducted by us, in an organisation where e-mail had not yet been introduced, commented: 'We need e-mail around here. Without it I feel like the Flintstones.'

Here, we focus on the challenges that this poses for effective writing. The informal nature of the medium can lead to problems such as misunderstanding and conflict. 'Netspeak' is neither written nor spoken language. Rather, it draws on aspects of both, forming a 'third medium' for communication.[55] Employees should understand that the way in which they communicate through e-mail is different to normal communication. They must appreciate the unique qualities of this new language. This has been recognised in many corporations. For instance, the New Jersey Hospital Association adopted a proactive approach, by providing training for all new recruits, encompassing the basics of communicating quickly but courteously, being careful not to write e-mails which could come back to haunt the sender, and the importance of proof-reading.[56]

However, the time devoted to writing e-mails is usually lower than that allocated to letters or memos, and therefore the content is often less precise. Spelling and grammatical errors that would be frowned upon in memos or letters are more readily accepted in e-mails. Indeed, with the epidemic of texting from mobile phones, e-messages are becoming even less formal. But confirming by e-mail a formal appointment with the CEO with 'OK4PowWowUrDenCUThen' is clearly not appropriate! In business contexts, words and phrases need to be chosen carefully. Box 10.5 presents guidelines for e-mail composition, which should be incorporated into employee training.

But all opportunities also bring dangers. Here, we focus on two issues. The first is that most of us assume – wrongly – that our office e-mails are private. In fact, at least two in three British employers monitor website access and incoming e-mail messages, while roughly 80 per cent of US employers have software capable of monitoring employee internet usage.[57] It is likely that these figures will grow. An obvious target is pornography. However, the software can also scan for such words as 'CV' or 'application', each of which might suggest that the employee is looking for a job elsewhere. The conclusion is simple. You should consider very carefully what you include in e-mail messages, and whether it could imperil your career or cost you your job. One in four British firms say they would fire employees who violate their internet policies,[58] and many have already done so. Caution is vital.

Second, a related problem is what has been dubbed 'flame mail' – angry e-mails that escalate conflict out of control. Part of the problem is that 'writing e-mail is a solitary activity. The reader is not there to

Box 10.5 Guidelines for writing business e-mails

1. Decide whether e-mail is the most effective medium for your purpose. Would other channels of communication be better?
2. Consider the needs of your audience. Adjust your style to that of the person to whom it is being sent.
3. Always use a signature as this gives vital contact details for follow-up.
4. Use a 'talking' subject line that tells the readers *what the message is about* and *how it concerns them*.
5. Only mark messages as 'urgent' when they really are.
6. Keep the message brief. Put the most important words and part of the message first, since this is what readers will see in their in-box display.
7. Keep emphasis to a minimum.
8. Check for spelling and grammar – this is often overlooked in casual e-mails.
9. Re-read messages to check for clear understanding.
10. Select the final distribution list before you write. If you do it later, you will not have composed the message with the audience's interests in mind. The odds are that most of it will pass most readers by.
11. Do not get involved in 'flaming'. There is a natural temptation to respond to rude e-mails in kind. This escalates conflict. Remember: if you lose your temper you lose the argument.

nod approval or frown when they disagree. Not surprisingly, then, e-mail writers, 'may state their messages bluntly, treating readers insensitively, or fail to explain fully, ignoring readers' needs.'[59] Accordingly, more than half of the 1000 users who responded to one major survey had received abusive e-mails (so-called 'flame mails'), which irreparably damaged working relationships.[60] Fifty-four per cent of antisocial e-mails were from managers to their staff and one in six of all respondents reported being officially disciplined via e-mail. Interestingly, flame mails were five times more likely to be written by men than by women. Forty six per cent of respondents also said that e-mail had reduced face-to-face communication in their workplace, and that this had led to less co-operation, greater internal conflict among colleagues, bullying and a more unpleasant working atmosphere. In short, e-mail lacks the nonverbal and tonal cues of face-to-face communication, on which we rely to interpret meaning. The rapid nature of e-mail also means that it provides for instant communication, at a time when tempers are running high and both parties require a cooling off period.

It has been suggested[61] that these problems can be reduced if we follow the simple guidelines contained in Box 10.6. These could form the basis of what is sometimes described as a 'netiquette statement'.

A clear danger with e-mail is the assumption that more communication is better communication. This can transform computer screens into slag heaps of discarded information, through which people forage in a futile quest to find something useful. The outcome is more likely to be isolation and despondency, rather than cohesion and enlightenment. The scale of the problem is illustrated by a survey of Information Technology directors and senior- and middle-ranking managers in the UK.[62] On average, managers reported receiving 52 e-mails a day, with seven per cent receiving 100 or more. But only 30 per cent of them were deemed essential, with a further 37 per cent regarded as important and the remainder being irrelevant or unnecessary.

Box 10.6 Composing fire proof e-mails

1. Resist the temptation to respond to the e-mail of another person when you are still angry.
2. Wait until you calm down before replying.
3. Consider whether you would say what you want to say to someone's face.
4. Do not use abusive language: a message cannot be rescinded once it has been transmitted, and the more discourteous your tone the more likely it is that this will become the issue, rather than whatever it is you should really be discussing with the other person.
5. Temper your overall enthusiasm for e-mail with an awareness of its defects and hazards.
6. Consider whether a face-to-face meeting might be more appropriate, or at least a useful follow up to your e-mail message.
7. Invest the same care in composing your message that you would do in writing a formal letter or memorandum.
8. Set the e-mail aside for an hour and then review it, before finally sending it.

All this can also mean that face-to-face communication becomes neglected. Precisely such a difficulty was reported with Apple Computers, which developed a culture of people having a computer on their desks.[63] In a dilemma that anyone who has become addicted to Macs will readily recognise, people loved the technology and came to rely on it so much that face-to-face communication was neglected. Apple's response was to hold a series of conferences for different levels of management, specifically to promote face-to-face communication. This led to systems for face-to-face briefings, the development of national publications and the convening of cross-functional communication meetings. The lesson is that the role and impact of e-mail should be carefully monitored, to ensure that it supplements rather than supplants the old 'technology' of people talking to people face-to-face.

An area where written communication is particularly pertinent is in dealing with complaints. A study by the Henley Centre for Forecasting[64] found that 95 per cent of complaining customers preferred their grievances to be dealt with in writing. Evidently, this reassures them that the issue is being treated seriously, and in most cases has the effect of discouraging further action, including litigation. Various writers on this question have suggested guidelines, and these are summarised in Box 10.7. In general, complaints are viewed as a litmus test of an organisation's commitment to genuine customer care. This holds true for 'internal' customers, as well as those outside its own ranks. Adherence to these guidelines is a vital means of nurturing those relationships most critical to overall success.

Box 10.7 Dealing with complaints

1. Don't delay – reply today. It is human nature to post-pone tasks we find unpleasant; it is equally human nature to seek a fast response when we feel aggrieved. Rapid action short circuits customer disillusionment.
2. Remember that it is easier to fire missiles in missives than it is face-to-face. Resist the temptation to declare war on the enemy.
3. Personalise your reply. Use the complainant's name. Otherwise, they are liable to feel they have received a standard form letter and that their complaint is not being taken seriously.
4. Thank the person for bringing the problem to your attention, however annoyed you feel by the complaint or however

Box 10.7 *continued*

irrational you assume it is. This might calm troubled waters: you must also reckon with the possibility that whatever you write will be read by many people other than the addressee. If people see you in full Blitzkrieg mode they will assume that this is your natural state, and take their business elsewhere.

5. Inform the complainant that you understand his or her point of view. Do this even if you think they are wrong – you can then explain the other point of view. However, most people want to be treated seriously and feel that they are understood. Acknowledging that you hear their grievance deflates aggression.
6. If an apology is in order, then express it whole-heartedly. Communicate your genuine desire to make amends.
7. Ensure that the letter is signed by the most senior person possible.
8. Resist the temptation to be curt. If a detailed reply is necessary to deal adequately with the issue – write it.
9. If the problem lies with some other department in your company avoid catching the virus of 'blameititis'. Customers detest organisations which treat complaints like an unexploded bomb, to be lobbed from Department to Department.
10. Err on the side of accepting responsibility, offering restitution and making placatory noises.

Overview

Communication must add value to information, rather than simply distribute it. Written communication, as this chapter has shown, has the potential to accomplish this in multiple ways. It can become a permanent form of recognition, and thus has high reward potential for staff. E-mail binds an organisation tighter together, speeds up the flow of information, increases its quantity and facilitates more rapid contact between a business and its customers. Well-crafted reports create a bias towards action, and help promote their authors' careers. Long ago, Confucius said it well: 'If language is not correct, then what is said is not what is meant; if what is said is not what is meant, then what ought to be done remains undone.'

Even if we lack his eloquence, most of us can improve our written communication skills. The guidelines outlined throughout this chapter will help. Practice may not make perfect, but it does make better. Remember – *Writing Matters*. Defective written communication leads to congestion on the information superhighway, causing traffic jams, multiple pile-ups and outbursts of road rage. Effective written communication keeps the traffic flowing freely, nurtures relationships and ensures a smoother journey towards business success. Used wisely, it will serve you and your organisation well.

Box 10.8 Model answer for reflective exercise 10.1

To: All employees of Rite Manufacturing Corporation
From: Managing Director
Date: 28th June, year

Come and find out how you can plan for a more comfortable retirement by taking out additional voluntary contributions to our existing pension scheme.

Date: Friday 5th July
Place: Boardroom
Time of meeting: 11.30a.m.
Total words: 48

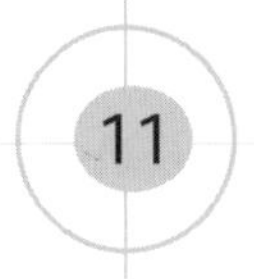

Tell it like it is ...: communicating assertively

Introduction

Conflict is a persistent feature of organisational life, as was pointed out in Chapter 7. When people share a workplace, such that their efforts are in some measure interdependent, differences in values, goals, strategies and priorities easily lead to tension, create unease and put individuals on their guard.[1] We tend to react in predictable ways when confronted by threatening situations. Put simply, we are inclined to either go on the offensive with all guns blazing or, alternatively, flee from the battlefield in disarray without firing a shot. We exhibit what is called the 'fight/flight response'. This is a well-established reaction to danger. Down through the ages, this predisposition has been passed from generation to generation. When confronted with a woolly mammoth or sabre-toothed tiger, there was obvious survival value for our ancestors in being well prepared for intense physical activity. This is just what the 'fight/flight response' does, it prepares us physiologically, psychologically and behaviourally to deal with potentially life-threatening challenges. Changes described by Paterson,[2] at the physiological level, include increases in heart rate, blood pressure, blood sugar levels, blood supply to large muscle groups, the release of endorphins and respiration. Psychologically, we become very focused on specific, unitary tasks, and may experience heightened emotional states of fear or anger. At the same time, dealing with complex, multifaceted tasks is hampered and creative thinking curtailed. Behaviourally, we grow edgy and restless in preparation for action.

In the present day world of business, commerce and public service, this conditioning for confrontation does not, however, serve us particularly well. Here threats to which managers are exposed are of an altogether different kind from the physical forms with which our ancestors were faced. This jungle is the Boardroom, the shop floor and the CEO's office. What is at stake is neither life nor limb, but monetary success, personal advancement, reputation and respect. In place of predatory beasts are myopic directors, ambitious colleagues, recalcitrant staff, fickle customers and ruthless competitors. 'Injuries' are the result of rejected visions, sabotaged projects, unfulfilled commitments, broken promises and lost contracts. Still, when managers' antennae begin vibrating to such workplace danger signals, the natural reaction is still channelled by the time-honoured fight/flight response. It is now acted out, though, in a different form. Violent physical counter-attack (although it still does happen) is reshaped into the delivery of an aggressive verbal mauling, or running away by withdrawal into sullen quiescence.

Despite the fact that these two options of fight or flight are, in a sense, the 'instinctive' way to react when confronted with conflict situations at work, both are often strikingly ineffective. Verbal attack often triggers reciprocation or, on the other hand, the victim makes an escape. Either way, the precipitating problem is left unresolved. Likewise, metaphorically fleeing from the situation, while bringing a temporary respite and sense of relief, does not help to advance a workable solution. But the negative effects can be even more telling. Put by Lindenfield,[3] this auto-response 'can and does threaten our bodies, relationships and even our ability to keep a job or drive a car safely'. But there is another option. We aren't compelled, in such instances, to fall victim to our evolutionary heritage. Being assertive is an alternative way of dealing with people problems that in most instances leads to more successful outcomes all round and a more committed and productive workforce.

Stated simply, assertion is a way of expressing one's needs, feelings and opinions honestly, openly, directly but respectfully, without being racked by negative emotions such as anxiety or guilt.[4] This chapter is about assertion and how it can advance more effectively communication in management. Assertiveness will be set against the contrasting styles of relating commonly found in work settings, namely aggressiveness and submissiveness. Causes and consequences of each will be explored. Verbal and nonverbal features of assertive behaviour will be outlined in some detail. The importance of knowing your rights in situations and moulding appropriate belief about yourself, others and what counts as acceptable conduct, will also be discussed. For the present, however, we will continue with some initial thoughts about assertiveness and why it is often the preferred way of dealing with people problems in management.

Assertiveness and management

Let us be clear at the outset about what assertiveness is *not*. It is not about always getting your way through bullying and intimidation. Admittedly this is how the term has come to be commonly used. Describing a boss as being very assertive typically conjures up an image of a person who is loud, brash, arrogant and roundly unpleasant. It must be stressed, this is *not* how assertiveness is being thought of here. Indeed the above description sketches one of the contrasting styles of communicating that we will look at – aggressiveness. Alberti and Emmons,[5] authors of *Your Perfect Right*, one of the classic self-help books in this area, pointed up this confusion between assertion and aggression but explained that, unlike the latter, 'assertive behaviour doesn't push others around, deny their rights, or ride roughshod over them'. A well-established way of thinking of this relationship is in terms of a continuum. If aggressiveness is at one end with submissiveness and passivity at the other, then assertiveness falls somewhere in the middle.[6]

So what is assertiveness? One of the earliest definitions by Lazarus[7] pointed to four key attributes. It is being able to:

- refuse requests
- ask for favours and make requests
- express positive and negative feelings
- initiate, continue and terminate general conversations.

Personal rights are also involved as we have seen – both those of the individual being assertive and the recipient. Lange and Jakubowski[8] stated that 'assertion involves standing up for personal rights and expressing thoughts, feelings and beliefs in direct, honest and appropriate ways which respect the rights of other people'. Furthermore, Rakos[9] believed that being properly assertive requires that the responsibilities attendant upon those rights be also acknowledged and brought into play. We will return to the issue of rights and responsibilities later in the chapter.

As well as including the stipulation of exercising and acknowledging personal rights, the assertive individual should feel emotionally comfortable behaving in this way. Assertion 'promotes equality in human relationships, enabling us to act in our own best interests, to stand up for ourselves without undue anxiety, to express honest feelings comfortably, to exercise personal rights without denying the rights of others'.[10] Hargie and Dickson[11] specified 12 main sub-types of assertion. Six of these have to do with handling negative situations and are also described as *conflict assertion*. Here the difficulty is in taking a line that is at odds with others or challenges them in some manner. The remaining six sub-types are essentially positive scenario that require the individual to become more prominent in the interaction through giving and receiving agreeable information, especially about self, that could cause embarrassment or awkwardness. All 12 are listed in Box 11.1. People differ in the ease with which they characteristically deal with situations such as those in Box 11.1. For some they cause no great concern while others avoid them if at all possible. Before moving on to outline the role of assertion in management, it may be useful to pause at this point to consider your present levels of assertion. Using Reflective exercise 11.1, decide if this style characterises your present handling of social situations.

Those who read this chapter in the vain hope that it will enable them to dominate, control and subjugate their workforce more effectively will be disappointed. As explained, assertiveness is not about that. But it is not only that they won't find this information – more importantly, they shouldn't need it. It flies in the face of communicative strategies and styles demanded by current principles of effective management.[12]

Box 11.1 Sub-types of assertion

Negative or conflict assertion

1. Making reasonable requests
2. Refusing unwanted or unreasonable requests
3. Asking others to change their behaviour
4. Giving personal opinions even if unpopular
5. Expressing disagreement or negative feelings
6. Responding to criticism from others.

Positive assertion

7. Expressing positive feelings
8. Responding to positive feelings expressed by others
9. Giving compliments
10. Accepting compliments gracefully
11. Admitting mistakes or personal shortcomings
12. Initiating and sustaining interactions.

Reflective exercise 11.1 Check your assertiveness

Consider each of the following statements about yourself and respond to each by circling the number that *in general* best represents your position in relation to it.

	Always	Often	Uncertain	Seldom	Never
1. I find it difficult saying 'No' to people.	1	2	3	4	5
2. I really look forward to meeting people for the first time.	1	2	3	4	5
3. I tend to go along with what others want.	1	2	3	4	5
4. I find it easy talking about my feelings.	1	2	3	4	5
5. I avoid conflict at all costs.	1	2	3	4	5
6. I lack confidence	1	2	3	4	5
7. Others take advantage of my good nature.	1	2	3	4	5
8. Making complaints is no problem to me.	1	2	3	4	5
9. I prefer to write rather than deal with awkward situations face-to face.	1	2	3	4	5
10. I pay compliments when appropriate	1	2	3	4	5
11. I usually drop hints that I am unhappy with others' performance, rather than mention it outright.	1	2	3	4	5
12. If others displease me I soon let them know.	1	2	3	4	5
13. Others put upon me.	1	2	3	4	5
14. I get my ideas accepted.	1	2	3	4	5
15. I get the respect that I deserve.	1	2	3	4	5
16. I dislike asking others for favours	1	2	3	4	5
17. I always have my say regardless of others	1	2	3	4	5
18. I'm relaxed about speaking in public	1	2	3	4	5
19. I give in rather than cause an argument	1	2	3	4	5
20. I'm happy to point out others' mistakes to them	1	2	3	4	5

See Box 11.7 at the end of the chapter for the scoring procedure.

Contemporary practice contrasts starkly with that from an earlier era when management was all about taking decisions, often with little or no consultation with the rest of the workforce, and then enforcing total compliance. Power and strength of leadership were measured in these terms. Communication was top down, from boss to staff. Workers acquiesced resentfully, left or were sacked. They did what they had to do but, typically, with no sense of ownership and hence little enthusiasm, commitment or dedication. Many managers were slow to recognise that this was scarcely the way to get the best out of people.

Changes in work have heralded a new set of values and principles shaping how management and employees now cast their relationship to their mutual benefit. These changes have direct and very real implications for how communication should be conducted.[13,14] They include the following:

- flattening of organisational structures and the devolution of responsibility leading to the greater autonomy of small teams of workers;
- replacement of an outdated culture of 'command and control' with an alternative that favours participative management and collective decision-making;
- entry of a generation into the workforce that is less prepared to reverentially obey orders, as previous generations have done, merely because they come from someone on a higher rung of the organisational ladder;
- a better-educated workforce more fully prepared to become involved in the decision-making process, expected to be entrepreneurial, and to take responsibility for its personal and professional development;
- staff who are less content than past generations with mere monetary rewards but who demand a strong sense of personal fulfilment from work;
- improved employment legislation protecting the rights of employees from practices that could be construed as harassment or bullying;
- wider dissemination of alternative management practices, through growing internationalisation of industry, that are at odds with those that took root in the first wave of industrialisation and persisted in many quarters until recently.

All of these changes point in the direction of styles of management with an emphasis on participation, facilitation and empowerment. Influencing workers rather than controlling them through subjugation is what counts. Maximising available resources and expertise in decision-making leads to more effective outcomes. Communicating in an open, inclusive and honest way that is direct yet respectful, is what is required. This calls for a style that is assertive rather than aggressive or passive.

Before moving on to examine assertiveness in greater depth, it will help to focus it more firmly if we briefly contrast it with the other two alternative styles already mentioned, aggressiveness and submissiveness.

Communicating aggressively

An aggressive style ignores, threatens or violates the rights of other people. Managers acting aggressively operate in accordance with just one set of personal considerations – their own. The working assumption is that their needs are more important, their concerns more pressing, their opinions more valid and their feelings more acute than those of the person being put upon. Aggressive types are out to get what they want rather than what is best for all concerned. The objective is to have things their way, to win at all costs. This may be done through bullying, threatening or making empty promises. It inevitably trades on the misuse of power and the exploitation of weakness or vulnerability. As such, in addition to being strategically short sighted, aggression is also ethically dubious.

Aggression can be direct and explicit or indirect and implicit.[15] We tend to think of it as the former, for the most part, and expressed in shouts, dire threats, red faces and savage looks. In soccer circles, at the hands of a tyrannical manager, it has become known as receiving the 'hair dryer' treatment.

Direct aggression

We have all most probably witnessed, experienced or perhaps even perpetrated an aggressive attack upon someone at work, at some time or other. In the most extreme case this can take a physical form with violence. Direct verbal aggression, in its full-blown form, is not difficult to spot. But other instances that are less 'hot' may be less easy to notice. Remember though that the manager behaving aggressively denies or in some way violates the rights of others. This is the key. The sensitivities of the other person are infringed or denied: their needs are disregarded.

Aggressive individuals typically place themselves centre stage and try to dominate proceedings to the exclusion of others. They tend to be closed-minded, opinionated and confrontational: they are right and all others are wrong and should be made aware of the fact. They are poor listeners, forceful, arrogant, demeaning and abrasive.[16] Typical verbal and nonverbal accompaniments of this style are noted in Box 11.2.

Box 11.2 Responding aggressively

Verbal cues

▸ Threat	'If that report is not on my desk by four o'clock, you can look for a job elsewhere.'
▸ Ridicule	'You never have your work done on time. I can never depend upon you to do anything.'
▸ Abuse	'Come on you prat, jump to it.'
▸ Foul language	'**** ****'
▸ Demands	'Get me the accounts for last year, and do it now.'
▸ Directives	'Never leave your desk before it is cleared and always make sure that I know where you can be contacted.'
▸ Interruption	'Stop right there! Before you say another word let me tell you what your rights are!'
▸ Blame	'It would have worked perfectly if you had done it properly.'
▸ Self-opinionation	'That is nonsense. The only workable solution is to move Johns into Sales, as I said at the start.'
▸ Intrusion	'I heard you mention the ZX34 model, a fine machine. I worked on them for three years. What I don't know about a ZX34 isn't worth knowing. The name 's Jones, by the way. Hope I'm not intruding, but let me tell you a thing or two about that machine.'

Box 11.2 *continued*

Nonverbal cues

▸ Tone of voice	Loud, strident, yelling, intense, strained
▸ Speed of speech	Fast
▸ Gaze	Staring, unbroken, intimidating
▸ Facial expression	Glaring, frowning
▸ Pallor	Florid, blanched
▸ Gestures	Animated
▸ Posture	Expansive, tense.

Various reasons for aggression in the workplace have been suggested.[17,18] Aggression may be:

- successful *in the short-term*. It can intimidate others into compliance or prevent them from making further demands. Apparent success leads to reinforcement and perpetuation of belligerence;
- modelled on the style of another senior figure in the organisation;
- a reaction to frustration;
- in response to perceived personal attack. For whatever reason, situations and cues may be read as posing personal threat. As such, the best defensive strategy becomes retaliation;
- more probable in situations where aggressors feel they can get away with it. This is the bullying aspect. It is likely to be directed at an underling rather than the boss;
- a feature of dysfunctional levels of personal control. People differ in the extent to which they can keep their hostile feelings under check;
- the result of the aggressor having been socialised into a work culture where such behaviour is relatively common and largely tolerated;
- an expression of hostility transferred from an entirely different situation. A manager may vent spleen on some undeserving junior member of staff in reaction to being carpeted by the CEO at an earlier meeting;
- mistaken for assertion because acceptable assertive skills have never been learned.

Regardless of why aggression occurs, an appreciation of its aftermath is crucially important. What are the consequences of this way of handling difficult situations and awkward people? Consequences are both short and long term and accrue to the perpetrator, the victim and the organisation.[19,20]

The perpetrator

Aggression may produce short-term advantages for the manager who adopts this style. The victim may acquiesce and comply with demands made. The precipitating problem may be sorted out, after a fashion, and at least for the moment. This is likely to lead to feelings of relief, perhaps even power and authority. The sheer reduction in tension that directly follows an aggressive outburst is also likely to be positively experienced.[21] (It should not be forgotten, on the other hand, that attack could provoke instant retribution by the other resulting in possible defeat and loss of face.)

The longer-term consequences of aggression, though, are largely unappealing. The emotional experience of the event may gradually be transformed, with positive feelings replaced by those of embarrassment, shame and guilt. There may be a growing paranoia that an enemy has been created with the person attacked now seeking opportunities to 'get even'. Perhaps more importantly there may be a justifiable concern about losing not only the goodwill, but the respect and trust of the workforce.

The victim

Depending upon the severity of the attack, there is a recognised sequence of emotional reactions. This begins with stunned shock, then anger which gives way to shame and guilt. Depression can set in if the victim begins to accept blame for what took place. A corollary of this emotional reaction is an acceptance of the perpetrator's right to act in this way. Repeated exposure to this form of abuse can eventually induce feelings of helplessness and worthlessness. But when the person on the receiving end refuses to succumb in this way, resentment is the more likely outcome, coupled with loss of creativity, low morale and perhaps a desire for revenge. Quality of work can suffer. Staff will play safe, for fear of failure, sticking to old habits and tested routines rather than risk fresh approaches and innovate thinking. Mistakes probably will not be reported or advice sought. Work processes or planning may be deliberately sabotaged. In all cases, prospects for productive teambuilding are poor.

The organisation

The effects of an endemically aggressive management style in an organisation can be truly devastating. Many members of the workforce, and usually the youngest and the brightest, leave while those that stay are less inclined to express their real opinions, present fresh ideas or take risks. Most of their time is spent 'covering their backs' and output suffers. Few are prepared to pop their heads up over the parapet in case they attract enemy fire from the front line of management.

A further risk, becoming increasingly common, is the possibility of legal action being taken by workers claiming compensation for damaged health as a result of bullying and victimisation. Workers exposed to unremitting harassment by rampantly aggressive managers, leading to emotional collapse through intolerable levels of stress, usually have their cases looked upon very favourably in the compensation stakes. Moreover, when the press get hold of the story, the reputation of the firm invariably suffers. As well as loss of business, increased recruitment difficulties are a probable effect. All of this ultimately impacts on the bottom line. Royal Mail put a figure of £247 million on costs incurred from aggression – what they labelled 'employee friction'.[22]

Indirect aggression

Aggression does not always have to be loud and oath-laden. The rights of others can be violated in altogether more subtle and insidious ways through emotional blackmail, manipulation, sulking or pouting.[23] Take the following situation where a manager has a report to get ready for the next morning.

Manager: 'Jane, I need you to work late this evening to finish off this report for Hawks. It should only take a couple of hours.'

Secretary: 'I'm afraid I can't, Mr Blackwell. I've got my drama group at 7.00 pm.'

Manager: 'Drama group! I don't believe this! Hawks needs this report for 9 o'clock tomorrow morning but he won't get it. And why not? Because you have a bloody drama group!' (*Direct aggression*)

alternatively

Manager: 'Oh dear! I'll just have to stay behind and do it myself. It's my wife's birthday as well. I suppose I'll have to phone and tell her that I won't be able to take her out for that special meal, after all. She'll be very disappointed, and give me dogs' abuse, but I suppose we'll eventually get over it ...'. (*Indirect aggression using emotional blackmail*)

alternatively

Manager: 'Oh that's most unfortunate, Jane, especially since you've already done so much work on the report and done it very well, if I may say so. With you keen to get promotion and so on, it would have been good if you had been able to set the finished document on old Hawk's desk tomorrow morning. You deserve the credit. Still if you can't do it, you can't do it. I don't think Sally has left yet. I'm sure she will finish it off. I suppose it's really down to the two of you as to who will fill Rosemary's post as his new PA.' (*Indirect aggression using manipulation*)

Indirect aggression using these sorts of Machiavellian tactics, although less intensely emotionally charged than a direct attack, can be just as corrosive of trust, respect and loyalty. Feelings of anger or shame can be just as consuming. The quest for revenge can be pursued with similar vigour. Some dub this a *passive–aggressive* style.[24] It enables perpetrators to get their way without having to confront the issue head-on or take direct responsibility for dealing with it. As such, it tends to be favoured by those who are particularly uncomfortable with conflict.[25] Here again, assertiveness is the more mature approach holding out greatest promise of a mutually satisfactory outcome to the problem. Before moving on to consider it in greater detail, however, let's take at look at a contrasting style of management at the other end of the spectrum from aggression.

Communicating submissively

People who are non-assertive due to over-passivity and over-submissiveness readily acknowledge the rights of others. This is not their problem. Their problem is that they do so at the expense of exercising their *own* rights in the situation. Typically they cannot say 'No', even to the most unreasonable of requests. They hesitate to present their views and opinions and when they do it is in such a self-effacing manner that they almost invite others to discount them. The majority position is usually the one voiced regardless of what they really think about an issue. True wants and feelings are rarely expressed in preference to those expected by others, or in some way anticipated to be more acceptable to them. What is said tends to be expressed apologetically and with little confidence: apprehension, anxiety and threat are constantly lurking on the horizons of their emotional experience.

Submissive people, therefore, downplay their own rights or at best attempt to advance them in a very half-hearted and ineffectual way.

Managers lacking assertion are inclined to let problems and difficulties continue in the forlorn hope that they will sort themselves out if left alone. They adopt a generally low profile. Avoiding conflict at all cost is an abiding quest. Submissive people have a tendency to be diffident and indecisive. Despite a desire to please, they often come across as weak and inconsequential. This style of relating has also been termed *protective*.[26] Characteristic cues of the submissive approach have been identified[27–29] and some are listed in Box 11.3.

Box 11.3 Responding submissively

Verbal cues

▸ Apologies *ad nauseam*	'I really am frightfully sorry for bothering you with this trivial matter'
▸ Hedges	'I'm pretty well sure that the figures are accurate. On the other hand, they were done in a bit of a hurry.'
▸ Waffle	'The vast number of right thinking people in positions of authority in industry would be very unlikely to fail to accept the majority view of experienced senior managers ...
▸ Prevarication	'I know that I almost made a decision but I didn't quite'
▸ Lack of self-referenced statements	'It might be better if you got back to work. One would expect all staff to be working at this time.'
▸ Self-deprecation	'I don't really know much about this and last time I made a bit of a mess if it.'
▸ Hesitations	'Would it be possible ... uh ... um ... to take ... ah ... some time ... um ... to sort the ... ah ... whole thing ... um ... out?'
▸ Obsequious politeness	'Excuse me, I hate to bother you but would you mind awfully moving your foot. You're standing on my toe.'

Box 11.3 *continued*

▶ Over-justification	'I wouldn't ask normally, but if I don't know when you intend to take your holiday, I won't be able to arrange cover, you see.'
▶ Hints	'I wonder who I could get to help me with the Rother's account.'

Nonverbal cues

▶ Tone of voice	Soft, quiet, tailing off towards the end
▶ Voice quality	Weak, thin, strained
▶ Speech pattern	Hesitant, uneven rate, frequent false starts and dysfluencies, lots of throat-clearing
▶ Gaze	Averted, downward, fleeting
▶ Facial expression	Fear, unease, apprehension
▶ Gestures	Jerky, fidgety
▶ Posture	Small, hunched, tense.

Of course there may be occasions when a submissive approach is the sensible course of action, just as there may be situations in which a more aggressive style is called for. It should not be thought that these contrasting ways of dealing with problems should never be contemplated under any circumstances. Richardson[30] argued that an unassertive, avoidance style of dealing with difference can actually be an *active* way of strategically pursuing goals. She gives, as an example, a situation involving staff in a higher education department where group cohesion and solidarity were strengthened when conflict was handled in this fashion. The point is, though, that assertiveness is the option likely to lead to a successful resolution most of the time. The other two are usually little more than short-term palliatives that do little to cure the underlying condition. Why then do some seem to inappropriately favour submissiveness as the preferred style? Amongst the reasons suggested[31,32] can be listed the following:

- *Ignorance of rights.* Submissive people may not appreciate that they too have rights deserving of respect or they may place greater emphasis on their attendant responsibilities. Alternatively they may 'know' in a remote, bookish way that they have rights, yet fail to embrace that knowledge sufficiently to act upon it. It seems, in any case, that non-assertive people take longer at the outset to reach decisions about issues like rights violation.[33]

- *Desire to please.* One manifestation of this desire is that submissives laugh much more at the humour of dominant individuals than vice versa.[34] The mistaken belief is that it is always more important to be liked than to be respected.
- *Avoidance of conflict.* The belief here is that confronting conflict only makes it worse. There is a failure to distinguish between confronting the problem and confronting the person with the problem. A blind eye is turned to both.
- *Lack of self-efficacy and poor self-esteem.* How we tackle difficult and challenging situations is partly shaped by our belief in our ability to cope successfully with them.[35] Without a sufficient sense of self-efficacy we are likely, in terms of the fight/flight response, to take flight. Doing so, however, reflects negatively on our sense of self-esteem. Next time around we will probably be even more convinced that this sort of situation is beyond us.
- *Cultural diversity.* What passes for submissiveness in one culture can be viewed, in another, as acceptable social protocol. Here managers, in being 'submissive', are merely abiding by the dictates of that particular social order. There are no absolute benchmarks for gauging aggression, submission or assertion. Indeed, some feel that assertive ways of behaving in the USA, come across as aggressive in the UK. The topic of culture will be returned to shortly.
- *Lack of skill.* Under circumstances where assertiveness is called for but not provided, it may be that the person simply has never learned the skills involved. While this way of relating may come more naturally to those of a less retiring predisposition, Rakos[36] echoed a general sentiment that we should think of assertion as a certain type of skilled behaviour rather than an underlying, immutable trait.

The consequences of a submissive style, as with aggression, can be both short-term and long-term and affect the person, the other workers and the organisation.

The person

Immediate effects of acting submissively can be quite positive. It may have obviated the need to challenge the unreasonable demands of another, and prevented a nasty scene, with corresponding reductions in anticipatory anxiety or guilt. Simply saying 'Yes' rather than 'No' is often the irresistibly easy way out at the time. In the longer term, however, submissiveness leads to broken promises, dishonoured contracts, unfilled orders, or unsustainable workloads. Either way, standards of work are likely to suffer, even leading to increased absenteeism through stress-induced sickness. Schwartz advocated assertiveness training as a way of fending off burnout from working beyond capacity.[37] Feelings about the submissive self are also likely to be essentially negative. What begins as a sense of relief and freedom from guilt eventually creates an abiding and overwhelming feeling of powerlessness, worthlessness and self-contempt.

The other workers

Again, how the submissive person is experienced typically changes over time, especially if that person is in a managerial role. Initially, and especially if the person is new to the job, there may be a reaction of benevolent sympathy. The gentler approach may be roundly welcomed. Not having someone constantly on top of you, checking your work closely, telling you what to do, often feels liberating. It can also be taken advantage of. In the long run, lack of guidance, support and direction produces a disgruntled, bickering, ineffective workforce with poor morale, that eventually turns its wrath on the manager they once cherished.

The organisation

Submissiveness can carry serious consequences at this level. Focussing specifically upon the airline industry, a review of major aviation accidents by the National Transport Safety Board[38] attributed the cause, in 80 per cent of cases, to the first officer failing to check on the captain and effectively challenging wrong decisions. Passive acquiescence had led to the loss of the aircraft in many instances. Jentsch and Smith-Jentsch[39] drew attention to a number of similar work situations, including health, fire control and police, where a lack of assertiveness amongst team members had life-threatening repercussions.

An organisation with a sizeable number of submissive people in pivotal positions cannot thrive. Important decisions are not taken, there is little sense of mission, dynamism is absent and internal strife rampant but largely ignored. The approach to management must either change quickly or the organisation fails. More broadly, LeMon[40] mandated assertiveness training as a corporate strategy to counteract a culture of dependence amongst staff.

Given that the long-term outlook is decidedly poor for those who routinely make use of aggression or submission to solve problematic situations with people at work, let us now consider assertiveness as a more promising alternative.

Communicating assertively

Michelli[41] neatly summed up the essential attributes of assertive communication by explaining that it 'does not diminish or put down another human being, it does not trespass on any human rights and it does not shy away from important issues. Rather it encourages satisfactory communication where everyone's needs are met in the best way.' An aggressive style cherishes the rights of others but at the expense of one's own. By contrast, submissiveness maximises respect for the former but trivialises the latter, as well as failing to deal with the issue. Those acting assertively, however, uphold both their own and the other's rights in equal measure. Moreover, they acknowledge and take on board the responsibilities that inevitably couple themselves to rights.

According to Leaper,[42] some assertive people are also affiliative while others are markedly less so, thus producing two contrasting interpersonal styles. The assertive and affiliative are *collaborative* individuals who only use assertion when necessary, but place a high value on having good relationships with others. On the other hand, assertive individuals who are nonaffiliative are not so concerned about being friendly, and use assertive skills to *control* and achieve their goal. Similarly, Darling and Walker[43] contrasted assertive individuals who are high, with those who are low, on emotional responsiveness. Manages who appear friendlier and are more expressive, people-oriented and casual in conversation and dress, typify the former *socializer* style. Those who exhibit the contrasting low-responsive, *director* style are characteristically independent, open, decisive, pragmatic and objective, in their manner.

In general, assertive managers:

- make known their wants and needs
- express their ideas and opinions openly and honestly and do so comfortably without feeling awkward, anxious or guilty

Box 11.4 Responding assertively

Acting assertively involves:

- Being comfortable expressing personal needs, wants, opinions and feelings
- Making reasonable requests of others without feeling awkward
- Refusing unreasonable requests without being guilty
- Being prepared to listen to others
- Disagreeing with the views and opinions of others, if necessary
- Giving and accepting praise and compliments without embarrassment
- Rejecting negative feedback that is considered to be unfair
- Initiating, maintaining and terminating contact with others without experiencing undue negative emotion
- Being open, honest and direct with others
- Respecting self and others
- Upholding the rights of self and others in equal measure
- Confronting rather than avoiding difficult situations that have to be resolved
- Being able to separate the person from the problem
- Admitting mistakes and shortcomings, if necessary, rather than perpetuating a false facade of infallibility
- Seeking the best possible outcome for all concerned, rather than blindly pursuing factional interests
- Acting non-assertively if it is felt that it is the best option under the circumstances.

- confront difficult situations that have to be dealt with rather than avoiding them
- attack the problem rather than the person
- seek the best outcome for all concerned (see Box 11.4).

The objective is 'to try to ensure fair play for everyone'.

Rights and beliefs about assertion

Assertiveness presupposes an awareness of rights and responsibilities. Without a firm appreciation of your rights and those of others, it is impossible to recognise when they are being violated, or what to uphold. Knowing how to assert yourself without this background is a bit like being gifted a chess set and taught the rudiments of how the different pieces move, without ever fully grasping the circumstances under which specific moves are called for. While pieces may admittedly get shifted around the board, defeat is the only outcome.

The Concise Oxford Dictionary defined a right in this sense, as 'fair treatment; a thing one may legally or morally claim; the state of being entitled to a privilege or immunity or authority to act…'. Many of those who have written about assertiveness have drawn up lists of those rights that legitimise this approach.[44–47] While these differ to some extent, they are all largely based around the United Nations' Universal Declaration of Human Rights. A composite of such rights is included in Box 11.5.

Box 11.5 Your Bill of rights

It is your right to:

- Hold and express views, opinions and ideas even though they may not be the same as those of others
- Have your views, opinions and ideas listened to and taken seriously
- Have and express feelings and emotions
- Experience needs and wants
- Request that these needs and wants be accommodated while acknowledging the right of others to refuse to do so
- Refuse a request without feeling awkward or guilty
- Respectfully disagree with the views, opinions and ideas of others without incurring attack or aggression from them or others
- Order your own life, as long as this does not infringe the rights of others to do likewise
- Be wrong sometimes; it is an unavoidable part of being human
- Sometimes not know the answer to a question or problem – no one can know everything
- Be respected by others, not necessarily on account of *who* you are, but rather *that* you are
- Assert yourself
- Not assert yourself, if you decide that this is best.

These are universal human rights. We can also think of more specific sets of rights peculiar to the work setting. Some of these may be enshrined in general employment legislation, others may form part of particular contractual arrangements and differ somewhat from employer to employer. Regardless, effective assertiveness depends upon a knowledge of where you stand in relation to them, so knowing your rights is crucial when it comes to acting assertively. Staff who are more assertive also have a clearer view of their work role. They tend additionally to express greater levels of job satisfaction.[48]

The flip side of rights is responsibilities and obligations. We may have a right to express our views but we also have an obligation not to impose them upon others if they are not welcomed. Rakos[49]cautioned that we ignore these obligations at our peril. Indeed, he argued, merely stating our rights can seem aggressive. Rather we have attendant obligations to establish the rights and circumstances of others, consider how our assertive action might affect them and, if need be, explain our actions in order to avoid or minimise hurt or humiliation.

Knowing your rights, in a matter-of-fact, detached way, is one thing, but you must also be able to take ownership of them. Some people 'know' their rights in a propositional way, but fail to act accordingly because those rights have not been fully embraced. This may be on account of this new knowledge failing to square with their beliefs about themselves, others and how the social world works. For instance, a strong assumption that intolerably nasty consequences will accrue unless the boss's demands are always complied with, can lead to permanent submissiveness. It has been found that assertive individuals typically believe that largely positive consequences will follow from their behaviour.[50] Their submissive counterparts, on the other hand, fully expect the outcomes to be negative. They also give themselves largely negative, defeatist messages. Their self-talk is along the lines of 'I'll sound awfully rude, if I say "No" ', 'I'll get so anxious refusing, that I'll stutter and stammer and look a fool', and so forth. It is only when more positive possibilities are recognised in assertive action that this style will be attempted. As put by Lindenfield,[51] in relation to becoming assertive, 'Our first task must therefore be to re-programme our minds by replacing the old unassertive values and thoughts with a more positive philosophy.'

Verbal assertive behaviour

Different verbal strategies for expressing assertiveness can be put to use as circumstances permit.[52–54] A common underpinning principle is that one begins with the least assertive response calculated to have the desired effect, moving on to more potent alternatives only if that doesn't work.

Basic assertion

This is a simple, straightforward statement of your wants, needs, views, feelings or rights, delivered directly and in a matter-of-fact fashion, without elaboration or embellishment. Paterson[55] commended the *bonsai principle* – prune your communication hard back to the basic message to avoid misunderstanding or evasion. Likewise, for Hayes[56] assertive expressions should be essentially brief and direct. In response to continual interruption, for example, basic assertion could take the form of a statement such as, 'I would like to continue with my point.'

Elaborated assertion

Basic assertion can on occasion seem brusque. Sometimes an embellished form is more acceptable and some alternatives are offered by Rakos:[57]

- *Empathy* – here recognition is given of the circumstances of the other person, and the impact that an assertive stance might have. Continuing with the example, the interrupted person might interject, 'I realise that, like me, you too have strong views on this matter and that you want to share these, but I would like to continue with my point'.
- *Apology* – this can be offered for any inconvenience caused to the other that may stem from an assertive line. Note, this is not an apology for *acting* assertively, merely for the *consequences*. Adding, 'I'm sorry if this means you will have to wait to have your say', could extend the previous example.
- *Explanation* – giving a reason for taking a stand may help to make assertion more agreeable. This probably works best when refusing a request. For example, 'I can't do the run to the airport because my car is being serviced today.'

Confrontive assertion

Here the assertive approach hinges around pointing out to others how their course of action is at odds with what was stated, understood or agreed. This is done to best effect in a matter of fact way, without any hint at accusation or attachment of blame. Indeed, all assertive behaviour accentuates fact and logic over emotional outburst. Still continuing with our example, confrontive assertion could be along the lines of, 'In debating this point, we agreed to abide by the normal conventions of turn-taking. Now, each time that I begin to speak, you interrupt. This flies in the face of what was agreed.' Indicating your *understanding* of the agreement can also be beneficial since it enables problems due to misinterpretation to be identified at an early stage and ironed out.

Drawing consequences

This involves making others aware of what will happen if they persist with their course of action, for example, 'If you continue to interrupt me, and I you, neither of us will be able to hear what the other has to say and both of our points of view will be lost.' This approach may take an even stronger form if you continue to the ultimate conclusion. For example, '... Under these circumstances, with these persistent interruptions, I would see no point in continuing our discussion and will therefore leave.' For Guirdham,[58] though, this type of assertion should only be used as a last resort since it can be perceived as a threat.

Assertive language

Recommended here is that speakers use the personal pronoun 'I', when they speak, to place themselves at the centre of their assertions. Referring specifically to PAs dealing with their bosses, the advantages of using 'I' statements in the office, according to Rouse,[59] included making explicit whose feelings, opinions and requirements were being referred to, thereby minimising confusion. But overuse of 'I' statements can lead to accusations of narcissism. Hargie and Dickson[60] suggested *We-language* as an effective alternative. The use of We-language helps to convey the impression of partnership in, and joint responsibility for, any problems to be discussed, for example, 'We need to sort out how we hold these conversations so that we both can have our say.'

Escalating assertion

Here a manager begins with a basic assertive response, gradually bringing into play more powerful alternatives as and when required, in the face of a persistent violation of rights. For instance, unremitting interruptions could be dealt with using a basic assertive response, followed by empathic assertion, confrontive assertion and finally drawing consequences.

Protective assertion

Three assertive tactics have been identified as a form of defence commonly used to counter hostility, manipulation, rudeness or unreasonable persistence.[61] They are called broken record, fogging and meta-level assertion.

- *Broken record.* This involves making a simple assertive statement and going on repeating it until it is complied with. It is as if the needle on the record had stuck. It has been described as repeating 'over and over again, in an assertive and relaxed manner, what it is you want or need, until the other person gives in or agrees to negotiate with you'.[62]
- *Fogging.* Here, negative comment is apparently accepted but without the emotional put-down that usually comes with it. The person using fogging seems to calmly 'hear the words' without rising to any emotional bait that may be dangled, and without accepting any possible negative implications for self-concept or self-esteem.

  For example:

  Director: 'You made an abysmal mess of that job for Seaport'.
  Manager: 'It's true that it probably didn't go as well as I had hoped'.

  Fogging reveals to the accuser that the accused is not prepared to be emotionally put upon in this way, to get involved in an argument or to engage in vigorous self-flagellation in a fury of self-blame. The consequence is quite often a shift to a more mature and assertive way of handling the situation.

- *Meta-level assertion.* Under circumstances where it becomes obvious that the bone of contention cannot be resolved within the current confines of the problem, meta-level assertion takes a broader view of the issue. Going back to our running example of persistent interruption, this reaction may be indicative of a deeper malaise in the relationship between the two people involved. In this case, a meta-level assertive response would be along the lines of:

  'John, since you still persist in interrupting me, and I have been aware of this before in meetings, we need to look more closely at our working relationship together to see if there is anything there that makes it difficult for you to listen to my point of view.'

Three-step assertion

This is one of the most comprehensive statements of assertion. It is particularly effective in situations where person B's behaviour is unacceptable to person A and A would like it changed. The three steps are:

- A factual description of B's troublesome behaviour
- The consequences of this behaviour for A

- The actual changes to B's behaviour that would resolve the difficulty.

Take the situation where a member of the office staff begins taking excessively long tea-beaks. The manager could employ the three-step approach as follows:

> *Manager*: 'The morning tea break should last 15 minutes, Jane, but I notice that you're never back at your desk before 10.45am (*factual description of B's troublesome behaviour*). This means that Janet has to take the calls and deal with the desk and some calls don't get answered, which I find unacceptable (*consequences of this behaviour for A*). Could you make sure that you are back at your desk by 10.30am from now on, along with the others?' (*actual changes to B's behaviour that would resolve the difficulty*).

Nonverbal assertive behaviour

For assertive behaviour to have the desired effect, it is crucial that the nonverbal elements of delivery are right. As with all aspects of effective performance, if the words spoken suggest one message while the rest of the body is signalling something entirely different, it is likely that the verbal message will be diluted or dismissed. People who find it difficult to be assertive in certain situations sometimes show their unease in how they act. Were the manager in the above example to deliver the three-step assertive statement with an apologetic smile, maybe out of a sense of unease with possible conflict in the office, the chances of Jane improving would be greatly reduced. Nonverbal behaviour that promotes assertion is outlined in Box 11.6.

Factors that shape assertiveness

There are situations and circumstances within which even the most aggressive individual adopts a quite submissive approach and, likewise, the submissive individual plays a more dominant part. Here we will consider several personal and situational factors that have a bearing upon the likelihood and the appropriateness of assertion.

Box 11.6 Nonverbal assertive behaviour

▶ Tone of voice	Intermediate modulation, relaxed but firm, confident
▶ Volume of voice	Medium, but slightly louder than that in normal conversation
▶ Speed of speech	Moderate but tending towards the slow and deliberate: neither gusting nor hesitant
▶ Response latency	No long pause before the delivery of the assertive response
▶ Gaze	Medium levels: flexible and intermittent eye-contact most appropriate
▶ Facial expression	Alert, yet avoiding uncontrolled movements or signs of negative emotion as well as smiles: should be consistent with what is being said
▶ Pallor	Neither flushed nor blanched
▶ Gestures	Relaxed, open gestures while speaking: inconspicuous when listening
▶ Posture	Generally upright, avoiding shifting, shuffling or fidgeting
▶ Head	Erect, avoiding excessive head nodding
▶ Interpersonal distance	Close enough to effect a presence but without gross violation of the other's personal space
▶ Orientation	Direct, face-to-face but not threatening

Gender

Traditionally, an assertive style has been more closely associated with masculinity than femininity,[63] although there is no clear picture from the research evidence as to an actual gender difference.[64] Indeed, in one study, females in Taiwan and Japan emerged as more assertive than their male counterparts.[65] Some feminist writers, however, have argued that the entire concept of assertion is male-centred and replete with demeaning assumptions of female 'weakness'.[66] Others take a more positive stance and accept that women would benefit from enhanced levels of skill in this area.[67] In any case, contemporary social changes have largely eroded the stereotypical view of women as 'the weaker sex'. In a survey of Japanese banking staff, reported by Alberti and Emmons,[68] 28 per cent reported that they would welcome a female boss. The corresponding figure a decade earlier had been only 12 per cent. Correspondingly, Twenge[69] plotted a rising profile of female assertion since the end of the Second World War. That said, Paterson[70] insisted that cultural barriers towards being an assertive woman are still high.

In professional circles, it seems that assertiveness is valued equally whether employed by male or female businesspersons,[71] corporate managers[72] or lawyers.[73] But there is evidence that when females are assertive there is an expectation that they use more 'caring' techniques, such as empathic assertion.[74] No doubt these norms will continue to change as women progressively occupy higher status positions in corporate life. Interestingly, but somewhat perversely, it seems that the increasing move towards 'feminising' companies through the promulgation of 'softer' values and management approaches, may actually work against female advancement. Wilson[75] reported a boomerang effect whereby competitive female job applicants are now looked upon less favourably than their male counterparts.

Relationship

The relationship shared by those involved in the assertive encounter is also highly pertinent. Expressing an unpopular opinion (as a form of assertion) tends to be more acceptable amongst friends than strangers. On the other hand, refusing a request from a stranger (another form of assertion) is viewed more positively than refusing a friend.[76]

Status

It could be predicted that assertiveness by senior members in an organisation would be more acceptable than similar behaviour by junior staff, and there is some research evidence to this effect. Acting assertively is also easier when directed towards those of lower than higher status.[77]

The situation

Certain types of assertion appear to have greater currency depending upon the situation in which they are employed. In the job interview, for example, having the interviewee subsequently write a letter of thanks expressing continued interest in the position, was viewed by employers as increasing the chances of offering employment. Requesting a second interview with a different interviewer, by contrast, had the opposite effect.[78]

As far as ease of expression is concerned, it is usually less difficult to adopt an assertive pose in one's own, as opposed to the other's, home or office.

Culture

Assertive behaviour is decidedly culture-bound. What passes as acceptable assertion in Europe and the USA, may be perceived quite differently in countries with markedly different sets of norms and values. Even within European countries and the USA, ethnic minorities that have largely perpetuated the culture of the country of origin, may abide by different standards of assertion. In the USA, Mexican, Japanese and Chinese communities report less use of this style than do the Caucasian culture.[79] That said, Bresnahan and her colleagues,[80] in contradiction to what was anticipated, found that US Americans were *less* assertive than Taiwanese and Japanese, in the samples studied.

There is evidence that individuals make adjustments for culture diversity in their use of an assertive style. Thus, a study in Germany of the manner in which Turkish immigrants handled conflict situations found that the preferred style varied depending upon the target person.[81] When dealing with someone from the Turkish community a more indirect, non-confrontational approach, typical of this cultural group, was usually employed. However, when dealing with a German, a more direct, instrumental style was used, again in keeping with the norms of that target group.

Age

Many people feel more comfortable being assertive towards others who are younger, rather than older. In addition, there seems to be a positive relationship between age and assertive expression. As people get older, this style of dealing with others appears to be more common.[82]

Benefits of assertion

We have already seen that the two contrasting styles of relating – aggression and submission – have some possible advantages in the immediate to short-term, but that long-term, the outcomes are counter-productive and frequently simply exacerbate the situation to be sorted out. The benefits of assertion are more enduring and are enjoyed by the manager, the staff and the organisation.

The manager

Managers who adopt an assertive approach feel good about themselves. They do not evade the issue to be tackled, neither do they lose face through losing their temper, as often happens in an aggressive out-burst. There is considerable truth in the claim that, 'The extent to which you assert yourself determines the level of your self-esteem.'[83]

While the issue to hand may not be 'resolved' instantaneously, as sometimes *seems* to happen with an aggressive assault, the chances are that when it is finally resolved, the solution will be enduring and to everyone's satisfaction. Being assertive means communicating directly, openly, honestly, unemotionally and therefore clearly. As such, the chances of a successful outcome to a situation of possible conflicting needs are strengthened.

A further advantage in this resolution, of course, is that it enables the manager to move on to other matters with energy freed up to now tackle them effectively. The earlier problem is not left festering, to erupt once more at probably the most inappropriate time, demanding attention that should be invested elsewhere. Nor is emotional energy consumed in ruminating upon the possible aftermath of an aggressive assault, and the paranoia that this can engender. Indeed, difficulties handled assertively frequently strengthen the working relationship amongst the key players, rather than erode it. As a result, the manager's confidence and motivation to extend this approach is enhanced.

It should also be mentioned, though, that assertive individuals, while respected, do not invariably win out in the popularity stakes. It seems that while assertiveness is evaluated positively in theory, assertive people may actually be rated as less attractive than those who are submissive.[84] In their review of this phenomenon, Buslig and Burgoon[85] noted, 'submissive behavior is often ineffective for reaching instrumental goals, but perceived more positively in terms of interpersonal impressions'. We may well like assertive people less than the non-assertive. Assertion needs to be used sensitively.

The staff

The word 'staff' is used here in a generic way to cover all those subjected to an assertive style. There can be no guarantee, of course, that the agreed solutions to the precipitating problems will always be *entirely* what staff want. Assertiveness is not a magical panacea. Those solutions will, however, be ones to which staff have contributed and by which they should be able to abide. Their views and concerns will have been given a full, even-handed and respectful hearing. In many cases, this alone goes a considerable way to placating the warring parties. Staff should, in consequence, recognise and appreciate the respect in which they are held by management. If encouraged, in turn, to act assertively, staff feel more at liberty to express ideas and opinions; to report mistakes; to ask for clarification when information is not understood; and to make known to managers when they are struggling to cope, without having their stress added to by the fear of blame or ridicule. In this way difficulties can be spotted at an early stage before they have an opportunity to catch hold and create worse problems. Lwehabura and Matovelo[86] argued persuasively that staff have an active role to play in effective management. Employees owe it to the organisation.

The organisation

An organisation with assertiveness as the preferred management style is typified by good communication, high staff morale, vibrancy and commitment. Internal disputes are kept to a minimum and when they do arise, tend to be resolved relatively quickly and to the broad satisfaction of most, if not all parties. Such organisations characteristically enjoy an enviable reputation for good employer–employee relations, working conditions and quality of product or service. They are ones to which staff have a sense of commitment and involvement, a feeling of being valued and of having a say in the totality of the operation.

Overview

When acting in accordance with the 'fight/flight' response, we often either metaphorically flee in the face of difficult problems and people, or we defend ourselves by going on the attack. These primitive routines give rise to two contrasting styles of communication in management, each of which tends to be just as counter-productive as the other, in the vast majority of instances. While both may have possible outcomes that are positive in the short-term, in the longer-term, consequences for the manager, staff and the organisation are negative.

In being submissive, one sets aside one's own rights in the situation in favour of those of the other party. Aggression, on the other hand, entails violating the rights of the other in favour of one's own. By contrast, assertiveness is the option presented in this chapter which typically upholds the rights of all, accepts attendant responsibilities and leads to positive payoffs for all parties sharing the problem or experiencing the difficulty. Reflective exercise 11.2 is designed to help you identify occasions at work when you have difficulty acting assertively and how these might be handled more effectively.

Reflective exercise 11.2 Becoming assertive

This exercise is intended to help you identify assertive opportunities at work.

1. Think of a situation at work that you find difficult to deal with assertively.
2. How do you presently handle it?
   What do you say?
   How do you say it?
   How do you behave?
   How do you feel?
   What goes through your mind?
3. What are the outcomes for:
   You?
   The other person/s involved?
   The organisation?
4. How could you handled this situation in a more assertive manner, thinking of both verbal and nonverbal elements?
5. Were this situation or one similar to it to recur, what would *help* you to act more assertively and what would *hinder* you doing so?

Exercise 11.2 ***continued***

6. How can you promote those factors that would help you act assertively in each situation while minimising the others that tend to hinder this course of action?

Box 11.7 Assertiveness scores for exercise 11.2

Having completed Execise 11.1 on page 290, now count up your total score. **Note** that the following items are reverse scored (i.e. 1 becomes 5, 2 becomes 4, etc.) – 2, 4, 8, 10, 12, 14, 15, 17, 18, and 20. Your total score may range from 20 to 100. The lower the score the less assertive you are likely to be *in general*. As a rough guide, a score under 70 suggests that a more assertive style could substantially improve your present levels of interpersonal effectiveness.

12 What's your problem? Helping in the workplace

Introduction

Until recently, organisations have been typically cast as essentially emotion-free zones – at least by those who write about them. This is surprising given that it is undoubtedly at odds with the first-hand experiences of the vast majority of staff who populate such places. Nevertheless, and leaving aside interest in stress and job satisfaction (together with the exception of one or two early pieces of work), it has been the rational, controlled, strategic, decision-making side of organisational life that has been accentuated to the neglect of the affective filigree that presents an ever-present back-cloth to most of what happens during it. As put by Lord and colleagues.[1] 'Although emotions influence every aspect of human life, their impact on work behavior has only recently received much attention.'

But perhaps 'back-cloth' as imagery suggests that emotion plays an essentially passive role. While admittedly it may sometimes be a mere by-product of management decisions and work practices, it also frequently comes front-stage to causally impact, both directly and indirectly, at a functional level.[2] Moreover, emotion may form part of what some workers, especially in service industries, are actually paid to do. Those required to be pleasant to customers, even when at odds with their true feelings' have been described as providing 'emotion labour'.[3] This in itself can be a source of difficulty and cause stress.[4]

Emotion in work can, of course, be positive as well as negative. It is typically the latter, though, that becomes problematic and hence a management concern. Indeed much of the manager's time is taken up dealing with employee problems. Such problems, whatever their cause, will have their own affective overtones of anger, anxiety, shame, guilt, confusion or depression. The larger the problem the stronger is likely to be the associated affectivity. Conversely, such feelings sometimes actually lie at the route of personal difficulties that get in the way of a fully functioning employee. Here emotions themselves are the ultimate problem. Regardless, the nature of employee difficulties differ from worker to worker and the actual role played in handling them varies from manager to manager. Some take a more direct hands-on approach than others. But irrespective of the strategy adopted for coping, these problems ultimately represent a management issue that cannot or must not be side-stepped.

Troubles experienced by employees in their job can be traced to a number of sources, one of which is the organisation itself. Work generates difficulties of contrasting types and at different levels. Some lie in the nature of the company's operation and how best to create quality solutions, perhaps in respect of design issues or technical challenges that are part-and-parcel of what it is about. Other problems may have more to do with how the work is organised than the actual work itself. An employee, for instance, requests a meeting with the line manager on account of intolerable stress experienced since departmental restructuring. Further work-based problems may emerge from dysfunctional interpersonal attitudes caused by poor working relationships. A production worker, perhaps, feels put-upon by a victimising supervisor and demands to see the section leader. None of these scenarios is likely to be solved satisfactorily by merely providing information or offering advice. What is required of the manager is the ability to facilitate the employee in reaching a resolution through the use of appropriate helping skills and procedures.

It is with counselling in the workplace, and offering help of this type, that the present chapter is concerned. Its relevance to the manager is two-fold. First, managers should be aware of the potential contribution that counselling provision in the workplace can have for both staff and the organisation. Second, managers should have a grasp of the basic skills and procedures that form the helping process. In the chapter, we will outline what counselling is, its potential benefits in organisations and the present level of provision in the workplace. Attention will be given to the extent to which the manager can and should counsel. Stages through which the helping process typically moves will be outlined and the qualities and skills of the effective helper presented. For the moment, however, we will return to the topic of problems at work.

Employee problems at work

Work can inflict problems upon workers, including the emotional trauma of economic downturn, downsizing and possible redundancy.[5]

Many other difficulties are imported from outside to adversely affect job performance. Sources of these include:[6–8]

- poor health, both physical and mental
- social relationship difficulties and family concerns
- financial worries
- substance abuse and drug dependency
- housing problems.

The important point is that, regardless of their source, these troubles inevitably find their way into the workplace to wreak an insidious and often highly corrosive effect. The comment was made by a manager, having attended a counselling skills training course,[9] that one of its effects was an altered vision of staff as 'not just people at work, but [as] human beings living their lives'. It is misguided and unreasonable to expect someone caught up in the throes of an acrimonious divorce procedure, in serious financial difficulty or nursing a sick relative at home, not to be affected at work by the resulting emotional turmoil or sheer physical exhaustion. Overlooking this fact can often unfairly lead to sloppy performance being attributed to incompetence or poor motivation.[10]

The extent to which workers suffer from problems at work is often under-estimated. Some of the conclusions reached by reviews of survey research[11,12] are captured in the statistics that:

- in the UK, approximately 90 million working days are lost per annum as a result of mental illness at a cost of some £3.7 billion
- when asked the real reason for absenteeism, more than 50 per cent of those taking time off point to some form of emotional/personal problem or stress
- 33 per cent of workers feel so vulnerable in their job that they are afraid to take time off when sick
- 20 per cent of the US workforce suffer from problems that affect how they do their job. These include alcohol and drug dependence, conflicts at home, and legal and financial complications.

Organisations that turn a blind eye to these statistics do so at their peril. The cost suffered can be measured in:[13,14]

- *work performance* – employees preoccupied with indomitable personal worries are unlikely to be in a fit state to make carefully thought-through decisions, or turn out quality work.

- *staff morale* – when workers sense that their concerns are ignored by the organisation, they begin to feel undervalued. This lowers morale and dissolves commitment and loyalty to the organisation.
- *staff turnover* – staff unhappy at work are likely to seek employment elsewhere, at a high cost to the company. Staff *really are* a company's most valuable asset.
- *compensation claims* – employees whose job difficulties have gone unheeded are increasingly litigious in their quest for monetary compensation. It may be deemed that an employer, in ignoring the worker's plight, was in breech of a duty of care to that individual. The recent upsurge in US work-related stress claims may set an increasing trend in the UK, verifying the prediction that 'Legal action against employers is expected to replace uncomplaining pill-popping as the remedy for occupational stress.'[15]
- *corporate image* – gaining the reputation of an uncaring, Dickensian exploiter of a workforce made to toil under intolerable conditions of abject misery, will do little for the corporate image of any organisation.
- *profit* – the effects of all the above consequences are reflected in high rates of absenteeism and withering financial success for the company.

What is counselling at work?

Let's start with the simpler (although not straightforward) question, 'What is counselling?' Distilled in its purest form in professional counselling circles it:

> ... includes work with individuals and with relationships which may be developmental, crisis support, psychotherapeutic, guiding or problem solving.... The task of counselling is to give the 'client' an opportunity to explore, discover, and clarify ways of living more satisfyingly and resourcefully.[16]

Nelson-Jones[17] explained that, in this sense, counselling proper is the exclusive purlieu of those who have been professionally trained and accredited. He used the term 'Helper', by contrast, to refer to all those who use counselling-type skills but as part of a secondary work role. Their primary function may be, for instance, to manage, instruct or supervise. Accordingly, the problems they help with are essentially practical (albeit with possible emotional overtones) rather than having emotional malfunction or psychopathology at their heart. Counselling skills, in turn, are regarded as ways of communicating by helpers that facilitate the development of a relationship with the helpee within which strategies for overcoming barriers to goal attainment can be developed and implemented.[18] We will outline some of the most central later in the chapter.

In the work context, the term 'counselling' has been used more loosely to refer to contrasting activities ranging from disciplining a member of staff, through offering advice and appraising, to providing emotional support.[19] Many managers seem to regard it as simply akin to advising, guiding or instructing,[20] and indeed may even eschew 'touchy-feely' connotations.[21] On the other hand, Minter and Thomas[22] differentiated counselling from, for instance, mentoring or coaching on the basis that counselling's outreach is more towards attitudinal or behavioural difficulties rather than those stemming from a lack of knowledge or skill. Some argue for a much broader vision of workplace counselling, operating not only at the level of the well-being of the individual worker, but as an agent of organisational change.[23] In practice, though, counselling at work is conceived much more circumspectly as:

- short-term
- problem/crisis centred and work focused (e.g. stress)
- geared to restoring employee effectiveness and efficiency.[24]

Conceived of narrowly in this way, as centring around problem management, counselling at work has been described in practical terms as, '... the manifestation of knowledge, attitudes, skills and behaviour, which are aimed at helping people to manage/solve their own problems, ideally by encouraging them to harness their own means'.[25] The process is underpinned by a set of values reflected in the following precepts:

- listen, for the most part, rather than tell
- always have the employee's best interests at heart
- help staff to clarify their thinking and understanding of the issues surrounding their problems rather than impose your constructions of those problems upon them
- assist individuals to work through their difficulties to a resolution rather than attempt to solve their problems for them
- respect people's rights to their own values, judgements and decisions as to what is best for them

- accept that staff, despite their possible confusion or emotional turmoil at present, know much more about themselves and the circumstances of their predicament than the manager does
- acknowledge that managers will often not have ready or easy answers to the difficulties brought to them
- act to strengthen the autonomy and independence of the other
- recognise that this type of involvement, if poorly handled, can hinder rather than help
- be constantly mindful of the possible need to refer the individual to someone with greater expertise.

Incidence and effects of counselling at work

Counselling in the workplace is not a new development. It can be traced back in the UK to the late nineteenth century when large family-owned companies such as Rowntree, inspired by humanitarian values, introduced a workers' welfare service. Later, several US firms introduced schemes designed to reduce the effects of alcohol abuse amongst the workforce on productivity. In time, such provision evolved into Employee Assistance Programmes (EAPs) which are now one of the main providers of counselling for employees particularly in the USA. It was estimated by Green that there the number of EAPs had grown from about 50 programmes in 1950 to more than 5000, just over 25 years later.[26] Most of the Fortune 500 companies in the US now have a counselling service in place for employees.[27] In Canada, Freiman[28] cited estimates of an uptake in the region of 80 per cent amongst larger organisations; about 50 per cent for medium-sized companies; and less than 50 per cent for smaller firms.

In the UK, the picture is somewhat different. In a survey by the Independent Counselling and Advisory Services,[29] only 4 per cent of the 1500 companies which were sampled, with more than one hundred employees, offered an EAP. However, counselling provision by other means was quite common:

- 85 per cent provided stress counselling
- 30 per cent provided retirement counselling
- 24 per cent provided redundancy counselling.

Carroll[30] suggested that the proportion of UK companies with active EAP policies could even be as high as 12 per cent.

The actual uptake of EAP provision by the workforce also seems to have increased. While figures are rather speculative, Freiman[31] reported a rise from roughly 3 per cent, 15 years ago, to about 12 per cent at present. Alternatively, Meyer and Davis[32] estimated current uptake more conservatively at from 4–8 per cent. What is beyond dispute, though, is the massive expansion in demand in the USA, particularly in the New York area, in the wake of the 9/11 attack on the World Trade Centre. One year on, Prince[33] reckoned it to be as high as 10–20 per cent over pre-9/11 figures. When it comes to usage by workers who were based in the Centre, the rise has been put at a massive 1000 per cent, by ComPsych Corp., an EAP and mental health provider with client companies whose offices were located there.[34] Meanwhile, the proportion of the UK workforce availing of EAP facilities would seem to be a more modest 6 per cent.[35]

The effects of counselling interventions in the workplace have been largely positive.[36–39] Some of the specific findings are presented in Box 12.1, and in summary form in Box 12.2.

Box 12.1 Workplace counselling outcomes

McDonnell Douglas estimated that the bottom line was a total savings of some $5.1 millions from their EAP over the four-year period of its evaluation.

General Motors calculated that it returned $67 for every dollar invested in its EAP.

The US Department of Health and Human Services reported that its EAP returned $7.1 per dollar of investment.

Johnston and Johnston, in the UK, found its rate of absenteeism reduced by 41 per cent with savings of almost a quarter of a million pounds, attributable to its EAP, over the first three years.

The Post Office reported a 66 per cent reduction in days lost through absenteeism during a three-year period following the introduction of a stress counselling programme with savings of about £5.7 for every pound spent.

A survey of UK workplace counselling programmes commissioned by the Health and Safety Executive and carried out by the Manchester School of Management, found a reduction in

Box 12.1 ***continued***

absenteeism. Workers also reported significant improvements in mental and physical health following counselling.

A Bureau of National Affairs survey revealed that 65 per cent of employers using EAPs drove down their health plan costs, 40 per cent reported lower workers' compensation costs and more than 50 per cent reduced their disability costs. Reductions in absenteeism and increases in productivity were also discovered.

Box 12.2 Summary of potential benefits of counselling in the workplace

For the employee:

- Less stress
- Improved morale
- Enhanced job satisfaction
- Increased effectiveness and efficiency
- Greater sense of being valued by the company
- Heightened sense of empowerment
- Fewer accidents.

For the employer:

- Lower absenteeism and sickness rates
- Reduced staff turnover
- Less litigation
- Better internal relations
- Improved corporate image
- Better quality work
- Increased profits
- Greater employee job commitment.

The manager as counsellor?

At present, counselling is either provided internally by companies or is bought in from external agencies. It is really only the former arrangement that concerns us here since it brings into sharper focus issues to do with the direct helping role of managers. If counselling is offered in-house, should it be provided by someone with professional levels of training and in a specialised role, or become a sub-role of the manager? Arguments for both options can be found. It will be recalled according to Nelson-Jones,[40] counselling proper is the exclusive domain of a specialist elite of professionally trained personnel equipped to deal with deep-seated emotional and psychological problems. 'Helpers' is the term used to refer to those who use counselling skills in lesser cases as part of a sub-role. As such, the manager would be more properly regarded as involved in helping rather than counselling. Others use the term 'counselling' in a much more inclusive way as it involves the manager with reference to work. MacLennan[41] not only labelled as a myth the belief that counselling required years of specialised training, but argued vehemently in a direct exhortation to managers that they, in fact, were the most appropriate people to counsel:

> 'You. Yes you, the manager, supervisor or director. You are best equipped to provide counselling at work because you know what it is like to work there. ... You know the organizational pressures, constraints, demands and deadlines. You've coped with them in the past and by enhancing your existing counselling skills you'll be more able to help others cope in the future.'

Likewise, de Board[42] declared that, 'It is my belief that the ability to counsel and to establish a counselling relationship is now a necessary addition to the managerial role ... .' Wells and Spinks[43] were also adamant that, in any case, managers actually do spend much of their time in this way. On the other hand, ethical dilemmas surrounding the line manager in counselling mode have been strongly voiced.

One of the preconditions of the counselling relationship, as decreed by the British Association for Counselling,[44] is that the counsellor be impartial, having no personal interest in any one particular outcome to the client's problem, other than what is believed to be best for the client. The line manager, it can be argued, is unavoidably compromised in this respect by the other demands of the managerial role.[45] Indeed in the USA there is legislation preventing managers from engaging in formal counselling relationships with those whom they manage.[46]

There are clearly unavoidable difficulties surrounding the concept of line managers as fully functioning counsellors. That said, there is widespread support for managers:[47,48]

- being familiar with the counselling process
- having high levels of, at the very least, basic counselling skills

- recognising problems amongst staff that could benefit from such help
- knowing when and where to refer employees for more specialised assistance.

Qualities of effective helpers

The qualities commonly held to be at the core of effective helping relationships are those espoused by Carl Rogers, one of this century's most influential figures in the counselling field. The three most pivotal of these he labelled *empathy, genuineness* and *unconditional positive regard*.[49] Not only are they championed as indispensable to counselling but more generally to 'probably most effective workplace management'.[50] Other qualities that are germane to counsellor effectiveness include concreteness, flexibility, sensitivity and knowledge of self.

Empathy

This is commonly held to be one of the most important qualities that a helper can have. Indeed, it is also an ingredient of communication competence, more broadly.[51] 'Empathy' derives from the ancient Greek word 'empathea' meaning affection and passion with an attribute of suffering. It should not be confused with sympathy. Empathy involves feeling *with* the other: sympathy feeling *for* the other. Someone who empathises with another makes an effort to enter the world of that person, to see things from that person's point of view: to look through that person's eyes. It is also important that the other person appreciates the fact they are being engaged with at this level of understanding.

Empathy then has three main elements:[52]

- *Sensing and understanding*. The manager must have the sensitivity to accurately tap into the employee's concerns and get to know them from that person's point of view.
- *Feeling*. Empathy has also a 'feelings' component. Indeed it has been described by Binder[53] as '... an interpersonal process whose level depends on emotional amenability to the perceived feelings of another person ...'. It is not enough to merely be *au fait* with 'the facts of the case' in a detached, intellectual way. The manager must be constantly tuned in to the emotional experiences that the employee is undergoing: feeling *with* the other person is what counts, without losing one's own sense of identity in the process.

- *Communicating*. Unless others realise that they are being empathised with, the process is pointless. It is crucial that the manager, in what is said and done, *conveys* empathy to the person seeking help. As put by Carl Rogers, empathy '... includes communicating your sensing of his world as you look with fresh and unfrightened eyes at elements of which the individual is fearful. It means frequently checking with him as to the accuracy of your sensings, and being guided by the responses you receive.'[54]

Empathy then is about: being alongside people requiring help as they work through their difficulty; trying to appreciate the world from their perspective; sensing how this emotionally affects them; and letting them know that this is happening. With this in mind, turn to Reflective exercise 12.1 and try to identify those responses most likely to reveal this empathic quality, from amongst the alternatives on offer. How empathy is conveyed depends ultimately upon how accurately the manager tunes in to the employee's experiences. As such it is not

Reflective exercise 12.1 Responding empathically

Scenario

Bill is a line manager in a manufacturing company that has recently undergone significant restructuring with major consequences for his job. He is off-loading some of his frustrations over a drink with his old friend, Bob. This is a snippet of the conversation:

> *Bill*: 'It has reached the stage where I simply detest the thought of having to go to work in the morning. I used to really enjoy what I do, but since the job's all changed I seem to spend most of my time trying to crawl out from under a mountain of paper. I seldom find time now to make contact with the production staff on the shop floor, the way I used to. It's important, you know, to maintain that type of relationship. The bloody phone goes non-stop ... never mind e-mails. I'm there late most nights trying to clear my desk ... if not, the next day's just impossible ...'.

Responses

Beneath are a number of ways that Bob could respond. Pick those that you feel convey a strong sense of empathy.

Reflective exercise 12.1 ***continued***

- Why don't you get some extra secretarial support?
- You're tired and frustrated because of the extra paperwork that's being piled on, to the point where you can hardly cope, and preventing you for doing those things that you believe really matter in the job.
- Sorry to hear that the old job isn't going so well these days, Bill.
- You never really could prioritise your commitments and now it's causing you all sorts of stress.
- Come on, let me cheer you up! Have you heard the one about ... ?
- You mustn't get down-in-the-dumps just because things are a bit tough at the moment.
- These things have a way of sorting themselves out, you'll see.
- Paperwork – tell me about it. Do you know that last week, I had to take two full cases home?

Now check your choices against the answers in Box 12.9.

possible to produce a categorical list of things to say or how to say them. More generally, though, using the following seems to be important:[55]

- appropriate nonverbal behaviour harmonising with the employee's mood state.
- reflections of feeling (these are statements that capture and reflect back the emotional message just communicated by the other).
- self-disclosures (in self-disclosing, the helper discloses personal detail which resonates with that revealed by the other. Together with reflecting feeling, it will be discussed more fully, later in the chapter).

Genuineness

This is sometimes also called *congruence or authenticity*. As explained by Thorne,[56] it depends on helpers being properly in touch with the stream of experiences, thoughts and feelings that flow through them as they engage with the worker. The effective helper should correspondingly be 'real' in the helping relationship – a sincere, authentic person, not someone pretending to be who or what s/he is not, or merely playing a role.[57] Being naturally oneself entails actually being what you appear to be. (See Box 12.3.) This does not mean, though,

Box 12.3 Being genuine

Genuineness requires managers to:

- be themselves rather than seek sanctuary in a role or take refuge behind a mask;
- have sufficient self-knowledge to ensure that there is no lack of consistency between feelings held, experienced and expressed;
- be spontaneous rather than merely mouthing the empty words of a well-rehearsed routine;
- remain open and receptive to what staff have to say and avoid becoming defensive, even if under attack from them;
- be prepared to share feelings and life experiences if this is thought to be in the client's best interests.

that the helper exercises no discretion as to what is said or done. However, since the intention is to encourage others to enter into a relationship of trust in which they are expected and encouraged to be open and honest, the helper must not be suspected of being less so.

According to Nelson-Jones,[58] genuineness is sensed by the client in the degree of consistency across the various elements of the helper's message. Is the same thing being 'said' verbally, vocally and non-verbally? If not, the client is likely to be suspicious. Being prepared to self-disclosure, as we shall see in the next section, is another way for the manager to manifest this quality.

Unconditional positive regard

This involves being receptive to, and accepting of other people, regardless of who they are or the nature of their difficulties. It has to do with recognising and responding to the inalienable 'personhood', the spark of human dignity, at the core of each of us. There are three components to this quality:[59]

1. Experiencing a warm, caring but non-possessive acceptance of the other

Indeed Carl Rogers went further to describe it as a 'prizing' of others, not because of *who* or *what* they are, but rather *that* they are. Thorne[60] goes as far as referring to it as a feeling of 'love'. It is the celebration of a shared humanity. While valuing another in this way, though, there should be no attempt to take away their independence or erode their autonomy: no desire to 'take them over'. This is what is meant by acceptance being 'non-possessive'.

2. *Constancy of acceptance* This entails that the individual seeking help must be accepted without 'ifs', 'buts' or 'maybes'. This is where the *unconditionality* of positive regard comes into play. It implies no judgement of that *person* by external standards: no approval or disapproval.

3. *Respect* People must be respected as unique autonomous individuals with the right to decide how to live their lives. Respect entails that what they have to say is worth listening to and that they deserve courtesy and consideration.

Concreteness

The nature of personal problems is such that we are seldom able to sit down to rationally and logically work through the details of our predicament. If we could we would probably reach an acceptable solution on our own. Rather, thinking and judgement is often clouded by intrusive emotion. This, in turn, comes through in what we say, leading to confusion, vagueness and contradiction. Feelings themselves are notoriously difficult to articulate. As such, much of their disclosure is obscure, abstract and imprecise. In working towards understanding, and beginning to tease out ways of assisting in a possible resolution of a problem, it is helpful if the manager can introduce a level of precision and specificity in discussing information and making decisions.[61]

Flexibility

Difficulties that perplex people are seldom neatly packaged, nor do they always have ready-made solutions. While we will come on to consider the stages through which the helping process can move, that route is rarely clear-cut. It is important to feel comfortable accommodating other people's agendas, being prepared to move at the pace they dictate, addressing the issues that they raise, when they raise them.

Sensitivity and self-knowledge

Managers who are good helpers possess considerable awareness both of self and of others. Unless you have some insight into your own needs, values, motives, fears, abilities, attitudes and biases, it is unlikely that you will be able to assist others to strike the match that will illuminate theirs. In addition to awareness of self, self-acceptance is an important requirement. This does not rule out change through growth and self-development, of course, but unless managers feel positive about themselves, it is unlikely that they will be accepting of others.

Helping skills

A range of skills involved in effective helping has been identified.[62,63] Regardless of whether or not managers should take on a formal counselling role, they should at least be able to draw upon counselling skills. Indeed, many of these ways of relating have a wider applicability beyond the narrow helping context, leading Wright[64] to contend that managers really cannot afford to be without them. The basic skills considered here are: active listening, reflecting feeling, paraphrasing, open questioning and self-disclosure.

Active listening

We tend to think of good communication as effective speaking, yet it is often poor listening that lets us down. It has been estimated that managers spend as much as 63 per cent of their total communication time listening to others[65] – but not always effectively. For example, in the business sphere, Stewart and Cash[66] reported how, 'Surveys of hundreds of corporations in the United States have revealed that poor listening skills are a major barrier in nearly all positions from accountants to supervisors ... .' Wright[67] believed that managers often talk when they should be listening and traces this to two sources: a frequent lack of confidence and fear of silence. Certainly, the helping relationship places a special premium upon quality listening.

Active listening is not just about hearing and seeing. It is much more demanding than that. It is about being able to tune in as fully as possible to the totality of the message being delivered, *and in turn communicating back that level of comprehension*. As such, listening in this concerted way has been described as listening with a 'third ear' and requires considerable sensitivity.

Two components are involved:

Tuning in This is about tuning in to, and picking up, the deep meaning and significance *for the other* of what has been communicated. Sensing what the employee is struggling to get across, or on occasion even actively trying to avoid disclosing, is a challenging task. It requires:

- listening carefully to what is being said and asking oneself, 'What does it mean from this other person's point of view, to have said this?' 'What is its significance at this time, at this juncture in the conversation?' 'Has this issue been mentioned before?' 'Does it fit into a theme or does it seem, on the other hand, to have come completely out of the blue?'
- being sensitive to *how* what is said, is said. Strong emotional cues can be picked up through paralanguage, in the tone of voice, voice inflection, speed of speech and voice quality.
- observing nonverbal behaviour. Important emotional and attitudinal information can be revealed in this way. Does the body language signal discomfort or unease with the topic? Does it complement or contradict what is being said?
- being mindful of what is *not* being said. Is there significance in the fact that the employee has not mentioned something that you would have expected under the circumstances? Could this be due to a bad experience with what is being avoided, or is it indicative of a lack of trust and confidence in the relationship with you?

Conveying understanding This is where the active bit of 'active listening' comes in. The manager may pick up more than is appropriate to communicate at that particular point. The employee may not yet be comfortable dealing with those issues at that depth of consideration. That apart, it is important that the manager conveys back to the staff member a sense of being listened to, a commitment to grasp as firmly as possible what is problematic for that individual and a resolve to work hopefully to achieve new insights for both. What is key is not that helpers must unerringly be accurate in what they sense during the interview, but that they are dedicated to getting it right and that this commitment is recognised by the other.

Active listening can be displayed both verbally and nonverbally, by the counsellor.[68] Verbal components are outlined in Box 12.4 and nonverbal components in Box 12.5.

Self-disclosure

In order to help others gain a full appreciation of what is troubling them, it is necessary to encourage them to openly and honestly disclose personal details about their situation and circumstances.

Box 12.4 Demonstrating active listening verbally

Verbal accompaniments include:

- *Verbal encouragers*. These are brief expressions like 'Right' and 'Yes', together with vocalisations such as 'Uh-huh' or 'Ah-hah', that provide feedback, convey attention and denote understanding. They encourage the speaker to continue.
- *Verbal following*. Good listeners conversationally follow the speaker rather than attempting to cut across the line of talk by, for instance, changing the topic. This facilitates the further development of the point being made.
- *Reference to past statements*. Bringing in some point made earlier in this or previous conversations is a very palpable way of showing that active listening is taking place.
- *Linguistic matching*. It was pointed out, in Chapter 2, that nonverbally matching the other in posture, gestures and such like, is a way of establishing rapport. Likewise using similar forms of expression as the speaker can create a sense of being listened to and engaged with.
- *Summarising*. Being able to neatly and succinctly summarise the main points covered by the speaker in a segment of the conversation, or in a more comprehensive way at the end, is a further tangible demonstration of effective listening.

Box 12.5 Demonstrating active listening nonverbally

Nonverbal accompaniments include:

- *Mirroring the facial expressions of the speaker*. This suggests that feelings are being recognised and empathised with.
- *Direct eye contact*. Averted gaze often indicates a lack of interest or unease with others and what they have to say.
- *Appropriate paralanguage*. As with other aspects of nonverbal communication, mirroring the paralanguage of speakers in tone of voice and speed of speech shows engagement with them and their problems.
- *Head nods*. These signal attention, interest and agreement and as such are examples of nonverbal encouragers, facilitating speakers in pursuing their lines of conversation.

Box 12.5 *continued*

- *Attentive posture*. A relaxed, open, forward-leaning posture is commonly regarded as indicative of deep involvement with another in dialogue.

Self-disclosure is also a way for helpers to constructively share some of their own experiences. In this sense, self-disclosure can be thought of as the act of verbally and/or nonverbally communicating to others some item of personal information that was previously unknown to them. Thus, self-disclosure can be nonverbal, given that it is possible either to hide feelings such as happiness, sadness and anger, or to express them through the use of facial expressions, gestures and so on. The verbal component of this skill is crucial since this aspect is less prone to misinterpretation, whereas we can be mistaken in our judgements about the nonverbal behaviour of others.[69]

Different types of self-disclosure have been suggested. Nelson-Jones[70] distinguished between: helper revelations about the client and/or the shared relationship; and information more directly about helpers themselves. More specifically, McKay and colleagues[71] identified four main disclosure categories:

1. *Observations*. Things done, witnessed or experienced.
2. *Thoughts*. These go beyond simple observations to reveal judgements about what has been experienced.
3. *Feelings*. These express affective states.
4. *Needs*. Here the focus is upon needs and wants.

Elements of self-disclosure

There are three features to be considered when evaluating the effectiveness of this technique.

1. Informativeness This relates to the amount (total number) of disclosures made and to their depth (or intimacy). Too much disclosing by the manager should definitely be avoided as it may shift the focus from the needs of the employee to those of the manager. The depth of self-disclosure offered is also important. It is common for people to reveal themselves in greater depth as relationships develop.

2. Appropriateness Manager self-disclosures that are done merely for some sort of self-serving effect are inexcusable. It should be appreciated that self-disclosures are most frequently used between people of equal status, followed by disclosures from low-status to high-status individuals. The more improbable usage is from those in high- to others in low-status positions.[72] This may make it more difficult for a manager to self-disclose, at any more than a superficial level, to a junior member of staff. That said, the truly helping relationship is one where differences in status are not played up.

3. Accessibility Certain individuals are more inhibited than others when presenting personal information. People usually find it more awkward discussing embarrassing, intimate problems. In addition to personal characteristics of the people and information content concerned, other factors that shape the likelihood and appropriateness of self-disclosure relate to the nature of their relationship and the particular situation in which they find themselves.

Effects of self-disclosure

Significant benefits are associated with self-disclosure in the helping setting.[73] Some of these are outlined in Box 12.6.

Box 12.6 Benefits of self-disclosure in helping conversations

- *opening dialogue* ('Hello, I'm John Brown and I'm happy for you to talk about anything that you feel will help …')
- *encouraging reciprocation and facilitating self-expression*. Self-disclosure by one interactor often leads to a similar response by the other. In so doing, self-expression is promoted.
- *providing reassurance*. Knowing that the helper has experienced and overcome similar difficulties can be immensely reassuring.
- *sharing common experiences*. It demonstrates that you are 'on the same wavelength', and can make the other feel empathised with.
- *providing new insights*. Information disclosed can help the other to view his/her predicament from a different angle.

Box 12.6 *continued*

- *demonstrating a useful skill.* The helper may act as a model to assist a taciturn client to open up.
- *developing and equalising relationships.* Self-disclosure plays a significant role in the development and maintenance of (especially egalitarian) relationships.

Guidelines for using self-disclosure

A number of recommendations to increase the effectiveness of the use of this technique in the helping process have been advanced.[74,75] Accordingly, self-disclosures should:

- *refer to self rather than personal experiences of a named third party.* The latter might raise suspicions about confidentiality and discretion.
- *be appropriate.* The benchmark here is, does it assist people to explore and understand their problems and find a way to manage them successfully? Be mindful of personal and circumstantial differences.
- *be selective and focused.* The revealed experience or feeling should resonate in harmony with that of the other, be offered for a specific purpose and with a particular effect in mind. Taking off on a long self-indulgent ramble down memory lane will only serve to abandon the helpee until your return.
- *not burden the individual being helped.* Managers should be careful in disclosing their own feelings and concerns. These may merely impose further pressure upon those seeking help who are already struggling to cope with their own difficulties.
- *be adaptable.* Not everyone in every situation will expect managers to self-disclose, want them to, or benefit from the experience.

Reflecting

This is perhaps the single most important skill in the counsellor's repertoire. Reflective statements both depend upon careful listening and are a further means of listening actively. They can be thought of as statements, in the manager's own words, that encapsulate and re-present the essential message conveyed in what the employee has just said. In doing so, they are a way of showing empathy. Additional functions can be found in Box 12.7.

Reflective statements can either address the factual content of what the employee has just said, in which case they are called *paraphrases*, or focus upon the feelings conveyed in the form of *reflections of feeling*.

Paraphrases

In paraphrasing the worker's preceding statement, managers should:

- use their own words rather than simply repeat, parrot fashion, the other's statement
- distil out the essential message in what was said rather than attempting to cover everything
- stick to the factual content, the thoughts, ideas and descriptions given, rather than the emotional melody behind the words.

To illustrate how this could work, let's take the example of a conscientious supervisor under stress through trying to be everywhere at once, making sure that everything and everyone is closely and constantly monitored.

> *Supervisor*: 'I know that some of the other supervisors are inclined to be slack, but that's not my way. You need to be on the floor and be seen to be about all the time. I seldom take a break, apart from lunch. I'm on my feet constantly, making sure things are being done as they should be. But is it appreciated? No way! I know that the staff talk about me behind my back.'
>
> [A suitable paraphrase of this could be]
>
> *Manager*: 'You are constantly on the floor, even to the extent of missing breaks, but the staff don't value your efforts.'

Reflections of feeling

The essential difference here is that feelings hinted at, rather than factual content, are picked up and mirrored back. Returning to the above example, the manager could have reflected the affective part of the message as follows:

> *Manager*: 'You feel frustrated, despondent and devalued because all your hard work is rejected by the staff.'

Responding in this way reveals that the emotional impact of the supervisor's experience has been recognised. The supervisor is thereby encouraged to continue exploring feeling states surrounding the problem.

Reflections can, of course, embrace elements of fact *and* feeling, if the helper senses that it is important for the other to consider both together.

Guidelines for using reflective statements include:

- use your own words
- do not go beyond the information just received by including your own interpretations of it
- be concise – remember it is only the core message that you are trying to catch and reflect
- be specific, it usually aids understanding
- be accurate
- do not over-use reflections – doing so may restrict the exploration of issues
- stick to the immediate message received, although more wide-ranging summaries of what has been communicated can also be useful.

Open questioning

The excessive use of questions of any type is sometimes frowned upon in counselling because it is felt that it has to do with helpers pursuing their own agendas, rather than allowing people with problems to tell their stories as they see fit. That said, however, open questioning, in particular, can be a beneficial tool. Open questions are ones that place few restrictions on how they should be responded to. In the extreme, they merely offer a topic for comment: for example, 'How do you find working here, generally?' Hill and O'Brien[76] contended that, as such, they generally have the effect of 'encouraging clients to talk longer and more deeply about their concerns'.

In addition, open questions tend to:

- be broad in nature
- leave the answer entirely up to the respondent
- encourage the other person to talk at length
- be particularly helpful in getting at more than just limited pieces of factual information. As such they are especially functional in exploring opinions, emotions and attitudes
- impose minimal control on the interaction.

Closed questions, by way of contrast, are better at unearthing limited pieces of factual detail, while the inquisitor retains firm control over the proceedings. Examples of open and corresponding closed versions of questions are given in Box 12.8.

Stages of the helping process

It is common to think of the helping process evolving through stages from initial contact with the troubled employee to the implementation of agreed strategies designed to effect a successful resolution. Different models exist of the intervening steps between beginning and ending, but one of the most robust is that proposed by Nelson-Jones and called the Relating–Understanding–Changing (RUC) model.[77]

Box 12.7 Functions of reflections

Reflective statements are a means of:

- demonstrating an interest in, and involvement with, the employee
- indicating close attention to the message
- showing that an effort is being made to fully understand the employee and that person's concerns
- checking perceptions and ensuring accuracy of comprehension
- facilitating employees in trying to come to grips with issues causing problems and thinking more clearly about them
- focusing attention in a selective way upon certain aspects of the employee's story
- communicating a deep concern for whatever the employee regards as important
- placing the employee rather than the manager centre stage in the situation
- indicating that it is acceptable for the employee to have and express feelings in the situation, and to facilitate their ventilation
- helping the employee to 'own' feelings
- enabling the employee to realise that feelings can be an important cause of behaviour
- helping the employee to scrutinise underlying reasons and motives for feelings and actions.[78]

Box 12.8 Open and closed questions

'Were you relieved, ecstatic or apprehensive when you discovered that you had landed the contract for the casing for the new C11 model?' *(Closed question)*
'How did you feel when you discovered that you had the contract for the casing for the new C11 model?' *(Open question)*

'Did the fabric get caught in the bearing just before the machine jammed?' *(Closed question)*
'What exactly happened just before the machine jammed?' *(Open question)*

'From which provider did you get your personal loan? *(Closed question)*
'What are your personal loan arrangements?' *(Open question)*

'Are you and Rebecca on better terms that when last we spoke?' *(Closed question)*
'How are things between you and Rebecca since we last met?' *(Open question)*

'Are you not confident about getting promotion because of your age?' *(Closed question)*
'Why do you think you won't get promotion?' *(Open question)*

'Come here every day, do you?' *(Closed question)*
'What's your attendance like here?' *(Open question)*

As such, helping is depicted as moving from initially engaging with people seeking help (Relating), to exploring and fully grasping the nature and circumstances of their problems (Understanding) and finally facilitating them in reaching decisions about how best to manage these difficulties together with implementing corresponding strategies to achieve these goals (Change).

Relating

This stage begins with the business of meeting, greeting and seating the person seeking help. How this is handled can create the successful beginnings of a beneficial association or alternatively turn that person away from the service on offer. The manner in which the interaction is opened will have an important bearing upon how that person responds. If the manager conveys the impression of having the time, disposition, energy and commitment to devote to it, the employee is more likely to be prepared to risk entering into an ultimately supportive, but perhaps initially uncomfortable, relationship. Careful attention through adopting an active listening style must be paid to the employee from the outset.

Since troubled individuals frequently open the discussion with a 'presenting' problem, and will often only reveal their real concerns when encouraged to do so later, it is important to be aware of verbal and nonverbal cues which may indicate a desire for a deeper level of involvement.

Furthermore, the portrayal of warmth, acceptance and respect, which involves communicating a liking for the other person and an indication of being willing to engage fully, is crucial to the establishment of a good rapport conducive to a helping encounter. The use of verbal and nonverbal encouragers are central to the communication of warmth.

Fundamental functions of this initial stage include laying down the beginnings of a suitably positive relationship, encouraging the employee to tell his/her story and establishing appropriate expectations surrounding what will take place.

Understanding

Following the initial relationship-development phase, the next step is to attempt to gain a full and accurate understanding of the member of staff's situation. This necessitates allowing freedom to talk, with as few restrictions as possible imposed by the manager. One way this can be achieved is through the use of reflections which, to a large extent, permit the employee to control the flow of the discussion. Where questions are used, these should be open rather than closed, again placing minimum restrictions upon the respondent. A further technique which is useful at the exploration stage is the use of spaced reviews. By employing this type of intermittent summary, the manager can ensure that both parties are in agreement about the information presented, before moving on to explore further issues at greater depth.

It is crucial to make sure that both parties are fully appreciative of issues, thoughts and feelings addressed. The manager should demonstrate empathy. Self-disclosure can also be introduced. This can either be about experiences which the manager has had, or has dealt with, which are similar to those being described by the employee, or it can involve commenting upon how the latter's situation is viewed. The employee also needs to feel fully accepted and the manager therefore must visibly convey positive regard and respect. In addition, the manager must be accepted as genuine and without facades: as not simply playing a role. Rather, for effective helping, there should ideally be consistency between how the manager feels about and relates to the employee.

Two important techniques that come into play at this stage are reframing and normalising.

Reframing Here the manager metaphorically puts a new frame round the picture being presented by the other, so that it can be viewed in a different way that offers possibilities for constructive action. This is particularly important where others get fixed into a particular viewpoint, seeing the world from a position of depression, anxiety or low self-esteem. Let's go back to the earlier example of the conscientious supervisor, over-stressed by trying to be everywhere at once, making sure that everything and everyone is closely and constantly supervised.

> *Supervisor*: 'I know that some of the other supervisors are inclined to be slack, but that is not my way. You need to be on the floor and be seen to be about all the time. I seldom take a break, apart from lunch. I'm on my feet constantly, making sure things are being done as they should be. But is it appreciated? No way! I know that the staff talk about me behind my back.'
>
> [The manager could reframe this as follows]
>
> *Manager*: 'Might it be possible to look at this another way? Could it be that you come across to your section, not as conscientious and hard working, but perhaps as having little trust or confidence in them, because they see you as always checking up?'

Note how in responding in this way, the manager moves outside the supervisor's frame. However, in re-framing, the manager must not deny the supervisor's point of view but merely offer an alternative for consideration. It therefore needs to be presented in a sensitive and tentative fashion.

Normalising The function here is to normalise the other's emotional state, by giving an assurance that it is not uncommon or inexplicable, under the circumstances. This is useful in response to questions such as 'Am I going crazy?' 'How could I feel like this?' 'Is it only me?' For example, those who have been recently bereaved may experience a mix of feelings, including anger, depression, guilt and despair. It can be made clear that this is part of a normal grief reaction, without diminishing the personal pain involved. Learning that one's emotions are experienced by others in similar circumstances can serve to reduce anxiety. At the same time, it is crucial that such feelings are not denied but the need for them to be worked through recognised.

Changing

By this stage, the problem will have been fully explored, and an in-depth understanding achieved, placing the employee in a position to consider the final phase of deciding how best to alleviate it and actually taking action so to do. The employee should be the decision-maker, knowing what needs to be achieved, with the manager acting in a supportive role. A range of possible ways to bring the goal about can be formulated and the one most likely to succeed selected. The employee should also be aware of those factors that will both facilitate (benefits) or hinder (barriers) goal realisation. Success usually occurs where the benefits can be engineered to clearly outweigh the barriers. Action may also include educating the employee to increase resources to bring about the chosen goal. Teaching and training can therefore be a part of the helping process at this final stage. Rehearsing agreed courses of action may be contemplated, prior to enactment, as part of a coaching involvement. A final aspect of the action stage may, on occasion, necessitate referring the person elsewhere for more specialist advice and guidance.

Conclusion

Contrary to the traditional picture portrayed by those who have researched and written about organisations, they are not cold, clinical, environments where the laws of dispassionate reason always hold sway. Rather, where numbers of people meet to complete tasks that are variously interdependent, emotion often finds a comfortable home. One manifestation of 'emotion at work' is in the problems of various kinds that frequently beset members of the workforce. These can have an adverse effect not only upon the quality of their work but on their lives and health. Some of these difficulties are caused by work, others have to do with personal matters, while yet more have family, social or financial concerns at their root. Nevertheless, none is left at the door as the worker enters the workplace each day.

Counselling at work is not a new provision, but it has become much more prevalent. Research carried out, especially in the USA, attests to its benefits for both the company and the individual member of staff. Cost–benefit analyses show that generally monies invested pay a very acceptable dividend. But apart from cold bottom-line statistics, today's organisations are expected to perform a duty of care towards their workers.

The precise role of the manager in a counselling service is a more contentious issue, however. Some hold that counselling should be an additional sub-role of the manager: others that it is ethically unacceptable for a line manager to contemplate entering into a true counselling relationship with an employee. All are in agreement, nevertheless, that it is important for managers to be familiar with the helping process and to command some of the core skills involved.

People who are effective helpers tend to possess qualities of empathy, genuineness, warmth, acceptance, respect, concreteness, flexibility, sensitivity and self-knowledge. Key skills and techniques through which these qualities are displayed include active listening, reflecting feeling, paraphrasing, open questioning and self-disclosure. The manager who is equipped with this portfolio of qualities and skills will be better placed to deal with the full gamut of encounters with employees. The days of management-by-shouting are long gone: an important part of modern management is managing-by-empathising.

Box 12.9 Answers to reflective exercise 12.1

Why don't you get some extra secretarial support?
(This response offers ADVICE and as such reflects Bob's, rather than Bill's frame of reference.)

You're tired and frustrated because of the extra paperwork that's being piled on, to the point where you can hardly cope, and preventing you for doing those things that you believe really matter in the job.

(This is an EMPATHIC response. It attempts to convey an understanding, from within his own frame of reference, of Bill's experiences of the job as disclosed by him.)

Sorry to hear that the old job isn't going so well these days, Bill.

(This is SYMPATHETIC, conveying Bob's feelings about Bill's predicament.)

You never really could prioritise your commitments and now it's causing you all sorts of stress.

(This is an INTERPRETIVE response, offering an explanation of the problem as Bob sees it.)

Come on, let me cheer you up! Have you heard the one about … ?

(This is a BLOCKING response. While possibly intended to chivvy Bill along and lift his spirits, it has the effect of cutting off further consideration of the topic.)

You mustn't get down-in-the-dumps just because things are a bit tough at the moment.

(This is a JUDGMENTAL response in which Bob imposes his values upon Bill and tells him what he ought and ought not do.)

These things have a way of sorting themselves out, you'll see.

(This is an attempt at REASSURANCE. However genuine problems need solutions, not glib platitudes.)

Paperwork – tell me about it. Do you know that last week, I had to take two full cases home?

(This is a ME-TOO reaction that shifts the focus from Bill to Bob. It can be helpful for Bill to know that he is not the only one with worries of this type … but before he knows it, all the talk will be about Bob's situation, with his forgotten!)

13 The war for talent: selection skills for busy managers

Introduction

Whatever the job opportunities immediately on offer, appointing the *right* people generally means appointing *bright* people. Those with positive attitudes will be more likely to exceed their immediate job brief, grow within the organisation concerned and make a long-term contribution to its bottom line. Researchers have thus generally agreed that top performing organisations pay particular attention to recruiting good people.[1] One study explored the distinguishing traits of those organisations that make the transition from being merely good in their field to sustained greatness.[2] Among their key attributes was a special emphasis on recruiting the right people, generally defined by their overall attitude. Indeed, the drive to recruit and retain the best has been dubbed 'The war for talent'.[3] In the struggle to get the right people on board, the interview remains one of the most common tools of selection.

It is an interpersonal encounter in which every practising manager will regularly engage, and one that they must master. As has been noted, 'There is perhaps no more widely used selection procedure than the employment interview.'[4] Indeed, some research suggests that it may be the only means used of selecting candidates in 85–90 per cent of companies.[5] A survey of 220 UK organisations found that 80 per cent regarded interviews as the most important part of their recruitment process, while 22 per cent said that interviews were a more important factor when picking someone to fill a post than they would have thought three years earlier.[6] This is despite many years of research that has questioned its validity as an instrument capable of predicting job performance. Interviews are also popular with candidates – or at least viewed more favourably than such alternatives as personality tests, biodata inventories or computerised tests.[7]

Thus, as countless studies have demonstrated, future performance is best predicted from past performance, aptitude tests or other information that can be quantified into statistical models, than from short face-to-face and unstructured interviews.[8] The problem with interviews is that most of us exaggerate our effectiveness as interviewers, imagine that we have a better insight into how personality can be assessed than most other people, and believe, quite wrongly, that our ability to predict how well people will do improves with time and experience.[9] The tenacity of such self-serving biases, in the face of the evidence, is simply explained:[10]

- *People tend to look for positive feedback on decisions that they have made.* There is no kudos attached to being acclaimed as an inexpert interviewer. We therefore look for evidence that most of our appointment decisions have worked, and ignore or downplay those instances where this is contradicted. We also trumpet our successes to colleagues, while suppressing any suspicion that such successes were exceptional. This is termed 'selective recall'.
- *Instances where our judgement is correct tend to be vividly remembered.* The rarer such judgements are the more vivid our recollections of them are likely to be. As the number of 'rare' instances accumulates during our career they become embellished in the telling. The process is similar to what happens when fishermen exchange tales about 'the one that got away'. The size of the fish grows in proportion to the number of times the story is told. This is called 'selective interpretation'. The effect, here, is that managers vividly recall successful appointments that they have made, and banish poor decisions to the remotest corners of their minds.
- *It is often difficult for managers to get honest feedback from subordinates on decisions that they make.* Research shows that ingratiation is the most commonly deployed tool of impression management, and that the greater the status differential between two people the more likely it is to be used by the junior partner in the interaction.[11] Ingratiation involves pumping up the ego of the message recipient with the hot air of flattery. Critical feedback is therefore limited. In this context, staff rarely tell managers when hiring decisions are wrong.
- *Attribution theory (discussed in Chapter 14) suggests that perception is distorted by an ultimate attribution error.*[12] In interview terms, this means that desirable outcomes are attributed to oneself, and undesirable ones to the situation. Thus, an interviewer reasons that 'I appointed Joe and he is excellent. This shows what an excellent interviewer I am.' If the same interviewer appointed someone who fails to make the grade, the likely reasoning will be: 'Fred didn't work out – it's a pity that he was so lazy, and that

> Department needs a review anyway.' Interviewers therefore sometimes also reason that the person they appointed did indeed have tremendous potential at the time, but they became in some way contaminated by the environment or people with whom they were then sent to work. In short, we like to claim the credit for success, but put the blame for failure on someone else's shoulders. Perception is distorted by a powerful self-serving bias.

The purpose of this chapter is to look critically at selection interviews, by-passing these four cul-de-sacs. Given that the interview is fundamentally 'a social interaction between the interviewer and applicant',[13] and consistent with the central thrust of this book, we focus most of the chapter on the communication dynamics involved. Research into the selection interview now dates back to the early twentieth century,[14] and the huge volume of studies that have been conducted enable us to make some suggestions as to what constitutes best practice.

A common mantra, chanted in some management circles, is that 'there are no bad soldiers – only bad generals'. We disagree. Many people are capable of making an outstanding contribution to industry, science, politics or the arts. However, in the event of a compulsory career change, they would make appalling soldiers, even if led by Alexander the Great. They should be weeded out before combat commences, and found a more appropriate niche for their talents. The role of selection is to put the right person in the right place at the right time for the right job.

Accordingly, this chapter explores the most common interview errors found in the selection process. In particular, a promising field of research into effective selection interviewing is outlined, focusing on what is known as 'Behaviour Description Interviewing' (BDI). The evidence suggests that, on the whole, this approach is an enormous improvement on the unstructured methods of the past. The main stages involved in such interviews are outlined, and the key skills that managers need in order to improve their effectiveness in them are addressed. In addition, we will also look at how such insights can help managers improve their effectiveness in their frequent role as interviewees.

The effectiveness of selection interviews

In general, selection interviews involve an encounter between a panel of interviewers and a solitary interviewee, during which questions are asked to determine whether the personality, skills and experience of the interviewee makes them the best applicant for a particular job. Common issues addressed during interviews include the following:[15]

1. Are candidates' qualifications relevant, adequate and genuine?
2. Is their alleged experience relevant and real?
3. Can they motivate people?
4. What have they improved (changed, prevented, stopped, started) in their previous jobs?
5. Do they communicate enough?
6. Do they communicate well in writing?
7. Are they assertive (but neither submissive nor aggressive)?
8. Do they have what it takes to get on in this organisation?
9. What sort of personality do they have, and will they fit in?
10. What is their record of success?
11. How do they react under pressure?
12. What is their level of maturity?

It is difficult to probe any of these issues, let alone all of them. For example, it has been found that although interviews can be effective in determining some personality attributes (such as extraversion), they are least effective for the two most job relevant personality traits – conscientiousness and emotional stability.[16] As a result, many interviews are directionless, skate over what is important, concentrate on the inessential and climax in poor decisions. In effect, we do the wrong thing, but we do it very carefully. A number of important biases have been identified in interviewer behaviour, which further confound the selection process. Some of the most important are:[17]

The 'similar to me' effect Research has generally found that candidates with similar biographical backgrounds, attitudes and perceived personalities to the interviewer are rated more favourably than candidates who are in some way different.[18] This leads to what is known as 'clone recruitment', in which only people identical to the interviewer have a chance of employment. There are two main problems with this. First, it enhances the process, discussed above, in which managers receive only positive feedback from subordinates and eventually come to believe in their own publicity, as do movie stars surrounded by a paid entourage. Second, if two people in an organisation do very little but agree with each other one of them is in effect redundant. Minority dissent improves decision-making (see Chapter 4), and selection interviews should facilitate the recruitment of people prepared to challenge the organisation's 'conventional wisdom'. This is also an essential condition for innovation.

Personal liking bias Positive correlations have been identified between the interviewer's personal liking for the candidate and the overall evaluations which they receive. Thus, it has been shown that people who are more physically attractive have a much better prospect of impressing an interview panel. In reality, there is no connection between merely liking someone (for whatever reason) and their actual ability to do a job.

Prototype bias Interviewers often possess notions of occupation-specific stereotypes of suitable personalities for particular job functions, and screen applicants against the extent to which they match these notions. Consider, for a moment, how you might feel if you were advertising a secretarial position. You would write the job description, draw up the personnel specification, visualise your ideal applicant in post, turn up to the interview – and as you read this sentence you most probably imagine a female (or a gay man) holding down the job. It is obvious that screening along such lines distracts us from the central task – determining who is the most effective applicant for the particular job.

The halo error The assumption here is that a desirable characteristic, skill or job success in one area equals the same in all areas.[19] This explains our constant surprise when we find that sporting heroes are incompetent at managing either money or their romantic lives, or find themselves in a courtroom charged with murder. We have made the quite unreasonable assumption that their excellence on the sports field translates into equal competence in everything else which they do. Similar errors proliferate during selection interviews.

The error of expectation Expectations are formed on the basis of documentary biographical information. This predisposes interviewers towards a decision, in advance of either the interview or of any other form of evaluation. It increases the possibility that someone with good communication skills (or easy access to desk-top publishing) will appear more job proficient than they actually are, and so bamboozle the panel into making an inappropriate appointment.

Primacy bias Interviewers often boast of their ability to know whether a candidate is 'the right stuff' at an early stage of the interview. Research supports the view that decisions are indeed often made within the first four minutes. Interviewers then spend the rest of the time justifying the decision which they have already reached. For example, one investigation has found that when negative impressions were formed during the first five minutes of an interview, 90 per cent of those applicants were not appointed. When positive impressions were formed during those five minutes applicants were hired 75 per cent of the time.[20] However, such practices are the result of pure bias. Opinions formed early in an interview are generally based on spurious criteria (such as physical attractiveness, or similarity to the interviewer), rather than criteria related to job effectiveness. They also reflect our innate need for closure, understood as a desire for definite answers and removal of ambiguity.[21] In particular, people with a high need for closure resort to *seizing* and *freezing*, in that they seize upon early information to make judgements and then freeze their opinion at that point.[22]

Unfavourable information makes more of an impression than favourable information It is difficult to set aside a negative impression, once it is formed. We are especially sensitive to negative information. For example, it has been found that negative self-disclosures are regarded as much more informative than positive ones.[23] The implications for interviews are striking. One study of interviewing found that on average 8.8 items of favourable information were required to change an initially unfavourable impression, but only 3.8 items of unfavourable information were required to alter an initially favourable impression.[24] Moreover, it takes more than twice as much positive as negative information to change an initial impression of a candidate.[25] A possible explanation for this, in the context of selection interviews, is that interviewers perceive their main task as being to select a good candidate and reject those who are poor. No one will really know if good candidates are rejected. However, they will know if we employ someone incapable of doing their job. This will damage the reputation of the interviewer, and other employees will grumble about poor interview decisions. In short, the costs of false positives are greater than the costs of false negatives. Other researchers have found, however, that interviewers are more influenced by positive information than negative when judging a candidate's abilities. But when judging morality related traits the opposite proved to be the case.[26] In general, it would seem that intense caution when evaluating either positive or negative information is advised, and that such information should be put in the overall context of what is known about the candidate's actual behaviour, both in previous jobs and in the context of the ongoing selection process.

Confirmatory bias This occurs when people seek out information that supports their starting hypothesis.[27] Thus, it has been found that when interviewers have a favourable pre-interview impression they spend more time recruiting the candidate; are more likely to form favourable post-interview impressions; and are more inclined to attribute favourable interview performance to the brilliance of the candidate, while attributing poor interview performance to external causes beyond the candidate's control.[28]

Overall, the traditional reliance on unstructured interviews has allowed such biases free reign. The evidence suggests that the more planned, structured, systematic and consistent the interview becomes the easier it is to eliminate the defects discussed above.[29] In particular, interviews which focus on past behaviours as a means of predicting future performance have been shown to work relatively well. We now look at this approach and how it might be more widely applied.

The Behaviour Description Interview (BDI)

Traditionally, standard questions have been asked during interviews, which probe the candidate's personality, family and educational background, previous job performance and future career intentions. Such questions usually focus on applicant opinions and generalities as opposed to what the applicant has actually done in the past. Since we tend to reduce uncertainty and ambiguity in our own minds by resorting to stock preconceptions, social stereotypes and unfounded social categorisation, the effect of this is to further activate the interviewer biases already discussed.

One study found that interviewers operating with traditional methods obtain *vague generalities* in around about 80 per cent of the responses to such questions.[30] Consider for a moment a question such as 'What is your biggest weakness?' Responses typically vary along a continuum from 'I can't think of any' to 'I work too hard.' In neither case is real information about actual performance likely to result: any useful information obtained is almost an accidental by-product of the question asked.

By contrast, behaviour description interviews *focus on past behaviour*.[31] The underlying assumption is, as Lord Byron once remarked, that 'the best prophet of the future is the past'. Research into this approach suggests that it is much more effective than traditional methods of interviewing, as a predictor of future job performance.[32] It also scores better than what has been described as 'situational interviewing', in which candidates are asked how they might respond to hypothetical situations in the future performance of their job. Figure 13.1 lists estimates of validity which demonstrates that the behaviour description interview is a more valid selection tool than other traditional approaches.[33]

The main principles of successful BDI are:

1. Interviewers are fully conversant with the job specification and person specification for each position being filled.
2. All questions are job related. Panels do not rely on a generic stock list of set questions. They develop job appropriate questions for each vacancy that arises.
3. The same questions are asked of all applicants, and follow-up questions not permitted. This ensures a consistent interviewer approach, which promotes inter-rater reliability in assessment and validity in terms of final panel decisions.
4. Questions focus explicitly on past performance. They should also be designed to obtain information for assessment against job related criteria. Questions which could be construed as unduly personal or discriminatory (including those relating to marital status, age, ethnic, gender or religious background) are avoided and

Figure 13.1 Selection interview validity

Selection tools	*Mean predictive validity*
Traditional one-to-one interview	0.20
Reference check	0.26
Assessment centres	0.36
Traditional board interview	0.37
Cognitive ability testing	0.53
Structured behaviour interview (i.e. BDI)	0.70

where information is requested for monitoring purposes, this is made clear to the applicant.

5. Rating scales should be anchored. This means that each item has precise weightings, determined through discussion with personnel and job experts. Such an approach ensures that each part of the job is assessed for its importance, with more weight attached to its most important function and so on, in descending order of importance. An example is provided in Box 13.1.

Box 13.1 Example of BDI rating scale

Name of applicant: ____________________

Position: ____________________

	Very poor	Little	Some	Good	Very good	Weight (%)
1. Written communication skills	1	2	3	4	5	25
2. Verbal communication skills	1	2	3	4	5	25
3. Ability to diagnose problems	1	2	3	4	5	15
4. Attention to detail	1	2	3	4	5	10
5. Team-building skills	1	2	3	4	5	10
6. Oral presentation skills	1	2	3	4	5	5
7. Knowledge of Pacific Basin	1	2	3	4	5	5
8. Marketing expertise	1	2	3	4	5	5

Recommendation

Hire __________ Not Hire __________

Additional comments: ____

____

____

Signature of panel chairperson ________________

Date ____________

6. Panels should be composed of at least three people, familiar with the job and trained in this method of interviewing. People are not permitted to drive a car without passing a test: why allow them to determine your organisation's future without appropriate training?
7. All candidates should experience the same process, and panel members should not discuss questions, answers or candidates between interviews. In this way, premature judgements are avoided.
8. The process should be as job related as possible. Full documentation should be maintained. This ensures that each candidate is treated fairly and the reliability of the interview is improved.

Beyond these points, general good practice would also suggest that recruiters must ensure that:

9. Candidates are kept fully informed of changes in interview times and consideration is given to their time constraints.
10. Applicants are informed of the interview process, test procedures where applicable, the terms and conditions of employment, the time scale of the recruitment process and the appointment procedure.
11. All members of the organisation with whom the interviewee comes into contact are kept fully aware of recruitment procedures and policies.

Key steps in the construction of a BDI

The above principles can be turned into practice by following a number of important steps. These are:

1. Analyse the job and determine its key result areas This means asking the following questions:

- What are the job's core areas?
- What additional activities would you expect the post-holder to undertake?
- What value do you see it adding to the organisation?
- What does the job 'look like', in terms of the day-to-day activities the employee will engage in?
- How will you assess performance?

The answers to such questions should then be turned into a *skills profile* of the ideal candidate. Such a profile might include reference to numeracy, leadership skills, writing ability, creativity, team building skills, interpersonal skills or other performance areas directly pertinent to the job concerned. The areas identified should relate directly and specifically to the job in question, and to the overall strategic goals of the organisation. The fundamental questions are:

- What does success in this job look like?
- How will we know whether the person appointed in helping or hindering us to achieve our strategic goals?
- What precisely do we want them to do, and how will we measure their performance?

Such an exercise involves more than compiling a 'hit list' of desirable qualities, which most people would compile for almost any job. It presumes that each of the component areas will be analysed in-depth. As an example, let us consider the area of interpersonal skills – cited as of vital importance in many jobs. A BDI approach would develop the notion of interpersonal skills so that it becomes specific for each vacancy being filled. Thus, a panel might decide that a high level of interpersonal skills in Case A would mean that a candidate is well versed in:

- Conflict and conflict resolution
- Relationship building
- Influence
- Negotiation
- Assertiveness
- Presentation
- Listening
- Selling
- Empathy, awareness, sensitivity.

The panel can then spend time during the interview looking for solid evidence that the candidate has, in their previous career, demonstrated the effective use of precisely these skills. In consequence, interviews become a precision search rather than a stab in the dark.

Reflective exercise 13.1 is designed to enable you to apply the above principles to the task of analysing key result areas.

2. Identify evidence that applicants have in the past demonstrated an ability to perform and produce in these key result areas At this stage, key result areas

Reflective exercise 13.1 Assessing your job's core result areas

The job you know most about is the one which you currently do, or have most recently done.

- Analyse your chosen job and identify its key result areas, as if you were about to embark on a job search for your successor.
- How would such a person's success or failure be identified?
- What would they actually do?
- What gains would you expect from their appointment?

Be as detailed and as precise as possible.

are detailed further, so that clear pictures emerge of what successful activities in these areas look like. One example is the area of written communication skills. The task is to identify the precise form successful written communication would have taken in the past, so providing evidence that the candidate is capable of fulfilling the needs of the job in the future. For some jobs evidence of having produced press statements would be appropriate; for others, the evidence might take the form of written reports; for still others, the evidence might be a number of highly focused summaries of various strategic reports produced by outside agencies. In terms of influence (one of the key interpersonal skills identified above), the panel could look for evidence of successfully introducing a major reorganisation; convincing an organisation to compete in challenging new markets; or resolving an intractable industrial dispute.

The task is to identify *critical incidents* in which an individual performed a key task and exhibited one or more of the behaviours regarded as crucial for success. What the person did, how they did it and the results obtained are all identified. During the resulting interview, such behaviours are then ranked in terms of their effectiveness (see Box 13.1 again, for one suggested rating method).

3. Formulate the job analysis and notion of evidence into appropriate job-related questions Most people prefer to rely on questions as a means of getting information during interviews. In consequence, research has found that questioning is often used inappropriately and fails to deliver its intended objectives.[34] As one writer has pointed out in relation to the interview process:

> ... we ask too many questions, often meaningless ones. We ask questions that confuse the interviewee, that interrupt him. We ask

> questions the interviewee cannot possibly answer. We even ask questions we don't want the answers to, and, consequently, we do not hear the answers when forthcoming.[35]

In contrast, consider designing questions which address the real needs of the organisation and the job under consideration. Box 13.2 contains

Box 13.2 BDI questions

Questions about effort/initiative

- Tell me about a project you initiated. What prompted you to begin it?
- Give an example of when you did more than was required.
- Give an example of when you worked the hardest and felt the greatest sense of achievement.

Planning and organising skills

- What did you do to get ready for this interview?
- How do you decide priorities in planning your time? Give examples.
- What are your objectives for this year? What are you doing to achieve them? How are you progressing? How will you measure whether each has been attained?

Interpersonal skills

- Describe a situation where you wished you'd acted differently with someone at work. What did you do? What happened?
- Can you describe a situation where you found yourself dealing with someone whom you felt was over-sensitive. How did you handle it?
- What unpopular decisions have you recently made? How did people respond? How did that make you feel?

Sales ability/persuasiveness

- What are some of the best ideas you ever sold to a superior/subordinate? What was your approach? Why did it succeed/fail?
- Describe your most satisfying (disappointing) experience in attempting to gain support for an idea or proposal?

Box 13.2 *continued*

- Select a situation where you met with a lot of resistance to a proposal. What did you do to overcome the objections?

Diagnosing problems in complex situations

- Tell me about the last time you recognised a problem in an organisation in which you were involved.
- How did you recognise the problem?
- How did you analyse the problem?
- How did you determine a solution to the problem?

Leadership skills

- What are some of the most difficult one-to-one meetings you have had with colleagues? Why were they difficult?
- Have you been a member of a group where two of the members did not work well together? What did you do to get them to do so?
- What do you do to set an example to others?

examples of questions that are widely recognised as meeting the criteria of BDI.[36] *We are not suggesting here that these be used in all interviews for all candidates*. However, they demonstrate a different approach to interviewing which focuses in detail on past performance. They are therefore useful in suggesting a different approach, and offer the prospect of interviewers receiving answers which assist them in making effective employment decisions.

Having studied these questions, it might also be useful to devise your own, for a post you are very familiar with – either a job you hold now, or have held in the past. Reflective exercise 13.2 will assist you with this process.

Overall, it has been suggested here that BDI represents a means of improving the hiring decisions which result from selection interviews, by focusing on the past behaviours and achievements of applicants. There is, however, an important qualification to be made. A significant body of research suggests that despite the overall superiority of BDIs, unstructured interviews (in which behaviour is more free to vary) are better at enabling interviewers to assess the personality of interviewees.[37] This does not mean that prospective interviewers should throw

Reflective exercise 13.2 Devising BDI questions for your own replacement

Working from your job analysis, your key result areas and the evidence that you have decided is needed in order to appoint your own replacement, identify detailed questions addressing each of the key areas. Remember:

- You need questions that can be asked of all candidates.
- Follow-up questions during the interview are not allowed.
- Your questions must therefore be as probing and precise as possible – you will not have a second and third chance to cover the ground required.

their hands up in despair. Rather, it is a question of recognising that:

> ... there is no one sure-fire way of accurately predicting a job candidate's standing on every trait. However, by implementing multiple methods and procedures ... the interviewer can increase his or her chances of garnering enough clues to piece together a usefully accurate portrait of the job candidate's personality.[38]

This means that some combination of structured and unstructured interviews may be most effective, particularly if used in conjunction with other selection tools. In addition, there are a number of phases common to most interviews. These complement the approaches outlined above, and it is to an exploration of these phases that we now turn.

Planning and preparation

Success in selection interviewing is largely dependent on preparation, as the above discussion of BDI has shown. Turning up without a script and with no previous rehearsal sets the stage for disaster. Further preparatory steps involve:[39]

Considering whether a replacement is really necessary The job might now be superfluous for many reasons. We no longer employ town criers, yelling the time for a citizenry that has no access to clocks and watches. In many cases, it may be that the need for the job concerned has been eliminated by computerisation. A main project that formed its core may now be complete. Appointing a direct replacement is sometimes like hiring a new architect when you have reached a stage where you really need a bricklayer. Thus, job descriptions in many organisations are often works of fiction. They disorient staff by providing the wrong signal of what the job's priorities should be, confuse managers during the selection process and, most crucially, send the wrong messages to the organisation's customers.

Compiling the job specification The need, here, is to compile a detailed picture of what the post-holder will actually do, where they fit into the organisational hierarchy, to whom they will be accountable and what their key result areas will be. Such revision is time consuming, and the temptation is to run with the job specification drawn up 10 years ago for the previous post-holder's predecessor. However, all jobs either evolve over time – or they should do. Jobs which remain static serve yesterday's market rather than tomorrow's. In turn, organisations which don't change go out of business. In addition, an updated job specification is a vital means of ensuring a relevant, probing and appropriate interview. This stage should not be missed.

Transforming the job specification into a personnel specification/person profile Normally, this addresses the following dimensions:

1. *Physical requirements.* Issues of legislation and equal opportunity must be borne in mind here. It is inappropriate to exclude people from jobs on grounds of disability, height, age, race, colour, religion or other distinguishing characteristics: the sole criteria must be their ability to do the job. It is, however, vital to identify whatever physical attributes are necessary in order to ensure that the job can be done. Thus, it is reasonable to assume that applicants for a University lectureship should not have a severe speech dysfunction, that those who work in warehouses possess a minimum level of physical strength and that house painters are not colour blind.
2. *Educational attainments/other qualifications.* The guiding principle here is to specify the lowest possible level of qualifications which are required, thereby ensuring that a sufficient pool of people capable of doing the job apply. A University degree is not required to collect rubbish, but would be justified for a research assistant. A clean driving license may not be needed for a Director of Human Resources, but will be needed for a travelling sales representative.

3. *Work attainments* This is a question of specifying the required level of previous experience which candidates must hold. Should the applicant have served an apprenticeship? Must they have had five years previous experience at a senior management level? Should they have been the key budget holder in their last job? Ought they to have already guided a large organisation through fundamental restructuring?
4. *Intelligence* The difficulty with this is clear. Intelligence, like beauty, is hard to define, even though we know the real thing when we encounter it. It is even more difficult to explore during an interview, and yet it is crucial for most jobs. (A colleague of ours once discovered a factory administering aptitude tests to a host of eager job applicants, all of whom invested their best effort in doing well. Unknown to them, the company was planning to employ only those who achieved the lowest scores, reckoning the jobs concerned were so menial that no one with any intelligence could tolerate them. We trust that such circumstances are rare.) The personnel specification should turn the general notion of intelligence into specified attainments and outcomes which will be evident from the candidate's past record.
5. *Disposition* This is as difficult but important to assess as intelligence. The key, again, is to identify what the candidate should have accomplished in the past in terms of team-building skills, leadership skills and interpersonal skills in general. It might be appropriate to look for solid evidence of team-building successes under adverse conditions – a candidate who held together a team which conquered Everest would certainly be worth a second glance, while someone who always seems to be working alone might not suit the post concerned. In essence, all such considerations need to be made explicit. The challenge is to identify those attributes vital to the job, but no more. Normally, a personnel specification would under each criterion list the personal attributes of the ideal candidate under two headings – that which is 'desired' and that which is 'essential'. For example, a University degree might be desirable for a particular post and attract a correspondingly higher weighting, but it might not be essential.

Examining the CV/application form CVs and application forms should be rigorously examined before the interview begins.[40] The overall task is '... to learn as much as possible about the candidate before the interview'.[41] In the first place, the task is to ensure that prospective interviewees match the personnel specification already drawn up. If they do not meet all of the essential criteria outlined the applicant should not be invited for interview. Applications should also be probed for weak areas which might either influence the interview or be discussed by the panel during its final decision-making meeting. Box 13.3 contains model guidelines of what in general should be looked for.

Box 13.3 Key issues in evaluating CVs

- Be aware of 'functional' CVs – look out for general statements with little content, no dates of employment, missing employer addresses.
- Be aware of 'qualifiers' – phrases such as 'knowledge of', 'assisted with', rather than evidence of solid achievement and real responsibilities.
- Look for signs of bitterness about past jobs, previous managers or work colleagues, rather than evidence of team-building skills and a problem-solving orientation.
- Notice sloppiness – misspelled words, a copy of the CV rather than an original, wrong addresses. Minor errors here show the lack of attention to detail which derails bigger projects.
- Don't read more into a CV than is there – assume that if a skill, attribute or experience is not listed that the applicant doesn't have it. It is the applicant's job to sell themselves, not yours.
- Look for a willingness to work hard. What evidence is there that this applicant goes beyond the minimum threshold of satisfactory performance? What added value do they habitually bring?
- Do not be dazzled by CVs which have been expensively produced. Someone other than the applicant may have drawn them up. Format should not overshadow content. Look hard for evidence of substantial achievement rather than access to desk-top publishing.
- Look for skill and logic in providing information on an applicant. How much effort has been spent in highlighting those aspects of the applicant's career which are directly relevant to the job in hand?
- Look for an ability to write intelligently on an application and resume.

Box 13.3 *continued*

- Search for signs of self-reliance and initiative. Is this the sort of person who always waits for direction from others, or do they routinely take the initiative themselves?
- Review reasons for leaving previous jobs. Is there evidence of seeing things through and positive career progression? Tell tale signs include long lists of jobs held for a few weeks or months.
- Do not pass final judgement in advance. In short, use your evaluation of the CV as a guide to interviewing rather than a determinant of your eventual decision. The most important task still lies ahead.
- Check. For many people embroidering CVs is a major hobby. There are now professional companies who check CVs – consider using them. One or two phone calls may save you enormous trouble in the future.

Conducting the interview

The opening phase of most interactions is generally regarded as crucial to its success or failure (see Chapters 6 and 12). As discussed above, it is also true that research into selection interviews shows that interviewers tend to make up their minds about applicants during the first few minutes of an interview. It is therefore important to manage the opening stage so that premature decision-making is delayed, a supportive atmosphere conducive to self-disclosure is created and clear expectations about the progress of the interview are established for both sides. This vital opening stage of an interaction has been termed set induction.[42] In the context of selection interviews, it is best accomplished by attending to:[43]

Social opening At this stage, rapport is built and the climate of the interview established. Non-task statements are employed, such as trivial comments about the weather, traffic congestion or the length of time the applicant has had to wait. The task is one of meeting, greeting, seating and exchanging small talk. Although short in duration, this gives everyone the opportunity to relax, become acclimatised to the interpersonal atmosphere and exchange supportive nonverbal cues.

Factual opening Here, the nature, purpose and format of the interview is explained. The candidate is informed how long the interview will last, which members of the panel will be asking questions and in which order and when the applicant will be able to ask questions of their own.

Shaping perceptions This involves manipulating the environment so that favourable and constructive first impressions are created. We make instant judgements about whether we like people, want to work with them and whether we will be able to give our best in the interview situation. Positive favourable initial impressions are created by comfortable chairs, a pleasant decor, the smell of coffee, the presence of flowers, soft lighting and the absence of chaos. We know of specially set aside interview rooms in some organisations where flip charts litter the room, the interview panel sits with its back to windows so that light shines in the applicants' faces, where there is no air conditioning in summer and poor heating in winter. The message here is: this interview is not important. Such situations predispose applicants to leave feeling aggrieved by what they have been through. It also prevents them giving their best in the interview. This is in no one's interest.

Listening Ninety per cent of talk in an interview should come from the interviewee. The following principles of effective listening are particularly pertinent to selection interviews:[44]

1. *Provide an environment that permits concentration.* There should be privacy and quiet. For example, there should be no distractions such as the sound of a lawnmower outside or a workman attempting to drill through the wall.
2. *Give applicants your full interest.* This means that note taking should be explained in advance but kept to a minimum. Interviewers should look at the applicant rather than at paper work or at each other. Under no circumstances should the panel whisper to one another or break into sub-groups, while one of them engages in a private dialogue with the applicant.
3. *Questions should be asked in their proper sequence.* In the sequence originally agreed by the panel, private hobby-horses and pet obsessions should remain – private. By way of contrast, we have observed an interview for a senior position in which one panel

member asked a candidate only one question: 'Are you related to the X family in London?'

4. *Listen for the meaning behind the words.* Note signs of anxiety about future performance, or evasion in accounting for the past.
5. *Avoid the fast rebuttal.* Listen objectively, with a deliberate attempt to postpone judgement. Give the applicant time to assimilate your questions, think what they mean and formulate a reply.
6. *Listen for basic ideas.* What is most important in the answers given? What is not said as well as what is said?
7. *Welcome and utilise pauses.* Don't rush in to fill a silence: when an interviewer allows a pause to occur, most interviewees resume talking within an acceptable period of time.

Interviewer wrap up This stage is short, but important. A final opportunity is usually afforded to the candidate to raise any issues which they feel are outstanding. Interviewers might ask: 'Is there anything that you wanted to tell us about yourself which you haven't had the chance to say?' The candidate is thanked for attending, informed when a decision will be made, when they will hear the outcome and is escorted from the room. Some interviewers find such closure difficult, and are inclined to retread familiar ground by asking new questions even as the candidate vacates the room. Such practices are essentially symptoms of poor preparation. Using the BDI format, the closure stage is reached when essential ground is covered, and should be devoted to straightforwardly terminating the interaction.

Post interview action This is decision time. Normally, a panel should reach a decision as soon as the interview is over. The general rule is that each panel member individually completes the interview evaluation schedule. This leads to each member producing a weighted score. The scores are then added up, and divided by the number of panel members to produce a mean score for each candidate. Discussion takes place on those candidates with a tied top score, if such a tie takes place, until agreement emerges on the best candidate for the job. Again, such discussion should focus on job-related characteristics, experiences and statements made by the candidates, rather than on idiosyncratic personal tastes of panel members.[45] At this stage, if the BDI format has been followed, the panel should be in the happy position of choosing between a number of people all eminently capable of satisfactorily filling the vacancy.

At this point, having considered all the ramifications of the interview process, we want to return to the principles of BDI. Reflective exercise 13.3 encourages you to reconsider some basic interview

Reflective exercise 13.3 Devising questions that get answers

Read the questions below carefully. Tick those that you think are questions which follow guidelines for BDI questioning and those that are not. (Answers can be found at the end of this chapter).

Typical interview questions	*BDI questions*	*Non-BDI questions*
1. *Why did you leave …?*	☐	☐
2. *How are/were X as employers?*	☐	☐
3. *What are your greatest strengths/weaknesses?*	☐	☐
4. *What have been your best achievements?*	☐	☐
5. *What are the qualities needed in a good JOB TITLE?*	☐	☐
6. *If we offer you a job what can you bring to our organisation?*	☐	☐
7. *What area of work do you feel least confident about?*	☐	☐
8. *What would colleagues see as your greatest weakness?*	☐	☐
9. *How would you describe your career progress to date?*	☐	☐
10. *What do you see yourself doing in 5/10/15 years' time?*	☐	☐
11. *Why did you become a …?*	☐	☐
12. *How do you take direction?*	☐	☐
13. *Why do you want this job?*	☐	☐
14. *Why should we offer you this job?*	☐	☐
15. *Are you being interviewed for any other jobs? Which one do you want?*	☐	☐
16. *How would you expect your results to be judged if you were appointed to this job?*	☐	☐
17. *What is the best measure of performance in this job?*	☐	☐

questions, often used, and assess whether they accord with the guidelines which we have outlined in this chapter.

An interviewee's perspective

All interviewers are also, on many occasions, interviewees. However much experience we have, most of us still approach this role with great anxiety. We face the pressure of evaluation apprehension. How, therefore, can the insights into the interview process outlined above also help us in our role as interviewees?

One psychologist has proposed that people remember short anecdotes, packed with concrete detail, very well. Such information is usually specific to a particular individual, and is stored in what has been termed episodic memory.[46] On the other hand, interviewees often provide information of a very general kind and which is either readily known to everyone or shared with all other applicants. For example, many interviewees will claim in their CVs that they enjoy 'reading'. However, they do not identify precisely what it is that they read. The information offered is therefore something that is shared by most applicants, and by failing to stand out as a unique selling point confers no competitive advantage on the interviewee. Interviewers find it more difficult to connect such information to particular individuals: it is stored in what has been called semantic memory. Thus, a vivid account of a fire in corporate headquarters which concluded with the interviewee bodily carrying the Chief Executive from the engulfing flames will be memorable (*it is stored in episodic memory*) – and will favourably influence a panel. On the other hand, someone who merely claims to 'keep my head in a crisis' will make little impression on interviewers (*this account is stored in semantic memory*).

The conclusion is that, to prepare effectively for interviews, you should:

- Identify crucial incidents. These should relate to the main achievement areas of the job for which you are applying.
- Ask yourself questions about what you found easiest, most difficult and about what you liked most and least in your previous career.
- Think of concrete examples, relating to major job successes. Concentrate on those associated with powerful feelings, and which are therefore likely to be particularly vivid.

- Ask whether the stories identified are relevant illustrations of the qualities required for the job being sought.

Having done this, answer as many questions as possible in the actual interview with specific and concrete examples of compelling achievements in your previous career. Now is the time to cast all modesty aside. Box 13.4 contains some examples of typical interview questions, and the beginnings of interviewee answers which correspond to this method of approach.

In addition, applicant questions themselves serve many important purposes in the interview.[47] Recruiters have ranked these questions as

Box 13.4 Responding to interviewer questions

Q. *What is your greatest strength?*
A. This position requires someone capable of X. In my last job when I was Xing, I did the following ....

Q. *What is your greatest weakness?*
A. Perhaps I can best answer this by referring to Crisis X last month, when I initially found that I had Y problem. This led to Z difficulties, which eventually I managed to overcome by ABC methods ....

Q. *How would you feel about moving to New York?*
A. Well, my present job meant that I had to move from X to Y. What happened was ...

Q. *What do you think about your current job?*
A. My best moment recently was when ...

Q. *Tell us about a significant failure you have had and what you did about it.*
A. Well, the following incident occurred. My mistake was ... I corrected it by the following steps (XXX), and learned the following lessons (ZZZ).

Q. *Have you ever lied or cheated?*
A. Well, surveys show that everyone does to some extent! However, I think there is a difference between minor omissions and outright lying. For example, recently when a particularly difficult employee asked if I wanted to fire him, I talked mostly about the need to improve his performance. But the truth is that I think it will eventually come to dismissal. Of course, I couldn't say so openly.

third in an inventory of twelve important factors which influence the final interview decision. In general, difficult questions at this stage are designed to 'test your ability to respond gracefully under pressure'.[48]

Interviewee questions should focus on the tasks of the job rather than vague generalities, and show a concern for how the candidate can contribute to the organisation's overall effort. Conversely, applicant questions which concentrate on promotion prospects, pay or how the job will better position the applicant in the wider job market, suggest someone whose mind is more on their next move than the present task.

Overall, it is clear that this approach also corresponds to the BDI format discussed earlier in this chapter. The challenge for interviewees, as much as for interviewers, is to generate specific examples of successful past performance. These will be seen as the best predictor of future performance, and will determine whether the job, promotion and opportunities being sought will be attained.

It is also worth noting that interviewees can derive substantial benefits from being trained in interview techniques. Investigations of training that utilised a skills approach have found that it often has very positive outcomes for candidates, particularly in terms of reducing stress and anxiety and thereby enhancing eventual performance.[49]

Finally, interviewees need to pay careful attention to impression management techniques. The interview is a game and both sides are expected to play by set, yet unspoken, rules. Meta-analysis has confirmed that ingratiation (praise, compliments, opinion conformity) and self-promotion positively affect how interviewers evaluate job candidates.[50] Self-promotion is therefore positively related to higher ratings, more job offers and fewer rejections. Of all the impression management options open to us, research suggests that self-promotion is the technique most likely to convince interviewers of a strong fit between the candidate and the demands of the job.[51] Thus, a norm of the interview process is that candidates are expected to sell themselves positively – in a sense, to boast shamelessly. Moreover, such tactics work, at least to the advantage of the candidate – it is, of course, clear that successful impression management may not be the same thing as actually displaying competence to do the job. Issues of clothing and weight have also been investigated, and found to exercise a significant impact on hiring decisions.[52] For example, one study found that candidates judged to be obese conveyed a negative impression of their personality traits, to such a degree that it explained 35 per cent of the variance in hiring decisions.[53] Individuals who act in a manner which does not conform to expected norms are regarded as 'bad applicants'. In particular, successful candidates have been shown to:[54]

- self-disclose freely
- present fluently and with few hesitations
- give direct and relevant answers to questions
- use powerful speech ('I would' rather than 'I might')
- employ intensifiers (such as 'extremely', 'absolutely', 'definitely')
- maintain high levels of eye contact with all members of the panel
- use smiles and other positive facial expressions
- be in control of gestures and posture
- dress smartly and appropriately.

It is also worth noting that managers are increasingly aware that many candidates they interview are, as one researcher has put it, 'overprogrammed'.[55] In other words, most of us now know the top dozen questions that are likely to be faced. A number of best-selling books have been published, promising great answers to interview questions. Hence candidates can arrive with pre-rehearsed answers. They should be aware that such over-preparation creates an interview which becomes so stupefyingly boring they are unlikely to stand out from the crowd. Interviewers lulled to sleep by soporific answers will be unlikely to offer you the dream job you crave. Remember the virtues of candour, honesty and spontaneity. Practice them in the interview – and you will stand out from the crowd. In short, the mission of candidates must be not merely to *survive* the interview experience, but to *excel* at it.

Overview

Selection interviews show no sign of losing their prime importance in business life. Indeed, the range of issues they are often utilised to measure has enormously expanded, and now includes citizenship,[56] emotional intelligence,[57] honesty[58] and much more besides. However, as this chapter has demonstrated, they have often been a ramshackle vehicle for achieving their intended objectives. It is little wonder that most managers attribute whatever successes they enjoy to luck and intuition, rather than the intrinsic value of the selection process.[59] In particular, unstructured interviews allow free reign to a variety of disabling interviewer biases and result in many poor appointment decisions. This has not been in the interests of either managers or those appointed: there are few fates more miserable than landing a job for which one's talents, abilities and interests are ill-suited. Thus, interviewers and interviewees have often found themselves dancing back to back, in the vague but unrealistic hope that each of them is performing the same moves.

More recently, the development of the BDI has transformed the conduct of selection interviews and led to much more satisfactory outcomes. The key principle is that the best predictor of future performance is past performance. Interviewers should systematically probe the past experiences of candidates for evidence of job behaviours which are in line with those needed in the job for which they have applied. Given such an approach, high validity scores have been reported in the research literature, which translates into satisfied managers, fulfilled employees and successful organisations. As this chapter shows, considerable effort needs to be invested in making such a process work. It remains the case that for most businesses their most important, as well as their most expensive, asset is their people. Second-class appointments prepare the ground for failure in the marketplace, and relegation to the ranks of the bankrupt. First-class appointments signal success, achievement and increased profitability. Time spent on improving selection interviews is a vital investment in the future of your organisation.

Box 13.5 Answers for reflective exercise 13.3

Only questions one and two fall within a behaviour description format. The central rule is that such questions always ask candidates 'What did you do WHEN?' The emphasis throughout is on what people did in the past, rather than what they think or what they might do in the future.

14 Feedback time: performance appraisal and management

Introduction

All of us enjoy passing judgements on other people. For this reason, gossip is a central ingredient of much of human communication. The informal appraisals in which we routinely engage are often concerned with making ourselves feel better at the expense of someone else, rather than honestly examining the facts. Such judgements are frequently based on flimsy evidence: in effect, a verdict is pronounced before any testimony has been heard. This was well shown by a newspaper report on the appointment of General Boonthin Wrongakmit as Assistant Police Director in Thailand some years ago.[1] Speaking after his appointment he said 'I shall be introducing an all-round shoot-to-kill policy towards our criminals. As police chief of North-East Thailand for 37 years I always used this policy.' Asked how he could be sure his men always shot the right people, the General replied: 'You could tell by the look of them.'

Once such judgements have been formed (even if on a less terminal level) they are difficult to abandon. We have a tendency to seek out and remember information that confirms our prejudices, while ignoring or forgetting anything that suggests we might be wrong.[2] For example, if we expect someone to be a poor performer in their job it is likely that we will see only evidence of this when we examine what they do. Furthermore, this perception is communicated to the person concerned by our overall bearing, and the tension created results in actual poor performance. Our expectation has created a self-fulfilling prophecy, which of course only confirms our view that what we thought at the beginning was right all along.[3]

Examples of such problems abound in the workplace. In the UK, the organisation once known as the Royal Mail, responsible for the national mail distribution system, was mystifyingly rebranded as Consignia, before once more reverting to its traditional title.

One investigation into its workings found a sorting office with a corridor suspended above the sorting area. The corridor had long slits from which supervisors could watch employees for evidence of malpractice. At other sorting offices, managers posted signs that informed employees 'You are the weakest link.'[4] The effects of such informal appraisals can be readily imagined.

Formal performance appraisal, when run well, is a powerful defence against these dangers. There are three main reasons for this:

1. It promotes open and honest two-way communication between managers and staff. This reduces the risk that opinions will be formed on the basis of the manager's personal prejudices, through gossip or through an inadequate scrutiny of insufficient information. These are real dangers. With an expanding span of control in more and more organisations, most managers are no longer familiar with every detail of what their people do.
2. Open and honest communication ensures that when misunderstandings occur an opportunity is provided for their resolution. This prevents disagreement festering into destructive and deeply embedded conflict.
3. Open communication means that both sides discuss their expectations of the other. There is less scope for hidden agendas, and more space for a constructive focus on key business issues. An appraisal scheme should therefore liberate people's sense of creativity, empower them, promote involvement and result in greater cohesion.

Accordingly, we would define appraisal as:

> A means for managers to identify and reward positive performance, promote a unified focus on the achievement of business goals and provide support for the personal development needs of employees.

As defined above, it has six commonly agreed functions.[5] These are to:

1. Provide adequate feedback to staff about their performance;
2. Serve as a basis for changing behaviour towards more effective working methods;
3. Provide managers with information which they can use to judge future job assignments;
4. Motivate people through offering recognition and support;

5. Strengthen supervisor–subordinate relationships;
6. Assist in the diagnosis of organisational problems.

Appraisal, in one form or another, has been widely used in industry since the 1930s, although the formal monitoring of performance is as old as commerce itself. Robert Owen, the renowned nineteenth-century industrialist, used what were called 'silent monitors', a piece of wood above machines with one of four colours attached to show daily performance. The scope of appraisal is now developing rapidly. A Superboss report,[6] which surveyed over 120 businesses in the UK, found that 89 per cent had a formal performance appraisal system in place. It has been estimated that over 94 per cent of US companies use some form of formal performance appraisal.[7] A survey of 280 midwest companies in the US found that 25 per cent used annual upward appraisals, 18 per cent peer appraisals and 12 per cent what are known as 360 degree appraisals, in which people evaluate themselves, and then receive feedback from their immediate peers, managers and subordinates.[8] Key companies such as AT&T, the Bank of America, Caterpillar, GTE and General Electric have been pioneers with this latter approach.

Given the expanding role of appraisal, and its increasingly supportive rather than punitive intentions, we would argue that managers should eliminate the term 'appraisal' in favour of the word 'feedback'. The former implies one-way communication, and never entirely escapes the judgmental connotations of a courtroom. The latter term suggests dialogue, partnership and participation. It also emphasises the importance of ongoing feedback, rather than something happening on one formal occasion.

But we are still a long distance from a position where feedback is generally conducted well. In the words of the Superboss report, many appraisals are 'demotivational, divisive, pseudo-scientific and counter-productive'. In an all too typical study of the field, an investigation of performance appraisal in one public sector organisation found over 40 per cent of staff dissatisfied with the system, including many who received good or outstanding ratings as result of it.[9] In Box 14.1, we list some of the most common complaints made about appraisals, derived from a number of sources.[10]

Thus, appraisals often consume vast amounts of time and use up acres of rain forest in paper-work, raise expectations that cannot be met, focus on negative behaviours while forgetting to reward the positive and produce a boiling resentment towards all those associated with the process.

Box 14.1 Common defects in appraisal systems

- Lack strategic focus
- Take too much time
- Are too subjective
- Are all the same
- Merely 'go through the motions', on the basis that it is the organisation's policy so it must be done
- Make distinctions between people, without making a real difference to performance
- Challenge managers who may not have the necessary skills to conduct effective appraisals
- Give too much power to little Hitlers, who relish the opportunity to pass judgement on others
- Are not timely enough – for example, criticism of poor performance arrives too long after the event to impact on outcomes
- Belittle people
- Ignore systemic factors that impact on performance while exaggerating the role of individuals
- Are used for too many purposes that are often at odds with each other
- Review criteria are often inconsistent, with different managers evaluating widely different things
- Only have value at the extreme ends of the performance scale, for those who are either exceptionally able or exceptionally poor.

However, as suggested above, the assessment of behaviour is *unavoidable*. An official appraisal/feedback scheme should merely formalise what is already an informal process. Unless carefully prepared, formal schemes may simply become a means of apportioning blame, shame and disgrace. This will not promote business success or organisational cohesion.

This chapter seeks to guide you past such quicksands. We start by examining some of the biases in interpersonal perception which lead feedback astray, outline the key principles of effective feedback, look at some of the things which go wrong most often and then explore how our knowledge of best practice can be applied to create feedback systems which identify good performance, celebrate it and so reward and enhance achievement.

Biases in interpersonal perception

It is said that when Sir Walter Raleigh was imprisoned in the Tower of London in the sixteenth century he wrote a history of the world. While he was doing so, a fight broke out between some workmen under the window of his cell and one of them was killed. Raleigh himself witnessed the fight and tried to find out what had caused it. But despite being an eyewitness and despite making extensive inquiries he never could discover what had sparked it off. Legend has it that this failure caused him to burn what he had written and abandon the whole project.

What this story shows is that facts rarely speak for themselves – we have to interpret them. And the problem is that no two people interpret a set of facts in the same way. This is particularly true when our own self-interests are at stake. Most of us possess a powerful reflex of self-justification, which would put us in the running for a gold medal if blaming others were to become an Olympic event. Many of the biases discussed in Chapter 14 pertaining to selection interviewing also apply here, along with many others. Indeed, it can be argued that 'the biggest challenge that impedes an effective performance review is the biases we all have'.[11] How might such biases create problems in a feedback interview?

The perspective of the interviewee

- A survey of British drivers found that 95 per cent thought they were better than the average driver.[12] This explains why so many relationships founder when we try to give driving lessons to our friends or, worse still, our spouses. In general, we have a high opinion of our own behaviour, and a correspondingly poor opinion of that of others. Furthermore, we tend to assume that others see us in the same rose-tinted light in which we see ourselves. Thus, critical feedback is generally seen as threatening. Those messengers offering it are more likely to be shot than greeted with applause.
- Another study found that people were 100 per cent confident of the correctness of their answers in a series of tests, even when they were correct only 78 per cent of the time.[13] People tend to be particularly certain of their decisions when they have been made in a group. By the same token, we are acutely aware of defects in the decision-making of others, particularly in that of other groups.

- Most of us think that we contribute more to group discussions than the average input of everyone else involved, and that more people agree with our opinions than is actually the case. A major reason for this may be that we are intrinsically motivated to develop a positive evaluation of ourselves, as a means of shoring up our sense of identity.[14] This is easily achieved when we exaggerate our role, general level of influence and contribution to group discussions. Each of us becomes our own spin-doctor. In short, success has many fathers, while failure is an orphan. It is a case of I/we succeeded, but you failed.
- We are inclined to explain the behaviour of the people around us as the result of global (i.e. what is true of them in one situation is true of them in all) personality characteristics which are also assumed to be permanent, while we excuse our own behaviour as the result of the situation we find ourselves in.[15] People often feel that their organisation is mired in the mud despite their own superb navigational skills, while everyone else is viewed as an incompetent driver. The tendency to overestimate the role of personality in the behaviour of others while exaggerating the role of situation in our own has been termed 'the fundamental attribution error'.[16] Moreover, we attribute our failure to the situation, but our successes to personal factors ('I passed because I am bright: I failed because the teacher was terrible'). This also tempts us into a process of what could be called *blame realignment*, in which our primary concern is to plead innocence of all charges while putting complete responsibility for disaster on someone else's shoulders. An interesting illustration of this comes from Oscar Wilde, who on being asked by a friend how the opening night of his new play had been received responded: 'My play was a complete success, but the audience was a disaster.'
- Organisations are often uneasy coalitions of conflicting professional tribes. Research shows[17] that intense prejudice between groups is induced when they compete with each other, especially if valued rewards are at stake. In addition, when people have a pride in their group they tend to denigrate other groups, thereby exaggerating the virtues of their own. Furthermore, bad behaviour is more easily noticed in minority groups than in majority ones, since we associate bad behaviour with minority groups because both bad behaviour and the minority group itself are rare. This suggests that if appraisal is introduced into an organisation with a history of poor working relationships it will, initially at least, exacerbate rather than ease the tension.

The above, in short, inclines most of us to exaggerate the extent of our contribution to organisational success. It also renders us resistant to critical feedback. A study found that attempts to assist people by pointing up improvement needs in their work were perceived as threatening to employees' self-esteem and resulted in defensive behaviour.[18] Seventy five per cent of people in any event saw the evaluations they received as less favourable than their own self-estimates and therefore regarded appraisal as a deflating experience. Furthermore (and this is the crunch) follow up studies found that aspects of performance most criticised showed the least improvement. Another experimental study offered people feedback after completing a survey, while withholding feedback from others. It found *no* significant positive changes in those receiving feedback.[19] People are especially sensitive to negative input – what has been termed *the automatic vigilance effect*.[20] It seems that, overall, negative feedback creates resentment and places obstacles in the path of personal development. Research in general suggests that reactions towards feedback are more positive in a supportive environment. Thus, when criticisms have to be made they should focus on specific behaviours, be linked to realistic action plans capable of achieving improvements and occur in the context of a supportive organisational culture. In any event, the main emphasis should be on positive feedback. This is more likely to create focus, clarity and a bias in favour of action to secure significant change.

The perspective of the interviewer

- We tend to slot people into categories based on immediately obvious stereotypical traits, such as the colour of their skin, height, accent and mode of dress.[21] If you doubt this, consider why you never turn up for a top executive job interview dressed in jeans and tee shirt. First impressions count. This inevitably means that we perceive many people based on our own personal prejudices, rather than as they really are. For example, studies have found that those rated as more physically attractive are assumed to possess a range of other desirable attributes, such as intelligence, power and charisma (see Chapter 3).
- We frequently fall victim to *the halo effect*.[22] This has already been identified, in the previous chapter, as a fundamental problem in selection interviews. In the context of appraisal, we tend to assume that a positive attribute or a job related success in one area automatically implies success in others. An example of this occurred

recently, when a colleague of ours was assessed by students on the effectiveness of her teaching. Among the scores obtained was a rating of 'excellent' for her use of flip charts. However, the colleague concerned never uses flip charts. Evidently, students considered her effective overall, and assumed that she must be excellent in this category too. Of course, this also illustrates the power that results from a major job related success – one initial triumph may well provide enough lift off to sustain a whole career. In short, glossy bodywork can blind us to serious defects under the engine hood. (Many romantic relationships run aground from precisely this sort of miscalculation!)

- *Personal liking bias* means that when supervisors like a subordinate, for whatever reason, they generally give them higher performance ratings, their judgement of the subordinate's work performance becomes less accurate and they show a disinclination to punish or deal with poor performance.[23] We also now live in an increasingly litigious age. There have been a growing number of lawsuits claiming that poor appraisals relative to those of others were influenced more by the personal biases of managers than by the actual performance of the employee.[24]
- *The horn effect* arises when a problem in one area is assumed to be representative of defects elsewhere.[25] If we see a scratch on the bodywork of a new car it might well be that everything else is perfect, but it is unlikely that we will be able to set aside our initial poor impression. As an old Russian proverb puts it: 'A spoonful of tar spoils a barrelful of honey.' In turn, we feel compelled to focus our attention on such negatives rather than positives. One consequence is what has been termed the 10–90 effect, in which 90 per cent of time in an interview is spent discussing the 10 per cent of the job where the employee is performing badly.
- *The consistency error* suggests that we have an exaggerated need to feel consistent in our opinions and judgements, and to assume that people and circumstances are more stable than they actually are.[26] Thus, when we form an initial impression of someone it is very difficult to change it.[27] This predisposes us to interpret new evidence in the light of our existing assumptions, while ignoring anything that contradicts our most cherished beliefs. So, if we assume that Fred is a lazy and incompetent employee, Fred will have to do much more than his more fortunate colleagues to convince us otherwise.

- The fundamental attribution error, discussed above, means that an appraiser tends to attribute poor performance to the personality of the interviewee, rather than to the situation. It may be assumed that there is low ability to begin with, perhaps compounded by lack of effort. However, if the employee has successes managers are likely to conclude that it is their inspired leadership, judgement and competency that has caused it.[28] The employee, meanwhile, is likely to have exactly the opposite perception. This replaces discussion with trench warfare. Peace becomes progressively more elusive, since each side uses the same words but attaches different meanings to what is said. In truth, managers and employees are often two sides divided by a common language.
- *The similarity bias* means that we are attracted to people who look like us, sound like us and form a convenient echo chamber for our own ideas.[29] In appraisal terms, this leads to a crony effect, in which yes men have a natural advantage in the competition for promotion, *and the Doppelganger effect*, in which appraisal ratings reflect the similarities between the person being appraised and the appraiser. The challenge here is to seek out, cherish and reward difference. If five people on a team do nothing but agree with each other at least four of them are, for all practical purposes, redundant.

Overall, these perceptual biases suggest that we have a high confidence in our judgements of other people, but that many of these judgements are inaccurate. However, we find it difficult to pay attention to anything that suggests that this might be the case. Thus, giving feedback often leads to communication roadblocks, multiple pile-ups and outbreaks of road rage. But if approached with an awareness of the various pitfalls discussed here appraisal becomes an invaluable means of institutionalising two-way feedback into all relationships within the workplace. Managing feedback is like cycling on a tightrope, stretched across a pit of crocodiles: survival depends entirely on achieving a sense of balance.

The principles of effective appraisal

We have suggested that performance appraisal is a fraught and error prone process. However, positive outcomes can be achieved if our movements are guided by a number of fundamental principles.[30]

These are:

- Organisations work better when they have clear business goals, widely disseminated and understood by everyone. The chief saboteur of efficient performance is secrecy.
- Employees are entitled to know how well they are contributing to the achievement of important business goals, and should feel able to communicate how they feel about the support they receive to this end. Open, honest communication and all round feedback are critical ingredients of business success.
- The main focus of the interview should be on *behaviour* and *results*.[31] That is, it should focus on what the employee has done in the past year, the results that were obtained and the behaviours required for the coming year. In this way performance feedback ceases to be a sad meditation on missed opportunities, and becomes what has been termed 'performance management'.[32]
- Managers should regularly sit down with each member of their staff and discuss (a) how well the organisation is doing (b) how the individual concerned is contributing to the overall effort and (c) what else the organisation in general and the manager in particular could do to enhance the employee's effort.
- These discussions should be frequent. Regular feedback gives people the opportunity to change their behaviour as they go along.[33]
- Regular feedback of the kind suggested here should be overwhelmingly informal, simple and free of paperwork. As we mention in Chapter 10, paperwork is an organisation's cholesterol. For many of us a diet is in order. Less is best.
- Managers are entitled to have opinions about the individual's performance, and should communicate such opinions during these informal discussions. This feedback should focus on behaviours rather than personalities, be highly specific and emphasise successes which the person has had as well as areas where performance could be improved.
- Similar opportunities to comment on the manager's performance should be afforded to staff. Securing accurate upward feedback is the biggest single problem faced by many organisations. Critical upward feedback is so often met with a hostile response that most people simply give up. The problem is well illustrated in Sam Goldwyn's fabled comment to his staff, after his studio had produced a string of six flops: 'I want you to tell me what's wrong

with me and MGM – even if it means losing your jobs.' Effective appraisal creates two-way feedback and clears this arterial blockage.

- Informal appraisal/ feedback should focus overwhelmingly on examples of excellent performance. Excellent performance, publicly appreciated, is emulated. Poor performance, publicly upbraided, promotes an atmosphere of defeat, resignation, fear and resentment. It creates a receptive context for failure. Managers should praise publicly, but criticise privately.
- Poor performance should be discussed with the individuals concerned, privately and at once. The focus should be on agreeing an action plan to prevent its recurrence, rather than securing confessions, convictions and public floggings.
- A culture of openness, honesty and trust is essential if feedback schemes are to succeed. Otherwise, public compliance is combined with private defiance. An organisation at war with itself conquers no new markets.
- Training must be given to help both managers and other employees accept and offer feedback. Most organisations train managers in appraisal: very few train staff in how to respond.

These principles suggest that appraisal is in essence concerned only with *the management of two-way feedback*. This should be unthreatening, action oriented and supportive. However, it will help us to understand how these principles should be applied if we also look at how appraisal so often goes wrong.

The perils of feedback

A variety of major problems with feedback have been identified. These are as follows:

1. Feedback is often restricted to small numbers of staff in key managerial positions The Superboss report, already referred to, found that only 14 per cent of organisations appraised all their employees, with front line employees mostly left out of the loop. The rationale for such restrictions is invalid, if appraisal is reconceptualised as the promotion of feedback.

2. Feedback has often been linked to evaluation of performance in the form of 'rating systems' Here, performance is graded on a scale of 1 to 5, with 5 representing excellent performance and 1 representing grounds for dismissal. Problems with this are legion,[34] and are worth examining since so many feedback schemes still make use of rating schemes. They include:

- The grave difficulty in accurately assessing the details of someone's performance. Results are frequently a team effort. How do we disentangle the extent of Bob's contribution from Jill's? What happens if we credit Bob with all the achievement, when Jill will think that she put in more effort than him? If ratings are awarded which people think are unfair, the 'unfair rating' will become the issue, rather than necessary improvements in performance.
- How does one measure intangible factors such as motivation, creativity, team spirit, responsibility and loyalty? Subjective impressions of performance on these issues tend to govern the ratings that we award. However, the impossibility of escaping subjective assessments makes the eventual 'grade' appear arbitrary to the person receiving it, and so leads to destructive conflict over the assessment awarded.
- When everyone knows that a grade is at stake, the emphasis of the meeting shifts from an open discussion of performance (in which both strengths and weaknesses can be honestly discussed) towards the optimum presentation of the self, the covering up of errors and inflated claims for one's own performance. Naturally, this will also involve a greater reluctance to accept feedback on areas where performance needs to improve.

3. Feedback has often been linked to the award of performance related pay
Many of the points made in opposition to the use of rating schemes also apply here. In the first place, such practices contradict what is known about motivation. *Intrinsic* motivation, which is most closely correlated with superior performance, flows from performing the task at hand, rather than doing it to obtain rewards *extrinsic* to the task itself. Our performance is likely to deteriorate when the emphasis shifts from intrinsic motivation to the gaining of extrinsic rewards. There is, therefore, no evidence that tying performance to pay actually improves performance – rather, the opposite is the case.[35]

Linking feedback to pay transform the process into one of confrontation. It heightens status differentials between managers and employees, and threatens working relationships. Consider the following. In practice, organisations find it difficult to pay more than a limited proportion of people much more than the budgeted average for any given job. The financial gains on offer from such systems therefore tend to be nominal, and/or restricted to a small number of people. The majority of an organisation's employees are more likely to emerge from what almost inevitably becomes an adversarial process bearing feelings of resentment. One reason is that most people do not rate their own performance as either average or below average – in fact, they exaggerate their contribution to organisational success.[36] The use of performance related pay as part of the appraisal process means that managers will be telling the majority of their people that their performance is much weaker than they themselves imagine it to be – an outcome which may also activate a large number of destructive self-fulfilling prophecies. For these reasons, the evidence suggests that such innovations as performance related pay demotivates rather than motivates people, that it does not help organisations to retain high performers, does not encourage poor performers to leave and creates widespread perceptions of unfairness.[37]

An illuminating example may be in order. Enron was an organisation that combined both a ranking system and the linking of performance to pay. Its bankruptcy in 2001 stands (at the time of writing) as the biggest in US corporate history. Enron had a reputation for aggressive recruitment practices, based on the notion that it was engaged in a 'war for talent'. An internal performance review committee rated employees twice a year.[38] They were graded on a scale of 1 to 5, on ten separate criteria, and then divided into one of three groups – 'A's, who were to be challenged and given large rewards; 'B's, who were to be encouraged and affirmed, and 'C's, who were told to shape up or ship out. The process was known as 'rank and yank'. The company's propensity to disproportionately reward those who were high achievers and risk-takers was widely acclaimed by business gurus.[39] Faculty from the prestigious Harvard Business School produced 11 case studies, uniformly praising its successes. However, problems multiplied. People chased high rankings because the potential rewards were enormous, while low rankings imperilled both their salaries and eventually their jobs. The appearance of success mattered more than its substance. In addition, internal promotions due to the appraisal system reached 20 per cent a year. This made further evaluation more difficult, and inevitably more subjective – how could you honestly rank someone's performance when they did not hold a position long enough to render sound judgement possible? Paradoxically, Enron had a punitive internal regime ('rank and yank') but loose control (those adjudged to be top performers moved on too fast to be pinned down). In this case, ratings and performance pay formed a lethal mix. Internal staff churn, and a relentless emphasis on achieving high performance ratings in the interests of obtaining ever-greater personal rewards, contributed to the lax ethical atmosphere that precipitated the company's downfall (see also Chapter 15).

Versions of rank and yank have been used by many organisations, including General Electric and IBM. IBM, in the early 1990s, actually required that one out of every 10 employees be allocated a poor rating, and given three months to improve or be fired.[40] The research evidence overwhelmingly suggests that such practices produce only defiance, defensiveness and rage.[41] As one writer has noted, 'Threatening people can make them anxious about the consequences of doing poorly, but the fear of failure is completely different from the desire to succeed'.[42] Praise can be used to emphasise that a culture of retribution belongs to the past, and is therefore much more likely to have a positive impact on performance.[43] It is, however, important that praise is not over-done. If it is, people may begin to perform tasks for the praise involved, and so find that their intrinsic motivation goes down. Its main value, it appears to us, is a signal that authoritarian management holds no sway in the organisation concerned. The main enemy of innovation, effort and achievement in the workplace is fear. In short, there is absolutely no evidence that either threatening to cut people's pay, or offering to significantly increase it, improves the quality as opposed to possibly the quantity of what they do.

However, illusions still linger, and some organisations now seek sustenance in technology. It has been argued that new software systems enable companies to monitor individual productivity more accurately (and less subjectively), and so target rewards on genuine top perform-ers.[44] Among the companies taking this route are Hewlett-Packard, General Electric and DuPont. Moreover, it has been suggested that peo-ple experience less evaluation apprehension and less emotion when they receive feedback via a computer system. Such systems can also focus the attention of raters on job-relevant behaviours, thereby reducing inter-personal biases.[45] However, it has also been found that self-ratings are more inflated and less accurate in electronic communication compared to face-to-face interaction.[46] Greater objectivity could be at the expense of sensitivity, since it removes the direct opportunity to monitor the reaction of recipients.[47] Thus, appraisal remains primarily a human issue. People's feelings about it are unlikely to change at the sight of managers brandishing spreadsheets. Technology has yet to overcome the problems associated with rating systems and the linking of performance to pay.

In short, the research on appraisal suggests two hard won lessons:

- Do not use rating systems for the evaluation of performance.
- Do not link appraisal interviews to performance related pay.

Both of these are landmines, primed to disable the whole feedback process. If they are disarmed the territory to be covered is immediately made safer. What steps can then be said to characterise the conduct of effective appraisal schemes?

The types of feedback interview

It has been suggested that there are four main types of performance appraisal interview: *tell and sell, tell and listen, problem solving* and *mixed-model interviews*.[48] Each has a different set of aims:

Tell and sell interviews

Here, the supervisor or appraiser is in complete control. They do most of the talking. It is assumed that the evaluation on offer is fair. The objective is to communicate this cogently to the employee, gain their acceptance of the evaluation and secure their compliance with the manager's plan for improvement. It is a model widely used in the military. However, the one-way nature of the dialogue can create defensiveness, hostility and anger, alongside permanently ruptured relationships. For most people, most of the time, it is an inappropriate model – however widely it is used.

Tell and listen interviews

Here, the appraiser communicates his or her evaluation of the employee's strengths and weaknesses. Possible points of disagreement are deferred until later in the interview. As the interview progresses, more time is devoted to the employee's feelings and views about the evaluation they have received. The main difference from tell and sell interviews is that although they both start as one-way communications, eventually the manager assumes the role of a non-directive counsellor. The clear gain from this approach is an increased emphasis on active listening.

Problem solving interviews

The aim here is to use exploratory questions and the skills of active listening to help employees identify their own strengths and weaknesses, and devise appropriate action plans for improvement. It is consistent with perspectives that see the management role as one of coaching. Evaluation is discouraged, since the manager's evaluation supplants the employee's own analysis of what is required. In theory, this precludes such age-old problems as employee defensiveness, since issues raised will be exclusively those identified by the employee. We suspect that this advantage is more theoretical than real. Questions, by their very nature, also set agendas and constrain an interviewee's response options. This is especially the case for what are known as *closed questions* and *leading questions*,[49] both of which are often used by unskilled interviewers.

Mixed-model interviews

Clearly, problem solving is a vital part of an effective appraisal process, as is an open two-way exchange between those being appraised and their appraiser. This requires the in-depth exploration of job performance and personal issues. Mixed-model interviews combine the above approaches, to achieve the objectives of open and honest two-way communication across a range of issues. The process summarised in Box 14.2, consistent with this approach, can also serve as an overall template for the entire interview process.

Box 14.2 The mixed-model interview

Schedule the interview:
Notify all parties well in advance of when and where the interview will be held. Ensure that there will be no external interruptions.

Agree on content:
Agree the nature of the interview and what will be discussed – for example, what aspects of performance will be addressed. This facilitates mutual preparation.

Agree on process:
This should include discussion of ground rules for communication. It should also include agreement on sequencing – for example, first

Box 14.2 ***continued***

we will discuss last year's agreed action points, then what worked well in this regard, then where the organisation helped or hindered the work effort, what will be agreed for next year.

Agree location and space:
Some sources advise that the best location for a feedback interview is either a neutral space, or the employee's work venue. In any event, the manager's office is more likely to activate anxiety and inadvertently communicate unhelpful status differentials that inhibit open discussion.

Open the interview/start the discussion:
This should involve open questions (e.g. 'How do you feel your job is going?' 'How do you see your performance?'). The primary purpose is to give the employee maximum initiative in agenda setting. In particular, it is helpful if the employee is given the opportunity to raise potential problems before the manager.

Exchange feedback:
Focus on specific behaviours that can be changed (i.e. what was said and done; what can be changed). Avoid personality judgements. (e.g. 'You are lazy.') Model openness to positive and critical feedback. Use both advocacy (i.e. the clear statement of your own position, based on *evidence*) and inquiry (i.e. the use of active listening and questions to explore the views of the other party).

Develop a plan for improvement:
Again, let the person being appraised take the lead. Suggestions offered in terms of how to improve another person's action plan are more likely to be favourably received. Be more directive if the other person shows an inability or reluctance to come up with any ideas. (We have worked in more than one organisation, in which particularly recalcitrant employees have responded to the question: 'Is there any one behaviour you can change that would improve your performance?' by baldly asserting: 'I can't think of a single thing!')

Close the discussion:
Summarise what has been agreed; envisage a future, of whatever kind that is appropriate, for the employee. Provide some sense of direction.

Managing the feedback interview

All good interviews start before the interview begins: success is 90 per cent preparation. Effective preparation means:

Eliminating the mystery As discussed above, informal feedback should be a routine part of relationships between managers and employees, all year round. The final interview then becomes nothing more than the formal climax to an ongoing informal process. It will be helpful for employees to receive a feedback preparation form, well in advance of the scheduled meeting. Box 14.3 contains a sample of what this could look like, derived from a variety of such forms commonly in use. This is not intended to be either prescriptive or exhaustive. It can, however,

Box 14.3 Feedback preparation form

1. What aspects of your job give you the greatest satisfaction?

____

____

2. Are there additional skills you have developed in any other job or organisation that you feel you aren't getting to apply here?

____

____

3. What have been your most important objectives over the past 12 months?

____

____

4. In which objectives have you done well? Why?

____

____

5. Which objectives have been the most difficult? Why?

____

____

6. What could the organisation do to help you achieve your objectives more effectively?

____

____

Box 14.3 *continued*

7. What sort of problems make it more difficult for you to perform your work (deadlines, type of manager, bureaucratic obstacles, team work etc.)

____

____

8. What are your key job skills and areas of strength?

____

____

9. What skills or knowledge do you feel you lack? What extra training would be of help?

____

____

10. How if at all has your job changed significantly over the past 12 months?

____

____

11. What are your key job priorities over the next 12 months?

____

____

12. Is there any further information we need to discuss to help you make a realistic action plan for the coming year?

____

____

be used as a template, which organisations should amend so that the documentation used meets their own unique needs. A key guideline is that all such forms should be as simple as possible. The problem with many forms is that they '... are so complicated, with so many ridiculous categories, that managers get totally stressed out trying to decide which box to check off. The employee often reads the review in anger and disgust, totally disagreeing with at least some of the review.'[50] It is helpful to involve as many people as possible in the design of the form, on the assumption that this will promote ownership of the process and hence greater enthusiasm. The manager should receive the completed form in advance of the feedback interview, so guarding against unpleasant and unnecessary surprises.

Steps towards preparation Appraisal/feedback is all about recognising job achievement, identifying areas for further improvement, and agreeing action to improve job effectiveness.[51] More broadly, it is also an opportunity to improve staff–management relationships, standards of communication and organisational climate. A feedback preparation form contributes to this, by setting a supportive tone. However, it is imperative that everyone approaches the actual interview in a similar spirit.

Consider the following dialogue. What do you think the intentions are of those involved? What would be the likely outcome of an interview approached in this spirit?

Ms Jones: *'Well, I'm seeing Ted tomorrow.'*
Production Director: *'How do you think it will go?'*
Ms. Jones: *'Just great. I've been collecting evidence all week. He won't know what's hit him. The figures are really appalling. Did you know that production was down 5% last week alone? He doesn't have a leg to stand on.'*

The guiding motivation here is the desire for revenge. In the short term, it might well make the manager feel better, but it is unlikely to improve performance. You cannot come in peace, while brandishing a gun and screaming threats. It is also certain that such hostile attitudes will be reciprocated on the shop floor. As Indira Gandhi once remarked: 'You cannot shake hands with a clenched fist.'[52] Thus, we could imagine that those ranged on the other side might gird themselves for a feedback interview as follows:

Worker 1: *'Well, Ted, I hearing you're seeing the Production Director tomorrow. Are you all ready?'*
Ted: *'I can't wait. When he hears about the state that new machine he bought is in he won't know what to do. I told him it was a daft idea. It lost us more production last week. He won't have a leg to stand on.'*

On the other hand, the gains derived from having a constructive feedback preparation form can be consolidated if managers approach the interview in the following spirit:[53]

Prepare mentally Here, you need to consider how you feel about the person you are meeting, what you think of their work and how you normally communicate with them. You also need to reflect on the balance you usually strike between positive and negative feedback, particularly where this person is concerned. Of course, this requires some ability to identify and to set aside your own prejudices and biases.

Understand the job The world expert on any particular job is the person doing it. They live with it, day in and day out. In particular, job descriptions are often a poor guide as to what a job consists of. Each job has a core area, consisting of activities which the organisation insists must be carried out. Beyond that, many of us have considerable latitude as to what we do and in which direction we can develop our work. It is not unusual for jobs to change radically over time, as a person stamps their own authority and personality on what they do. You must therefore consider the purpose of the job and its key result areas, both as originally defined and as they might now be. How clear are these to everyone? Is there a possibility that you might think Janet's key area of responsibility is still developing the new computer system, while she now feels that it is running so well she can move on to a new marketing strategy? *How much do you really know?* Of course, if informal and ongoing feedback is working well the scope for misunderstanding is reduced. In any event, both sides should be clear about such issues before a formal interview commences. It is also critical, at this stage, to consider what is often described as extrarole behaviour. In today's business environment it may be necessary for people to demonstrate behaviours consistent with such notions as flexibility, a willingness to take charge and a tolerance for uncertainty, beyond what describes their immediate tasks in a job description.[54] Managers thus need to consider issues associated with the construct of organisational citizenship, and integrate them into the feedback process.

Highlight training and development needs An attempt should be made to anticipate the training and development needs of the individual concerned. Obviously, these must be linked to the business goals of the organisation. A desire to learn fluent Mandarin Chinese or come first in a Morris Dancing competition might well boost individual self-esteem, but prove irrelevant to the development of a marketing strategy for Latin America. Nevertheless, the more that both sides can anticipate here, and the more the manager may be primed to offer in advance, the smoother the feedback interview will proceed. As with the rest of the process, the main objective is to eliminate unpleasant surprises.

Consider the discussion Finally, the manager needs to consider the basic logistics of the discussion. An appraisal/feedback interview, like all interviews between managers and staff, requires a set time, a designated venue, a hassle free atmosphere and creature comforts (such as warmth, suitable chairs, coffee and biscuits). There should be no distractions, such as ringing telephones or secretaries bustling in with 'important' messages. Attending to these elementary needs communicates interest, concern and respect. Ignoring them sets the stage for disappointment, rage and conflict.

Handling the interview

The opening of an interview is its most vital point, and determines the prospects for success or failure. This is because the opening triggers further expectancy effects – we tend to assume that how people behave when we first meet them will be typical of how they behave the rest of the time.[55] This forms an expectation which may be positive or negative. Such an expectation then governs our own behaviour, and creates self-fulfilling prophecies which often determine the outcome of the interaction. Our first concern at the beginning of an interview (especially if we approach it in an anxious frame of mind) is to reduce feelings of uncertainty. This predisposes us all the more to pay attention to the other person's opening behaviours, and use them as a framework within which to organise our perceptions of what is happening. The following approaches will therefore be particularly appropriate at the beginning of a feedback interview:[56]

- Arrange for relaxed, informal seating. Avoid sitting behind a desk, imposing a physical barrier between yourself and the interviewee.
- People bring social needs into the interview context with them. A short period of informal chat is appropriate, possibly combined with tea or coffee. If this period becomes too extended the interview loses focus: it should not become an extended gossip. However, some small talk reinforces the informal and human connection which underlies the staff–manager relationship.
- Review what both of you already know and have agreed about the process – for example, the amount of time available, the forms that the interviewee will have filled in and returned to you, the key issues that you want to address. Make positive statements such as 'This is a very important discussion for me. I've been looking forward to hearing how well your last project is doing.' Describe the interview,

stress its positive purpose, explain how you intend to conduct it, and invite comments from the interviewee. In this way you are shaping and agreeing an agenda for action.

Beyond this, the rest of the interview time is spent reviewing the issues covered in the feedback preparation form. The key here is to ask lots of open questions, thereby allowing the interviewee the maximum amount of space and opportunity to raises issues which concern them. Some of the most typical questions asked in such interviews are included in Box 14.4.

The emphasis throughout should be on supportive, two-way communication, and the interview should be regarded as an opportunity not only to give feedback but also receive it. Box 14.5 identifies some communication approaches which will achieve this end.

Box 14.4 Some of the most typical questions asked in feedback interviews

1. What was the most interesting task you had to do this year?
2. What was the most successful thing that you accomplished in the past year?
3. How do you feel you handled X in retrospect?
4. What areas of your work would you say require most attention?
5. What extra help do you need to improve in these areas?
6. What do you think you need to learn now to develop the job further?
7. How have you found dealing with X has worked out?
8. How do you see your future in this company?
9. What do you think was your greatest success?
10. What was most disappointing for you?
11. What are your priorities for the next 12 months?
12. What have you most enjoyed working on recently?
13. Where did you have the most fun?
14. What was most difficult project you've worked on since our last meeting?
15. What have you most disliked in the last year about working here?
16. Where do you think you could most improve in your work?
17. What could I improve as your manager that would make things better?

Box 14.5 Developing supportive communication

- Listen more than talk.
- Seek the interviewee's views rather than impose your own.
- Give information, but keep it limited and do so only as necessary.
- Seek the other person's views, feelings, proposals, suggestions and opinions.
- Test understanding, by frequently summarising what has been said or agreed. Pause and repeat, if some issue is causing difficulty.
- Propose rather than impose. Action plans that are not mutually agreed create resentment. Plans genuinely agreed through open discussion are more likely to be internalised, owned and acted upon.
- Encourage as much self-assessment by the interviewee as possible.

Agreeing objectives

A central part of the interview will be the agreeing of objectives for the forthcoming year. There are two key points to be made about this. First, too many objectives creates disorientation. At the decisive moment, an army needs one battle plan rather than the choice of twenty. Therefore, a small number of agreed objectives which should be restricted to the most important business requirements of the organisation is sufficient. Second, these objectives should be as specific as possible. Box 14.6 explores how one well known acronym (SMART) can be adopted in this context to achieve this end.

Reflective exercise 14.1 contains a list of objectives, and it is worth while going through it to ascertain how many of them fit the 'SMART' description in Box 14.6. How could each of them be improved, so that they meet all of the criteria suggested here?

Offering critical feedback, and giving instructions

As stated above, the overwhelming focus of the interview should be on positive feedback and agreeing action for the future. However, in some cases serious problems will exist which must be addressed. How this is done is crucial. If dealt with well, the underlying relationship

Box 14.6 Agreeing specific objectives

S*pecific*: Can the objective be visualised? What will success look like? Will everyone recognise dry land when they get there?

M*easurable*: Suggesting that 'new product launches will improve' is not the same as saying 'we will have 10 new products launched in Japan by Christmas.' The figure 10 makes the objective measurable – we will either be there, or we won't.

A*greed*: All parties crucial to the objective's success should be openly committed to it, and convinced that it is achievable. Imposed objectives inspire dejection rather than achievement.

R*ealistic*: It must be genuinely within the person's and organisation's capacity to achieve the goals concerned. *Good generals never give an order that cannot be obeyed.* Targets set and missed suggest failure, and undermine the credibility of future business plans.

T*imebounded*: The objectives should have a time frame attached. Otherwise, they always find their way to the bottom of everyone's 'to do' lists.

Reflective exercise 14.1 Setting objectives

Study each of the following objectives carefully. How many of them do you think fit the 'SMART' criteria outlined in Box 14.6?

Now, take each objective that you think does not meet the criteria we have suggested, and adapt it so that it does. Ensure that each of the criteria is met as fully as possible. How much more likely is it that the new objectives you have developed at the end of this exercise could be implemented and evaluated in your organisation? (We identify those objectives that meet the criteria at the end of this chapter).

1. Absenteeism in the human resources department will be reduced.

Reflective exercise 14.1 ***continued***

2. Sales will improve over a 10-year period by a significant percentage.
3. Morale will improve.
4. Inventory will be reduced by 30 per cent by the end of the current financial year.
5. Budget savings will be made on consumables.
6. We will eliminate waste, cut costs and improve profits by 300 per cent within six weeks of this action plan being agreed by the senior management team.
7. Staff resistance to the reorganisation plan will be overcome and the new structure will be in place by the new financial year.

can actually be improved, and the person concerned will emerge with a much clearer picture of what needs to be changed. Mishandled, the manager's feedback becomes the issue, rather than the job performance of the employee. In general, critical feedback should be accompanied with precise instructions designed to solve the underlying problem. The following guidelines should help:[57]

Give employees plenty of opportunity to raise issues themselves Most people are well aware of problem areas in their performance, although they may be slow to appreciate their full significance. If managers are always the first to raise such problems they undermine self-confidence and are viewed as aggressive: the messenger is contaminated by the bad news delivered. Few undertakers enjoy a parallel career on the comedy circuit. However, if employees get the chance to raise problems first managers will be viewed as coaches engaged in joint problem solving, rather than unpopular oracles of doom. Ask questions such as:

- 'Are there any difficulties in your job that you wish to discuss?'
- 'Where do you need most help to improve in the year ahead?'
- 'Is there anything that has proved more difficult than you expected in the last year?'
- 'We certainly had some successes with that project, but is there any way that we could have done even better?'

When your feedback is critical, let the person know what is wrong in clear and unambiguous language Having done this, explain why you think the issue is a problem. This is particularly important if the employee has shown little sign of anticipating the criticism made. You should then summarise and repeat back to the person the response to the criticism, so that it is clear their response is being heard. However, you should also reassert the underlying point that is being made.

Focus your criticism on specific behaviours which can be changed, rather than on personality traits which are more resistant to change People perceive negative judgements of their personality as an attack.[58] However, they are likely to see comments on specific behaviours as constructive feedback which they can use to make things better. The key here is to assess feedback in terms of the 'DVD' test. Can the person actually 'see' in their mind's eye the behaviour that you are describing? The statement 'You are always aggressive' is a judgement on the recipient's personality. It is also hard to 'see'. What exactly does this aggression look like, and what can be done to change it? On the other hand, you could say: 'At yesterday's meeting you walked out and slammed the door behind you, and that was the second time this week.' Such behaviour can certainly be visualised, and immediate steps taken to avoid its recurrence.

Couple criticism with guidelines to solve the problem Criticism by itself changes nothing. People need to know what you now expect them to do, and believe that what you are suggesting is fair, viable and possible to implement. The SMART acronym, discussed above in relation to setting objectives, applies fully in this context as well. Offer guidelines which can be achieved (rather than which are desirable, but impossible), which are within the employee's range of competence, which relate to specific behaviours and which both parties are committed to reviewing within a specified time frame.

Handling critical feedback

Inevitably, in at least some feedback interviews, the manager will also receive criticism. This will often be emotional, wrong-headed, highly personalised and aggressive. It will also sometimes be constructive, specific, well intentioned and accurate. It is vital that managers themselves model effective approaches to handling criticism. Otherwise, it will be even harder for them to offer it to others.

Fundamentally, the normal rules of supportive communication, as discussed in Chapter 5, still apply in this context. Critical feedback should be listened to and examined honestly to see whether there is any substance to it. The Four R method[59] is one useful means of using criticism to strengthen the relationship, and ensure that the channels of communication remain open in the future. This proposes that we should:

1. **R***eceive* the other person's comments without interruption, denying the validity of the criticism, launching immediate counter-attacks or engaging in other defensive behaviours. This shows an openness to discussion, and an interest in what the other has to say.
2. **R***epeat* what has been said as objectively as possible. This is a core means of building empathy, and shows that what has been said has been understood.
3. **R***equest* the other person's ideas about how the difficulty should be dealt with. This helps escape a spiral of defend/attack, and moves the critic into the constructive position of helping to identify solutions. It also ensures that the discussion deals with specifics rather than generalities.
4. **R***eview* at the end the different options available and agree the best way forward.

Closing the interview

Research suggests that we are inclined to remember very well the beginning of an interaction and its end – but lose most of what occurs in the middle. This has been termed the primacy/recency effect (see Chapter 8). Therefore, it is imperative that the key points that have been agreed are summarised at the end. It is useful to pause after each point made until the other party involved signifies their agreement.

As discussed in Chapter 3, it has also been shown that when people make a public commitment to a particular course of action it is more likely that their attitudes will shift to agree that it is indeed appropriate.[60] In turn, this prepares the way for future actions in line with the agreement reached. Therefore, one option here is for both parties to formally 'sign off' on any documentation used during the interview. This is an important symbolic gesture and a very useful point of departure for what is ultimately at stake – the securing of significant improvements in work performance, in the ability of the organisation to achieve its goals and in the relationships between managers and staff.

360-degree appraisal – a new way forward?

We noted, at the beginning of this chapter, that the popularity of 360-degree appraisals has grown enormously in recent years. Nearly all the Fortune 500 companies in the USA now utilise it, while a growth trend has also been observed in the UK.[61] 360-degree appraisal, or multisource feedback, involves people evaluating themselves, and then receiving feedback from an immediate supervisor, peers and (if the person is a manager) direct reports. This differs from traditional upward appraisals, where feedback is only solicited from subordinates.[62] Some concern has been expressed about its burgeoning popularity. For example, one investigation found that 360-degree appraisal was associated with a 10.6 per cent decrease in shareholder value.[63] Evidently, many such programmes have arisen as a straightforward imitation of what competitors are doing, and have been hurriedly implemented without sufficient attention to such 'minor' details as how feedback should be managed and delivered, and how the process should support bottom line organisational goals. For example, one survey discovered that over half the companies that introduced 360-degree appraisal quickly abandoned it, in the face of inflated ratings and hostility from employees.[64] Merely doing something because everyone else does it is a forlorn quest to find inspiration amidst a surfeit of mediocrity.

It is critical to remember that performance appraisal, upward appraisal and multisource feedback all share one common characteristic – a person is receiving feedback from others about her or his performance. Therefore, the problems with biases and reactions to feedback that we have discussed earlier in this chapter will also apply to 360-degree feedback. Negative feedback, or feedback which departs widely from the person's own perception of their performance, is unlikely to stimulate positive change.[65] These are formidable problems – but they can be managed.

There are many suggestions as to how this can be done. In Box 14.7 we summarise some of the best practice guidelines derived from the relevant research.[66]

Box 14.7 Guidelines for effective 360-degree appraisal

- *Keep the process simple*. As with traditional appraisals, the more complex the paper work and the more overwhelming the feedback, the less likelihood there is of sustained behaviour change.
- *Develop your own instrument*. Many 360 instruments are available. However, it is best to design one customised for your own organisation, and that meets its own unique needs. Involve people in this effort, and so generate their participation, understanding and support.
- *Provide written feedback*. Research suggests that, when multisource feedback is at stake and thus many people have contributed to the evaluation, most people prefer to receive their feedback in writing.
- *In addition to written feedback, train people to act as coaches*. Most people need someone with whom they can discuss the results they have obtained. People formally allocated this role can function as coaches. They should be trained in active listening, focused interviewing, dealing with feelings and goal setting.
- *Ensure that those doing the appraising are afforded anonymity*. People are more likely to offer honest opinions if their identity is protected. This depersonalises the nature of the feedback, and helps focus attention on the behaviour changes that are required.
- *Select peer appraisers on the basis of objective criteria*. If the person being appraised is charged with this responsibility they are more likely to select people who will give them inflated praise rather than suggest how they can do better.
- *Train appraisers*. This should focus on the objectives of the process, the errors associated with it (such as the halo error) and contain scope for questions and discussion regarding the whole process.
- *Train appraisees*. People need training in how to analyse the data, set improvement targets, deal with feelings associated with receiving negative feedback, how to discuss summary action plans with appraisers and in setting specific goals and action plans. *Research clearly suggests that merely receiving feedback does not improve performance* – rather, it is how this feedback is managed and internalised that determine eventual outcomes.

Box 14.7 *continued*

- *Train people in self-awareness.* When people over-rate their own performance relative to the perceptions of others, they are more likely to dismiss corrective feedback. A more balanced approach to self-assessment is necessary. Some research has found that even warning people of the danger of over-rating their own performance significantly diminishes the problem.

Overview

Appraisal is now widely used in business, and is rapidly growing to embrace both upward appraisal and 360-degree appraisal. It is therefore imperative that managers hone their skills in giving and receiving feedback. The lack of such feedback, in both directions, is a recipe for communication breakdown and organisational dysfunction. Accordingly, we have argued that, where possible, the term 'appraisal' should be dropped in favour of 'feedback'. This is much less threatening.

The benefits of such two-way feedback are increasingly confirmed in the literature. For example, Ricardo Semler reported the following innovations in his organisation, Semco, based in Brazil:[67]

- Factory workers set their own production quotas;
- Employees set their own salaries, with no strings attached;
- Before people are hired or promoted into management positions they are interviewed and approved by those they will be managing;
- Managers are reviewed on their performance every six months, by those who work under them;
- Semco has grown six-fold, despite buffeting recessions;
- Productivity has increased seven-fold;
- Profits have risen five-fold.

Feedback interviews are an integral part of innovative new management styles (such as those adopted by Semco), and more traditional management approaches. In whatever context they occur, they should only be the formal conclusion of an informal and ongoing process. It is vital that they be conducted in as supportive a manner as possible. Their main emphasis should be on successful behaviours, which can be praised publicly and thus are perceived as having been rewarded. Where negative issues are concerned, it is important that feedback is on specific behaviours which can be changed, is constructive, is linked to important business goals, is highly specific and is conducted in private.

With these approaches in mind feedback becomes a tool for improving relationships, strengthening organisational cohesion and achieving business success. Everyone's efforts will be geared towards common goals, and a perilous journey in the face of death defying obstacles will have reached a safe conclusion.

Answer to reflective exercise 14.1

NONE of the objectives listed meets ALL of the criteria identified in the SMART acronym. For example:

1. This contains no *timescale* as to when the objective will be met.
2. This does not *specify* the percentage improvement that will be attained within 10 years.
3. How will we *measure* the improvements in morale, when will we do it and who has *agreed* to implement this plan?
4. This looks good, but by not mentioning who will be responsible for reducing inventory it conveys the impression that the objective has not really been *agreed* with anybody, and therefore will probably become *unrealistic*.
5. *How*, by *whom*, and *when* will budget savings be made on consumables?
6. It is highly questionable whether the objective of improving profits by 300 per cent within 6 weeks could be a *realistic* objective for any organisation!
7. This last objective suggests that managers see themselves on a collision course with staff, and that therefore the objective has not been *agreed* by anyone, least of all those capable of implementing it.

15 Following the correct path: the guiding lights of ethics and audits

Introduction

The focus of this book has been upon communication in organisations, and, in particular, the pivotal role played by managers in maintaining an effective communicative flow within the workplace. In the previous chapters we provided a comprehensive analysis of a wide range of managerial skills and strategies. Following a general introduction in chapter one, each of the following chapters examined a separate dimension of managerial communication, as follows.

- Communicating nonverbally
- Persuading
- Team-building
- Leading motivated teams
- Making presentations
- Negotiating
- Selling
- Using the telephone in business
- Writing skills
- Asserting oneself
- Helping
- Selecting staff
- Appraising and giving feedback.

The manager who has mastered these dimensions of communication will undoubtedly be more effective across a wide range of one-to-one and group situations. The implementation of these skills on a day-to-day basis helps the organisation to achieve its main goals.

In this final chapter we examine two important approaches to 'doing the right thing'. Given that communication is not a neutral, value-free process, we will first discuss core ethical issues that should guide

Box 15.1 Case study 1 – Enron

Energy giant Enron became a household name in 2002 when it crashed spectacularly, from a high-flying energy giant to filing for bankruptcy, with the loss of 4500 jobs. They had operated what they termed a 'rank and yank' employee policy for years,[2] where under-performers (who were termed 'shipwrecks') were dismissed ('yanked') with the minimum statutory payoff. It was the norm in many Departments that one in seven staff would be sacked every year. Former CIA and FBI agents were employed to snoop on staff, checking e-mails and monitoring phone calls. On the other hand, high flyers were rewarded with annual bonuses of hundreds of thousands of dollars. Company concierges looked after mundane matters for these executives, from taking care of their dry cleaning to arranging their holidays. Free massages were available in the corporate health centre six days a week from 7.00 a.m. until 10.00 p.m. For party conferences no expense was spared with props such as elephants and Harley-Davison motorbikes being hired to spice up the event.

On one occasion a party of Wall Street analysts visited to find out about a new venture called Enron Energy Services. The company had misled them about the progress of this operation, so in a scene reminiscent of one from the famous movie *The Sting*, they constructed a fake trading room on the sixth floor of the Houston headquarters at a cost of $500 000. Banks of big-screen televisions and state-of-the-art computers were provided. To complete the scam, the company had a full dress rehearsal, which lasted for an entire day, before the visit. When the analysts arrived the dummy 'energy traders' were busily rapping keyboards and yelling into telephones. Visits such as these usually ended with a trip to a lap-dancing club, after which the analysts would return to New York and push the stock price even higher. All of this was fuelled by accounting scams to disguise the true trading figures. Enron senior executives were give stock options, which they rapidly sold. For example in 2001, just before the crash, the company founder Ken Lay alone made more than $16 million from selling his shares. In the four-year period before bankruptcy senior executives sold a total of $600 million worth of stock. As one former employee put it: 'Enron went belly up because of some crooked people.'

managerial behaviour. Second, since knowledge of the results of communication initiatives is central to success, we will illustrate how and in what ways managers should measure and monitor the effectiveness of, and develop a strategy for, organisational communication.

Communication ethics

We spend a large part of our lives in organisations. They, therefore, influence us in all types of ways. One important part of this is how they affect our ethical views and moral code. As expressed by Brandon,[1] a business has: 'a profound impact on souls. No one can remain unaffected by how he or she is treated eight hours a day, five days a week – nor by the ethical behavior witnessed in associates and superiors.' For example, in unethical organisations we may become personally corrupted by collusion in devious dealings (by 'cheating and maltreating' others) or react to the bad practices with rectitude by exposing them to wider society (by 'naming and shaming' the offenders). It is therefore important to examine the role of ethics in organisational communication. In recent years the image of many corporations has plummeted in the eyes of the general public. Scandal after scandal has hit the headlines. We give two examples in Box 15.1 and Box 15.2.

But these two case examples are far from exceptional. It has been well documented[6,7] how many other companies were also up to their necks in dubious dealings. In April 2002, another well-known corporation, Xerox, was charged by the US financial regulator, the Securities Exchange Commission (SEC), with overstating profits over a four-year period to the tune of $3 billion. Xerox agreed to pay a $10 million fine (the largest ever imposed by the SEC) and restate the trading statements for the four-year period, while neither accepting nor denying wrongdoing. One of the pioneers of the telecommunications industry, WorldCom, was another conglomerate contaminated by the odour of corruption. In 2002 it laid off 17 000 staff after admitting that it had inflated its profits by a staggering $3.8 billion between January 2001 and March 2002. In a scenario redolent of *Alice in Wonderland*, it emerged that the founder and former Chief Executive, Bernie Ebbers, had borrowed hundreds of millions of dollars from the company in order to boost stock price by then paying inflated prices for the corporation's own shares. The SEC declared WorldCom's accounting malpractices to be of 'unprecedented magnitude'. Linked to the activities

Box 15.2 Case study 2 – Tyco

Dennis Kozlowski was paid millions of dollars to run Tyco as Chief Executive. As part of his salary entitlement he regularly received shares in the company – which he then sold as soon as possible. But this was not enough for him. He believed that shareholders should pay for his little luxuries as well. Among the items he bought on company expenses were a $15 000 dog umbrella stand, a $6 000 gilded shower curtain, and coathangers costing $2 900. For the fortieth birthday of his wife, Karen, he held a jamboree on the island of Sardinia. Guests were greeted by gladiators with lions and taken to an ice statue of Michelangelo's David. Vodka flowed from the ice sculpture's penis into crystal glasses and this was served to guests by waiters in togas. The statue was surrounded by caviar. The cost of this junket was a staggering $2 million, for which Tyco claims it unwittingly picked up half of the bill.[3] Likewise he was never short of a bed for the night. He had a £13.5 million estate in Florida, a $5 million home in Massachusetts, an $18 million apartment (paid for by Tyco) on Fifth Avenue, New York (furnished at a cost of $11 million) and an $875 000 house in New Hampshire. If he felt like sleeping on water, he owned a yacht bought for $16 million in 2000, which cost $700 000 per annum to run.

Investigations revealed that Kozlowski owed Tyco $52.7 million in loans, some $25 million of which may have been 'forgiven'. He was also charged with avoiding $1 million in New York state sales taxes on purchases of artwork worth £13 million, some of which was actually paid for by Tyco. He donated millions of Tyco dollars to schools and colleges – often in his own name. Ironically, one of these was a donation of $2 million to Cambridge University to fund a chair in boardroom ethics.[4] He was a very devout Catholic, who in 2002 told students in a speech at St Anselm Catholic College in New Hampshire: 'You will be confronted with questions every day that test your morals. Think carefully, and for your sake do the right thing, not the easy thing.' Shortly after this, the truth about Tyco was revealed. Unfortunately, Kozlowski evidently did not follow his own advice and as one commentator in an article aptly entitled 'The Wages of Sin',[5] put it: 'when he wasn't praying to God, it seems he was preying on shareholders'. Interestingly, and by contrast, his predecessor at Tyco, John Fort, had been the antithesis of Kozlowski. He had driven a Pontiac car with no air conditioning and had grounded the company jets.

of some of these companies was the accounting firm Andersen, whose involvement in cooking the company books in some of these debacles (including both Enron and WorldCom) resulted in their own demise. When the Enron scandal broke, Andersen destroyed key documents and were convicted of obstruction of justice – a conviction that put it out business.

These are just a sample of the raft of business imbroglios that welcomed the dawn of the new millennium. We could give many other examples, but the point has been made. Some commentators have even argued that we should not be surprised by such dealings, as business ethics is inherently incompatible with corporate life[8,9]. This perspective holds that the underpinning raison d'être of any business is simply to make profits, and so anything goes – at least anything that is legal or businesspersons feel fairly sure they can get away with. It is therefore hardly surprising that the term 'business ethics' is often perceived to be an oxymoron.[10] Such a perspective on business morality is reinforced by an unending stream of highly publicised tales of company fraud, dark dealing, deceit and subterfuge. However, these practices are both dubious ethically and damaging financially. In her book on business ethics, Sternberg[11] illustrated how: 'most dramatic business failures ... have been the result of unethical conduct. In almost all cases "bad ethics is bad business": the short-term gains which may be won by unethical conduct seldom pay in the end.' Among the identified[12] consequences of unethical behaviour are a tarnished corporate reputation, the failure to sell what should be a desirable service or product, and inexplicably high staff turnover. This was graphically charted by Punch in his analysis[13] of numerous case studies of organisational misbehaviour that resulted in financial catastrophe for the companies involved. Indeed, Boyle[14] has shown how ethical business is good business in every sense, since some £3 billion is invested ethically in the UK alone. Furthermore, when a company wins an environmental award its share price is raised by an average of 0.82 per cent, whereas when it is faced with bribery or corruption allegations the share price drops by some 2.3 per cent. As noted by Beck[15] ethical misdemeanours can have far-reaching consequences since 'The audience for ethical action spans all levels affected by the organization.'

It is also important to note that it is not only managers who engage in unethical practices. Employees display a variety of these as well, ranging from malicious gossip to pilfering. In fact the latter issue of employee theft is a huge problem for businesses, with retailers losing around 2 per cent of their total sales volume as a result of insider theft.[16] In the UK it is estimated that small-scale pilfering (e.g. stationery theft) and minor expenses fraud (e.g. inflated travel claims) alone amounts to some £831 million annually.[17] In some cases this figure can rise to as high as a 10 per cent loss of takings and stock.[18] As a result, companies have to devote considerable efforts to attempt to minimise such losses by installing various forms of internal monitoring, ranging from rigorous systems of stock control and financial auditing to Closed-Circuit Television (CCTV) surveillance of employees.[19] Likewise, there is often a lax view to ethical matters among consumers. Mitchell and Chan,[20] in noting that consumer theft and fraud costs some £1.8 billion annually in the UK, carried out a major survey, using an age and gender quota sample of the UK population, in which they found that many people readily engage in ethically questionable practices. In Box 15.3 we have summarised those items from this research that 50 per cent or more of those surveyed admitted having

Box 15.3 Some unethical choices of UK consumers

	%
Recording a movie off the television and keeping it	90
Copying a CD instead of buying it	78
Receiving too much change and saying nothing	78
Lying about a child's age in order to get a reduced price	78
Returning a product after trying and not liking it	77
Taking the coins mistakenly left by others in a vending machine	76
Using work telephone to make private calls	75
Jumping a long queue	66
Not paying for travel fares (bus or train) if the conductor doesn't check	66
Lying about one's age to get a pint of beer	65
Spending time in a book shop reading a book and not buying it	59
Occupying seats in a bus that are meant for the disabled or elderly	54
Giving an unused car parking ticket to another user	52
Taking advantage of trial periods	50
Using computer software or games that you did not buy	50

(Source: Adapted from Mitchell and Chan, 2002)

carried out. There is clearly much scope for improving ethical behaviour from every side of business.

In fact, the majority of corporations have codes of ethics as a way of avoiding litigation and 'doing good business'.[21] To secure the SA 8000 social accountability certification standard, developed by the Council on Economic Priorities Accreditation Agency, the company must audit a range of areas including *inter alia*, discrimination, health and safety, working hours, child and forced labour, compensation and disciplinary practices. Yet, unethical ways of doing business persist.[22] So why is this pattern of malfeasance endemic in many organisations?

Why do unethical business practices occur?

There are a number of reasons for the existence of unethical approaches to business.

1. As mentioned earlier, the hard capitalist view is that businesses are simply about profit or loss. The rationale here is that of 'no profit no company'. The balance sheet then becomes the God to be worshipped above all others. Small profits are not enough as the primary goal becomes that of maximising returns. The problem is that this then determines all actions. 'Good business' is defined by such companies as that which achieves a measurable economic end product in terms of the bottom line, and concepts to do with moral rectitude have low persuasive power.[23]
2. Profit-driven managers in the commercial world equate ethics at best with what is legal, and at worst with what they can get away with. The only sin is in being found out. This view was colourfully epitomised by the lubricious Gordon Gekko character, as depicted by Michael Douglas in the film *Wall Street*, whose maxim was 'Greed is good'. It is believed that 'ethics is for wimps', and that having a conscience is all well and good, but at the end of the day business is business. Given this backdrop it is small wonder that a large majority of the American public regard business executives as having suspect ethical codes of practice.[24] This is not surprising, since many managers themselves view business as analogous to a game of poker, where a certain degree of bluff and deceit are acceptable.[25] They would do well to remember the advice of Confucius that: 'A gentleman takes as much trouble to discover what is right as the lesser men take to discover what pays.'

3. The above problem is compounded by the fact that we live in an era of short-termism. Just as a boxer is seen as only as good as the last fight, so a company is increasingly viewed as only as good as its last share price listing. Executive pay is directly related to stock value, and as assessment always drives effort, managers spend their time devising ways to maximise the share price so as to increase their own pay. In this moral haze, Company Boards appoint Chief Executives whom they think will maximise share-holder profits.[26] The CEO in turn promotes managers in a similar mould. Impossible targets are often set, and ways have to be found to meet them. Temptations then enter the fray, as corners begin to be cut and lines stepped over. Like a drug addict each 'fix' is only a small one in the eyes of the driven executive. The earlier example of chief executive Bernie Ebbers borrowing hundreds of millions from WorldCom to buy its own shares at the resulting inflated prices shows where this madness can lead. It is like the behaviour of a mad gambler, but with one important difference. Few executives play with their own money. It is the shareholders who stand to pick up the losses.
4. Organisations operate in a world where 'getting the job done' is understandably the main focus of day-to-day attention. Any consideration of 'other things' can be seen to get in the way of operational matters. Managers and employees do what they have to do to achieve task goals, and ethical issues can get lost in the daily round of corporate functionalism. To obtain a clear perspective people must stand back regularly from what they do and ask if it is being done 'right' – in every sense. This requires that ethical considerations have to be built in to the strategic planning cycle. Systems should be introduced to allow employees and managers to review the morality of their operations. As Seeger[27] has clearly illustrated most organisations do not have strategies to enable such discussions, and so they rarely happen. Some theorists[28] even argue that this is deliberate, as it allows companies to function in a context of moral ambivalence. Dubious practices may then be carried out because no one asks any questions. If bad chickens then come home to roost, managers can plausibly argue either that these are not their chickens, or that no one said it was their duty to look after them and so they are not responsible for their poor state of health. When silence is the guiding organisational code, ethical problems will fester unattended beneath the surface[29] until they become an open, visible and dysfunctional corporate sore.

5. Given the above situation, an effective ethical policy means that issues of responsibility and accountability have to be clearly demarcated.[30] At the Nuremberg trials after the Second World War, the Nazi leaders famously pleaded in defence of their actions that they were 'only following orders'. In other words, they were not responsible or accountable, as they had been told what to do by others. Likewise, in many organisations, responsibility is a post hoc construction when things go wrong. Blame becomes a very portable commodity that is quickly given to someone else. To circumvent such problems, clear lines of ethical accountability must be put in place.
6. One problem in all of this is that often managers are not trained in ethics, or at best receive only a cursory input on this topic.[31] The main reason for this is simply that 'Too many business schools don't take ethics training seriously.'[32] Consequently, managers do not feel equipped to monitor practices or lead discussions in this field. This contributes to a prevailing organisational silence on ethics. At best there is ambivalence, in that managers may recognise that they have to make moral compromises to optimise financial gain.[33] But the end is seen to justify the means.

Another difficulty in the study and practice of organisational communication is that ethics has been relegated to a subsidiary topic, with a host of other issues predominating.[34] As summarised by Taylor *et al.*, 'ethics suffers from neglect in organizational communication research and consulting'.[35] In a sense, academics have tended to follow the lead of industrialists. Concrete operational issues such as information flow, decision-making, leadership and the impact of technology, have predominated[36] at the expense of what can be seen as the abstract and indeed esoteric world of morality and ethics. The dangers of this state of affairs have been highlighted by several communication scholars.[37,38] Some business schools have also begun to address this hiatus with interesting schemes, such as having MBA students spend a day in prison as a salutary warning of where they may end up if they engage in corrupt practices. However, ethical education still remains the Cinderella of most business schools.

Personal ethical principles and practices

The other side of the coin is that there are many ethical companies employing upright managers. There is also an increasing public desire for scrupulous practices in companies, as evidenced by the growth in corporations which publicly proclaim their ethical commitments in written codes of practice,[39] and the linked expansion (and financial success) of ethical investment trusts which deal only with such firms. For an organisation to have high ethical standards, managers must both be moral people and moral managers.[40,41] As moral individuals they must have and display a strong personal ethical code. As moral managers they should communicate regularly about ethics, and have systems in place to hold all staff accountable to the company's values and standards. While one bad apple can spoil the organisational barrel, if this is a big apple at managerial level, the damage is likely to be very much greater. To prevent such a state of affairs, managers must:

- be people-centred, valuing the integrity of individuals and caring for their well-being rather than seeing them as expendable cogs in the corporate machine
- focus on the interests of multiple stakeholders including the wider community
- be aware of the importance of achieving profitable returns, but care as much about the *means* to success as well as the *ends*
- be good ethical role models, practising what they preach
- have an effective system whereby rewards for good behaviour and punishments for wrongdoing are fully and fairly implemented.

Knowledge of the interactive skills outlined in this book should be used to *good* effect. For example, it would be possible for a manager to use skills of selling, negotiating and persuading in a Machiavellian fashion to manipulate staff. This would be unethical, and in the long run counter-productive, since employees who have been manipulated against their true interests will bear a grudge. In general, once manipulated twice hostile. Managers therefore need to be guided by higher-order values. When the managerial rubber hits the organisational road, ethical treads need to be firmly embedded to keep leadership on the straight path. There are three broad values[42] that managers must possess, and clearly display to others, namely integrity, honesty and respect for people. More specifically, in communicating with internal and external stakeholders, the following core ethical principles and practices[43,44] should be used to guide behaviour.

Be honest

The basic principle here is that *you should not attempt to deceive others.* This is easier said than done. 'White lies' are ubiquitous. For example, *CV Check*, a CV verifying company reported that when it contacts candidates to inform them it has been employed by an organisation to verify the details in job applicants' CVs, some 20 per cent immediately withdraw their applications.[45] A similar finding was reported by the University of California at Berkeley's Haas Business School, which rejected 5 per cent of candidates it had initially accepted for admission into its MBA programme, when CV checks revealed inaccuracies in their resumes.[46] It seems that many people regard CVs as flexible entities when it comes to truth-telling. Likewise, in everyday conversations, when asked, we are more likely to say yes we really like that new hat, than no actually it is hideous; or that we are glad to see someone, when in truth we are so busy we wish we hadn't. Social rules dictate that we do not always say what we think, but say what is polite. In fact, studies[47] have shown that some form of deception occurs in 25 per cent of all conversations. There are sins of commission and sins of omission. As well as telling overt falsehoods, as the former UK Cabinet Secretary Sir Robert Armstrong famously put it, one can be 'economical with the truth' by omitting crucial facts. Other euphemisms include 'putting a different spin on it', 'creative accounting', 'accentuating the positive' and 'massaging the figures'. In relation to the latter, as Mark Twain famously noted, 'There are lies, damned lies and statistics.'

In the business world, where rival companies are working on similar projects, it is obviously not prudent to be always open with information and trade secrets when communicating with another company. Furthermore, within organisations, legal constraints may mean that certain information cannot be disclosed to staff before specified procedures have been gone through. As a rule, however, with one's own staff honesty is the best policy. Apart from the moral perspective here, it is prudent for managers to be truthful since research has shown[48] that employees have a high ability to detect deceptive messages from others within the same organisation. One survey[49] of 2600 UK employees, carried out in 2002, showed low levels of trust in managers, and 82 per cent of respondents felt that more honesty from their bosses would improve trust and morale. Where people cannot be given certain information, they should be told why. Indeed, it has been found that when managers explain the reasons and motives for their actions, rather than merely describing what was or would be done, they are regarded as more trustworthy by employees.[50] The *why* is just as important as the *what* of communication.

Care about the greater good

This may involve *whistleblowing*, which occurs when people release information in the interests of wider society, even though to do so may be detrimental to the company. An important question, therefore, is when *should an employee break written or unwritten codes of loyalty to the organisation* by going public about some aspect of its operation that may be dangerous or immoral? As a rule, this should only occur once internal attempts to remedy the problem have been rebuffed. In the Enron scandal mentioned earlier, an executive, Sherron Watkins, sent memos to senior management warning of the dangers of the company 'imploding' as a result of the accounting scandal in which it was involved.[51] When she began to question the $1 billion of debts hidden in off-balance partnership sheets, the reaction of the chief financial officer, Andrew Fastow, was to want to fire her and impound her computer. Watkins had initially tried to handle the matter in-house, and even devised a plan to save the company. Despite some criticism of her own role in the Enron affair,[52] in recognition of her ethical stance, Congressional investigators praised her as a corporate hero who had done her country a great service.

So how can managers circumvent and obviate the need for whistleblowing? An open-door policy and a culture where criticism is seen as positive are conducive to problems being accepted and resolved in-house. Contentious issues should be recognised, accepted and openly debated. The converse of whistleblowing is what is known as *swallowing the whistle* where the employee keeps silent about identified problems. This is often through fear of telling the truth, and again can be overcome through a conducive communication climate. The Public Interest Disclosure Act, which gives legal protection to employees who raise genuine concerns about crime, negligence, miscarriage of justice or dangers to health and safety or the environment, was introduced into the UK in 1999. However, three years later a survey of 281 companies by the *Work Foundation* found that only one in three firms in the private sector had a formal policy with regard to the provision of adequate internal channels for whistleblowers to use, rather than going external with the information. In the voluntary and public sectors three out of four organisations did have such channels in place.

Treat people justly

The principle of justice is concerned with affording others their just rights and dues. Again, however, it is not always easy to operationalise. For example, is it just that some individuals earn more than others? Is it right that downsizing means that some staff lose their jobs while others do not? Is it moral to have some workers on short-term contracts while others are in permanent positions? In theory we should value all humans equally, but the effort factor enters the equation, so that those who carry a managerial load or perform at a higher rate of output may be paid more than their colleagues.

However, there should be limits to pay discrepancies, and these have increasingly been overstepped. In 1982, chief executives in the USA on average earned 40 times more then their lowest paid employee, but by 2002 this figure had grown to 100 times more.[53] To take another statistic, in the 30 years between 1970 and 1999 the annual salary of the average employee in the USA rose by around 10 per cent (to some $35 864), whereas that of the top 100 CEOs increased by a staggering 2785 per cent (to about $37.5 million). For example, in 2001, Shell doubled the pay of chairman Phil Watts to £1.6 million, despite the fact that both their share price and profits had fallen. The following year, 2002 was a bad year for Corus Group (formerly British Steel) employees, as 6000 lost their jobs and those that remained were asked to accept a pay freeze. Not such a bad year for the Corus chairman, Sir Brian Moffat, as he was awarded a 130 per cent pay increase.

Such double standards proliferate and give business a bad name. Indeed, when it was announced that the BP chief executive Lord Browne had received a package worth £3.04 million in 2001 the *Daily Mirror* newspaper printed a cartoon in which he was christened 'Big Pig' and depicted guzzling banknotes coming out of a petrol pump. Not surprisingly, shareholders, unions and the media have expressed great concern about the ethical behaviour of many companies in this regard.[54] In fact, senior managers have also expressed concerns about the behaviour of the so-called 'fat cats'. Thus, Gloria Stuart, a member of the executive management board at the industrial gas giant BOC resigned in protest at the size of bonuses, salaries and golden handshakes being given to her colleagues. One example she cited[55] was that despite the fact that profits had fallen in 2002 the remuneration of the BOC chief executive rose by 47 per cent, to £1.8 million. It is clear that more justice in terms of distribution and equity of rewards is required in many companies.

Norms of justice also dictate that staff should be kept informed about what is happening within the organisation on the basis of having a *right to know*, rather than only being told what management ordain they *need to know*. While it is not always possible to treat all staff *equally*, they can and should all be treated *justly*.[56] There are two types of organisational justice.[57]

1. *Distributive justice* refers to the extent to which there is equity in the division of rewards, resources, duties and so on across all employees.
2. *Procedural justice* is to do with the fairness of the processes and procedures used to make decisions about the allocation of these resources. This in turn has two components. First, *formal procedures* in the form of rules and regulations laid down by the organisation, that are supposed to guide managerial decisions. Second, *interactional justice*, which relates to the perceptions of employees about how their supervisors actually implement the procedures. For example, do they spend more time communicating with their 'personal favourites', give them better resources, and more encouragement to apply for rewards?

Leader–member exchange (LMX) theory[58] argues that leaders have limited amounts of personal (e.g. time) and functional (e.g. financial) resources available, and so are forced to distribute these selectively. This selectivity of allocation in turn affects the quality of the LMX, as employees soon become aware of differential treatment. Research has shown that subordinates who experience positive LMXs, compared to those in low quality LMXs, receive a range of benefits,[59] including better appraisals, greater influence in decisions, higher pay, more rapid promotion and increased job satisfaction. It has also been found[60] that employees who perceive less fairness in organisational justice are more likely to retaliate by reducing their workrate, spreading gossip about co-workers and withholding information and co-operation from others. They are also more likely[61] to experience negative emotional states (anger, stress, resentment, etc.). For harmonious organisational functioning, there must therefore be transparent justice in terms of both the distribution of rewards and the procedures used in their allocation.

Be open and do not engage in subterfuge or gossip

Leaks are often used to sabotage plans, or force changes in direction. Here, someone in the organisation decides to release information through informal channels, and on a confidential or anonymous basis. Trade unions may initiate leaks to scupper possible management decisions. Likewise, managers may use deliberate leaks to assess staff reactions to proposed initiatives. Leaks are similar to whistleblowing, but the difference is that information is leaked simply to serve selfish personal interests rather than the wider public good. But *are leaks ethical*? The answer is 'no'. They are reflective of subterfuge and dark dealing, and in general should be avoided. The remedies proffered to circumvent whistleblowing can be applied to help prevent leaks.

In relation to gossip, there are two ethical questions. First, *should you spread a rumour?* Second, *should you listen to rumour?* The ethical answer to both is 'no', but in reality in relation to the latter question it is difficult to avoid hearing the rumour mill as it grinds relentlessly. While formal channels of communication only take place during working hours the gossip channel stays open much longer, for example, as employees travel to and from work or meet socially after work. Organisations are fertile breeding grounds for gossip and hearsay. Rumours are almost always more fascinating and engrossing than reality, and so they spread rapidly along the grapevine like some form of viral infection. With the advent of e-mail, cybergossip now zooms through the ether to ensure all parts of the organisation are up-to-date with the latest unofficial news. One reason for the power of this channel is that while it at times disseminates false stories, in fact the grapevine has been shown[62] to be an accurate source of information for around 80 per cent of the time.

Like the poor, the grapevine will always be with us. Since managers did not have it installed it in their organisation they cannot simply have it removed. Indeed, many commentators argue that rather than trying to dampen down the grapevine, managers should use it to their own benefit (a) to ensure that information is rapidly disseminated, and (b) to check on current employee concerns. There are in fact four types of rumour.

1. *'Great news' stories*. Here, rumours are about the best hopes of employees being fulfilled (e.g. impending large pay increase, more holidays), or positive stories about colleagues (forthcoming promotion, achievement outside work, etc.). They are harmless, but can be informative as they reflect employees' 'best case' hopes and wishes.
2. *'Bad tidings' rumours*. These are driven by the fear of negative outcomes ahead (e.g. redundancies, loss of orders). While negative,

again they provide important feedback for managers about what workers fear most and see as believable.

3. *Divisive innuendos*. These involve derogatory stories about the actions of other individuals or sub-groups. They serve to divide the workforce. Managers who are aware that such rumours are circulating need to take steps to bring people together and team-build. Where the rumours involve malicious attacks on individuals, or unsubstantiated tittle-tattle about them, they need to be dealt with rigorously and rapidly.
4. *Gap-fillers*. These involve gossip at times of uncertainty. They occur when employees know that important decisions are imminent (e.g. restructuring) but the organisation is slow to involve staff in the decision-making process or inform them of what is to happen. People then invent plausible scenarios and disseminate these to fill the information hiatus. Here, managers should swiftly move to fully inform employees of the true position by disseminating information widely.

Thus, some rumours are harmless, while others can be very damaging. When they involve the discussion of unsubstantiated matters that may be harmful to particular individuals or the company as a whole, then it is unquestionably wrong to be part of it.

Be straight rather than evasive

Politicians are very good at obfuscation, equivocation and general vagueness, but should managers use these tactics? There is an old expression that in certain circumstances the best advice is 'Whatever you say, say nothing.' In other words, no direct or forthright information should be given. However, *while there may be occasions when evasion or ambiguity could be justified, it should certainly not be policy*. Likewise, while euphemisms play a useful role in everyday communication (for example 'passed away' sounds less harsh that 'died'), they can also distort the true reality. Thus, rightsizing is often a euphemism for getting rid of staff. Over-use of ambiguity and euphemism will result in a decrease in trust in the communicator.

Where a manager, or indeed an organisation, makes a mistake, then there is an ethical issue as to *whether an apology is in order*. In everyday social encounters apologies are widely used and are expected. When we accidentally bump into someone, spill their drink or commit some other form of *faux pas*, we say we are sorry and the apology is usually graciously accepted. These are norms of politeness and manners, which also serve to prevent aggression. From a moral standpoint, where a mistake has been made, resulting in someone feeling offended or hurt, then the proper form of communication is a genuine apology. In the business context, some managers are loath to apologise to staff because they fear a loss of face. However, there is evidence that public apology is an effective tactic[63] both for managers and for organisations as a whole, leading to improved perceptions of the person or the organisation.[64] Six strategies are used[65] by those who have been publicly accused of responsibility for a negative event.

1. *Denial*. The person simply denies that the event occurred and questions the motives of the accusers.
2. *Dissociation*. The accused accepts that the act did take place but denies personal culpability. Someone else was to blame.
3. *Reframing*. A new 'frame' is constructed around the event. This purports that while it did happen, it was not as serious as it has been made out to be.
4. *Excuse*. The tactic here is to argue that while the event did occur, no one could have foreseen it, or realised what the outcome would have been.
5. *Justification*. This approach 'explains' that the event occurred because it was the only possible course of action – there was simply no alternative.
6. *Apology and remediation*. This involves accepting full and personal responsibility for the action, apologising to those affected for any untoward consequences, and asking for forgiveness. When remediation (in the form of recompense and restitution for damage suffered) is offered, as well as credible assurances that the event will not recur, public perceptions of the individual are more positive.[66]

Care about others and cause them no harm

The rule that your communication should not purposefully harm other members of staff is referred to as the *non-maleficence* (literally 'do no harm') *principle*. Engaging in scurrilous gossip about a colleague is an example of how this principle might be broken. However, as with many things in life, non-maleficence is not always black and white. For example, at a disciplinary interview it may be necessary to relate some home truths which the other person may find hurtful or even harmful. The important dimension here is that the *intention* should not be to cause harm. Employees should also be treated with dignity and respect. As expressed[67] by one Chief Executive:

> If there is one thing I have learned in my career as an industrialist which I would wish to share with others, it is that business should always strive to operate to the highest moral standards. This has a wide meaning, but in particular it means treating your people properly, and with respect.

These are the main ethical issues that need to be borne in mind for most managers. For those who work as communication professionals, offering a consultancy service to others, there are specific ethical issues to be considered.[68] We have summarised 10 key concerns for this group in Box 15.4.

Box 15.4 Ten ethical concerns for communication professionals

1. Respect and concern for clients as fellow humans.
2. Protection of client rights and autonomy at all times, including the avoidance of inappropriate relationships (sexual, monetary, etc.).
3. Open acknowledgement of any conflicts of interest.
4. Honesty with respect to the benefits and limitations of one's services.
5. Responsibility to third parties who may be adversely affected in any way by your work.
6. Achieving and maintaining (through continuing education) high levels of professional competence.
7. Full disclosure about one's true qualifications, experience and so on.
8. Fairness with regard to fees, payments and all financial dealings.
9. Behaving with a sense of duty to one's profession and one's professional colleagues.
10. Involvement in pro bono activities for the good of the wider community.

It is also important to recognise that we sometimes have to face considerable ethical conflict. Such occasions have been termed[69] 'defining moments'. An ethical decision typically involves choosing between an option which is right and one that is wrong. A defining moment involves choosing between two options both of which you believe to be right. They are so-called because the decisions we make help us to define who we are and what exactly we stand for. An example is provided in Box 15.5. There is clearly no simple answer to such dilemmas. With good forward planning, collisions between two rights can be minimised, but where they occur there will inevitably be moral debris of some sort left behind in the emotional wreckage at the scene of the crash. Sometimes we also have to decide upon the lesser of two evils. For instance, should you make a few workers (all of whom are very conscientious) redundant in the hope of saving the jobs of the rest of the workforce? Again, there are no easy solutions.

In conclusion, ethical behaviour is clearly desirable. But it has to be encouraged by a rigorous system of rewards for good behaviour and punishments for infringements. In fact, many businesses have recognised the importance of corporate citizenship,[70] and the most forward-thinking have developed specific measures and targets in this field for senior managers. Remuneration is linked to performance in areas such as employee satisfaction, health and safety, environment and corporate social responsibility. Organisations clearly need such incentives to encourage and sustain an ethical approach.[71] If ethical practices are not seen to be rewarded or profitable, and if people feel they can get away with unethical behaviour, then they will be less inclined to follow the right path. One of the most notorious unethical businessmen was the infamous Chicago racketeer and mobster Al Capone. Interestingly, he was not convicted either for his many illegal business practices, which included prostitution, bootlegging and gambling, or for his involvement in the St Valentine's Day Massacre. Rather, he was jailed in 1931 for tax evasion. The moral of this story is that checks on breaches of corporate standards should be many and varied.

Measuring and monitoring communication

While it is important for managers to know how to communicate skilfully and to do so ethically, they also must be keenly aware of the current state of communications generally within the workplace. Just because things seem calm on the bridge and the ship is moving ahead,

Box 15.5 Defining moments – an example

Your colleagues are depending on you as the key member of the team making a specially arranged Saturday afternoon presentation for a major contract to the company's biggest client. The team has worked on this for weeks, with you as keynote presenter. The Chief Executive keeps reminding you all about its importance. To your horror, you then discover you promised your 10-year-old son that on that same afternoon, and at the same time, you would be at the school's cup final since he is captain of the team, and every other parent will be there. There has been considerable excitement in the family about this for weeks. You cannot fulfil both commitments. What do you do? Is your duty to your employer and colleagues higher than your moral responsibilities to your son and family?

- You could go down the unethical road by *lying* either to your colleagues (by saying you are ill) or to your family (pretending your car broke down on the way to the game). The ultimate destination of this road is Tensiontown! Relational breakdown is very probable, and lying is therefore not an option to be recommended.
- An alternative is to take the *apology* trail. Explain to the company that your family must come first and prepare others fully to stand in for you (not good for your future promotion prospects!). Or, try to explain to your child that work must come first (the emotional and loyalty damage is probably immense) and you will make up for it (how?!)
- You could try to *compromise* by for example attending the first part of the presentation and the end of the cup final. Neither party will be entirely satisfied.
- A better solution is to try to *avoid* such occasions through good forward planning. Once they arise, there is never an easy solution to large ethical dilemmas.

does not mean that the journey will be smooth. The Titanic operated successfully for most of its only voyage. It is better to chart and circumvent the icebergs than to hope that your ship will miss them. As John F. Kennedy, using another analogy, put it: 'The time to repair the roof is when the sun is shining.' To further vary the metaphor, if a communication malaise sets in, the corporate body suffers badly. Thus, it has been shown[72] that: 'when systems of communication begin to deteriorate within a given organization, the likelihood increases that the collective set of individuals will fragment into subgroups whose structures reflect their own internal communication needs and dynamics, rather than those of the total organization'.

Just as a vehicle operates best when serviced regularly, so do organisations need frequent check-ups. Prevention is always preferable to cure. It is therefore crucial for managers to know the current state of communication within their organisation so that they can take rapid steps to address identified problems. They cannot simply rely on their own perceptions, or upon what others tell them, to give them a comprehensive, objective and true picture regarding the current state of communications. One portrayal of organisational life, that has been widely circulated via e-mail, is that contained in Box 15.6. As this illustrates, managers are often told the good news that subordinates think they want to hear – no one wants to be a dead messenger. This, in turn, results in a process known[73] as 'the boss's illusion', whereby managers mistakenly believe that this defective feedback is honest, well meant and accurate. To avoid this vicious circle, steps need to be taken to ensure that staff can openly express what they really think, as opposed to what they feel is politically correct or safe to express. This necessitates an objective, confidential and anonymous mechanism for accessing and assessing employee views.

A common error made by many managers is to focus upon efficiency rather than effectiveness. The distinction between these two concepts was neatly encapsulated by Clampitt and DeKoch:[74] 'Someone posing an efficiency question asks, "Are you doing things the right way?" A person enquiring about effectiveness asks, "Are you doing the right things?" It is entirely possible to be very efficient while

Box 15.6 One portrayal of organisational life

'An organisation is like a tree full of monkeys, on different branches, at various levels, some climbing up, some doing little and watching others who seem always to be very busy, some falling off, and some hanging on for dear life. The monkeys on the top look down and their perception is of smiling faces looking up. The monkeys at the bottom look up and only see ass-holes!'

being completely ineffective.' The best method for obtaining accurate information about the effectiveness of internal communications is the *communication audit.* An audit has been described[75] as providing 'an objective picture of what is happening compared with what senior executives think (or have been told) is happening'. Such knowledge empowers managers to realistically evaluate how communication relationships can best be transformed to meet the needs of the organisation. The results of an audit shed bright light on the dark back alleys of organisational dysfunction, and enable managers to see clearly the path along which they should be going.

The term 'audit' is used widely in the world of business.[76] Financial audits are long established, and terms such as medical audit, clinical audit and organisation audit have all filtered into the lexicon in various sectors. While there is some debate about how and in what ways organisational communication should be measured, in essence all forms of audit have the following general characteristics:

1. *The accumulation of information* – the **diagnostic** phase of the auditing process. Managers need *information* about who they are communicating with, through what channels and to what productive and qualitative effect.
2. *The creation of management systems* – the **prescriptive** phase of the audit. Once information has been obtained, *systems* must then be developed to overcome identified problems and to build upon existing best practice.
3. *Accountability* – the **functional** aspect of auditing. Specific individuals should be made *accountable* for different aspects of the flow of information within the organisation. At a practical level, this means that if vital information is not getting through to its key audiences the blockages in the channels of communication must be identified and dealt with.

Organisations require all three of these strands to be applied to their internal and external communication systems. An audit is the organisational equivalent of a medical check-up, since it examines the health of the company. It highlights where the corporate body is functioning well, but also ascertains if some communication arteries are clogged, if blood pressure is high in certain departments and whether signs of growing malignancy are evident. Accurate diagnosis then informs decisions about an exact prescription tailored to cure the identified problems.

Audit measures

The term 'organometrics' is used[77] to refer to the methods employed in the measurement of organisational functioning. There is a range of organometric tools that can be applied in communication audits. The measures employed in any particular audit will vary depending upon its exact objectives. Some audits are more collaborative than others. In essence there is a continuum of involvement.[78] At one end the audit is 'done with' employees, who actively participate in establishing the objectives and methodologies for the exercise, play a key role in data collection, and contribute centrally to the report and recommendations. At the other, the audit is 'done to' employees by independent external consultants, who carry out the entire assessment operation, write the report and make recommendations. In practice, most audits fall somewhere in between these two extremes.

The following are the main methods used in organisational assessments.

Questionnaires The organisational survey is a widely used method for measuring employee attitudes and satisfaction. Indeed, in his review of the area, Clampitt[79] noted that organisational surveys are now as ubiquitous as weather forecasts. There is a range of validated questionnaires that can be readily adapted for any specific communication audit context[80,81]. The two most widely used are the *Communication Satisfaction Questionnaire*[82] and the *International Communication Association Audit Survey*.[83] The advantages of questionnaires are that they:

- allow for a high degree of control over the focus of the research
- can gauge the views of a large sample of respondents
- produce approval ratings[84] for each element of the organisation
- provide quantitative data to act as benchmarks against which future performance can be measured and extent of improvement assessed.[85]

One disadvantage with surveys is that while they can cover a breadth of topics, they are limited in the extent to which they produce deeper levels of employee insight and analysis. However, the inclusion of open questions provides a certain degree of freedom of expression for respondents to air their wider views.[86]

Interviews The structured interview is a tried and tested approach to data collection.[87] It is now widely recognised that different people form markedly differing impressions of the same events. To gain a full understanding of these interpretations it is necessary to probe under the surface of initial employee responses. The narratives that emerge can paint an insightful picture of corporate life.[88] The interview is the ideal tool for such exploration. Of course, it is not a unitary phenomenon. As summarised by Young and Stanton[89] 'The interview is a highly flexible and adaptable tool'. Like humans, interviews come in different guises.[90] They can be highly structured and restricting for respondents at one extreme, or completely unstructured and facilitative at the other. Furthermore, there are specialised types of interview that can be used in audits, such as the Retrospective Interview Technique.[91]

When skilfully executed, the interview encourages full, open and honest freedom of expression from employees. However, it is also a very time-consuming, and therefore costly, method especially where large numbers are involved in the audit. Another drawback of interviews as opposed to questionnaires is that the responses obtained are not anonymous, and so respondents may be reluctant to give certain information or express particular opinions. But overall, given a trusting relationship between interviewer and interviewee, coupled with firm guarantees of confidentiality, interviews generate a rich and deep seam of valuable information.

Focus groups These are, in some respects, an extension of interviews, being defined[92] as 'a non-directive interview technique which encourages discussion between participants'. Here, a small group (usually between five and eight representative staff) participates in discussion. The general 'focus' of the discussion is guided by a facilitator, although the emphasis is upon allowing members as much freedom as possible to verbalise their opinions, engage in member–member interchanges and spark ideas off one another.[93] The discussion is recorded, either on tape or by a colleague of the facilitator, and content analysed for recurring themes. Focus groups can be used[94] to gather information about reactions at a micro level (e.g. views about a particular communication channel) or to obtain insights at a macro level (e.g. the impact of downsizing on the corporation). Their chief advantages[95] are that they:

- can produce a rich harvest of data in a relatively short period of time
- allow both reported and observed data to be obtained; the auditor has access to the reported experiences of the group but also can gain insights from the way in which employees interact with one another

- are adaptable and so can be used in a range of contexts and for differing purposes
- reveal a kaleidoscope of information on employee experiences, ideas, opinions, attitudes and feelings, that may be missed by other more directive approaches.

Among the main disadvantages are that:

- some employees may be unwilling to express honest opinions in the presence of colleagues
- less assertive respondents can find it difficult to air personal views that do not concur with the general group consensus
- focus groups are more difficult to control than interviews; some participants may try to dominate while others are less vocal, there can be overtalk, and so on
- the data collected can be difficult to analyse, especially where there is overtalk.

Data collection log-sheets This method involves the use of a structured proforma (a 'diary' or 'log') on which respondents itemise and evaluate communicative activities over a set period.[96] Thus, when used in audits, for each communication, respondents are requested to list the source, topic, channel (telephone, e-mail face-to-face, etc.), its length or duration, whether it was one- or two-way, and finally rate its effectiveness.[97] Alternatively, rather than analysing each communication, a 'time sampling' or 'experience sampling' approach may be used,[98] whereby employees make notes on their reactions to experiences at set periods during the day. The advantages of log-sheet methods are that they:

- are familiar – most people understand the notion of 'keeping a diary'
- offer the most realistic way of obtaining representative descriptions of actual communication events
- provide interesting idiographic or 'insider' insights into actual communication events not readily achieved by other methods.

However, there are disadvantages, including the following:

- high demands are placed on the time and effort of respondents; for rigorous applications this can amount[99] to over 20 hours per participant (including preparatory meetings, etc.)
- the results depend upon respondents regularly completing the task – the auditor has no control over data collection
- sample maintenance is often low using this method – in other words there can be a high drop-out rate

Episodic Communication Channels in Organisations (ECCO) Analysis This is a method that has been used[100] for over half a century in organisational research. It is a specially designed questionnaire, which tracks the progress of a specific piece of information through the organisation. Respondents are asked to list whether or not they know of the information, if so when they received it, where they were when they first heard it, through which channel (memo, phone call, grapevine) and from what source (manager, colleague). As such, it specifically educes aspects such as, 'rates of flow, distortion of messages, and redundancy'.[101] From the results, a pattern emerges of where communication is flowing well and where blockages are occurring.[102] An ECCO questionnaire only takes a few minutes to complete and its ease of analysis means that it can be administered to a large sample of the workforce.[103] Drawbacks are that some staff are reluctant to identify sources, while others are loath to admit that they have not heard what is perceived to be an important piece of information.

Social network analysis This methodology identifies and charts the frequency and type of contact between individuals and groups. It highlights the strengths or weakness of working bonds between people – in other words, how often and how well individuals communicate with one another. There is a range of instruments for use in network analysis,[104] and this method has been employed in a broad range of organisational settings.[105] Dimensions investigated include employee evaluations of one another (liking, trust, etc.), task relationships (who individuals interact with to complete tasks), informal relationships (e.g. who goes for coffee breaks with whom), information exchange (who sends messages to whom) and physical linkages (who shares offices or facilities). The relationships that exist can be depicted diagrammatically using *sociograms* or *communicograms*.[106] This approach is based upon numerical ratings. As such, it provides valuable information about the direction, volume and frequency of communications, a major drawback is that it does not in itself offer explanations or interpretations for these. The latter can be provided by augmenting the network analysis with a qualitative form of evaluation (such as interviews).

Critical Incident Technique The Critical Incident Technique (CIT) involves respondents recalling and describing personal experiences to an interviewer, or putting them down on paper. Respondents are asked to select instances that are 'out of the ordinary', in either a positive or negative fashion, from the norm and describe these in detail.[107] The chosen 'critical' effective and ineffective instances are then believed to reflect more general opinions about that which is under scrutiny. CIT pinpoints precise sources of functional and dysfunctional performance in organisations. It produces a detailed in-depth analysis of what staff regard as the main issues. Employees can also be asked to rate these, so that the degree of seriousness attached to each can be evaluated. Furthermore, minority views can be taken into account in a way that may be overlooked when relying upon strict quantitative analysis and large statistical effects.[108] One problem is that even when notification of topic is given, interviewees may find it difficult to recall examples of effective and ineffective communication. The CIT technique has been found[109] to be not so well suited to hard-nosed, hierarchical, organisations, especially in the manufacturing sector.

Surveillance techniques Increasingly, companies use some form of what has been called *undercover auditing*[110] to check on staff. These include techniques such as CCTV recording, customer feedback questionnaires and mystery shopping. The latter method, also known as mystery customer research, involves a trained inspector posing as a customer and visiting or telephoning outlets to assess the effectiveness of various aspects of service. Surveillance methods are designed both to check on how employees are communicating, and motivate them to maintain high levels of performance in the knowledge that they are being monitored. There are clear ethical problems with surveillance techniques, and where they are used strict guidelines need to be in place to ensure employee rights are protected.[111]

These then are the main organometric audit tools. The decision about which to employ depends upon a range of factors including the purpose and scale of the audit, the accessibility of respondents and their responsiveness to being recorded. It is also the case[112] that a combination of quantitative and qualitative approaches is usually most appropriate. As Boyle[113] has clearly shown, numbers only matter in relation to what they reflect or represent. Thus, while figures furnished by surveys are useful to provide benchmarking against which future performance can be compared, they lack the depth of insight that can be gleaned from interviews or focus groups. Regardless of methods used, once the audit is completed the results should then feed in to an overall communication strategy.

Developing a communication strategy

To achieve high levels of performance, organisations must have clearly formulated strategies for all aspects of the business and communicate these effectively to staff.[114] In general terms[115] strategic planning requires 'broad yet effective information gathering, development and exploration of strategic alternatives, and an emphasis on future implications of present decisions'. As part of this, organisations must develop a coherent communication strategy, which can be defined[116] as the process that enables managers to evaluate the communication consequences of the decision-making process, and integrate this into the normal business planning cycle and psyche of the organisation. If an organisation does not have a coherent strategy for managing communication, ad hoc and often dysfunctional methods will develop. A strategy is the business equivalent of a steering wheel to control the communicating vehicle. There are five key stages in the development of a communication strategy.

1. Secure senior management commitment This is the cornerstone of change in any organisation. Without the backing of the chief executive nothing concrete will be achieved. The senior management team should clearly endorse the importance of a strategy for effective communications, and cascade this down the hierarchy.

2. Identify current practice Managers need to start from a clear picture of where the organisation is in communication terms. This means that some form of objective audit of existing communication practices must be carried out. To be credible, it should be conducted by independent auditors, rather than by anyone within the organisation. In-house auditing leads to the related twin problems of perceived vested interest and staff suspicions of the results.

3. Have a clear policy to guide communications This includes taking strategic decisions[117] regarding:

- with whom managers should communicate, and about what
- when, where and under what circumstances, this should happen
- which channels of communication should be used for what purposes
- how to secure the optimum involvement of employees in the communication process.

A communication strategy should guide decisions about the communication of both good and bad news. Policies should cover the celebration of success as well as the handling of crises. To take but one example, if the company is downsizing and people are being made redundant, communication has been shown[118] to be of paramount importance in minimising the potential damage for all involved. Important choices also have to be made about communication channels including, inter alia: When should senior managers interface with employees? What information is it appropriate to send to staff by e-mail, put on the intranet, or publicise in the Newsletter? What form of 'meetings structure' should the organisation have, and what objectives will they serve?

4. Set standards to measure success This operates on two levels. First, explicit links between communication and organisational outcomes should be made by all business units. Second, staff 'satisfaction with communication' targets should be set. Ongoing audit research should track the extent to which these standards are being achieved. Strategic communication must impact at various levels, including information dissemination, decision-making, employee empowerment, leadership performance, implementation of personnel policies and so on. The extent to which current communication strategy is achieving these results needs to be tracked. Identified weaknesses in existing communication patterns may then require investment, such as in the training of managers or the introduction of new technologies.

5. Incorporate this process into the business planning cycle (and psyche) of the organisation A genuine communication strategy means involving all managers and ultimately all staff in identifying goals, standards of good practice and methods of evaluation. When business plans are being drawn up, their communication consequences should be highlighted. All forms of strategy must also be flexible, to meet changing needs and shifting circumstances. Communication is no different. What worked 50 years ago in companies would simply not be tolerated by employees today. Like dress, communication has to fit in with current trends. This means that the costs and benefits of communication initiatives have to be regularly evaluated.

A communication task force and a communication committee can both be useful in regulating strategy.[119] The task force is given a short-term remit, usually to investigate specific problems identified by an audit and to make recommendations about how these can best be resolved. The communication committee is a more permanent structure, comprised of managerial and non-managerial staff from across the different sections of the organisation. It has the remit of continually monitoring communication practices, diagnosing issues of concern and taking steps to rectify these. One useful technique is for membership of the task force to be rotated, so that as wide a range of staff as possible recognise communication as a core area of interest and carry this perspective back into their working practice.

Overview

The topic of organisational communication has become a vast field of study with a voluminous amount of literature being published in recent years. This is not surprising, given that effective communication is central to goal achievement in almost every dimension of organisational functioning. In this book, we have attempted to cull from this burgeoning work the key facets of effective managerial communication. Managers have to decide which strategies to employ within the given context in which communication is taking place, bearing in mind the nature of those with whom they are interacting. The information contained in this text provides invaluable guidelines to shape better behavioural decision-making across a broad range of situations. As emphasised in this chapter, two broader aspects which are important for managers to keep in mind are:

- doing what is right, in terms of communicating ethically; and
- knowing exactly how you are doing, by regularly auditing your communications.

In concluding, we recognise that life is not always within our control, and sometimes regardless of how well we communicate the result is not as we would have hoped. As the Scottish poet Robert Burns put it:

> 'The best laid schemes o' mice an' men
> Gang aft a-gley'.

In other words, circumstances can conspire to frustrate even the most carefully worked-out plans. However, it is the case that the more skilled we are in the realm of communication and the more carefully we plan what we intend to do, the more likely we are to be successful in life. Organisations are like families. Those in trouble are characterised by dysfunctional communication, while successful ones have harmonious relationships. Managers are similar to the heads of the family. They need to lead by example and encourage a congenial atmosphere in which all members can achieve their true potential. The outcome will be success and stability. Conversely, where managers rule like tyrannical parents, the consequence is typified by constant strife and ultimate breakdown. By judiciously employing the skills and strategies discussed in this book, managers will achieve much more positive results from their staff. In the end, it is the employees who determine the success or failure of any business.

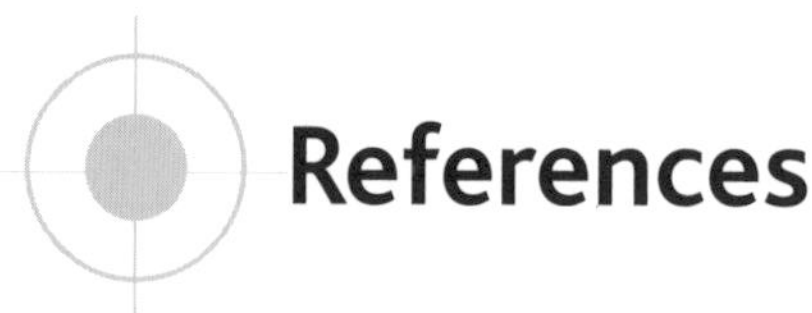

References

1 The world of the communicative manager

1. Schermerhorn, J.R. (1996) *Management and Organizational Behavior*, New York: Wiley.
2. O'Hair, D. Friedrich, G. and Dixon, L. (2002) *Strategic Communication in Business and the Professions*, 4th edition, Boston: Houghton Mifflin, p. 3.
3. Eglin, R. (2001) 'Graduates become more demanding', *The Sunday Times Appointments Section*, 2 September, p. 12.
4. Reed Employment Services (2002) *Motivating People at Work: What is to be Done*? London.
5. Caulkin, S. (1998) 'How that pat on the back can mean money in the bank', *The Observer: Work Section*, 19 April, p. 1.
6. Withers, P. (2002) 'The sweet smell of success', *HR Magazine*, June, pp. 76–92.
7. Ocasio, W. (2001) 'How do organizations think?', in T. Lant and Z. Shapira (eds) *Organizational Cognition: Computation and Interpretation*, Mahwah, NJ: Lawrence Erlbaum, p. 42.
8. Huczynski, A. and Buchanan, D. (2001) *Organizational Behaviour: An Introductory Text*, Harlow: Pearson, p. 5.
9. Talcott Parsons (1963) *Structure and Process in Modern Societies*, New York: Free Press.
10. Clampitt, P. (1991) *Communicating for Managerial Effectiveness*, Newbury Park: Sage.
11. Hargie, O. and Tourish, D. (eds) (2000) *Handbook of Communication Audits for Organisations*, London: Routledge.
12. Tourish, D. and Hargie, O. (eds) (2004) *Key Issues in Organisational Communication*, London: Routledge.
13. Berger, B. (1994) 'Revolution at whirlpool', *Internal Communication Focus*, November, pp. 8–11.
14. Moskowitz, M. and Levering, R. (2002) 'Nurturing staff helps your profits grow', *The Sunday Times 100 Best Companies to Work For*, Supplement, 24 March, pp. 4–5.
15. Moskowitz, M. and Levering, R. (2002) ibid., p. 4.
16. *The Sunday Times* (2003) *100 Best Companies To Work For* (Supplement), p. 14.
17. Morley, D., Shockley-Zalabak, P. and Cesaria, R. (2002) 'Organizational influence processes: perceptions of values, communication and effectiveness', *Studies in Communication Sciences*, 2: 69–104.
18. Schermerhorn, J.R. (1996) op. cit., p. 2.
19. Beck, C. (1999) *Managerial Communication: Bridging Theory and Practice*, Upper Saddle River, NJ: Prentice-Hall.
20. Forrest, A. (1997) *5 Way Management*, London: The Industrial Society.

21. Quirke, B. (1995) 'Internal communication', in Hart, N. (ed.) *Strategic Public Relations*, Houndmills: MacMillan.
22. Hanna, M. and Wilson, G. (1998) *Communicating in Business and Professional Settings*, 4th edition, New York: McGraw-Hill.
23. Guest, D., Michie, J., Sheehan, M., Conway, N. and Metochi, M. (2000) *Effective People Management*, London: Chartered Institute of Personnel and Development, p. ix.
24. Hanna, M. and Wilson, G. (1998) op. cit.
25. Davey, K. and Liefhooghe, P. (2003) 'Voice and power: a critical investigation of accounts of bullying in organizations', in A. Schorr, W. Campbell and M. Schenk (eds) *Communication Research and Media Science in Europe*, Berlin: Mouton de Gruyter, p. 443.
26. McGregor, D. (1960) *The Human Side of Enterprise*, New York: McGraw-Hill.
27. Kassing J. (2000) 'Exploring the relationship between workplace freedom of speech, organizational identification, and employee dissent', *Communication Research Reports*, 17: 387–96.
28. Quirke, B. (1995) op. cit.
29. McKeans, P. (1990) 'GM Division builds a classic system to share internal information', *Public Relations Journal*, 46: 24–41.
30. Smith, A. (1991) *Innovative Employee Communication: New Approaches to Improving Trust, Teamwork and Performance*, Englewood Cliffs: Prentice-Hall.
31. Hargie, O., Tourish, D. and Wilson, N. (2002) 'Communication audits and the effects of increased information: a follow-up study', *Journal of Business Communication*, 39: 414–36.
32. Hargie, O. and Tourish, D. (2004) 'How are we doing? measuring and monitoring organisational communication', in D. Tourish and O. Hargie (eds) *Key Issues in Organisational Communication*, London: Routledge.
33. Hargie, O. and Tourish, D. (eds) (2000) op. cit.
34. Shockley-Zalabak, P. and Ellis, K. (2000) 'Perceived organizational effectiveness, job satisfaction, culture, and communication: challenging the traditional view', *Communication Research Reports*, 17: 375–86.
35. Zorn, T. and Taylor, J. (2004) 'Knowledge management and/as organisational communication', in D. Tourish and O. Hargie (eds) *Key Issues in Organisational Communication*, London: Routledge.
36. Tourish, D. and Hargie, O. (2004) 'Motivating critical upward communication: a key challenge for management decision-making', in D. Tourish and O. Hargie (eds) *Key Issues in Organisational Communication*, London: Routledge.
37. Clampitt, P.G. (2001) *Communicating for Managerial Effectiveness*, 2nd edition, Newbury Park: Sage.
38. Tourish, D. and Hargie, O. (1993) 'Don't you wish sometimes you were better informed?' *Health Service Journal*, 103: 28–9.
39. Johlke, M. and Duhan, D. (2001) 'Testing competing models of sales force communication', *The Journal of Personal Selling and Sales Management*, 21: 265–77.
40. Clampitt, P., DeKoch, R. and Cashman, T. (2000) 'A strategy for communicating about uncertainty', *Academy of Management Executive*, 14: 41–57 (p. 43).
41. Scott, C., Connaughton, S. Diaz-Saenz, H., Maguire, K., Ramirez, R., Richardson, B., Shaw, S. and Morgan, D. (1999) 'The impacts of communication and multiple identifications on intent to leave: a

multimethodological exploration', *Management Communication Quarterly*, 12: 400–35.
42. Hargie, O. and Tourish, D. (eds) (2000) *Handbook of Communication Audits for Organisations*, op. cit.
43. Hargie, O. (ed.) (1997) *The Handbook of Communication Skills*, 2nd edition, London: Routledge.
44. Oldham G. and Cummings, A. (1996) 'Employee creativity: personal and contextual factors at work', *Academy of Management Journal*, 39: 607–34.
45. West, M. (2000) 'State of the art: creativity and innovation at work', *The Psychologist*, 13: 460–4.
46. Hargie, O. (1992) *Communication: Beyond the Crossroads*. Monograph, University of Ulster, Jordanstown, p. 10.
47. Hargie, O. and Dickson, D. (2004) *Skilled Interpersonal Communication: Research, Theory and Practice*, Routledge: London.
48. Axelrod, S. (1999) *Work and the Evolving Self: Theoretical and Clinical Considerations*, Hillsdale, NJ: The Analytic Press, p. 116.
49. Downs, C.W. (1988) *Communication Audits*, Glenview, Illinois: Scott, Foresman & Co.
50. Axelrod, S. (1999) op. cit., p. vxii.
51. Valås, V. and Sletta, O. (2004) 'Blending attitudes and motivation: a key cocktail', in D. Tourish and O. Hargie (eds) *Key Issues in Organisational Communication*, London: Routledge.
52. Tourish, D. and Hargie, O. (2000) 'Communication and organisational success', in O. Hargie and D. Tourish (eds) *Handbook of Communication Audits for Organisations*, London: Routledge.
53. Axelrod, S. (1999) op. cit., p. 1.
54. West, M. (2000) op. cit., p. 464.
55. Hargie, O. and Tourish, D. (1999) 'Internal communications and the management of change', in R. Baker, H. Hearnshaw and N. Robertson (eds) *Implementing Change with Clinical Audit*, Chichester: Wiley.
56. West, M. (2000) op. cit.
57. Hargie, O. and Tourish, D. (1999) 'The psychology of interpersonal skill', in A. Memon and R. Bull (eds) *Handbook of the Psychology of Interviewing*, Chichester: Wiley.
58. Goleman, D. (1997) *Emotional Intelligence*, London: Bloomsbury.
59. Dickson, D. (1999) 'Barriers to communication', in A. Long (ed.) *Interaction for Practice in Community Nursing*, Houndmills, Hampshire: MacMillan.
60. Stewart, J. and Logan, C. (1998) *Together: Communicating Interpersonally*, 5th edition, Boston, MA: McGraw-Hill.
61. Carlone, D. and Taylor, B. (1998) 'Organizational communication and cultural studies', *Communication Theory*, 8: 337–67.
62. Huczynski, A. and Buchanan, D. (2001) *Organizational Behaviour: An Introductory Text*, Harlow: Pearson, p. 624.
63. Robbins, S. (2001) *Organizational Behavior*, 9th edition, New Jersey: Prentice Hall.
64. Deal, T. and Kennedy, A., 1999 *The New Corporate Cultures: Revitalizing the Workplace after Downsizing, Mergers and Reengineering*, London: Orion.
65. Dixon, J. and Durrheim, K. (2000) 'Displacing place-identity: a discursive approach to locating self and other', *British Journal of Social Psychology*, 39: 27–44 (p. 27).

66. Deal, T. and Kennedy, A. (1999) op. cit., p. 4.
67. Deal, T. and Kennedy, A. (1999) op. cit., p. 9.
68. O'Shea, J. and Madigan, C. (1997) *Dangerous Company: The Consulting Powerhouses and the Businesses they Save and Ruin*, London: Nicholas Brealey.
69. Rolfsen, M. (2004) 'The tyranny of trends: towards an alternative perspective on fads in management', in D. Tourish and O. Hargie (eds) *Key Issues in Organisational Communication*, London: Routledge.
70. Daniels, T., Spiker, B. and Papa, M. (1997) *Perspectives on Organizational Communication*, 4th edition, Boston: McGraw-Hill, p. 203.
71. Helm, T. (2000) 'Service with a smile frowned upon by Germans', *Daily Telegraph*, 28 October, p. 23.
72. Rushe, D. (2001) 'Wal-Martians', *The Sunday Times Business Focus*, 10 June, p. 5.
73. Saporito, B. (2003) 'Can Wal-Mart get any bigger?', *Time Magazine* (Canadian edition), 13 January, pp. 26–31 (p. 30).
74. Hargie, O. and Morrow, N. (1995) 'An evaluation of a presentation skills course for pharmacists', *International Journal of Pharmacy Practice*, 3: 101–5.
75. Hanna and Wilson (1998) op. cit., p. 1.

2 It's not what you say ... communicating nonverbally

1. Abercrombie, K. (1968) 'Paralanguage', *British Journal of Disorders of Communication*, 3: 55–59 (p. 55).
2. Fletcher, W. (2000) 'Let your body do the talking', *Management Today*, March, 30, p. 30.
3. Richmond, V. and McCroskey, J. (2000) *Nonverbal Behaviour in Interpersonal Relations*, 4th edition, Boston: Allyn and Bacon.
4. Remland, M. (2000) *Nonverbal Communication in Everyday Life*, Boston: Houghton Mifflin.
5. Anderson, P. (1999) *Nonverbal Communication: Forms and Functions*, Mountain View, CA: Mayfield Publishing Company.
6. Jones, S.E. and LeBaron, C.D. (2002) 'Research on the relationship between verbal and nonverbal communication: emerging integrations', *Journal of Communication*, 52: 499–521.
7. Mehrabian, A. (1972) *Nonverbal Communication*, Chicago, IL: Aldine-Atherton.
8. Burgoon, J., Buller, D. and Woodall, W. (1996) *Nonverbal Communication: The Unspoken Dialogue*, New York: McGraw-Hill.
9. Bull, P. (2002) *Communication under the Microscope: The Theory and Practice of Microanalysis*, London: Routledge.
10. Fineman, S. (2001) 'Emotions and organizational control', in R.L. Payne and C.L. Cooper (eds) *Emotions at Work: Theory, Research and Applications for Management*, Chichester: John Wiley & Sons.
11. Goman, C.K. (2002) 'Cross-cultural business practices', *Communication World*, 19: 22–5 (p. 24).
12. Hiemstra, K. (1999) 'Shake my hand: making the right impression in business with nonverbal communications', *Business Communication Quarterly*, 62: 71–4 (p. 74).
13. Graham, G., Unruth, J. and Jennings, P. (1991) 'The impact of nonverbal communication in organizations: a survey of perceptions', *The Journal of Business Communication*, 28: 45–62.

14. Warfield, A. (2002) 'Your body speaks volume, but do you know what it is saying?' *Business Credit*, 104: 20–1 (p. 20).
15. Carnevale, A., Gainer, L. and Meltzer, S. (1991) *Work-place Basics: The Essential Skills Employers Want*, San Francisco, CA: Jossey-Bass.
16. Vrij, A., Edward, K., Roberts, K. and Bull, R. (2000) 'Detecting deceit via analysis of verbal and nonverbal behavior', *Journal of Nonverbal Behavior*, 24: 239–63 (p. 241).
17. Vrij, A. (2001) 'Detecting the liars', *The Psychologist*, 14: 596–8.
18. Kristof-Brown, A., Barrick, M. and Franke, M. (2002) 'Applicant impression management: dispositional influences and consequences for recruiter perceptions of fit and similarity', *Journal of Management*, 28: 27–46.
19. Trethewey, A. (1999) 'Disciplined bodies: women's embodied identities at work', *Organization Studies*, 20: 423–50 (p. 438).
20. Bavelas, J.B., Coates, L. and Johnson, T. (2002) 'Listener responses as a collaborative process: the role of gaze', *Journal of Communication*, 52: 566–80.
21. Bull, op. cit.
22. Argyle, M. (1994) *The Psychology of Interpersonal Behaviour*, London: Penguin.
23. Burgoon, op. cit.
24. Warfield, op. cit., p. 21.
25. McElroy, J. and Loundenback, L. (1981) 'Personal space and personal selling: customer reactions to personal space invasion', *Proceedings of the Educator Seminar*, 38, 52.
26. Bente, G., Donaghy, W. and Suwelack, D. (1998) 'Sex differences in body movement and visual attention: an integrated analysis of movement and gaze in mixed-sex dyads', *Journal of Nonverbal Behavior*, 22: 31–58.
27. Remland, op. cit.
28. Bull, op. cit.
29. Hall, E.T. (1966) *The Hidden Dimension*, Garden City, NY: Doubleday.
30. Mead, R. (1992) *Cross-Cultural Management Communication*, New York: Wiley.
31. Zahn, G.L. (1991) 'Face-to-face communication in an office setting: the effects of position, proximity and exposure', *Communication Research*, 18: 737–54.
32. Hall, op. cit.
33. Cook, M. (1970) 'Experiments on orientation and proxemics', *Human Relations*, 23: 61–76.
34. Blake, G. (1999) 'E-mail with feeling', *Research Technology Management*, 42: 12–13.
35. Friesen, W. (1972) *Cultural Differences in Facial Expression: An Experimental Test of the Concept of Display Rules*, PhD thesis, University of California, San Francisco.
36. Matsumoto, D. (1990) 'Cultural similarities and differences in the display rules', *Motivation and Emotion*, 14: 195–214.
37. LaFrance, M. and Hecht, M. (1999) 'Option or obligation to smile: the effects of power and gender on facial expression', in P. Philippot, R. Feldman and E. Coats (eds) *The Social Context of Nonverbal Behavior*, Cambridge: Cambridge University Press.
38. Hecht, M. and LaFrance, M. (1998) 'License or obligation to smile: the effect of power and sex on the amount and type of smiling', *Personality and Social Psychology Bulletin*, 24: 1332–42.

39. DePaulo, P. (1992) 'Applications of nonverbal behaviour research in marketing and management', in R. Feldman (ed.) *Applications of Nonverbal Theories and Research*, Hillsdale, NJ: Lawrence Erlbaum.
40. Knapp, M. and Hall, J. (1997) *Nonverbal communication in human interaction*, 4th edition, Forth Worth: Harcourt Brace College Publishers.
41. Adler, I. (1999) 'Let's get physical', *Business Mexico*, 9: 24.
42. Ekman, P. and Friesen, W. (1969) 'The repertoire of non-verbal behaviour: categories, origins, usage and coding', *Semiotica*, 1: 49–98.
43. Kendon, A. (1984) 'Some use of gestures', in D. Tannen and M. Saville-Troike (eds) *Perspectives on Silence*, Norwood, NJ: Ablex.
44. Trethewey, op. cit.
45. Bull, op. cit.
46. McGinniss, J. (1969) *The Selling of the President 1968*, NY: Simon & Schuster.
47. Kalin, R. and Raydo, D. (1978) 'Discrimination in evaluative judgements against foreign-accented job applicants', *Psychological Reports*, 43: 1203–9.
48. Pugh, S.D. (2002) 'Emotional regulation in individuals and dyads: causes, costs and consequences', in R.G. Lord, R.J. Klimoski and R. Kanfer (eds) *Emotions in the Workplace: Understanding the Structure and Role of Emotions in Organizational Behaviour*, San Francisco, CA: Jossey-Bass.
49. Sundstrom, E. (1986) *Work Places: The Psychology of the Physical Environment in Offices and Factories*, Cambridge: Cambridge University Press.
50. Gladwell, M. (2000) *The Tipping Point: How Little Things Can Make a Big Difference*, London: ABACUS, p. 183.
51. Becker, F. and Steele, F. (1995) *Workplace by Design: Mapping the High-performance Workscape*, San Francisco, CA: Jossey-Bass.
52. Korda, M. (1975) *Power! How to Get It, How to Use It*, New York: Random.
53. Ornstein, S. (1989) 'Impression management', in R. Giacaolone, and P. Rosenfeld, (eds) *Impression Management in the Organization*, Hillsdale, NJ: Lawrence Erlbaum.
54. Beck, C. (1999) *Managerial Communication: Bridging Theory and Practice*, Upper Saddle River, NJ: Prentice-Hall.
55. Ornstein, op. cit.
56. Ellis, P. (1986) 'Functional, aesthetic, and symbolic aspects of office lighting', in J.D. Wineman (ed.) *Behavioral Issues in Office Design*, New York: Van Nostrand Reinhold.
57. Andersen, op. cit.
58. de Craen, A.J., Roos, P.J., de Vries, A.L. and Kleijnen, J. (1996) 'Effect of colour of drug: systematic review of perceived effect of drugs and of their effectiveness', *British Medical Journal*, 313: 1624–6.
59. Smith, E. and Mackie, D. (2000) *Social Psychology*, 2nd edition, Philadelphia, PA: Psychology Press.
60. Wilson, G. and Nias, D. (1999) 'Beauty can't be beat', in L. Guerrero and J. DeVito (eds) *The Nonverbal Communication Reader: Classic and Contemporary Readings*, Prospect Heights, IL: Waveland Press.
61. Adler, R. and Towne, N. (1996) *Looking Out, Looking In*, 8th edition, Fort Worth: Harcourt Brace.
62. Barnard, M. (2002) *Fashion as Communication*, 2nd edition, London: Routledge, p. 29.
63. Grattan, G. (1997) 'Telegraph Education', *Belfast Telegraph*, 1 July, p. 18.
64. Baird, M. (2002) 'Smart set say suits are back', *Sunday Times Public Appointments Section*, 24 February, p. 9.

65. Baird, ibid.
66. Leigh, T.W. and Summers, J.O. (2002) 'An initial evaluation of industrial buyers' impressions of salespersons' nonverbal cues', *The Journal of Personal Selling & Sales Management*, 22: 41–53.
67. Molloy, J. (1975) *Dress for Success*, New York: Peter H. Wyden.
68. Golden, N. (1986) *Dress Right for Business*, New York: McGraw-Hill.
69. Molloy, J. (1977) *The Women's Dress for Success Book*, Chicago, IL: Follett.
70. Sundaram, D.S. and Webster, C. (2000) 'The role of nonverbal communication in service encounters', *The Journal of Services Marketing*, 14: 378–85.
71. Trethewey, op. cit.
72. Wallach, J. (1986) *Looks that Work*, New York: Viking Penguin.
73. Hamilton, C. and Parker, C. (1990) *Communicating for Results*, Belmont, CA: Wadsworth.
74. Fulfer, M. (2001) 'Nonverbal communication: how to read what's plain as the nose ... or eyelid ... or chin ... on their faces', *Journal of Organizational Excellence*, 20: 19–27 (p. 19).
75. Goffman E. (1959) *The Presentation of Self in Everyday Life*, New York: Anchor Books.

3 They could be persuaded: using your managerial influence

1. Forgas, J. and Williams, K. (2001) 'Social influence: introduction and overview', in J. Forgas and K. Williams (eds) *Social Influence: Direct and Indirect Processes*, Philadelphia: Psychology Press, p. 4.
2. Bragg, M. (1996) *Reinventing Influence: How to Get Things Done in a World Without Authority*, London: Pitman.
3. Morris, M., Podolny, J. and Ariel, S. (2001) 'Culture, norms, and obligations: cross-national differences in patterns of interpersonal norms and felt obligations toward coworkers', in W. Wosinska, R. Cialdini, D. Barrett and J. Reykowski (eds) *The Practice of Social Influence in Multiple Cultures*, Mahwah, NJ: Lawrence Erlbaum, p. 98.
4. Keys, B. and Case, T. (2003) 'How to become an influential manager', in R. Lewicki, D. Saunders, J. Minton and B. Barry (eds) *Negotiation: Readings, Exercise and Cases*, 4th edition, New York: McGraw-Hill, p. 202.
5. Pearson, J. and Nelson, P. (2000) *An Introduction to Human Communication: Understanding and Sharing*, 5th edition, Boston: McGraw-Hill, p. 430.
6. Hargie, O. and Dickson, D. (2004) *Skilled Interpersonal Communication: Research, Theory and Practice*, London: Routledge.
7. Hsiung, R. and Bagozzi, R. (2003) 'Validating the relationship qualities of influence and persuasion with the family social relations model', *Human Communication Research*, 29: 81–110.
8. Allen, M. and Stiff, J. (1998) 'An analysis of the sleeper effect', in M. Allen and R. Preiss (eds) *Persuasion: Advances Through Meta-analysis*, Cresskill, NJ: Hampton Press.
9. Peau, M., Szabo, E., Anderson, J., Morrill, J., Zubric, J. and Wan, H. (2001) 'The role and impact of affect in the process of resistance to persuasion', *Human Communication Research*, 27: 216–52.
10. Pearson, J. and Nelson, P. (2000) *An Introduction to Human Communication: Understanding and Sharing*, 5th edition, Boston: McGraw-Hill.
11. McGuire, W.J. (1981) 'Theoretical foundations of campaigns', in R. Rice and W. Paisley (eds) *Public Communication Campaigns*, Beverly Hills: Sage.

12. Turner, J. (1991) *Social Influence*, Buckingham: Open University.
13. Kipnis, D. and Schmidt, S. (1990) 'The language of persuasion', in I. Asherman and S. Asherman (eds) *The Negotiation Sourcebook*, Amherst, MA: Human Resource Development Press, p. 50.
14. Buchanan, D. and Huczynski, A. (1997) *Organizational Behaviour*, 3rd edition, London: Prentice Hall, p. 695.
15. Allen, M. and Preiss, R. (eds) (1998) *Persuasion: Advances Through Meta-analysis*, Cresskill, NJ: Hampton Press.
16. Allen, M. (1998) 'Comparing the persuasive effectiveness of one- and two-sided messages', in M. Allen and R. Preiss (eds) *Persuasion: Advances Through Meta-analysis*, Cresskill, NJ: Hampton Press.
17. Allen, M., Bruflat, R., Fucilla, R., Kramer, M., McKellips, S., Ryan, D. and Spiegelhoff, M. (2000) 'Testing the persuasiveness of evidence: combining narrative and statistical forms', *Communication Research Reports*, 17: 331–6.
18. Cruz, M. (1998) 'Explicit and implicit conclusions in persuasive messages', in M. Allen and R. Preiss (eds) *Persuasion: Advances Through Meta-analysis*, Cresskill, NJ: Hampton Press.
19. Barry, B. and Bateman, T. (1992) 'Perceptions of influence in managerial dyads: the role of hierarchy, media and tactics', *Human Relations*, 45: 555–74.
20. Lewicki, R., Barry, B., Saunders, D. and Minton, J. (2003) *Negotiation*, 4th edition, Boston, MA: McGraw-Hill, p. 208.
21. O'Keefe, D. and Hale, S. (2001) 'An odds-ratio-based meta-analysis of research on the door-in-the-face influence strategy', *Communication Reports*, 14: 31–8.
22. O'Keefe, D. (2002) *Persuasion: Theory and Research*, 2nd edition, Thousand Oaks, CA: Sage.
23. Dawson, P. (2004) 'Managing change: communication and political process', in D. Tourish and O. Hargie (eds) *Key Issues in Organisational Communication*, London: Routledge.
24. Dawson, P. (2003) *Understanding Organizational Change: The Contemporary Experience of People at Work*, London: Paul Chapman Publishing.
25. Cialdini, R. (2001) *Influence: Science and Practice*, Boston: Allyn and Bacon.
26. Morley, I. (1997) 'Negotiating and bargaining', in O. Hargie (ed.) *The Handbook of Communication Skills*, 2nd edition, London: Routledge.
27. Ohme, R. (2001) 'Social influence in media: culture and antismoking advertising', in W. Wosinska, R. Cialdini, D. Barrett and J. Reykowski (eds) *The Practice of Social Influence in Multiple Cultures*, Mahwah, NJ: Lawrence Erlbaum.
28. Cialdini, R. (2001) 'Harnessing the science of persuasion', *Harvard Business Review*, October: 70–80.
29. Gibb-Clark, M. (1997) 'People with "hot skills" can "call the shots" on wages, survey finds', *The Globe and Mail*, October 29, B6.
30. Forgas, J. 2001 'On being moody but influential: the role of affect in social influence strategies', in J. Forgas and K. Williams (eds) *Social Influence: Direct and Indirect Processes*, Philadelphia: Psychology Press.
31. Vaes, J., Paladino, M. and Leyens, J. (2002) 'The lost-mail: prosocial reactions induced by uniquely human emotions', *British Journal of Social Psychology*, 41: 521–34.
32. Mongeau, P. (1998) 'Another look at fear-arousing persuasive appeals', in M. Allen and R. Preiss (eds) *Persuasion: Advances Through Meta-analysis*, Cresskill, NJ: Hampton Press.

33. Hargie, O. and Dickson, D. (2004) op. cit.
34. Davey, K. and Liefhooghe, P. (2003) 'Voice and power: a critical investigation of accounts of bullying in organizations', in A. Schorr, W. Campbell and M. Schenk (eds) *Communication Research and Media Science in Europe*, Berlin: Mouton de Gruyter.
35. Lewicki, R., Barry, B., Saunders, D. and Minton, J. (2003) op. cit.
36. Garko, M.G. (1992) 'Physician executives' use of influence strategies: gaining compliance from superiors who communicate in attractive and unattractive styles', *Health Communication*, 4: 137–54.
37. Craig, O. (1997) 'Focus', *Sunday Telegraph*, 29 June, p. 21.
38. Iyengar, S. and Brockner, J. (2001) 'Cultural differences in self and the impact of personal and social influences', in W. Wosinska, R. Cialdini, D. Barrett and J. Reykowski (eds) *The Practice of Social Influence in Multiple Cultures*, Mahwah, NJ: Lawrence Erlbaum.
39. Dillard, J. and Peck, E. (2001) 'Persuasion and the structure of affect: dual systems and discrete emotions as complementary models', *Human Communication Research*, 27: 38–68.
40. Kleinke, C. (1986) *Meeting and Understanding People*, New York: Freeman, p. 179.
41. Hayes, N. (1998) *Foundations of Psychology*, Walton-on-Thames, Surrey: Thomas Nelson.
42. Bohner, G., Ruder, M. and Erb, H. (2002) 'When expertise backfires: contrast and assimilation effects in persuasion', *British Journal of Social Psychology*, 41: 495–519.
43. Clampitt, P. (2001) *Communicating for Managerial Effectiveness*, 2nd edition, Thousand Oaks, CA: Sage.
44. Di Blasi, Z. (2003) 'The crack in the biomedical box', *The Psychologist*, 16: 72–5.
45. Dixon, M. and Sweeney, M. (2001) *The Human Effect in Medicine: Theory, Research and Practice*, Abingdon, Oxon: Radcliffe Medical Press.
46. 'Workers prefer title to pay', *Belfast Telegraph*, 18 April, 2000, p. 9.
47. Daily Telegraph Correspondent (2002) 'Grander job titles but no more pay', *The Daily Telegraph*, 7 March, p. 15.
48. Cialdini, R. (2001) *Influence: Science and Practice*, op. cit.
49. Barrow, B. (2002) '£3 million wasted as Royal Mail makes comeback', *The Daily Telegraph*, 14 June, p. 6.
50. Sapsted, D. (2002) 'Firm's £1 m search for a 10-minute name', *The Daily Telegraph*, 1 March, p. 13.
51. Bragg, M. (1996) op. cit.
52. Schweiger, D. and Denisi, A. (1991) 'Communicating with employees: a longitudinal field experiment', *Academy of Management Journal*, 34: 110–35.
53. Bennett, H. (1996) 'Communicating change – a case for multiple method's, *Corporate Communications: An International Journal*, 1: 32–9.
54. Hargie, O. and Tourish, D. (eds) (2000) *Handbook of Communication Audits for Organisations*, Routledge: London.
55. Tourish, D. and Wohlforth, T. (2000) *On the Edge: Political Cults Right and Left*, Amherst, NY: M.E. Sharpe, p. 17.
56. Cialdini, R. and Rhoads, K. (2001) 'Human behavior and the marketplace', *Marketing Research*, Fall: 9–13.
57. Little, A. and Perett, D. (2002) 'Putting beauty back in the eye of the beholder', *The Psychologist*, 15: 28–32.

58. Hargie, O. (1997) 'Interpersonal communication: a theoretical framework', in O. Hargie (ed.) *The Handbook of Communication Skills*, 2nd edition, London: Routledge.
59. Duck, S. (1995) 'Repelling the study of attraction', *The Psychologist*, 8: 60–3.
60. Feeley, T. and Barnett, G. (1997) 'Predicting employee turnover from communication networks', *Human Communication Research*, 23: 370–87.
61. Cialdini, R. (2001) *Influence: Science and Practice*, op. cit., p. 176.
62. Hargie, O. and Dickson, D. (2004) op. cit.
63. Rackham, N. and Morgan, T. (1977) *Behaviour Analysis in Training*, London: McGraw-Hill, p. 233.
64. Smith, D. and Higgins, S. (1997) 'Call me "Sir", demand British bosses', *The Sunday Times*, July 13.
65. Foot, H. (1997) 'Humour and laughter', in O. Hargie (ed.) *The Handbook of Communication Skills*, London: Routledge.
66. Meyer J. (2000) 'Humor as a double-edged sword: four functions of humor in communication', *Communication Theory*, 10: 310–31.
67. Campbell, K., Martin, M. and Wanzer, M. (2001) 'Employee perceptions of manager humor orientation, assertiveness, responsiveness, approach/avoidance strategies, and satisfaction', *Communication Research Reports*, 18: 67–74.
68. Kipnis, D. and Schmidt, S. (1990) 'The language of persuasion', in I. Asherman and S. Asherman (eds) *The Negotiation Sourcebook*, Amherst, MA: Human Resource Development Press.
69. Morris, M., Podolny, J. and Ariel, S. (2001) 'Culture, norms, and obligations: cross-national differences in patterns of interpersonal norms and felt obligations toward coworkers', in W. Wosinska, R. Cialdini, D. Barrett and J. Reykowski (eds) *The Practice of Social Influence in Multiple Cultures*, Mahwah, NJ: Lawrence Erlbaum.
70. Orpen, C. (2000) 'The interactive effects of role uncertainty and accountability on employee use of upward influence tactics', *Psychology: A Journal of Human Behavior*, 37: 2–4.
71. Krone, K. (1992) 'A comparison of organizational, structural, and relationship effects on subordinates' upward influence choices', *Communication Quarterly*, 40: 1–15.
72. Strack, F. and Mussweiler, T. (2001) 'Resisting influence: judgmental correction and its goals', in J. Forgas and K. Williams (eds) *Social Influence: Direct and Indirect Processes*, Philadelphia: Psychology Press, p. 208.
73. Mitchell, M. (2000) 'Able but not motivated: the relative effects of happy and sad mood on persuasive message processing', *Communication Monographs*, 67: 215–26.
74. Meyers-Levy, J. and Malaviya, P. (1999) 'Consumers' processing of persuasive advertisements: an integrative framework of persuasion theories', *Journal of Marketing*, 63: 45–60.
75. Huczynski, A. (1996) *Influencing Within Organizations*, London: Prentice Hall.

4 Let's get together: teams at work

1. Zaiger Roberts, V. (1994) 'The organization of work: contributions from open systems theory', in A. Obholzer and V. Zaiger Roberts (eds) *The Unconscious at Work*, London: Routledge.

2. Orsburn, J. and Moran, L. (2000) *The New Self-Directed Work teams: Mastering the Challenge*, New York: McGraw Hill.
3. Katzenbach, J. and Smith, D. (1993) *The Wisdom of Teams*, Boston: Harvard Business School Press.
4. Glassop, L. (2002) 'The organizational benefits of teams', *Human Relations*, 55: 225–49.
5. Bacon, N. and Blyton, P. (2000) 'High road and low road teamworking: perceptions of management rationalises and organizational and human resource outcomes', *Human Relations*, 53: 1425–58.
6. Ashmos, D. and Nathan, M. (2002) 'Team sense-making: a mental model for navigating uncharted territories', *Journal of Managerial Issues*, 14: 198–217.
7. Knights, D. and McCabe, D. (2000) 'Bewitched, bothered and bewildered: the meaning and experience of teamworking for employees in an automobile company', *Human Relations*, 53: 1481–517.
8. Sprigg, C., Jackson, P. and Parker, S. (2000) 'Production teamworking: the importance of interdependence and autonomy for employee strain and satisfaction', *Human Relations*, 53: 1519–43.
9. Glassop, L. (2002) op. cit.
10. Mueller, F., Proctor, S. and Buchanan, D. (2000) 'Teamworking in its context(s): antecedents, nature and dimensions', *Human Relations*, 53: 1387–424.
11. Tourish, D. (1997) 'Transforming internal corporate communications: the power of symbolic gestures and barriers to change', *Corporate Communications: An International Journal*, 2: 109–16.
12. Reichfield, F. (2001) *Loyalty Rules: How Today's Leaders Build Lasting Relationships*, Boston: Harvard Business School Press.
13. Fukuyama, F. (1995) *Trust: The Social Virtues and the Creation of Prosperity*, London: Hamish Hamilton.
14. D'Aprix, R. (1996) *Communicating for Change*, San Francisco: Jossey-Bass.
15. Tourish, D. and Hargie, O. (2004) 'The communication consequences of downsizing trust, loyalty and commitment', in D. Tourish and O. Hargie (eds) *Key Issues in Organisational Communication*, London: Routledge.
16. Pfeffer, J. (1998) *The Human Equation*, Boston: Harvard Business School Press.
17. Banker, R., Field, J., Schroeder, R. and Sinha, K. (1996) 'Impact of work teams on manufacturing performance: a longitudinal field study', *Academy of Management Journal*, 39: 867–90.
18. Pfeffer (1998) op. cit.
19. Kanter, R. (1983) *The Change Masters: Innovation and Entrepreneurship in the American Corporation*, New York: Simon and Schuster.
20. Parker, G. (1990) *Team Players and Teamwork: The New Competitive Business Strategy*, San Francisco, CA: Jossey-Bass.
21. Kharbana, O. and Stallworthy, E. (1990) *Project Teams: The Human Factor*, Oxford: Blackwell.
22. Arnott, M. (1987) 'Effective employee communication', in N. Hart (ed.) *Effective Corporate Relations*, London: McGraw-Hill.
23. Pappa, M. and Tracy, K. (1988) 'Communication indices of employee performance with new technology', *Communication Research*, 15: 524–44.
24. Kirkman, B., Rosen, B., Gibson, C., Tesluk, P. and McPherson, S. (2002) 'Five challenges to virtual team success: lessons from Sabre, Inc.', *Academy of Management Executive*, 16: 67–79.

25. Elkins, T. (2000) 'Virtual teams: connect and collaborate', *IIE Solutions*, 32: 26–32.
26. Lipnack, J. and Stamps, J. (2000) *Virtual Teams: People Working Across Boundaries With Technology*, 2nd edition, New York: Wiley.
27. Morris, S. and Johnson McManus, D. (2002) 'Information infrastructure: centrality in the agile organization', *Information Systems Management*, 19: 8–12.
28. Kirkman *et al.*, op. cit.
29. Hackman, J. (2002) *Leading Teams: Setting the Stage for Great Performances*, Boston: Harvard Business School Press. Kirkman *et al.*, op. cit.
30. Coles, M. (1997) 'Firm plays it by ear', *Sunday Times*, 19 October, p. 28.
31. Tuckman, B. and Jensen, M. (1977) 'Stages of small group development revisited', *Group and Organization Studies*, 2: 419–27.
32. Alper, S., Tjosvold, D. and Law, K. (2000) 'Conflict management, efficacy, and performance in organizational teams', *Personnel Psychology*, 53: 625–42.
33. Brown, K., Klastorin, T. and Valuzzi, J. (1990) 'Project performance and the liability of group harmony', *IEEE Trans Eng Management*, 37: 117–25.
34. Peters, T. and Austin, N. (1985) *A Passion for Excellence*, Glasgow: Collins.
35. Katzenbach and Smith, op. cit.
36. Hayes, N. (1997) *Successful Team Management*, London: Thomson Business Press.
37. Hackman, J. (2002) *Leading Teams: Setting the Stage for Great Performances*, Boston: Harvard Business School Press.
38. Hackman, ibid., p. 41.
39. Cited by Hackman, ibid., p. 63.
40. Hackman, ibid., pp. 116–22.
41. Meyer, C. (1994) 'How the right measures help teams excel', *Harvard Business Review*, May: 95–103.
42. Quoted in Evans, R. (1997) 'Hollow the leader', *Report on Business Magazine*, November, p. 60.
43. Hargie, O. and Dickson, D. (2004) *Skilled Interpersonal Communication: Research, Theory and Practice*, 4th edition, London: Routledge.
44. 'Boss buys workers free drinks', *Newsletter*, 30 April 1998, p. 13.
45. O'Reilly, C. and Pfeffer, J. (2000) *Hidden Value: How Great Companies Achieve Extraordinary Results with Ordinary People*, Boston: Harvard Business School Press.
46. Adapted from Whetten, D. and Cameron, K. (2001) *Developing Management Skills*, 5th Edition, New York: Prentice Hall.
47. Brown, R. (2000) *Group Processes*, 2nd edition, Oxford: Blackwell.
48. Janis, I. (1982) *Groupthink*, 2nd edition, Boston: Houghton Mifflin.
49. Tourish, D. and Wohlforth, T. (2000) *On the Edge: Political Cults, Right and Left*, New York: Sharpe.
50. Steiner, I. (1972) *Group Process and Productivity*, New York: Academic Press.
51. Discussed in Brown (2000) op. cit., pp. 173–4.
52. Ingham, A., Levinger, G., Graves, J. and Peckham, V. (1974) 'The Ringlemann effect: studies of group size and group performance', *Journal of Experimental Social Psychology*, 10: 371–84.
53. Hambrick, D. (1995) 'Fragmentation and the other problems CEOs have with their top management teams', *California Management Review*, 37: 110–27.

54. Katzenbach, J. (1997) 'The myth of the top management team', *Harvard Business Review*, 75: 83–91.
55. Parker, S., Wall, T. and Jackson, P. (1997) ' "That's not my job": developing flexible employee work orientations', *Academy of Management Journal*, 40: 899–930.
56. Yeatts, D. and Hyten, C. (1998) *High Performing Self Managed Work Teams*, Thousand Oaks, CA: Sage.
57. Kirkman, B. and Rosen, B. (2000) 'Powering up teams', *Organizational Dynamics*, Winter: 48–65.
58. Sinclair, A. (1992) 'The tyranny of a team ideology', *Organization Studies*, 13: 611–26.
59. Geary, J. and Dobbins, A. (2001) 'Teamworking: a new dynamic in the pursuit of management control', *Human Resource Management Journal*, 11: 3–23.

5 Steering the way: leading meetings that work

1. Seibold, D. (1979) 'Making meetings more successful: plans, formats, and procedures for group problem solving', *Journal of Business Communication*, 16: 3–20.
2. Mintzberg, H. (1973) *The Nature of Managerial Work*, New York: Harper and Row.
3. Lynn, J. (2001) 'Managing meetings', *Commercial Law Bulletin*, 16: 12–13 (p. 12).
4. Carney, K. (1999) 'Making meetings work', *Harvard Management Update No. U9910C*, Boston: Harvard Business School Publishing.
5. Smith, D. (1997) 'Managers lack proper skills', *The Sunday Times (Business Section)*, 14 September, p. 12.
6. Council for Excellence in Management and Leadership (2002) *Managers and Leaders: Raising Our Game. Summary Report*. London: Council for Excellence in Management and Leadership, p. 3.
7. Doh, J. (2003) 'Can leadership be taught? Perspectives from management educators', *Academy of Management Learning and Education*, 2: 54–67.
8. Essery, E. (2002) 'Reflecting on leadership', *Works Management*, July: 54–7.
9. Article, The Economist (2001) 'Churning at the top: the nature of corporate leadership', *The Economist*, 7 March.
10. Kets de Vries, M. (2001) *The Leadership Mystique*, London: Prentice Hall.
11. Collins, J. (2001) *Good to Great*, London: Random House Business Books (p. 21).
12. Grint, K. (2001) *Literature Review on Leadership* (Commissioned by the Performance and Innovation Unit of the Cabinet Office), Oxford: Templeton College.
13. Cooper, G. (2001) 'Wanted: leaders to transform public services', *Sunday Times (Business Section)*, 13 January, p. 17.
14. Mintzberg, H. (1973) *The Nature of Managerial Work*, New York: Harper and Row.
15. Wilke, H. and Meertens, R. (1994) *Group Performance*, London: Routledge.
16. Pfeffer, J. (1992) 'Understanding power in organizations', *California Management Review*, 34: 29–50 (p. 41).
17. Kotter, J. (1988) *The Leadership Factor*, New York: Free Press, p. 5.

18. Messe, L., Kerr, N. and Sattler, D. (1992) '"But some animals are more equal than others": The supervisor as a privileged status in group contexts', in S. Worchel, W. Wood, and J. Simpson (eds) *Group Process and Productivity*, London: Sage.
19. Brown, R. (2000) *Group Processes*, 2nd edition, Oxford: Blackwell.
20. Yukl, G., op. cit.
21. Brooks, I. (2003) *Organisational Behaviour: Individuals, Groups and Organisation,* 2nd edition, London: Prentice-Hall.
22. Yukl, G. (2002) *Leadership*, 5th edition, London: Pearson Education
23. Scase, R. and Goffee, R. (1989) *The Reluctant Managers*, London: Unwin-Hyman.
24. Harvard Business Review (2001) 'All in a day's work', December: 55–66.
25. McKee, L., Mauthner, N. and Galilee, J. (2001) 'Corporate men in late middle age: re-assessing work and life', University of Aberdeen: Department of Management Studies.
26. Collins, J. and Porras, J. (2000) *Built to Last*, 3rd edition, London: Random House Books.
27. Ashmos, D. and Duchon, D. (2000) 'Spirituality at work: a conceptualisation and measure', *Journal of Management Inquiry*, 9: 134–45.
28. Pfeffer, J. (2001) 'Business and the spirit: management practices that sustain values', Research Paper No. 1713, Stanford University: Graduate School of Business.
29. Collins, J. and Porras, J. (1996) 'Building your company's vision', *Harvard Business Review*, September–October: 65–78 (p. 76).
30. Doucouliagos, C. (1995) 'Worker participation and productivity in labor-managed and participatory capitalist forms: a meta-analysis', *Industrial and Labor Relations Review*, 49: 58–77.
31. Tourish, D. and Hargie, O. (1998) 'Communication between managers and staff in the NHS: trends and prospects', *British Journal of Management*, 9: 53–71.
32. Tropman, J. (2003) *Making Meetings Work Even Better: Achieving High Quality Group Decisions*, London: Sage.
33. Evans, R. (1997) 'Hollow the leader', *Report on Business Magazine*, November: 66.
34. Napier, R. and Gershenfeld, M. (1989) *Groups: Theory and Experience*, Dallas: Houghton Mifflin.
35. Whetten, D. and Cameron, K. (2001) *Developing Management Skills*, 5th edition, London: Prentice-Hall.
36. Carney, K., op. cit., p. 3.
37. Huber, G. (1980) *Managerial Decision Making*, Glenview, IL: Scott Foresman.
38. Rackman, N. and Morgan, T. (1977) *Behavior Analysis in Training*, Maidenhead: McGraw-Hill.
39. Hartley, P. and Bruckman, C. (2002) *Business Communication*, London: Routledge.
40. Craumer, M. (2001) 'The effective meeting: a checklist for success', *Harvard Management Communication Letter No. C0103A*, Boston: Harvard Business School Publishing.
41. Hattersley, M. (1996) 'Checklist for conducting a perfect meeting', *Harvard Management Update No. U9607D*, Boston: Harvard Business School Publishing.
42. Ostrander, S., Schroeder, L. and Ostrander, N. (1994) *Superlearning 2000: New Triple-fast Ways You Can Learn, Earn, and Succeed in the 21st Century*, New York: Dell.

43. Pattison, S. (2001) 'Staff meetings: an opportunity for accelerated training of employees', *Journal of Workplace Learning*, 13: 172–8.
44. Hargie, O. and Dickson, D. (2004) *Skilled Interpersonal Communication*, 4th edition, London: Routledge.
45. Harvard Management Communication Letter (2000) *Coping with conflict*, Reprint No. C0011A, Boston: Harvard Business School Publishing.
46. Jarboe, S. (1996) 'Procedures for enhancing group decision making', in R. Hirokawa and M. Poole (eds) *Communication and Group Decision making*, 2nd edition, London: Sage, p. 356.
47. Hawkins, C. (1997) *First Aid For Meetings: Quick Fixes and Major Repairs for Running Effective Meetings*, New York: Bookpartners.
48. This and the next two suggestions are discussed in detail in Krattenmaker, T. (2000) Before and after the meeting, *Harvard Management Communication Letter, No. C0010A*, Boston: Harvard Business School Publishing.
49. Smythe, J. (2001) 'The chief entertainment officer: the new CEO', *E-Preview*, 1: 1–9.
50. Bennis, W. (1989) *On Becoming a Leader*, London: Century Business.
51. Goleman, D., Boyatzis, R. and McKee, A. (2001) 'Primal Leadership', *Harvard Business Review*, December: 42–51.
52. Manzoni, J. and Barsoux, J. (2002) *The Set-Up-To-Fail Syndrome*, Boston: Harvard Business School Press.

6 That silver-tongued devil ... making presentations matter

1. Moody, J., Stewart, B. and Bolt-Lee, C. (2002) 'Showing the skilled business graduate: expanding the tool kit', *Business Communication Quarterly*, 65: 21–36.
2. Maes, J., Weldy, T. and Icenogle, M. (1997) 'A managerial perspective: oral communication competency is most important for business students in the workplace', *The Journal of Business Communication*, 34: 67–80.
3. Hartley, P. and Bruckmann, C.G. (2002) *Business Communication*, London: Routledge.
4. Cosnett, G. (1990) 'A survival guide to public speaking', *Training and Development Journal*, 44: 15–19.
5. Guirdham, M. (2002) *Interactive Behaviour at Work*, 3rd edition, Harlow: Prentice Hall.
6. Sherman, R. (2002) '10 presentation skills top executives live by', *Business Credit*, 104: 46–7.
7. Pullin, J. (2002) 'Unaccustomed as I am ...', *Professional Engineering*, 15: 43.
8. Aziz, K. (1999) 'How to wow an audience', *Management Today*, August: 56–9 (p. 56).
9. Ibid., p. 59.
10. Janner, G. (1989) *Janner on Presentation: An Essential Guide to the Theory, Tricks and Techniques of Business Presentation*, London: Business Books, p. 4.
11. Hamilton, C. and Parker, C. (1999) *Communicating for Results: A Guide for Business and the Professions*, Belmont: Wadsworth.
12. Mandel, S. (1987) *Effective Presentation Skills: A Practical Guide for Better Speaking*, Los Altos, CA: Crisp Publications.

13. DeVito, J. (1990) *The Elements of Public Speaking*, New York: Harper and Row.
14. Simon, T. (2001) 'Public speaking isn't natural, and your body knows it', *Presentations*, 15: 8.
15. Aziz, op. cit.
16. McCurry, P. (2002) 'Stand and deliver', *Director*, 54: 23.
17. Mandel. S., op. cit.
18. McCarthy, P. and Hatcher, C. (1996) *Speaking Persuasively*, St. Leonards, NSW: Allen and Unwin.
19. Cristina Stuart cited in Pullin op. cit., p. 43.
20. Pullin, op. cit.
21. Zigelstein, T. (2002) 'Developing effective presentation skills', *CMA Management*, 76: 8.
22. Simons, C. and Naylor-Stables, B. (1997) *Effective Communication for Managers: Getting Your Message Across*, London: Cassell.
23. Williams, G.A. and Miller, R.B. (2002) 'Change the way you persuade', *Harvard Business Review*, 80: 65–73.
24. Williams and Miller, op. cit.
25. Baker, G. (2001) 'Lasting impressions', *New Zealand Management*, 48: 74–6.
26. Davies, J.W. (2001) *Communication Skills: A Guide for Engineering and Applied Science Students*, Harlow: Prentice Hall, p. 117.
27. Daniels, L. (1999) 'Introducing technology into the classroom: PowerPoint as a first step', *Journal of Computing in Higher Education*, 10: 42–56.
28. O'Hair, D. and Friedrich, G. (1998) *Strategic Communication in Business and the Professions*, 3rd edition, Boston: Houghton Mifflin.
29. Chaney, L. and Green, G. (2002) 'Presenter behaviours: actions often speak louder than words', *SuperVision*, 63: 17–19.
30. Downing, J. and Garmon, C. (2002) 'A guide to implementing PowerPoint and overhead LCD projectors in communication classes', *American Journal of Communication*, 5, http://www. acjournal.org/holdings/vol5/iss2/articles/ guide.pdf.
31. Baker, op. cit.
32. Simons and Naylor-Stables, op. cit.
33. Chaney and Green, op. cit.
34. Pathak, op. cit.
35. Sherman, op. cit., p. 46.
36. O'Hair, op. cit.
37. DeVito, J. (1990) *The Elements of Public Speaking*, New York: Harper and Row.
38. Tiersma, P. (2001) *The Problem of Jury Instructions*, Paper presented at the Annual Meeting of the American Association for the Advancement of Science, San Francisco, February.
39. Hargie, O. and Dickson, D. (2004) *Skilled Interpersonal Communication*: Research Theory and Practice, 4th edition, London: Routledge.
40. Steven, M. (1989) *Improve your Interpersonal Skills: A Complete Action Kit*, London: Kogan Page.
41. Brown, G. and Atkins, M. (1997) 'Explaining', in O. Hargie (ed.) *The Handbook of Communication Skills*, London: Routledge.
42. Turk, C. (1985) *Effective Speaking: Communicating in Speech*, London: Spon.
43. Chaney and Green, op. cit.
44. Dickson, D., Hargie, O. and Morrow, N. (1997) *Communication Skills Training for Health Professionals*, 2nd edition, London: Chapman and Hall.

45. Morgan, N. (2001) 'The kinesthetic speaker: putting action into words', *Harvard Business Review*, 79: 113–20.
46. Brosius, H. and Bathfelt, A. (1994) 'The utility of exemplars in persuasive communication', *Communication Research*, 21: 48–78.
47. Chaney and Green, op. cit.
48. Simons, op. cit., p. 8.
49. Conradi, M. and Hall, R. (2001) *That Presentation Sensation*, Upper Saddle River, NJ: Prentice Hall.
50. Hartley and Bruckmann, op. cit.
51. Blundel, op. cit.
52. Baker, op. cit.
53. Nadeau, R., Jablonski, C. and Gardner, G. (1993) *Speaking Effectively in Public Settings*, Lanham, MD: University Press of America.

7 We can work it out: negotiating and bargaining

1. Simons, T. and Tripp, T.M. (2003) 'The negotiation checklist', in R.J. Lewicki, D.M. Saunders, J.W. Minton and B. Barry (eds) *Negotiation: Readings, Exercises, and Cases*, Boston: McGraw-Hill, p. 50.
2. O'Hair, D., Friedrich, G.W. and Shaver, L.D. (1998) *Strategic Communication in Business and the Professions*, 3rd edition, Boston: Houghton Mifflin Company, p. 372.
3. Fraser, C. and Zarkada-Fraser, A. (2002) 'An exploratory investigation into cultural awareness and approach to negotiation of Greek, Russian and British managers', *European Business Review*, 14: 111–27.
4. Wilmot, W.W. and Hocker, J.L. (1998) *Interpersonal Conflict*, 5th edition, Boston: McGraw Hill, p. 2.
5. Thomas, K. (1976), 'Conflict and conflict management', in M. Dunnette (ed.) *Handbook of Industrial and Organizational Psychology*, Chicago: Rand McNally.
6. Lawyer, J. and Katz, N. (1985), *Communication and Conflict Management Skills*, Dubuque, Iowa: Kendall/Hunt.
7. Darling, J.R. and Walker, W.E. (2001) 'Effective conflict management: use of the behavioural style model', *Leadership & Organizational Development Journal*, 22: 230–42 (p. 231).
8. Fraser and Zarkada-Fraser, op. cit., p. 114.
9. LePoole, S. (1995) *Never Take No for an Answer: A Guide to Successful Negotiating*, London: Kogan Page.
10. Thompson, L. (1992), 'Negotiation behaviour and outcomes: empirical evidence and theoretical issues', *Psychological Bulletin*, 108: 515–32.
11. Lewicki, R.J., Saunders, D.M. and Minton, J.W. (2001) *Essentials of Negotiation*, 2nd edition, Boston: McGraw-Hill.
12. Rubin, J.Z. (2003) 'Some wise and mistaken assumptions about conflict and negotiation', in R.J. Lewicki, D.M. Saunders, J.W. Minton and B. Barry (eds) *Negotiation: Readings, Exercises, and Cases*, Boston: McGraw-Hill.
13. Brandenburger, A.M. and Nalebuff, B.J. (2003) 'The right game: use game theory to shape strategy', in R.J. Lewicki, D.M. Saunders, J.W. Minton and B. Barry (eds) *Negotiation: Readings, Exercises, and Cases*, Boston: McGraw-Hill.
14. Ibid., p. 67.
15. Brandenburger, A. and Nalebuff, B. (1996) *Co-opetition*, New York: Doubleday.

16. Berlew, D. (1990), 'How to increase your influence', in I. Asherman and S. Asherman (eds) *The Negotiating Sourcebook,* Amherst, MA: Human Resource Development Press, p. 33.
17. McRae, B. (1998) *Negotiating and Influencing Skills*, Thousand Oaks, CA: Sage, p. 2.
18. Woo, H.S., Wilson, D. and Liu, J. (2001) 'Gender impact on Chinese negotiation: "some key issues for Western negotiators"', *Women in Management Review*, 16: 349–56 (p. 350).
19. Morley, I. (1981) 'Negotiating and bargaining', in M. Argyle (ed.) *Social Skills and Work*, London: Methuen.
20. Mnookin R., Peppet S. and Tulumello, A. (1996) 'The tension between empathy and assertiveness', *Negotiation Journal,* 12: 217–30.
21. Rubin, op. cit., p. 135.
22. Woo *et al.*, op. cit., p. 352.
23. Savage, G.T., Blair, J.D. and Sorenson, R.L. (2003) 'Consider both relationship and substance when negotiating strategically', in R.J. Lewicki, D.M. Saunders, J.W. Minton and B. Barry (eds) *Negotiation: Readings, Exercises, and Cases*, Boston: McGraw-Hill.
24. Wilmot and Hocker, op. cit.
25. Webber, A.M. (2003) 'How to get them to show you the money', in R.J. Lewicki, D.M. Saunders, J.W. Minton and B. Barry (eds) *Negotiation: Readings, Exercises, and Cases*, Boston: McGraw-Hill, p. 7.
26. Dawson, R. (1995) *Secrets of Power Negotiating*, Franklin Lakes, NJ: Career Press.
27. Thompson, L. (2001) *The Mind of the Negotiator*, 2nd edition, Upper Saddle River: Prentice Hall.
28. Stepp, J.R., Sweeney, K.M. and Johnson, R.L. (2003) 'Interest-base negotiation: an engine-driving change', *The Journal for Quality and Participation*, 21: 36–41.
29. Solnick, S. (2001) 'Gender differences in the ultimate game', *Economic Inquiry*, 39: 189–200.
30. Olekalns, M. and Smith, P.L. (2000) 'Understanding optimal outcomes: the role of strategy sequences in competitive negotiations', *Human Communication Research*, 26: 527–57.
31. Fisher, R., Ury, W. and Patton, B. (1991) *Getting to Yes: Negotiating an Agreement Without Giving In*, 2nd edition, London: Random House.
32. Scott, B. (1988), *Negotiating: Constructive and Competitive Negotiation*, London: Paradigm Press.
33. Holmes, M.E. (1997) 'Optimal matching analysis of negotiation phase sequences in simulated and authentic hostage negotiations', *Communication Reports*, 10: 1–8.
34. Kennedy, G. (1998) *Kennedy on Negotiation*, Aldershot: Gower.
35. Lewicki, R.J., Barry, B., Saunders, D.M., and Minton, J.W. (2003) *Negotiation*, 4th edition, Boston: McGraw Hill, p. 54.
36. Karrass, C. (1970) *The Negotiation Game*, New York: Thomas Y. Crowell.
37. Jordan, J.M. and Roloff, M.E. (1997) 'Planning skills and negotiator accomplishment: the relationship between self-monitoring and plan generation, plan enhancement, and plan consequences', *Communication Research*, 24: 31–63.
38. Fells, R. (1996) 'Preparation for negotiation: issues and process', *Personnel Review*, 25: 50–60.
39. Fisher *et al.*, op. cit.
40. Stepp *et al.*, op. cit.

41. Lewicki, Barry *et al.*, op. cit.
42. Simons and Tripp, op. cit.
43. Mattock, J. and Ehrenborg, J. (1996) *How to be a Better Negotiator*, London: Kogan Page.
44. Webber, op. cit.
45. Davies, J. (1998) 'The art of negotiating', *Management Today*, November: 126–8 (p. 128).
46. Anderson, T. (2003) 'Step into my parlor: a survey of strategies and techniques for effective negotiation', in R.J. Lewicki, D.M. Saunders, J.W. Minton and B. Barry, (eds) *Negotiation: Readings, Exercises, and Cases*, Boston: McGraw-Hill.
47. Fisher *et al.*, op. cit.
48. LePoole, op. cit.
49. Mattock and Ehrenborg, op. cit.
50. Hendon, D.W., Roy, M.H. and Ahmed, Z.U. (2003) 'Negotiation concession patterns: a multi-country, mulyiperiod study', *American Business Review*, 21: 75–83.
51. Lewicki *et al.* (2001) op. cit.
52. Salacuse, J.W. (1999) 'Intercultural negotiation in international business', *Group Decision and Negotiation*, 8: 217–36.
53. Salacuse, J. (1998) 'Ten ways that culture affects negotiating style. Some survey results', *Negotiation Journal*, 14: 221–39.
54. Brett, J.M., Shapiro, D.L. and Lytle, A.L. (1998) 'Breaking the bonds of reciprocity in negotiation', *Academy of Management Journal*, 41: 410–24.
55. Mattock and Ehrenborg, op. cit.
56. Anderson, op. cit.
57. Wilson, S., Paulson, G. and Putnam, L. (2001) 'Negotiating', in W.P. Robinson and H. Giles (eds) *The Handbook of Language and Social Psychology*, Chichester: John Wiley & Sons, p. 305.
58. Scott, op. cit.
59. Brett *et al.*, op. cit.
60. Taylor, P. (2002) 'A cylindrical model of communication behavior in crisis negotiations', *Human Communication Research*, 28: 7–48.
61. Weingart, L., Prietula, M., Hyder, E. and Genovese, C. (1999) 'Knowledge and the sequential processes of negotiation: a Markov chain analysis of Response-in-kind', *Journal of Experimental Social Psychology*, 35: 366–93.
62. Berry, W. (1996) *Negotiating in the Age of Integrity: A Complete Guide to Negotiating Win/Win in Business*, London: Nicolas Brealey.
63. Lewicki *et al.* (2001) op. cit., p. 89.
64. Thompson (2001) op. cit.
65. Hamilton, P.M. (2000) 'Attaining agreement: a rhetorical analysis of an NHS negotiation', *The International Journal of Public Sector Management*, 13: 285–300.
66. Dunne, H. (2001) 'One wrong word and we lose him', *Daily Telegraph*, 29 October, p. 15.
67. Ritov, I (1996) 'Achoring in simulated competitive market negotiation', *Organizational Behavior and Human Decision Processes*, 67: 16–25.
68. Scott, op. cit.
69. Lewicki, Barry *et al.*, op. cit.
70. Falls, R. (1996) 'Preparation for negotiation: issues and process', *Personnel Review*, 25: 50–60.
71. LePoole, op. cit.

72. Thompson (2001) op. cit.
73. Hendon *et al.*, op. cit.
74. Galinsky, A. and Mussweiler, T. (2000) 'Promoting good outcomes: effects of regulatory focus on negotiation outcomes'. Working Paper, Northwester University, Evanston, IL.
75. Mills, H. (1991) *Negotiate: The Art of Winning*, London: BCA.
76. Dawson, op. cit.
77. Fisher *et al.*, op. cit.
78. Hendon *et al.*, op. cit.
79. Pruitt, D. (1981) *Negotiating Behavior*, New York: Academic Press.
80. Lewicki, Barry *et al.*, op. cit.
81. Halpern, J. (1994) 'The effect of friendship on personal business transactions', *Journal of Conflict Resolution*, 38: 647–64.
82. Jeffries, K. and Reed, R. (2000) 'Trust and adaptation in relational contracting', *Academy of Management Review*, 25: 873–82.
83. Robinson, R.J. (1995) 'Defusing the exploding offer: the farpoint gambit', *Negotiating Journal*, 11: 277–85.
84. Woo *et al.*, op. cit.
85. Olekalns, M. and Smith, P. (2001) 'Understanding optimal outcomes: the role of strategy sequences in competitive negotiations', *Human Communication Research*, 26: 527–57.
86. Cairns, L. (1996) *Negotiating Skills in the Workplace: A Practical Handbook*, London: Pluto Press.
87. Kennedy, op. cit.
88. Dawson, op. cit.
89. Webber, op. cit.
90. Fortgang, R.S., Lax, D.A. and Sebenius, J.K. (2003) 'Negotiating the spirit of the deal', *Harvard Business Review*, 81: 66–75.
91. Goman, C.K. (2002) 'Cross-cultural business practices', *Communication World*, 19: 22–5.
92. Mills, op. cit.
93. Taylor, P. (2002) 'A cylindrical model of communication behavior in crisis negotiations', *Human Communication Research*, 28: 7–48.
94. McRae, B. (1998) *Negotiating and Influencing Skills*, Thousand Oaks, CA: Sage.
95. Koh, T.T. (1996) 'American strengths and weaknesses', *International Negotiation*, 1: 313–17 (p. 317).
96. Thompson, op. cit.
97. Rackham, N. (2003) 'The behavior of successful negotiators', in R.J. Lewicki, D.M. Saunders, J.W. Minton and B. Barry (eds) *Negotiation: Readings, Exercises, and Cases*, Boston: McGraw-Hill.
98. Adler, R., Rosen, B. and Silverstein, E. (1998) 'Emotions in negotiation: how to manage fear and anger', *Negotiation Journal*, 14: 161–79.
99. Rackham, op. cit.
100. McAllister, D. (1995) 'Affect- and cognition-based trust as foundations for interpersonal cooperation in organizations', *Academy of Management Journal*, 38: 24–59 (p. 25).
101. Rackham, op. cit.
102. Mnookin *et al.*, op. cit.
103. Rackham, op. cit.
104. Rackham, ibid.
105. Rackham, ibid.

8 Will they buy it? Why managers must be able to sell

1. Brodie, S., Stanworth, J. and Wotruba, T. (2002) 'Comparisons of salespeople in multilevel vs. single level direct selling organizations', *The Journal of Personal Selling and Sales Mangement*, 22: 67–75.
2. Peterson, R. and Wotruba, T. (1996) 'What is direct selling? Definition, perspectives, and research agenda', *Journal of Personal Selling and Sales Management*, 16: 1–16 (p. 2).
3. O'Hair, D. Friedrich, G. and Dixon, L. (2002) *Strategic Communication in Business and the Professions*, 4th edition, Boston: Houghton Mifflin, p. 446.
4. Hersey, P. (1988) *Selling: A Behavioral Science Approach*, Englewood Cliffs, NJ: Prentice Hall.
5. Lund, P.R. (1987) *Compelling Selling: A Framework for Persuasion*, London: MacMillan Papermac.
6. Rich, M. and Smith, D. (2000) 'Determining relationship skills of prospective salespeople', *Journal of Business and Industrial Marketing*, 15: 242–59.
7. Comstock, J. and Higgins, G. (1997) 'Appropriate relational messages in direct selling interaction: should salespeople adapt to buyers' communicator style?', *Journal of Business Communication*, 34: 410–18.
8. Miles, M., Arnold, D. and Nash, H. (1990) 'Adaptive communication: the adaptation of the seller's interpersonal style to the stage of the dyad's relationship and the buyer's communication style', *Journal of Personal Selling and Sales Management*, 10: 21–7.
9. Doyle, S. and Roth, G. (1992) 'Selling and sales management in action', *Journal of Personal Selling and Sales Management*, 12: 59–64.
10. Hawes, J., Mast, K. and Swan, J. (1989) 'Trust earning perceptions of sellers and buyers', *Journal of Personal Selling and Sales Management*, 9: 1–8.
11. McCarthy, P. and Hatcher, C. (1996) *Speaking Persuasively: Making the Most of Your Presentations*, St. Leonards, Australia: Allen and Unwin, p.163.
12. Hargie, O. and Morrow, N. (1987) 'Interpersonal communication: the sales approach', *Pharmacy Update*, 3: 320–4.
13. Hargie, O. and Dickson, D. (2004) *Skilled Interpersonal Communication: Research, Theory and Practice*, London: Routledge.
14. Swan, J., Trawick, I. and Silva, D. (1985) 'How industrial salespeople gain customer trust', *Industrial Marketing Management*, 14: 203–11.
15. Lassk, F., Marshall, G., Cravens, D. and Moncrief, W. (2001) 'Salesperson job involvement: a modern perspective and a new scale', *The Journal of Personal Selling and Sales Management*, 21: 291–302.
16. Barker, A. (2001) 'Salespeople characteristics, sales managers' activities and territory design as antecedents of sales organization performance', *Marketing Intelligence and Planning*, 19: 21–8.
17. Cialdini, R. (2001) 'Harnessing the science of persuasion', *Harvard Business Review*, October: 70–80.
18. Cody, M. and Seiter, J. (2001) 'Compliance principles in retail sales in the United States', in W. Wosinska, R. Cialdini, D. Barrett and J. Reykowski (eds) *The Practice of Social Influence in Multiple Cultures*, Mahwah, NJ: Lawrence Erlbaum.
19. Kossen, S. (1982) *Creative Selling Today*, New York: Harper and Row.
20. Shoemaker, M. and Johlke, M. (2002) 'An examination of the antecedents of a crucial selling skill: asking questions', *Journal of Managerial Issues*, 14: 118–31.

21. Rackham, N. (1995) *Spin Selling*, Aldershot: Gower.
22. Poppleton, S.E. (1981) 'The social skills of selling', in M. Argyle (ed.) *Social Skills and Work*, London: Methuen.
23. Shepherd, C., Castleberry, S. and Ridnour, R. (1997) 'Linking effective listening with salesperson performance: an exploratory investigation', *Journal of Business and Industrial Marketing*, 12: 315–22.
24. Ingram, T., Schwepker, C. and Hutson, D. (1992) 'Why salespeople fail', *Industrial Marketing Management*, 21: 225–30.
25. Rosenbaum, B. (2001) 'Seven emerging sales competencies', *Business Horizons*, 44: 33–6.
26. Scott, R. (1999) 'The art of consultative selling', *Accounting Technology*, 15: 18–22.
27. Maslow, A. (1954) *Motivation and Personality*, New York: Harper and Row.
28. Smith, R. and Dick, G. (1984) *Getting Sales*, London: Kogan Page.
29. Donaldson, J. (1999) 'Tailoring sales style to suit prospect personality', *Trusts and Estates*, 138: 8–10.
30. Rohrer, R. (1999) 'Is it better to buy or be sold?' *The American Salesman*, 44: 3–7 (p. 3).
31. Shepherd, D., Tashchian, A., Dabholkar, P. and Ladd, R. (2002) 'A measure of selling skill: scale development and validation', *The Journal of Personal Selling and Sales Management*, 22: 13–21.
32. Saporito, B. (2003) 'Can Wal-Mart get any bigger?' *Time Magazine* (Canadian edition), 13 January, pp. 26–31.
33. Williams, G. and Miller, R. (2002) 'Change the way you persuade', *Harvard Business Review*, 80: 65–73 (p. 65).
34. Cialdini, R. (2001) 'Systematic opportunism: an approach to the study of tactical social influence', in J. Forgas and K. Williams (eds) *Social Influence: Direct and Indirect Processes*, Philadelphia: Psychology Press, p. 28.
35. Armitstead, L. (2002) 'Firms sold short by bad sales technique', *The Sunday Times (Business Section)*, 20 October, p. 17.
36. Leigh, T. and Summers, J. (2002) 'An initial evaluation of industrial buyers' impressions of salespersons' nonverbal cues', *The Journal of Personal Selling and Sales Management*, 22: 41–53.
37. Thompson, J., Courtney, L. and Dickson, D. (2002) 'The effect of neurolinguistic programming on organisational and individual performance: a case study', *Journal of European Industrial Training*, 26: 292–8.
38. Robinson, L., Marshall, G., Moncrief and Lassk, F. (2002) 'Toward a shortened measure of adaptive selling', *The Journal of Personal Selling and Sales Management*, 22: 111–18.
39. Davis, W. (1986) *The Supersalesman's Handbook*, New York: Sidgwick and Jackson.
40. Withers, P. (2002) 'The sweet smell of success' *HR Magazine*, June, pp. 76–92.
41. Hargie, O. and Tourish, D. (1999) 'Internal communications and the management of change', in R. Baker, H. Hearnshaw and N. Robertson (eds) *Implementing Change with Clinical Audit*, Chichester: Wiley, p. 149.
42. Williams, A. (1983) *All About Selling*, London: McGraw-Hill, p. 99.
43. Hargie, O. (1997) 'Interpersonal communication: a theoretical framework', in O. Hargie (ed.) *The Handbook of Communication Skills*, London: Routledge.
44. Leong, S., Busch, P. and Roedder John, D. (1989) 'Knowledge bases and salesperson effectiveness: a script-theoretic analysis', *Journal of Marketing Research*, 26: 164–78, (p. 174).
45. Ellis, K. (2002) 'Deal Maker', *Training*, April: 34–7.

46. Jackson, D., Cunningham, W. and Cunningham, I. (1988) *Selling: The Personal Force in Marketing*, New York: Wiley.
47. Marks, R. (1985) *Personal Selling: An Interactive Approach*, Boston: Allyn and Bacon.
48. Miller, R. and Heiman, S. (1988) *Conceptual Selling*, London: Kogan Page.
49. Festinger, L. (1957) *A Theory of Cognitive Dissonance*, Stanford: Stanford University Press.
50. Hargie, O. and Dickson, D. (2004) op. cit.
51. Pettijohn, C., Pettijohn, L. and Taylor. A. (2002) 'The influence of salesperson skill, motivation, and training on the practice of customer oriented selling', *Psychology and Marketing*, 19: 743–57.
52. Frankwick, G., Porter, S. and Crosby, L. (2001) 'Dynamics of relationship selling: a longitudinal examination of changes in salesperson–customer relationship status', *The Journal of Personal Selling and Sales Management*, 21: 135–46.
53. Jacobs, R., Evans, K., Kleine, R. and Landry, T. (2001) 'Disclosure and its reciprocity as predictors of key outcomes of an initial sales encounter', *The Journal of Personal Selling and Sales Management*, 21: 51–61.
54. Brown, G., Boya, U., Humphreys, N. and Widing, R. (1993) 'Attributes and behaviors preferred by buyers: high socializing vs. low socializing industrial buyers', *Journal of Personal Selling and Sales Management*, 13: 25–33.
55. Crosby, L., Evans, K. and Cowles, D. (1990) 'Relationship quality in services selling: an interpersonal influence perspective', *Journal of Marketing*, 54: 68–81.
56. Liu, A. and Leach, M. (2001) 'Developing loyal customers with a value-adding sales force: examining customer satisfaction and the perceived credibility of consultative salespeople', *The Journal of Personal Selling and Sales Management*, 21: 147–56.
57. Hayward, S. (1998) 'Sales executives still struggle to sell themselves', *Sunday Times*, 11 January, p. 36.
58. Ehninger, D., Gronbeck, B. and Monroe, A. (1984) *Principles of Speech Communication*, Glenview, IL: Scott, Foresman & Co.
59. Yoder, D., Hugenberg, L. and Wallace, S. (1993) *Creating Competent Communication*, Madison, WI: Brown and Benchmark.

9 Calling all organisations: the business of the telephone

1. O'Kane, P., Hargie, O. and Tourish, D. (2004) 'Communication without frontiers: the impact of technology upon organizations', in D. Tourish and O. Hargie (eds) *Key Issues in Organizational Communication*, London: Routledge.
2. Bishop, S. (2000) *The Complete Feedback Skills Training Book*, Aldershot: Gower, p. 175.
3. Carroll, R. (2002) 'Bell did not invent telephone, US rules', *The Guardian*, 17 June, p. 14.
4. Office of Population Censuses and Surveys (1992) *General Household Survey*, London: OPCS.
5. Irwin, A. (1998) 'Calls to mobile phones "a rip off"', *The Daily Telegraph*, 6 March, p. 6.

6. Uhlig, R. (2003) 'Video games and photos push mobile sales to 50 m', *The Daily Telegraph*, 11 March, p. 8.
7. Jagoda, A. and de Villepin, M. (1993) *Mobile Communications*, Chicester: Wiley.
8. Plant, S. (2002) 'How the mobile changed the world', *Sunday Times*, 5 May, p. 9.
9. Meek, J (2002) 'Hi, I'm in G2', *The Guardian G2*, 11 November, pp. 2–5.
10. Smith, D. (2000) 'UK goes upwardly mobile', *Sunday Times (Business Section)*, 10 December, p. 4.
11. Gillen, J. (2003) 'Engaged from birth: children under two talking on telephones', in A. Schorr, W. Campbell and M. Schenk (eds) *Communication Research and Media Science in Europe*, Berlin: Mouton de Gruyter.
12. Womack, S. (2002) 'Would you buy an insurance policy from this TV screen', *Financial Mail on Sunday*, 10 March, pp. 30–1.
13. Kennedy, D. (1998) 'Millions call for privacy', *The Times*, London, 14 February, p. 10.
14. Freephone (1997) *The Daily Telegraph* (Special Supplement), 4 July.
15. Advertising feature by Kent County Constabulary and BT (1997) *The Times*, 24 December, p. 5.
16. Short, J., Williams, E. and Christie, B. (1976) *The Social Psychology of Telecommunications*, London: John Wiley & Sons.
17. Kellerman, A. (1998) 'Sociospatial aspects of telecommunications: an overview', in H. Sawhney and G. Barnett (eds) *Progress in Communication Sciences. Vol XV. Advances in Telecommunications*, Stamford, CT: Ablex, p. 221.
18. Fischer, C. (1992) *America Calling: A Social History of the Telephone to 1940*, Berkley: University of California Press.
19. Postmes, T., Spears, R. and Lea, M. (2000) 'The formation of group norms in computer-mediated communication', *Human Communication Research*, 26: 341–71.
20. Frey, J.H. (1989) *Survey Research by Telephone*, 2nd edition, Newbury Park: Sage, p.16.
21. Hargie, C. and Tourish, D. (1997) 'Relational communication', in O. Hargie (ed.) *The Handbook of Communication Skills*, London: Routledge.
22. Argyle, M. and Henderson, M. (1985) *The Anatomy of Relationships*, Harmondsworth: Penguin.
23. Rutter, D.R. (1979) *Communicating by Telephone*, Oxford: Pergamon Press.
24. Argyle, M. (1988) *Bodily Communication*, 2nd edition, London: Methuen, p. 118.
25. McLuhan, M. (1964) *Understanding the Media*, New York: McGraw-Hill.
26. Hopper, R. (1998) 'What do we know about telephone communication?' in H. Sawhney and G. Barnett (eds) *Progress in Communication Sciences. Vol XV. Advances in Telecommunications*, Stamford, CT: Ablex, p. 30.
27. Beattie, G. (1983) *Talk: An Analysis of Speech and Non-verbal Behaviour in Conversation*, Milton Keynes: Open University.
28. Hargie, O. (1997) 'Interpersonal communication: a theoretical framework', in O. Hargie (ed.) *The Handbook of Communication Skills*, London: Routledge.
29. Goddard, J. (1973) *Office Linkages and Location*, London: Pergamon Press.
30. Hargie, O. and Tourish, D. (1996) 'Auditing communication practices to improve the management of human resources: an inter-organisational study', *Health Services Management Research*, 9: 209–22.

31. Smoreda, Z. and Licoppe, C. (2000) 'Gender-specific use of the domestic telephone', *Social Psychology Quarterly*, 63: 238–52.
32. Short, J., Williams, E. and Christie, B. (1976) *The Social Psychology of Telecommunications*, London: John Wiley & Sons.
33. Frey, J.H. (1989) *Survey Research by Telephone*, op. cit.
34. Reed Employment Services (1997) *Telephone Techniques: Maximising Customer Satisfaction in Telephone Transactions*, London.
35. La Rose, R. (1998) 'Understanding personal telephone behavior', in H. Sawhney and G. Barnett (eds) *Progress in Communication Sciences. Vol XV. Advances in Telecommunications*, Stamford, CT: Ablex, p. 5.
36. MacErlean, N. (1997) 'How to deal with rudeness on the telephone', *The Observer*, London, 31 October.
37. Tracy, K. and Tracy, S. (1998) 'Rudeness at 911', *Human Communication Research*, 25: 225–51.
38. Barry, B. and Bateman, T. (1992) 'Perceptions of influence in managerial dyads: the role of hierarchy, media and tactics', *Human Relations*, 45: 555–74.
39. Lyman, G.C. (1984) 'Voice messaging comes of age', *Speech Technology*, 2: 45–9.
40. 'Don't touch that phone' (1989) *Wall Street Journal*, 25 July, A1.
41. Hopper, op. cit.
42. Kleinke, C. (1986) *Meeting and Understanding People*, New York: Freeman.
43. Feldman, R. and Rime, B. (eds) (1991) *Fundamentals of Nonverbal Behaviour*, Cambridge: Cambridge University Press.
44. Cotton, I. (2000) 'You don't have to be mad to work here ... ', *Daily Telegraph Magazine*, 12 August, pp. 34–9.
45. Hopper, R. (1992) *Telephone Conversation*, Bloomington, IN: Indiana University Press, p. 5.
46. 'High price of call hang-ups' (1997) *Mail on Sunday*, 6 January.
47. Ward, M. (2000) 'How phone firms keep callers hanging on', *Daily Telegraph*, 4 May, p. 16.
48. Kemeny, L. and Rushe, D. (2001) 'Switch to India puts jobs at risk', *Sunday Times (Business Section)*, 18 February, p. 3.
49. Dawe, T. (2002) 'A call to arms against the rivals', *The Times*, 13 September, p. 35.
50. Margullis, D. (2002) 'Smarter call centers: are they at your service?' *International Herald Tribune*, 16–17 March, p. 10.
51. Neill, M. (2001) 'Union critical of call centre pay', *Belfast Telegraph*, 12 February, p. 9.
52. Costello, M. (2002) 'Curse of the call centres', *Financial Mail on Sunday*, 10 March, pp. 6–7.
53. Vandevelde, H. (2001) 'Call centres don't have to be hellish', *The Sunday Times (Appointments Section)*, 25 November, p. 9.
54. Cameron, D. (2000) *Good to Talk? Living and Working in a Communication Culture*, London: Sage.
55. Irwin, A. (1999) '"Brain strain" risk for telephone staff', *The Daily Telegraph*, 6 January, p. 8.
56. Tomlinson, A. (2002) 'Call centres work to shed their negative image', *Canadian HR Reporter*, 15, 24–5.
57. Rosenfield, R. (1997) *Counselling by Telephone*, London: Sage.
58. Suh, K. (1999) 'Impact of communication medium on task performance and satisfaction: an examination of media-richness theory', *Information and Management*, 35: 295–312.

59. Burgoon, J., Buller, D. and Floyd, K. (2001) 'Does participation affect deception success? A test of the interactivity principle', *Human Communication Research*, 27: 503–34.
60. Rice, R., D'Ambra, J. and More, E. (1998) 'Cross-cultural comparison of organizational media evaluation and choice', *Journal of Communication*, 48: 3–26.
61. Fulk, J., and Collins-Jarvis, L. (2001) 'Wired meetings: technological mediation of organizational gatherings', in F. Jablin and L. Putnam (eds) *The New Handbook of Organizational Communication: Advances in Theory, Research and Methods*, London: Sage.
62. O'Sullivan, P. (2000) 'What you don't know won't hurt me: impression management functions of communication channels in relationships', *Human Communication Research*, 26: 403–31.
63. Westmyer, S., Di Cioccio, R. and Rubin, R. (1998) 'Appropriateness and effectiveness of communication channels in competent interpersonal communication', *Journal of Communication*, 48: 27–48.
64. Rice, R. and Shook, D. (1990) 'Relationships of job categories and organizational levels to use of communication channels, including electronic mail: a meta-analysis and extension', *Journal of Management Studies*, 27: 195–229.
65. Goddard, op. cit.
66. Uhlig, R. (2000) 'Mobile phone mania spreads as phones become the must-have gadget', *Daily Telegraph*, 6 January, p. 3.
67. Schegloff, E. (1987) 'Identification and recognition in interactional openings', in I. Pool (ed.) *The Social Impact of the Telephone*, Cambridge, MA: MIT Press.
68. Roman, E. (1993) *How to Use the Telephone: Effectively and Economically*, London: Business Books.
69. Shafiroff, M. and Shook, R.L. (1982) *Successful Telephone Selling in the '80s*, New York: Harper & Row.
70. Tourish, D. and Hargie, O. (2000) 'Auditing the communications revolution', in O. Hargie and D. Tourish (eds) *Handbook of Communication Audits for Organisations*, London: Routledge.
71. Cairncross, F. (1998) *The Death of Distance: How The Communications Revolution Will Change Our Lives*, Orion Business Books: London.
72. Pool, I. (ed.) (1987) *The Social Impact of the Telephone*, Cambridge, MA: MIT Press.

10 Writing matters: how to create the write impression

1. Smart, K., Whiting, M. and DeTienne, K. (2001) 'Assessing the need for printed and online documentation: a study of customer preference and use', *Journal of Business Communication*, 38: 285–314.
2. Mabrito, M. (1997) 'Writing on the front line: a study of workplace writing', *Business Communication Quarterly*, 60: 58–70.
3. Wardrope, W. (2002) 'Department chairs' perceptions of the importance of business communication skills', *Business Communication Quarterly*, 65: 60–72.
4. Hobson, R. (1997) 'Getting the message: we value your custom', *The Times*, Special Supplement: Communicating with your customer, p. 2.

5. Jones, T. (1997a) 'Retaining the thrill of the letter', *The Times*, Special Supplement: Communicating with your customer, 18 February, p. 8.
6. Jones, T. (1997b) 'Create the write impression', *The Times*, Special Supplement: Communicating with your customer, 18 February, p. 8.
7. Sutherland, S. (1992) *Irrationality*, London: Constable.
8. Jones (1997b) op. cit.
9. Jones (1997b) ibid.
10. Jones (1997b) ibid.
11. Jones (1997a) op. cit.
12. Bovee, C. and Thill, J. (2000) *Business Communication Today*, Upper Saddle River, NJ: Prentice Hall.
13. Peters, T. (1988) *Thriving on Chaos*, London: MacMillan.
14. Tourish, D. and Hargie, O. (1996) 'Auditing communication practices to improve the management of human resources: a regional study', *Health Services Management Research*, 9: 209–22.
15. Dawes, R. (2001) *Everyday Irrationality*, New York: Westview Press.
16. Huettman, E. (1996) 'Writing for multiple audiences: an examination of audience concerns in a hospitality consulting firm', *Journal of Business Communication*, 33: 257–73.
17. Ley, P., Flaherty, B., Smith, F., Martin, J. and Renner, P. (1985) *A Comparative Study of the Effects of Two Warning Messages About Volatile Substances*, Sydney, NSW: New South Wales Drug and Alcohol Authority.
18. Young, L. and Humphrey, M. (1985) 'Cognitive methods of preparing women for hysterectomy: does a booklet help?', *British Journal of Clinical Psychology*, 24: 303–4.
19. Tourish, D. and Hargie, O. (1998) 'Communication between managers and staff in the NHS: Trends and prospects', *British Journal of Management*, 9: 53–71.
20. This Box is adapted from an excellent discussion of channel usage in Chapter 5 of Clampitt, P. (2001) *Communicating for Managerial Effectiveness*, 2nd edition, London: Sage.
21. Pratkanis, A. and Aronson, E. (1991) *Age of Propaganda*, New York: WH Freeman.
22. Suchan, J. and Colucci, R. (1989) 'Analysis of communication efficiency between high-impact and bureaucratic written communication', *Management Communication Quarterly*, 2: 454–84.
23. Bailey, E. (1997) *The Plain English Approach to Business Writing*, Oxford: Oxford University Press.
24. Clayton, J. (2000) *The Ten Principles of Good Business Writing*, Harvard Management Communication Letter (Reprint No. C0009F), Boston: Harvard Business School Publishing.
25. Harvard Management Communication Letter No. C0008D (2000), Boston: Harvard Business School Press.
26. Bierck, R. (2001) *Find the Right Tone for Your Business Writing*, Harvard Management Communication letter (Reprint No. C0109D), Boston: Harvard Business School Publishing.
27. Guirdham, M. (2002) *Interactive Behaviour At Work*, London: Prentice Hall.
28. Orwell, G. (1970) 'Politics and the English language', in I. Angus and S. Orwell (eds) *The Collected Essays, Journalism and Letters: Volume 4*, London: Penguin.
29. Plotkin, H. (1999) *A Nine-Step Guide to Fast, Effective Business Writing*, Harvard Management Communication Letter (Reprint No. C9909B), Boston: Harvard Business School Publishing.

30. Lynch, D. and Golen, S. (2003) '10 steps to writing clear documents', *Internal Auditor*, February: 53–7.
31. Bailey (1997) op. cit.
32. Clayton, J. (2001) *A Call to Action for Business Writing*, Harvard Management Communication Letter (Reprint No. C0110C), Boston: Harvard Business School Publishing (p. 1).
33. Ogilvy, D. (1987) *Confessions of an Advertising Man*, London: Pan.
34. St Maur, S. (2002) *Powerwriting*, London: Prentice Hall.
35. Hartley, P. and Bruckman, C. (2002) *Business Communication*, London: Routledge.
36. Rouse, M. and Rouse, S. (2002) *Business Communications: A Cultural and Strategic Approach*, London: Thomson Learning.
37. Ogilvy, D. (1983) *Ogilvy on Advertising*, London: Pan.
38. Bailey (1997) op. cit.
39. Roman, K. and Raphaelson, J. (1981) *Writing that Works*, New York: Harper and Row.
40. Poulton, E., Warren, T. and Bond, J. (1970) 'Ergonomics in journal design', *Applied Ergonomics*, 13: 207–9.
41. Baker, W. (2001) 'HATS: a design procedure for routine business documents', *Business Communication Quarterly*, 64: 65–76.
42. Cited in Hartley, P. and Bruckman, C. (2002) op. cit., p. 165.
43. See the website of the Plain English Campaign for these and other examples: http://www.plainenglish.co.uk/
44. Rouse and Rouse, op. cit., p. 149.
45. Cutler, S. (2001) *Designing and Writing Message-based Audit Reports*, New York: Institute of Internal Auditors.
46. Netzley, M. and Snow, C. (2002) *Guide to Report Writing*, Upper Saddle River, NJ: Prentice-Hall.
47. Kramlinger, T. (1998) 'How to deliver a change message', *Training and Development*, April: 44–7 (p. 46).
48. Wissema, H. (2002) 'Driving through red lights: how warning signals are missed or ignored', *Long Range Planning*, 35: 521–39.
49. Tourish, D. and Hargie, O. (2000) 'Crafting the audit report', in O. Hargie and D. Tourish (eds) *Handbook of Communication Audits for Organisations*, London: Routledge.
50. Sutherland, S. (1992) op. cit.
51. Murray, H. (1989) 'Training in giving and receiving criticism', *Training and Development*, January: 19–20.
52. O'Kane, P., Hargie, O. and Tourish, D. (2004) 'Communication without frontiers: the impact of technology upon organisations', in D. Tourish and O. Hargie (eds) *Key Issues in Organisational Communication*, London: Routledge.
53. Samuels, P. (1997) 'The impact of computer-based communications networks', in E. Scholes (ed.) *Gower Handbook of Internal Communication*, Aldershot: Gower, p. 35.
54. O'Kane, P., Hargie, O. and Tourish, D. (2004) op. cit.
55. Crystal, D. (2001) *Language and the Internet*, Cambridge: University Press.
56. Poe, A.C. (2001) 'Don't touch that "send" button!', *HR Magazine* 46, July, pp. 74–80.
57. Summerskill, B (2002) 'Bosses step up e-mail spying', *The Observer (News Section)*, 13 October, p. 15.
58. Summerskill, ibid.

59. Munter, M., Rogers, P. and Rymer, J. (2003) 'Business e-mail: guidelines for users', *Business Communication Quarterly*, 66: 26–40 (p. 28).
60. Utley, A. (1997) 'Abusive e-mails ignite work fury', *Times Higher Education Supplement*, 30 May, p. 1.
61. Angell, D. and Heslop, B. (1994) *The Elements of E-mail Style*, London: Addison-Wesley.
62. British Computer Society (2002) *Information Overload: Organisation and Personal Strategies*, Wiltshire: BCS and Henley Management College.
63. Quirke, B. (1996) *Communicating Corporate Change*, Maidenhead: McGraw-Hill.
64. Jones (1997a) op. cit.

11 Tell it like it is ... communicating assertively

1. Nurmi, R.W. and Darling, J.R. (1997) *International Management Leadership: The Primary Competitive Advantage*, New York: International Business Press.
2. Paterson, R. (2000) *The Assertiveness Workbook: How to Express Your Ideas and Stand Up for Yourself at Work and in Relationships*, Oakland, CA: New Harbinger Publications.
3. Lindenfield, G. (2001) *Assert Yourself: Simple Steps to Getting What You Want*, London: Thorsons, p. 11.
4. Rakos, R. (1997) 'Asserting and Confronting', in O. Hargie (ed.) *The Handbook of Communication Skills*, London: Routledge.
5. Alberti, R. and Emmons, M. (2001) *Your Perfect Right: Assertiveness and Equality in Your Life and Relationships*, Atascadero, CA: Impact Publishers, p. 6.
6. Guirdham, M. (2002) *Interactive Behaviour at Work*, Harlow: Pearson Education Limited.
7. Lazarus, A. (1971) *Behaviour Therapy and Beyond*, New York: McGraw-Hill.
8. Lange, A. and Jakubowski, P. (1976) *Responsible Assertive Behaviour*, Champaign, IL: Research Press, p. 38.
9. Rakos, op. cit.
10. Alberti and Emmons, op. cit., p. 6.
11. Hargie, O. and Dickson, D. (2004) *Skilled Interpersonal Communication: Research, Theory And Practice*, London: Psychology Press.
12. Beck, C.E. (1999) *Managerial Communication: Bridging Theory and Practice*, Upper Saddle River, NJ: Prentice Hall.
13. Gillen, T. (1992) *Assertiveness for Managers*, Aldershot: Gower.
14. Back, K. and Back, K. (1992) *Assertiveness at Work: A Practical Guide to Handling Awkward Situations*, London: McGraw-Hill.
15. Green, R. (2001) *Human Aggression*, Buckingham: Open University Press.
16. Burley-Allen, M. (1995) *Managing Assertively: A Self-Teaching Guide*, New York: John Wiley & Sons.
17. Back and Back, op. cit.
18. Paterson, op. cit.
19. Back and Back, op. cit.
20. Willcocks, G. and Morris, S. (1996) *Putting Assertiveness to Work: A Programme for Management Excellence*, London: Pitman.
21. Hilpern, K. (1999) 'Secretarial demands with menaces. Treated badly at work? Take a course on how to cope', *The Independent*, 19 May, p. 12.

22. Bynes, J. (2000) 'The aggression continuum: a paradigm shift', *Occupational Health & Safety*, 69: 70–1.
23. Stubbs, D. (1985) *How to Use Assertiveness at Work*, Aldershot: Gower.
24. Paterson, op. cit.
25. Ibid.
26. Schutz, A. (1998) 'Assertive, offensive, protective, and defensive styles of self-presentation: a taxonomy', *The Journal of Psychology,* 132: 611–28.
27. Zuker, E. (1983) *The Assertive Manger: Positive Skills at Work for You*, New York: American Management Association.
28. Burley-Allen, op. cit.
29. Back and Back, op. cit.
30. Richardson, J. (1995) 'Avoidance as an active mode of conflict resolution', *Team Performance: An International Journal*, 1: 19–25.
31. Gillen, op. cit.
32. Willcocks and Morris, op. cit.
33. Collins L., Powell, J. and Oliver, P. (2000) 'Those who hesitate lose: the relationship between assertiveness and response latency', *Perceptual and Motor Skills*, 90: 931–43.
34. Provine, R. (2000) *Laughter: A Scientific Investigation*, London: Penguin.
35. Bandura, A. (1997) *Self-efficacy: The Exercise of Control*, New York: Freeman & Co.
36. Rakos, op. cit.
37. Schwartz cited in Brewer, G. (2000) 'How to banish burnout', *Sales and Marketing Management*, 152: 90.
38. National Transport Safety Board (1994) *Safety Study: A Review of Flightcrew-involved, Major Accidents of US Carriers, 1978 through 1990* (Rep. No. NTSB/SS–94/01). Washington, DC: National Technical Information service.
39. Jentsch, F. and Smith-Jentsch, K. (2001) 'Assertiveness and team performance; more than "just say no"' in E. Salas, C.A. Bower and E. Edens (eds) *Improving Teamwork in Organizations*, Mahwah, NJ: Lawrence Erlbaum Associates.
40. LeMon, C. (2000) 'Motivating adult employees to grow up', *Employment Relations Today*, 27: 89–98.
41. Michelli, D. (1997) *Successful Assertiveness*, Hauppauge, NY: Barron's Educational Series, p. 5.
42. Leaper, C. (2000) 'Gender, affiliation, assertion, and the interactive content of parent–child play', *Developmental Psychology*, 36: 381–93.
43. Darling, J.R. and Walker, W.E. (2001) 'Effective conflict management: use of the behavioral style model', *Leadership & Organization Development Journal*, 22: 230–42.
44. Burley-Allen, op. cit.
45. O'Brien, P. (1992) *Positive Management: Assertiveness for Managers*, London: Nicholas Brealey Publishing.
46. Lindenfield, op. cit.
47. Hargie, O. and Dickson, D. (2004) *Skilled Interpersonal Communication*: Research Theory and Practice, 4th edition, London: Routledge.
48. Rabin, C. and Zelner, D. (1992) 'The role of assertiveness in clarifying roles and strengthening job satisfaction of social workers in multidisciplinary mental health settings', *British Journal of Social Work*, 22: 17–32.
49. Rakos, op. cit.

50. Piccinin, S., McCarrey, M., Fairweather, D., Vito, D. and Conrad, G. (1998) 'Impact of situational legitimacy and assertiveness-related anxiety/discomfort on motivation and ability to generate effective criticism responses', *Current Psychology: Developmental, Learning, Personality, Social*, 17: 75–92.
51. Lindenfield, op. cit., p. xiii
52. Lange and Jakubowski, op. cit.
53. Stubbs, op. cit.
54. Guirdham, op. cit.
55. Paterson, op. cit.
56. Hayes, J. (2002) *Interpersonal Skills at Work*, 2nd edition, Hove: Routledge.
57. Rakos, op. cit.
58. Guirdham, op. cit.
59. Rouse, R. (2001) 'Assertiveness doesn't mean making enemies', *The Times*, 16 May, p. 4.
60. Hargie and Dickson, op. cit.
61. Fry, L. (1983) 'Women in society', in S. Spence and G. Shepherd (eds) *Developments in Social Skills Training*, London: Academic Press.
62. Lindenfield, op. cit., p. 30.
63. Park, D. (1997) 'Androgynous leadership style: an integration rather than a polarization', *Leadership & Organizational Development Journal*, 18: 166–71.
64. Hargie and Dickson, op. cit.
65. Bresnahan, M.J., Ohasi, R., Nebashi, R., Liu, W.Y. and Liao, C.C. (2002) 'Assertiveness as a predictor of compliance and resistance in Taiwan, Japan, and the U.S.', *Journal of Asian Pacific Communication*, 11: 135–59.
66. Crawford, M. (1995) 'Gender, age and the social evaluation of assertion?', *Behavior Modification*, 12: 549–64.
67. Rakos, op. cit.
68. Alberti and Emmons, op. cit.
69. Twenge, J. (1998) 'Assertiveness, sociability, and anxiety', *Dissertation Abstracts International: The Sciences and Engineering*, 59 (2-B): 0905.
70. Paterson, op. cit.
71. Mullinix, S. and Galassi, J. (1981) 'Deriving the content of social skills training with a verbal components approach', *Behavioural Assessment*, 3: 55–66.
72. Solomon, L., Brehony, K., Rothblum, E. and Kelly, J. (1982) ' "Corporate managers" reaction to assertive social skills exhibited by males and females', *Journal of Organizational Behaviour Management*, 4: 49–63.
73. Sigal, J., Branden-Maguire, J., Hayden, M. and Mosley, N. (1985) 'The effect of presentation style and sex of lawyer on jury decision-making behaviour', *Psychology: A Quarterly Journal of Human Behaviour*, 22: 13–19.
74. Hargie and Dickson, op. cit.
75. Wilson, A. (2000) 'Women's ways work', *Psychology Today*, 33: 17.
76. Rakos, op. cit.
77. Bryan, A. and Gallois, C. (1992) 'Rules about assertion in the workplace: effects of status and message type', *Australian Journal of Psychology*, 44: 51–9.
78. Cianni-Surridge, M. and Horan, J. (1983) 'On the wisdom of assertive jobseeking behavior', *Journal of Counseling Psychology*, 30: 209–14.
79. Hargie and Dickson, op. cit.
80. Bresnahan *et al.*, op. cit.
81. Klinger, E. and Bierbraver, G. (2001) 'Acculturation and conflict regulation of Turkish Immigrants in Germany: a social influence perspective', in

W. Wosinska, R. Cialdini, D. Barrett and J. Reykowski (eds) *The Practice of Social Influence in Multiple Cultures*, Mahwah, NJ: Lawrence Erlbaum.
82. Pardeck, J., Anderson, C., Gianino, E. and Miller, B. (1991) 'Assertiveness of social work students', *Psychological Report*, 69: 589–90.
83. Fensterheim, H. and Baer, J. (1975) *Don't Say Yes When You Want To Say No*, New York: David McKay, p. 14.
84. McCartan, P. (2001) 'The identification and analysis of assertive behaviours in nurses', Unpublished Phd Thesis, Jordanstown: University of Ulster.
85. Buslig, A. and Burgoon, J. (2000) 'Aggressiveness in privacy-seeking behavior', in S. Petronio (ed.) *Balancing the Secrets of Private Disclosures*, Mahwah, NJ: Lawrence Erlbaum, p. 193.
86. Lwehabura, M. and Matovelo, D. (2000) 'Effective library management', *New Library World*, 101: 263–8.

12 What's your problem? Helping in the workplace

1. Lord, R., Klimoski, R. and Kanfer, R. (eds) (2002) *Emotions in the Workplace: Understanding the Structure and Role of Emotions in Organizational Behavior*, San Francisco: Jossey-Bass, p. 1.
2. Lord, R. and Kanfer, R. (2002) 'Emotions and organizational behavior', in R. Lord, R. Klimoski, and R. Kanfer, (eds) *Emotions in the Workplace: Understanding the Structure and Role of Emotions in Organizational Behavior*, San Francisco: Jossey-Bass.
3. Hochschild, A.R. (1983) *The Managed Heart: Commercialization of Human Feelings*, Berkeley: University of California Press.
4. Grandey, A. and Brauburger, A. (2002) 'The emotion regulation behind the customer service smile', in R. Lord, R. Klimoski, and R. Kanfer, R. (eds) *Emotions in the Workplace: Understanding the Structure and Role of Emotions in Organizational Behavior*,San Francisco: Jossey-Bass.
5. Fletcher, L. (2001) 'Communication important in economic downturn', *Business Insurance*, 35: 6–7.
6. Sworder, G. (1977) 'Counselling problems at work: where do we go from here?', in T. Watts (ed.) *Counselling at Work*, Plymouth: Bedford Square Press.
7. Pont, T. and Pont, G. (1998) *Interviewing Skills for Managers*, London: Piatkus.
8. Levine, D. (2001) 'Assisting employees around the world', *Business and Health*, 19: 23–6.
9. Martin, P. (1997) 'Counselling skills training for managers in the public sector', in M. Carroll and M. Walton (eds) *Handbook of Counselling in Organizations*, London: Sage, p. 245.
10. Tysoe, M. (1988) *All This and Work Too: The Psychology of Office Life*, London: Fontana.
11. Green, C. (1997) 'Employee counselling: historical developments and key issues', in Feltham, C. (ed.) *The Gains of Listening: Perspectives on Counselling at Work*, Buckingham: Open University Press.
12. Carroll, M. (1996) *Workplace Counselling*, London: Sage.
13. Green, C., op. cit.

14. Carroll, C., op. cit.
15. Buckingham, I. (1992) 'A headache that won't go away', *Guardian*, 31 October, p. 38.
16. British Association for Counselling (1984) *Code of Ethics and Practices for Counsellors*, Rugby: BAC, p. 2.
17. Nelson-Jones, R. (2003) *Basic Counselling Skills: A Helper's Manual*, London: Sage.
18. Nelson-Jones, R. (2000) *Introduction to Counselling Skills*, London: Sage.
19. Wells, B. and Spinks, N. (1997) 'Counselling employees: an applied communication skill', *Career Development International*, 2: 93–8.
20. Wheeler, S. and Lyon, D. (1992) 'Employee benefits from the employer's benefit: how companies respond to employee stress', *Personnel Review*, 21: 47–65.
21. Wright, A. (1998) 'Counselling skills: part 1 – can you do without them?', *Industrial and Commercial Training*, 30: 107–9.
22. Minter, R. and Thomas, E. (2000) 'Employee development through coaching, mentoring and counselling: a multidimensional approach', *Review of Business*, 21: 43–7.
23. Carroll, M., op. cit.
24. Feltham, C. (2002) 'Workplace counselling', in C. Feltham and I. Horton (eds) *Handbook of Counselling and Psychotherapy*, London: Sage.
25. MacLennan, N. (1998) *Counselling for Managers*, Aldershot: Gower, p. 6.
26. Green, C., op. cit.
27. Highley-Marchington, C. and Cooper, C. (1997) 'Evaluating and auditing workplace counselling programmes', in M. Carroll and M. Walton (eds) *Handbook of Counselling in Organizations*, London: Sage.
28. Freiman, C. (2001) 'Someone to talk to', *OH & S Canada*, 17: 79–80.
29. Reddy, M. (ed.) (1993) *EAPs and Counselling Provision in UK Organizations*, London: Independent Counselling and Advisory Services.
30. Carroll, M., op. cit.
31. Freiman, C., op. cit.
32. Meyer, J. and Davis, E. (2002) 'Workplace chaplains: filling a need traditional EAPs can't reach', *Benefits Quarterly*, 18: 22–6.
33. Prince, M. (2002) 'EAP use surges after 9/11', *Business Insurance*, 36: 14–16.
34. Wojcik, J. (2001) 'Helping employees cope', *Business Insurance*, 35: 1–24.
35. Berridge, J., Cooper, C.L. and Highley-Marchington, C. (1997) *Employee Assistance Programmes and Workplace Counselling*, NY: J. Wiley & Sons.
36. Bull, A. (1997) 'Models of counselling in organizations', in M. Carroll and M. Walton (eds) *Handbook of Counselling in Organizations*, London: Sage.
37. Highley-Marchington, C. and Cooper, C., op. cit.
38. Meyer, J. and Davis, E., op. cit.
39. Mayor, S. (2001) 'Review confirms that workplace counselling reduces stress', *British Medical Journal*, 322: 637.
40. Nelson-Jones, R. (2003) op. cit.
41. MacLennan, N., op. cit., p. 10.
42. de Board, R. (1983) *Counselling People at Work*, Aldershot: Gower, p. x.
43. Wells, B. and Spinks, N., op. cit.
44. British Association for Counselling, op. cit.
45. Nixon, J. (1997) 'Line management and counselling', in M. Carroll and M. Walton (eds) *Handbook of Counselling in Organisations*, London: Sage.
46. Carroll, M. op. cit.
47. Nixon, J. op. cit.

48. MacLennan, N. op. cit.
49. Rogers, C. (1957) 'The necessary and sufficient conditions of therapeutic personality change', *Journal of Counselling Psychology*, 21: 95–103.
50. Hannabuss, S. (1997) 'Counselling approaches and the workplace', *Library Management*, 18: 373–9.
51. Adler, R., Rosenfeld, L. and Procter II, R. (2001) *Interplay: The Processes of Interpersonal Communication,* 8th edition, Forth Worth: Harcourt College Publications.
52. Irving, P. (1995) *A Re-conceptualization of the Rogerian Core Conditions of Facilitative Communication*, Unpublished Phd Thesis, University of Ulster, Jordanstown.
53. Binder, U. (1998) 'Empathy and empathy development with psychotic clients', in B. Thorne and E. Lambers (eds) *Person-centred Therapy: A European Perspective*, London: Sage, p. 218.
54. Rogers, C. (1975) 'Empathic: an unappreciated way of being', *The Counselling Psychologist*, 5: 2–10.
55. Dutfield, M. and Eling, C. (1990) *The Communicating Manager: A Guide to Working Effectively with People*, Longmead: Element Books.
56. Thorne, B. (2002) 'Person-centred therapy', in W. Dryden (ed.) *Handbook of Individual Therapy*, 4th edition, London: Sage.
57. Egan, G (1998) *The Skilled Helper*, New York: Brooks/Cole.
58. Nelson-Jones, R. (1996) *Relating Skills*, London: Cassell.
59. Irving, P., op. cit.
60. Thorne, B., op. cit.
61. Egan, G., op. cit.
62. Brammer, L. and MacDonald, G. (1999) *The Helping Relationship,* 7th edition, Boston: Allyn and Bacon.
63. Nelson-Jones, R. (2000) op. cit.
64. Wright, A. (1998) 'Counselling skills: part 1 – can you do without them?', *Industrial and Commercial Training*, 30: 107–9.
65. Wolvin, A. and Coakley, C. (1996) *Listening*, 5th edition, Boston, MA: McGraw-Hill.
66. Stewart, C. and Cash, W. (2000) *Interviewing: Principles and Practice,* 9th edition, Boston, MA: McGraw-Hill, p. 39.
67. Wright, A. (1998) 'Counselling skills: part 2 – making sense of performance appraisal, coaching and mentoring', *Industrial and Commercial Training*, 30: 176–8.
68. Hargie, O. and Dickson, D. (2004) *Skilled Interpersonal Communication: Research, Theory and Practice*, London: Routledge.
69. Ibid.
70. Nelson-Jones, R. (2003) op. cit.
71. McKay, M., Davis, M. and Fanning, P. (1999) 'Expressing', in J. Stewart (ed.) *Bridges Not Walls*, 7th edition, Boston: McGraw-Hill.
72. Tardy, C. and Dindia, K. (1997) 'Self-disclosure', in O. Hargie (ed.) *The Handbook of Communication Skills*, 2nd edition, London: Routledge.
73. Nelson-Jones, R. (2003) op. cit.
74. Ibid.
75. Egan, G., op. cit.
76. Hill, C. and O'Brien, K. (1999) *Helping Skills: Facilitating Exploration, Insight and Actions*, Washington, DC: American Psychological Association, p. 113.
77. Nelson-Jones, R. (2000) op. cit.
78. Hargie and Dickson, op. cit.

13 The war for talent: selection skills for busy managers

1. Pfeffer, J. (1998) *The Human Equation*, Boston: Harvard Business School Press.
2. Collins, J. (2001) *Good to Great*, Boston: Harvard Business School Press.
3. Michaels, E., Handfield-Jones, H. and Axelrod, B. (2001) *The War for Talent*, Boston: Harvard Business School Press.
4. Judge, T., Higgins, C. and Cable, D. (2000) 'The employment interview: a review of recent research and recommendations for future research', *Human Resource Management Review*, 4: 383–406 (p. 383).
5. Bell, A. (1992) *Extraviewing: Innovative Ways to Hire the Best*, Homewood, IL: Business One Irwin.
6. Belfast Telegraph (1997) *Business Section* (News Item), 10 February, p. 9.
7. Posthuma, R., Morgeson, F. and Campion, M. (2002) 'Beyond employment interview validity: a comprehensive narrative review of recent research and trends over time', *Personnel Psychology*, 55: 1–81.
8. Moscoso, S. (2000) 'Selection interview: a review of validity evidence, adverse impact and applicant reactions', *International Journal of Selection and Assessment*, 8: 237–47.
9. Dawes, R. (1994) *House of Cards*, New York: Free Press.
10. Dawes, R. (2001) *Everyday Irrationality: How Pseudo-Scientists, Lunatics and the Rest of Us Fail to Think Rationally*, New York: Westview Press.
11. Rosenfeld, P., Giacalone, R. and Riordan, C. (1995) *Impression Management in Organizations*, London: Routledge.
12. Forsterling, F. (2001) *Attribution: An Introduction to Theories, Research and Applications*, Hove: Psychology Press.
13. Posthuma *et al.* (2002) op. cit., p. 4.
14. Buckley, M., Norris, A. and Wiese (2000) 'A brief history of the selection interview: may the next 100 years be more fruitful', *Journal of Management History*, 6: 113–20.
15. Hattersley, M. (1997) 'Conducting a great job interview', *Harvard Management Update (No. U9703C)*, pp. 1–5.
    Levant, J. (1995) *Selecting the Right People*, Hertfordshire: Technical Communications.
16. Barrick, M., Patton, G. and Haugland, S. (2000) 'Accuracy of interviewer judgments of job applicant personality traits', *Personnel Psychology*, 53: 925–51.
17. Anderson, N. and Shackleton, V. (1990) 'Decision making in the graduate selection interview: a field study', *Journal of Occupational Psychology*, 63: 63–76.
18. Posthuma *et al.* (2002) op. cit.
19. Kreitner, R., Kinicki, A. and Buelens, M. (2002) *Organizational Behaviour*, 2nd European edition, London: McGraw-Hill.
20. Hamilton, C. and Parker, C. (1990) *Communicating for Results*, 3rd edition, London: Wadsworth.
21. Hargie, O. and Dickson, D. (2004) *Skilled Interpersonal Communication: Research, Theory and Practice*, 4th edition, London: Routledge.
22. Kruglanski, A. and Webster, D. (1996) 'Motivated closing of the mind: "seizing" and "freezing"', *Psychological Review*, 103: 263–83.
23. Hargie and Dickson (2004) op. cit.
24. Bolster, B. and Springbett, N. (1981) 'The reaction of interviewers to favourable and unfavourable information', *Journal of Applied Psychology*, 45: 97–103.
25. Judge *et al.* (2000) op. cit.

26. Morton, K. (1994) 'A schema model of dispositional attribution in the employment selection process', Doctoral dissertation, Florida State University, *Dissertation Abstracts International*, 55: 1031.
27. Dougherty, T. and Turban, D. (1999) 'Behavioural confirmation of interviewer expectancies', in R. Eder and M. Harris (eds) *The Employment Interview Handbook*, Thousand Oaks, CA: Sage, pp. 217–28.
28. Phillips, A. and Dipboye, R. (1989) 'Correlational tests of predictions from a process model of the interview', *Journal of Applied Psychology*, 74: 41–52.
29. Barclay, J. (2001) 'Improving selection interviews with structure: organisations' use of "behavioural" interviews', *Personnel Review*, 30: 81–101.
30. Janz, J. (1982) 'Initial comparisons of patterned behaviour description interviews versus unstructured interviews', *Journal of Applied Psychology*, 67: 129–34.
31. Roth, P. and McMillan, J. (1993) 'The behaviour description interview', *The CPA Journal*, December: 76–9.
32. Barclay (2001) op. cit.
33. Van Clieaf, M. (1994) 'In search of competence: structured behaviour interviews', *Business Horizons*, 34(2): 51–5.
34. Hargie and Dickson (2004) op. cit.
35. Benjamin, A. (1981) *The Helping Interview*, 3rd edition, New York: Houghton-Mifflin, p. 17.
36. Hornby, M. (1991) 'How to succeed in recruitment interviews', *Training and Development*, 9: 17–20.
37. Ickes, W., Snyder, M. and Garcia, S. (1997) 'Personality influences on the choice of situations', in R. Hogan (ed.) *Handbook of Personality Psychology*, Orlando, FL: Academic Press.
    Blackman, M. (2002) 'Personality judgment and the utility of the unstructured employment interview', *Basic and Applied Social Psychology*, 23, pp. 241–50.
38. Blackman, M. and Funder, D. (2002) 'Effective interview practices for accurately assessing counterproductive traits', *International Journal of Selection and Assessment*, 10: 109–16 (p. 115).
39. Torrington, D., Hall, L. and Taylor, S. (2001) *Human Resource Management*, London: Prentice Hall.
40. Hackney, M. and Kleiner, B. (1994) 'Conducting an effective selection interview', *Recruitment, Selection and Retention*, 3: 10–16.
41. Hattersley (1997) op. cit., p. 3.
42. Hargie and Dickson (2004) op. cit.
43. Millar, R. and Gallagher, M. (1997) 'The selection interview', in O. Hargie (ed.) *A Handbook of Communication Skills*, 2nd edition, London: Routledge.
44. Black, J. (1982) *How to Get Results from Interviewing*, Malabar, FL: Robert Krieger Publishing Co.
    Hargie and Dickson (2003) op. cit.
45. Cooper, D. and Robertson, I. (1995) *The Psychology of Personnel Selection*, New York: Routledge.
46. Fisher, P. (1995) 'I'm glad you asked that', *The Guardian (Careers Supplement)*, 4 February, p. 2.
47. Dillon, J. (1990) *The Practice of Questioning*, London and New York: Routledge.
48. Morgan, N. (2002) 'A question of survival', *Harvard Management Communication Letter* (Reprint No. C0208B), pp. 1–3 (p. 3).

49. Tourish, D., Hargie, O. and Curtis, L. (2001) 'Preparing adolescents for selection interviews: The impact of a training intervention on levels of worry and locus of control', *International Journal of Adolescence and Youth*, 9: 273–91.
50. Judge *et al.* (2000) op. cit.
51. Brown, A., Barrick, M. and Franke, M. (2002) 'Applicant impression management: dispositional influences and consequences for recruiter perceptions of fit and similarity', *Journal of Management*, 28: 27–46.
52. Posthuma *et al.* (2002) op. cit.
53. Pingitore, R., Dugoni, B., Tindale, R. and Spring, B. (1994) 'Bias against overweight job applicants in a simulated employment interview', *Journal of Applied Psychology*, 79: 909–17.
54. Millar and Gallagher (1997) op. cit.
55. Mornell, P. (1998) 'How to shift the burden of hiring onto the candidate: an interview with Pierre Mornell', *Harvard Management Update (No. U9808B)*, pp. 1–5 (p. 4).
56. Facteau, C., Bordas, R. and Jackson, K. (2000) *Developing Structured Interviews to Assess Organizational Citizenship Behaviors*, Paper presented at the Annual Conference of the Society for Industrial and Organisational Psychology, New Orleans, LA, April.
57. Fox, S. and Spector, P. (2000) 'Relations with emotional intelligence, practical intelligence, general intelligence, and trait affectivity with interview outcomes: it's not all just g', *Journal of Organizational Behavior*, 21: 203–20.
58. Hollwitz, J. and Harrison, W. (2000) *Structured Interviews for Pre-employment Integrity Screening*, Paper presented at the Annual Conference of the Society for Industrial and Organisational Psychology, New Orleans, LA, April.
59. Nowicki, M. and Rosse, J. (2002) 'Managers' views of how to hire: building bridges between science and practice', *Journal of Business and Psychology*, 17: 157–70.

14 Feedback time: performance appraisal and management

1. Hargie, O. (1992) *Communication: Beyond the Cross-roads*, Monograph: University of Ulster, Newtownabbey.
2. Tourish, D. (1999) 'Communicating beyond individual bias', in A. Long (ed.) *Advanced Interaction for Community Nursing*, London: MacMillan.
3. Manzoni, J. and Barsoux, J. (2002) *The Set-up-to-Fail Syndrome: How Good Managers Cause Great People to Fail*, Boston: Harvard Business School Press.
4. Beckett, A. (2002) 'Out of Sorts', *The Guardian (G2)*, 23 January, pp. 2–4.
5. Levinson, H. (1976) 'Appraisal of *what* performance?', *Harvard Business Review*, 54: 30–46.
   Beer, M. (1997) 'Conducting a performance appraisal interview', *Harvard Business School Note No. 9-497-058.*
6. Freemantle, D. (1994) *The Performance of 'Performance Appraisal' – an Appraisal*: a Superboss Research Report, Berkshire: Superboss, p. 4.
7. Latham, G. and Wexley, K. (1994) *Increasing Productivity Through Performance Appraisal*, 2nd Edition, Reading, MA: Addison-Wesley.
8. Antonioni, D. (1996) 'Designing an effective 360-degree appraisal feedback process', *Organizational Dynamics*, 25: 24–38.

9. Mani, B. (2002) 'Performance appraisal systems, productivity, and motivation: a case study', *Public Personnel Management*, 31: 141–59.
10. Gray, G. (2002) 'Performance appraisals don't work', *Industrial Management*, 44: 15–17.
    Kennedy, P. and Dresser, S. (2001) 'Appraising and paying for performance: another look at an age-old problem', *Employee Benefits Journal*, 26: 8–14.
    Segal, J. (2000), '86 your appraisal process?' *HR Magazine*, October, p. 199–206.
    Strebler, M., Bevan, S. and Robinson, D. (2001) 'Performance review: balancing objectives and content', *Institute of Employment Studies Report 370*, London: IES.
11. Losyk, B. (2002) 'How to conduct a performance appraisal', *Public Management*, 84: 8–11 (p. 8).
12. Sutherland, S. (1992) *Irrationality*, London: Constable.
13. Sutherland, S., op. cit.
14. Wilke, H. and Meertens, R. (1994) *Group Performance*, London: Routledge.
15. Forsterling, F. (2001) *Attribution: An Introduction to Theories Research and Applications*, Hove, East Sussex: Psychology Press.
16. Kreitner, R., Kinicki, A. and Buelens, M. (2002) *Organizational Behaviour*, 2nd European Edition, London: McGraw-Hill.
17. Brown, R. (2000) *Group Processes*, 2nd edition, Oxford: Blackwell.
18. DeNisi, A. (1996) *A Cognitive Approach to Performance Appraisal*, London: Routledge.
19. Atwater, L., Waldman, D. and Brett, J. (2000) 'The influence of feedback on self and follower ratings of leadership', *Personnel Psychology*, 48: 35–60.
20. Pratto, F. and John, O. (1991) 'Automatic vigilance: the attention grabbing power of negative social information', *Journal of Personality and Social Psychology*, 51: 380–91.
21. Leyens, J., Yzerbyt, V. and Schadron, G. (1994) *Stereotypes and Social Cognition*, London: Sage.
22. Philp, T. (1983) *Making Performance Appraisal Work*, London: McGraw-Hill.
23. Lefkowitz, J. (2000) 'The role of interpersonal affective regard in supervisory performance ratings: a literature review and proposed causal model', *Journal of Occupational and Organizational Psychology*, 73: 67–85.
24. Goldstein, H. (2001) 'Appraising the performance of performance appraisals', *IEEE Spectrum*, 38: 61–3.
25. Philp (1983) op. cit.
26. Millar, R., Hargie, O. and Crute, V. (1992) *Professional Interviewing*, London: Routledge.
27. Fiske, S., Lin, M. and Neuberg, S. (1999) 'The continuum model: ten years later', in S. Chaiken and Y. Trope (eds) *Dual-Process Theories in Social Psychology*, New York: Guilford Press.
28. Heneman, R., Greenberger, D. and Anonyuo, C. (1989) 'Attributions and exchanges: the effects of interpersonal factors on the diagnosis of employee performance', *Academy of Management Journal*, 32: 466–76.
29. Millar *et al.* (1992) op. cit.
30. Grote, D. (2000) 'Performance appraisal reappraised', *Harvard Business Review* (January–February): p. 21.
    Randall, G. Packard, P. and Slater, J. (1984) *Staff Appraisal: A First Step to Effective Leadership*, 3rd Edition, London: Institute of Personnel Management.
    Wynne, B. (1995) *Performance Appraisal: A Practical Guide To Appraising the Performance of Employees*, Hertfordshire: Technical Communications.

31. Tziner, A., Joanis, C. and Murphy, K. (2000) 'A comparison of three methods of performance appraisal with regard to gaol properties, goal perception and ratee satisfaction', *Group and Organization Management*, 25: 175–90.
32. Cederblom, D. (2002) 'From performance appraisal to performance management: one agency's experience', *Public Personnel Management*, 31: 131–40.
33. Williams, M. (1997) 'Performance appraisal is dead: long live performance management!' *Harvard Management Update No. U9702A*, pp. 1–6.
34. Kennedy and Dresser (2001) op. cit.
35. Gray (2002) op. cit.
36. Rollinson, D. and Broadfield, A. (2002) *Organisational Behaviour and Analysis: An Integrated Approach*, 2nd edition, Prentice Hall.
37. Institute of Manpower Studies Report, No. 258 (1993) *Pay and Performance – The Employee Experience*, London.
38. Gladwell, M. (2002) 'The talent myth', *The Times* (T2), 20 August, pp. 2–4.
39. For a good example of this hagiographic approach, see Hamel, G. (2000) *Leading the Revolution*, Boston: Harvard Business School Press.
40. Gabor, A. (1992) 'Take this job and love it', *New York Times (F1)*, 26 January, p. 6.
41. Kohn, A. (1999) *Punished by Rewards*, New York: Houghton Mifflin.
42. Kohn (1999) ibid., p. 136.
43. Seddon, J. (2001) 'Perform a miracle – praise the workers', *The Observer Business Supplement*, 11 March, p. 13.
44. Conlin, M. (2002) 'The software says you're just average', *Business Week*, Issue 3771, 25 February, p. 126.
45. Fletcher, C. and Perry, E. (2001) 'Performance appraisal and feedback: a consideration of national culture and a review of contemporary and future trends', in N. Anderson, D. Ones, H. Sinangil, and C. Viswesvaran (eds) *International Handbook of Industrial, Work and Organizational Psychology*, Beverly Hills, CA: Sage.
46. Weisband, S. and Atwater, L. (1999) 'Evaluating self and others in electronic and face to face groups', *Journal of Applied Psychology*, 84: 632–9.
47. Fletcher, C. (2001) 'Performance appraisal and management: the developing research agenda', *Journal of Occupational Psychology*, 74: 473–87.
48. Beer (1997) op. cit.
49. Hargie, O. and Dickson, D. (2003) *Skilled Interpersonal Communication*, 4th edition, London: Routledge.
50. Losyk (2002) op. cit., p. 9
51. Anstey, E. Fletcher, C. and Walker, B. (1976) *Staff Appraisal and Development*, London: Allen and Unwin.
52. Quoted in Manzoni, J. and Barsoux, J. (2002) *The Set-Up-To-Fail Syndrome*, Boston: Harvard Business School Press (p. 161).
53. Lawson, I. (1989) *Notes For Managers: Appraisal and Appraisal Interviewing*, 3rd edition, London: The Industrial Society.
54. Pulakos, E., Arad, S., Donovan, M. and Plamondon, K. (2000) 'Adaptability in the workplace: development of a taxonomy of adaptive performance', *Journal of Applied Psychology*, 85: 612–24.
55. Eden, D. (1993) 'Interpersonal expectations in organisations', in P. Blanck (ed.) *Interpersonal Expectations: Theory, Research and Applications*, Cambridge: Cambridge University Press.

56. Millar *et al.* (1992) op. cit.
57. Goodworth, C. (1989) *The Secrets of Successful Staff Appraisal and Counselling*, Oxford: Heinemann.
    Hunt, N. (1994) *How to Conduct Staff Appraisals,* 2nd edition, Plymouth: How To Books.
58. Rakos, R. (1991) *Assertive Behaviour: Theory, Research and Practice*, London: Routledge.
59. Kolt, W. and Donohue, R. (1992) *Managing Interpersonal Conflict*, London: Sage.
60. Cialdini, R. (2001) *Influence*, 4th edition, New York: Harper Collins.
61. Mabey, C. (2001) 'Closing the circle: participant views of a 360 degree feedback programme', *Human Resource Management Journal*, 11: 41–53.
62. Atwater, L., Waldman, D. and Brett, J. (2002) 'Understanding and optimising multisource feedback', *Human Resource Management*, 2: 193–208.
63. Pfau, B., Kay, I., Nowack, K. and Ghorpade, J. (2002) 'Does 360-degree feedback negatively affect company performance?',*HR Magazine*, 47, June: 54–9.
64. Waldman, D., Atwater, L. and Antonioni, D. (1998) 'Has 360 degree feedback gone amok?' *The Academy of Management Executive*, 12, pp. 86–95.
65. Brett, J. and Atwater, L. (2001) '360 degree feedback: accuracy, reactions, and perceptions of usefulness', *Journal of Applied Psychology*, 86: 930–42.
66. Peiperl, M. (2001) 'Getting 360 degree feedback right', *Harvard Business Review*, January: 142–7.
67. Semler, R. (1993) *Maverick*, London: Century.

15 Following the correct path: the guiding lights of ethics and audits

1. Brandon, N. (1996) *Self-reliance and the Accountable Life*, New York: Simon & Schuster, p. 168.
2. Robinson, S. (2002) 'How Enron fooled the world', *Daily Telegraph Magazine*, 4 May, pp. 28–34.
3. English, S. (2002) 'Decline and fall of America's corporate emperors', *Daily Telegraph*, 21 September, p. 35.
4. Beaton, G. (2002) 'Ashcroft quits Tyco in boardroom cull', *Financial Mail on Sunday*, 10 November, p. 2.
5. Rushe, D. (2002) 'The wages of sin', *The Sunday Times Business Section*, 11 August, p. 5.
6. Bryce, R. (2003) *Pipe Dreams: Greed, Ego and the Death of Enron*, New York: PublicAffairs.
7. Partnoy, F. (2003) *Infectious Greed: How Deceit and Risk Corrupted the Financial Markets*, London: Profile.
8. Schwartz, H. (1990) *Narcissistic Process and Corporate Decay: The Theory of the Organizational Ideal*, New York: New York University Press.

9. Friedman, M. (1998) 'The social responsibility of business is to increase profits', in L. Pincus Hartman (ed.) *Perspectives in Business Ethics*, New York: McGraw-Hill.
10. Green, R. (1994) *The Ethical Manager: A New Method for Business Ethics*, New York: MacMillan College Publishing.
11. Sternberg, E. (1994) *Just Business: Business Ethics in Action*, London: Little, Brown & Company, p. 19.
12. Stewart, L. (2001) 'The importance of addressing issues of applied ethics for communication scholars and consultants', *American Communication Journal* (online), 5(1).
13. Punch, M. (1996) *Dirty Business: Exploring Corporate Misconduct*, London: Sage.
14. Boyle, D. (2000) *The Tyranny of Numbers: Why Counting Can't Make Us Happy*, London: Harper Collins.
15. Beck, C. (1999) *Managerial Communication: Bridging Theory and Practice*, Upper Saddle River, NJ: Prentice-Hall, p. 304.
16. Towler, J. (2002) 'Dealing with employees who steal', *Canadian HR Reporter*, 15: 4–6.
17. Bridge, R. (2002) 'Counting the cost of expenses fraud', *Financial Mail on Sunday*, 24 November, p. 55.
18. Thompson, H. (2002) 'Brothers find ways to win in coffee war', *The Times*, 9 March, p. 44.
19. Herman, M. (2002) 'Protect your resources from insider theft', *Nonprofit World*, 20: 35–7.
20. Mitchell, V. and Chan, J. (2002) 'Investigating UK consumers' unethical attitudes and behaviours', *Journal of Marketing Management*, 18: 5–26.
21. Kramer, M. (2001) *Business Communication in Context*, Upper Saddle River, NJ: Prentice-Hall.
22. Boylan, M. (2001) *Business Ethics*, Upper Saddle River, NJ: Prentice Hall.
23. Cheney, G. and Christensen, L. (2001) 'Organizational identity: linkages between internal and external communication', in F. Jablin and L. Putnam (eds) *New Handbook of Organizational Communication*, Thousand Oaks, CA: Sage.
24. Freeman, R. (ed.) (1991) *Business Ethics: The State of the Art*, Oxford: Oxford University Press.
25. Donaldson, T. and Gini, A. (1990) *Case Studies in Business Ethics*, Englewood Cliffs, NJ: Prentice Hall.
26. Kochan, T. (2002) 'Addressing the crisis in confidence in corporations: root causes, victims, and strategies for reform', *Academy of Management Executive*, 16: 138–41.
27. Seeger, M. (2001) 'Ethics and communication in organizational contexts: moving from the fringe to the center', *American Communication Journal* (online), 5(1).
28. Toffler, B. (1986) *Tough Choices*, New York: Wiley.
29. Deetz, S., Tracy, S. and Simpson, J. (2000) *Leading Organisations Through Transition*, Thousand Oaks, CA: Sage.
30. Johannesen, R. (1990) *Ethics in Human Communication*, 3rd edition, Prospect Heights, IL: Waveland Press.
31. Seeger, M. (1997) *Organizational Communication Ethics: Decisions and Dilemmas*, Cresskill, NJ: Hampton Press.
32. Gioia, D. (2002) 'Business education's role in the crisis of corporate confidence', *Academy of Management Executive*, 16: 142–4 (p. 143).

33. Deetz, S. (1995) *Transforming Communication, Transforming Business: Building Responsive and Responsible Workplaces*, Cresskill, NJ: Hampton.
34. Redding, C. (1996) 'Communication ethics: a case of culpable neglect', in J. Jaksa and M. Pritchard (eds) *Ethics of Technology Transfer*, Cresskill, NJ: Hampton Press.
35. Taylor, J., Flanagan, A., Cheney, G. and Seibold, D. (2000) 'Organizational communication research: key moments, central concerns, and future challenges', in W. Gudykunst (ed.) *Communication Yearbook 24*, Thousand Oaks, CA: Sage, p. 125.
36. Allen, M., Groucher, M. and Siebert, J. (1994) 'A decade of organizational communication research: journal articles 1980–1991', in S. Deetz (ed.) *Communication Yearbook 16*, Thousand Oaks, CA: Sage.
37. Stewart, L. (2001) 'The importance of addressing issues of applied ethics for communication scholars and consultants', *American Communication Journal* (online), 5(1).
38. Cheney, G. (1999) *Values at Work*, Ithaca, NJ: Cornell University Press.
39. Hoffman, W. and Moore, J. (eds) (1990) *Business Ethics: Readings and Case Studies in Corporate Morality*, New York: McGraw-Hill.
40. Trevino, L., Hartman, L. and Brown, M. (2000) 'Moral person and moral manager: how executives develop a reputation for ethical leadership', *California Management Review*, 42: 128–42.
41. Primeaux, P. (2001) 'Icons, and values: communicating ethical leadership', *American Communication Journal* (online), 5(1).
42. Broadhurst, A. (2000) 'Corporations and the ethics of social responsibility: an emerging regime of expansion and compliance', *Business Ethics: A European Review*, 9: 86–98.
43. Kreps, G. (1990) *Organizational Communication: Theory and Practice*, 2nd edition, New York: Longman.
44. Clampitt, P.G. (2001) *Communicating for Managerial Effectiveness*, 2nd edition, Newbury Park: Sage.
45. Howard, S. (2001) 'Gilding the lily with those little white lies', *The Sunday Times Appointments*, 28 January, p. 10.
46. 'Business curricula include learning from others' mistakes', *International Herald Tribune*, 24 March, 2003, p. 15.
47. Buller, D. and Burgoon, J. (1996) 'Interpersonal deception theory', *Communication Theory*, 6: 203–42.
48. Mattson, M., Allen, M., Ryan, D. and Miller, V. (2001) 'Considering organization as a unique interpersonal context for detecting deception: a meta-analytic review', *Communication Research Reports*, 17: 148–60.
49. Reed Employment Services (2002) *Motivating People at Work: What is to be Done?* London.
50. Clampitt, P., DeKoch, R. and Cashman, T. (2000) 'A strategy for communicating about uncertainty', *Academy of Management Executive*, 14: 41–57.
51. Swartz, M. with and Watkins, S. (2003) *Power Failure: The Inside Story of the Collapse of Enron*, New York: Doubleday.
52. Bryce, R. (2003) op.cit.
53. English, S. (2002) '2002: capitalism brought to book', *The Daily Telegraph*, 27 December, pp. 34–5.
54. Partnoy, F. (2003) op. cit.

55. Tooher, P. (2003) 'Disgusted BOC boss resigns over fat cats', *Financial Mail*, 5 January, pp. 1–2.
56. Hanna, M. and Wilson, G. (1998) *Communicating in Business and Professional Settings*, 4th edition, New York: McGraw-Hill.
57. Lee, J. (2001) 'Leader-member exchange, perceived organizational justice, and co-operative communication', *Management Communication Quarterly*, 14: 574–89.
58. Graen, G. and Uhl-Bien, M. (1995) 'Relationship-based approach to leadership: development of leader-member exchange (LMX) theory of leadership over 25 years: applying a multi-level multi-domain perspective', *Leadership Quarterly*, 6: 219–47.
59. Greenberg, J. (1990) 'Organisational justice: yesterday, today, and tomorrow', *Journal of Management*,16: 399–432.
60. Skarlicki, D. and Folger, R. (1997) 'Retaliation in the workplace: the roles of distributive, procedural, and interactional justice', *Journal of Applied Psychology*, 82: 434–43.
61. Sias, P. and Jablin, F. (1995) 'Differential superior–subordinate relations, perceptions of fairness, and coworker communication', *Human Communication Research*, 22: 5–38.
62. Karathanos, P. and Auriemmo, A. (1999) 'Care and feeding of the organizational grapevine', *Industrial Management*, 41: 26–30.
63. Clampitt, P. and Benson, J.A. (1988) 'Crisis revisited: an analysis of strategies used by Tylenol in the second tampering episode', *Central States Speech Journal*, 39: 49–66.
64. Hearit, K. (1995) 'From "We didn't do it" to "It's not our fault": the use of apologia in public relations crises', in W. Elwood (ed.) *Public Relations Inquiry as Rhetorical Criticism: Case Studies of Corporate Discourse and Social Influence*, Westport, CT: Praeger.
65. Schutz, A. (1998) 'Assertive, offensive, protective, and defensive styles of self-presentation: a taxonomy', *The Journal of Psychology*, 132: 611–28.
66. Seeger, M. (2004) 'Organisational communication ethics: directions for critical inquiry and application', in D. Tourish and O. Hargie (eds) *Key Issues in Organisational Communication*, London: Routledge.
67. Hasselkus, W. (1998) 'Manager's maxim', *The Observer: Work Section*, 29 March, p. 1.
68. Montgomery, D., Wiesman, D. and DeCaro, P. (2001) 'Toward a code of ethics for organizational communication professionals: a working proposal', *American Communication Journal* (online), 5(1).
69. Badaracco, J.L. (1998) 'The discipline of building character', *Harvard Business Review*, March–April, pp. 115–24.
70. Fisher, C. and Lovell, A. (2003) *Business Ethics and Values*, Harlow: Prentice Hall.
71. Montgomery, D. and DeCaro, P. (2001) 'Organizational communication ethics: the radical perspective of performance management', *American Communication Journal* (online), 5(1).
72. Church, A.H. (1994) 'The character of organizational communication: a review and new conceptualisation', *The International Journal of Organizational Analysis*, 2: 18–53 (p. 19).
73. Odom, M. (1993) 'Kissing up really works on boss', *San Diego Union-Tribune* 12, August, p. E12.
74. Clampitt, P. and DeKoch (2001) *Embracing Uncertainty: The Essence of Leadership*, Armonk, New York: M.E. Sharpe, p. 110.

75. Hurst, B. (1991) *The Handbook of Communication Skills*, London: Kogan Page, p. 24.
76. Tourish, D. and Hargie, O. (1998) 'Communication between managers and staff in the NHS: Trends and prospects', *British Journal of Management*, 9: 53–71.
77. Furnham, A. and Gunter, B. (1993) *Corporate Assessment: Auditing a Company's Personality*, London: Routledge.
78. Hargie, O. and Tourish, D. (2004) 'How are we doing? Measuring and monitoring organisational communication', in D. Tourish and O. Hargie (eds) *Key Issues in Organisational Communication*, London: Routledge.
79. Clampitt, P. (2000) 'The questionnaire approach', in O. Hargie, and D. Tourish, (eds) *Handbook of Communication Audits For Organizations*, London: Routledge.
80. Downs, C.W. (1988) *Communication Audits*, Glenview, Illinois: Scott, Foresman & Co.
81. Goldhaber, G. and Rogers, D. (1979) *Auditing Organisational Communication Systems*, Texas: Kendall-Hunt.
82. Downs, C. and Hazen, M. (1977) 'A factor analytic study of communication satisfaction', *Journal of Business Communication*, 14: 63–73.
83. Hargie, O. and Tourish, D. (eds) (2000) *Handbook of Communication Audits for Organisations*, London: Routledge.
84. Hargie, O. and Tourish, D. (1996) 'Auditing internal communication to build business success', *Internal Communication Focus*, November, 10–14.
85. Hargie, O., Tourish, D. and Wilson, N. (2002) 'Communication audits and the effects of increased information: a follow-up study', *Journal of Business Communication*, 39: 414–36.
86. Tourish, D. and Hargie, O. (1996) 'Communication in the NHS: using qualitative approaches to analyse effectiveness', *Journal of Management in Medicine*, 10: 38–54.
87. Millar, R. and Gallagher, M. (2000) 'The interview approach', in O. Hargie and D. Tourish (eds) *Handbook of Communication Audits for Organisations*, London: Routledge.
88. Meyer, J. (2002) 'Organizational communication assessment: fuzzy methods and the accessibility of symbols', *Management Communication Quarterly*, 15: 472–9.
89. Young, M. and Stanton, N. (1999) 'The interview as a usability tool', in A. Memon and R. Bull (eds) *Handbook of the Psychology of Interviewing*, Chichester: Wiley, p. 227.
90. Memon, A. and Bull, R. (eds) (1999) *Handbook of the Psychology of Interviewing*, Chichester: Wiley.
91. Sias, P.M. and Cahill, D.J. (1998) 'From coworkers to friends: the development of peer friendships in the workplace', *Western Journal of Communication*, 62: 273–99.
92. Hennink, M. and Diamond, I. (1999) 'Using focus groups in social research', in A. Memon and R. Bull (eds) *Handbook of the Psychology of Interviewing*, Chichester: Wiley, p. 114.
93. Dickson, D. (1999) 'The focus group approach', Hargie and D. Tourish (eds) (2000) *Handbook of Communication Audits for Organisations*, London: Routledge.
94. Daymon, C. and Holloway, I. (2002) *Qualitative Research Methods in Public Relations and Marketing Communications*, London: Routledge.

95. Dickson, D., Hargie, O. and Nelson, S. (2003) 'Communicating sensitive business issues: part 1', *Corporate Communications: An International Journal*, 8: 35–43.
96. Hargie, O. and Tourish, D. (2000) 'Data collection log-sheet methods', in O. Hargie, and D. Tourish, (eds) *Handbook of Communication Audits for Organizations*, London: Routledge.
97. Hargie, O. and Tourish, D. (1996) 'Auditing communication practices to improve the management of human resources: an inter-organisational study', *Health Services Management Research*, 9: 209–22.
98. Brandstatter, H. (2001) 'Time sampling diary: an ecological approach to the study of emotions in everyday life situations', in H. Brandstatter, and A. Eliasz (eds) *Persons, Situations, and Emotions*, Oxford: Oxford University Press.
99. Brandstatter, H. (2001) op. cit.
100. Davis, K. (1953) 'A method of studying communication patterns in organizations', *Personnel Psychology*, 6: 301–12.
101. Goldhaber, G.M. (1993) *Organizational Communication*, 6th edition, Madison, Wisconsin: WCB Brown and Benchmark, p. 374.
102. Dickson, D., Hargie, O. and Nelson, S. (2002) *Relational Communication Between Catholics and Protestants in the Workplace: A Study of Policies, Practices and Procedures*, Jordanstown: University of Ulster.
103. Hargie, O. and Tourish, D. (2000) 'Data collection log-sheet methods', op. cit.
104. Bass, L. and Stein, C. (1997) 'Comparing the structure and stability of network ties using the Social Support Questionnaire and the Social Network List', *Journal of Social and Personal Relationships*, 14: 123–32.
105. Hargie, O., Rainey, S. and Dickson, D. (2003) 'Working together, living apart: inter-group communication within organizations in Northern Ireland', in A. Schorr, W. Campbell and M. Schenk (eds) *Communication Research and Media Science in Europe*, Berlin: Mouton de Gruyter.
106. Wienshall, T. (1979) *Managerial Communication: Concepts, Approaches and Techniques*, London: Academic Press.
107. Bejou, D., Edvardsson, B. and Rakowski, J. (1996) 'A critical incident approach to examining the effects of service failures on customer relationships: the case of Swedish and US airlines', *Journal of Travel Research*, 35: 35–40.
108. Hargie, O. and Tourish, D. (2000) 'Auditing professional practice', in O. Hargie, and D. Tourish, (eds) *Handbook of Communication Audits for Organizations*, London: Routledge.
109. Hargie, O. and Tourish, D. (2004) 'How are we doing? Measuring and monitoring organisational communication', op. cit.
110. Hargie, O. and Tourish, D. (2000) 'Data collection log-sheet methods', op. cit.
111. Hargie, O. and Tourish, D. (2000) 'Data collection log-sheet methods' op. cit.
112. Salem, P. (2002) 'Assessment, change and complexity', *Management Communication Quarterly*, 15: 442–50.
113. Boyle, D. (2000) op. cit.
114. Cushman, D. and King, S. (eds) (2001) *Excellence in Communicating Organizational Strategy*, New York: State University of New York Press.
115. Bryson, J. and Moore, J. (1995) *Strategic Planning for Public and Nonprofit Organizations*, San Francisco: Jossey Bass, p. 5.
116. Hargie, C. and Tourish, D. (1996) 'Corporate communication in the management of innovation and change', *Corporate Communications: An International Journal*, 1: 3–11.

117. Clampitt, P., DeKoch, R. and Cashman, T. (2000), op. cit.
118. Hargie, O. and Tourish, D. (2004) 'The communication consequences of downsizing trust, loyalty and commitment', in D. Tourish and O. Hargie (eds) *Key Issues in Organisational Communication*, London: Routledge.
119. Frank, A. and Brownell, J. (1989) *Organizational Communication and Behavior: Communicating to Improve Performance*, New York: Holt, Rinehart and Winston.

Index